Choice Awareness:

A Systematic, Eclectic Counseling Theory

Richard C. Nelson

Professor, Counseling and Development
Purdue University
West Lafayette, Indiana

Publisher—
Educational Media Corporation®
P.O. Box 21311
Minneapolis, MN 55421-0311

Production editor—
Don L. Sorenson

Graphic design—
Earl Sorenson

Table of Contents
Choice Awareness:
A Systematic, Eclectic Counseling Theory

Dedication

To Robert and Hildreth Snodgrass

The bequest of Hildreth Snodgrass, in memory of her husband, made it possible for me to complete a draft of this manuscript while I was the Purdue University Robert L. Snodgrass Scholar.
I will always remain grateful for that opportunity.

Richard C. Nelson

To the Counselor

This book presents Choice Awareness as an eclectic counseling theory. Its focus is on providing to you an uncomplicated, direct, and concise approach through which you can enable your clients to make more effective choices and to exercise more responsibility in their lives—as a means of achieving a sense of inner well-being.

It has long been a stratagem of advertisers to convince us that we have a problem—halitosis, loose spots, body odor, ring around the collar—and then to offer their products as antidotes. Despite the great degree of freedom that abounds in our society, we believe a problem exists that we might, in the spirit of advertising, characterize as *choicelessness*, *powerlessness*, *irresponsibility*, or even *joylessness*. Our antidote is a greater breadth of choices—through Choice Awareness.

The language of advertising, which has become a part of our everyday communication, gives us an illusion of expanding our choices while it actually attempts to narrows them. Phrases like *The Right Choice* and *The Best Choice* imply that only one choice makes sense. Advertisers capitalize on the either-or, black-white, now-never, with-against language we so commonly use to point us in a specific direction. Choice Awareness encourages you as counselor to use a variety of approaches in helping your clients broaden the vision they have of the choices available to them—so that they might make more effective choices.

Many sources are available that present a variety of counseling theories that can be used to create an eclectic approach. Because this is so, and because we wish to focus on Choice Awareness theory *per se*, current theories are treated briefly. Attention is given to clarifying ways in which those theories are particularly relevant in building the sense of choice and of responsibility in clients.

One of the difficulties in most eclectic theories is that they provide too little guidance to the counselor in deciding which specific approach to use when, or they present too many complexities to the counselor to be useful. Choice Awareness has been designed to strip eclecticism of unnecessary complexities. It is easily understood and direct in its use of language; its concepts are readily utilized; and it complements what is currently known in the field of counseling.

Is Choice an Illusion?

Choice Awareness theory is based on a definition of choice as any behavior over which we have a reasonable degree of control (Nelson & Bloom, 1975; Nelson, 1976). We assume that freedom of choice exists. However, important questions deserve attention before we present a theory based on that assumption. Do we really have choices? Are choices merely illusions?

It seems vital in the development of any system or theory to consider the arguments that can be made for and against the positions taken—so that pitfalls can be avoided, and so that the ideas that support the theory are clearly presented. In the spirit of inquiry the issue of choice versus no-choice is explored briefly.

Skinner, a determinist, suggested that the environments of individuals control their choices; ". . .persons do not act upon the world, the world acts upon them" (Skinner, 1971, p. 211). In *Walden Two*, a leading character stated Skinner's view, "Our members are practically always doing what they want to do— what they 'choose' to do—but we see to it that they will want to do precisely the things which are best for themselves and the community. Their behavior is determined, yet they're free" (Skinner, 1948, pp. 296-297). Choice in Skinner's view is, then, largely an illusion.

Bandura, another behaviorist, took the same position early, but over the years changed his view concerning whether or not the individual acts upon the environment.

> On closer inspection, man [human beings] proved to be the more active and the environment less autonomous. . . behavior partly creates the environment, and the environment influences the behavior in a reciprocal fashion. It is just as important to analyze how man [humans] shapes [shape] environmental conditions as it is to assess how conditions modify his [their] actions. A distinguishing feature of man [human beings] is that he is [they are] capable of creating self-regulative influences. By functioning as an agent as well as an object of influence, man has [human beings have] some power of self-direction (Bandura, 1974, p. vi).

Aristotle, in his essay, "Choice, Deliberation, and the Limits of Responsibility," considered pro and con arguments concerning human freedom and concluded that it is ". . .absurd to make external circumstances responsible, and not oneself. . . for base acts" (Aristotle in Wolff, 1971, p. 97), thus lending his support to the argument that both the positive and the negative things we do are voluntary. The view held by Cicero, that if the individual's behavior is known in advance by God there is an inevitable chain of consequences and nothing depends on our free will, was challenged by St. Augustine; ". . .we assert both that God knows all things before they come to pass, and that we do by our own free will whatsoever we know and feel to be done by us only because we will it" (St. Augustine in Wolff, 1971, p. 107).

Wingo (1974) objected to determinism on two major grounds. First, that we cannot ignore our own compelling feelings that we do have choices among alternatives, and second, that determinism in human behavior strikes a fatal blow against moral responsibility and a system of ethics.

Sartre argued not only that individuals are free, but that they "...are condemned to be free... because once thrown into the world, they are responsible for everything they do" (Sartre in Wolff, 1971, p. 158).

A middle ground between the deterministic view of Skinner and the sense of absolute freedom and responsibility suggested by Sartre is offered by Kelley. "Determinism and freedom are two complementary aspects of structure. They cannot exist without each other any more than *up* can exist without *down* or *right* without *left*. Neither freedom nor determinism is absolute. A thing is free *with respect to something*; it is determined *with respect to something else*" (Kelley, 1955, p. 78).

The Choice Awareness position is that neither end of the continuum—the belief that all human behavior is determined, nor the belief that human beings are "condemned to be free"—describes experience adequately. We tilt toward the existential position: freedom rather than determinism. We contend that individuals in most circumstances have far more freedom to act than they themselves can imagine, and that behavior is limited far more by habit, perceptions, and an inclination to maintain a consistent view of self, than by external forces. Yet we also contend that limits exist on the choices of individuals—first, because their physical and intellectual powers are by no means infinite; second, because choices that affect their lives are made by others; and third, and most frequently, because they lack an awareness of alternative choices they might make. We accept Kelley's (1955) view: people tend to make free choices if they are not overly dependent on habits, are not narrow in their view of themselves, and are able to see the world without narrow limitations. Individuals tend to make choices that are determined to the extent that they are affected by physical and intellectual limitations, the force of choices made by others, and their awareness of alternative choices.

For most of us, at most times and in most circumstances, the question is not: *Is choice an illusion?* More properly the question is: *Are limitations an illusion?* Choice Awareness theory acknowledges that we do not have absolute freedom, nor do we have the capacity to do *anything* we might choose. At the same time it argues that our beliefs about our limits are far more constricting than they need to be.

Choice Awareness as a counseling theory is focused on helping people see the few, genuine limits that exist on their choices, while enabling them to reach beyond the many internal and external constrictions they feel. The goal is greater freedom and responsibility and a deepening sense of inner well-being through more effective choices.

The Organization

This book is designed to increase your options as a counselor while enabling you to increase your clients' options in turn. Throughout its pages you are provided opportunities to engage in a self-examination process through making journal entries. We encourage you to have a notebook at the ready and take some time to respond to each of these opportunities as they arise. It should be noted that an optional, companion source is available that develops the same concepts in an informal way, and uses a similar journaling approach. That source, *On the CREST: Journaling Your Way to Better Choices*, is designed for you to use with your clients as a supplement to the process of counseling, or for individuals to use on their own.

Part I of *Choice Awareness: A Systematic, Eclectic Counseling Theory* explores the nature of choices, sets forth the idea of creating a spa-like condition in counseling, and clarifies the major options you have available as you work with your clients. Part II considers the five CREST choices available to human beings: Caring, Ruling, Enjoying, Sorrowing, and Thinking/Working; and suggests how current counseling theories fit the Choice Awareness schema. Part III provides illustrations of how Choice Awareness may be integrated into specific counseling processes.

References

Bandura A. (1974). Foreword. In C. Thoresen and M. Mahoney, *Behavioral self-control*. New York: Holt Rinehart & Winston.

Kelley, G. A. (1955). *The psychology of personal constructs. Volume one. A theory of personality*. New York: W. W. Norton.

Nelson, R. C. (1976). Choice Awareness: An unlimited horizon. *Personnel and Guidance Journal, 54*, 462-467.

Nelson, R. C. & Bloom, J. W. (1976). *Choice Awareness: An innovative guidance process*. Boston, Houghton Mifflin.

Skinner, B. F. (1971). *Beyond freedom and dignity*. New York: Alfred A. Knopf.

Skinner, B. F. (1948). *Walden two*. New York: Macmillan.

Wingo, G. M. (1974). *Philosophies of education: An introduction*. Lexington, MA: D. C. Heath.

Wolff, R. P. (1971). *Philosophy: A modern encounter*. Englewood Cliffs, NJ: Prentice-Hall.

Part I
Developing
Awareness:
The Nature of Choices

What is Choice Awareness?
An Overview

Spa, Learning, and Relearning
Accenting Spa

Counselor Choices

Habits, Goals, and Meaning

OK and OD Choices

Chapter 1
What is Choice
Awareness?
An Overview

Five Guiding Principles

Choice Awareness is an eclectic counseling theory designed to help you reach more of your clients in a variety of significant ways. If you apply the principles of Choice Awareness dynamically, you should be able to: (1) help your clients become more aware of the choices they make; (2) assist your clients to make more effective choices involving their words, actions, thoughts, and feelings—that is, to choose more effectively in the three major realms of life—the behavioral, the cognitive, and the affective; and (3) enable your clients to gain a greater sense of inner well-being and joy in their lives.

Choice Awareness as a theory of counseling is founded on five major principles. In this brief section we enumerate those principles and the logical extensions that result from them—the bare bones of Choice Awareness—so that you can see how this theory may be useful to you, and to demonstrate that Choice Awareness meets the criteria of an effective theory.

Brammer (1986) set two primary criteria for evaluating theories: *simplicity* and *elegance*. When the word *elegance* is used in the scientific sense, it denotes precision and neatness. As you will see, precision and neatness are two of the greatest strengths of Choice Awareness. Other questions Stefflre (1965) suggested that you may ask of this or any other theory are: is it clear—are its principles in agreement; is it comprehensive—does it account for much behavior; is it explicit—can it be readily implemented; is it parsimonious—does it avoid over explaining behavior; and is it testable—does it generate useful research?

The five principles of Choice Awareness as a counseling theory are as follows:

The Choosing Principle

In Choice Awareness theory choice is seen as any behavior over which the individual has some reasonable degree of control. The choosing principle is served when counseling focuses on helping clients see that they are making choices, that they can exercise control.

The following are logical extensions of the choosing principle:

- Human beings are involved in a continuous process of making choices—that is, they choose their way through their lives—and choice is the basic currency of their exchanges with others.

- The words individuals speak, the actions they take, and many of their thoughts and feelings are choices—that is, people make choices in the behavioral, cognitive, and affective realms.

- Counseling may focus on helping clients understand that their words, actions, thoughts, and feelings involve choices, and on helping them develop alternative choice patterns.

The Five Choice Principle: CREST Choices

There are five basic choices that individuals make in the circumstances of life, either alone or in combination, and in ways that may either be positive (OK) or negative (OD—in the sense of the words overdone or overdose). The first letters of these five basic choices form the acronym CREST:

C   *Caring* involves individuals' attempts to meet their own needs and the needs of others.

R   *Ruling* includes any act of leadership involving self or others.

E   *Enjoying* includes those choices through which individuals express their positive feelings.

S   *Sorrowing* choices are those choices through which individuals express their negative feelings.

T   *Thinking/Working* choices are those that are primarily cognitive and/or action-oriented.

- Individuals can be helped in the process of counseling to determine which of the CREST choices they use effectively and which choices they use ineffectively in their relationships and for themselves.

- In most circumstances the individual can make any of the CREST choices in a way that is OK.

The Less is More Principle

Counseling should be governed by the less is more principle, the principle that help should not exceed that needed by the client. This is also known as the law of least effort or the law of parsimony.

- Effective counseling may be brief and the number of sessions limited.

- The amount of support given the client by the counselor should not exceed the client's need.

- The amount of direction given by the counselor should not exceed the client's need.

- For many clients, counseling may be focused on a single realm—the behavioral, the cognitive, or the affective. To specify that in greater detail in Choice Awareness terms:

- For many clients it will be sufficient if counseling is focused on one of the CREST choices, the direction of the expression of that choice, and the person or persons with whom that expression is a problem.

The Principle of Three Counseling Levels: Spa, Learning, and Relearning

Counseling tends to function primarily at one of three levels—spa, learning, or relearning—although all three levels may enter the counseling process with individual clients.

- Spa is counseling that enables clients to experience the joy of knowing themselves positively.

- Learning is counseling that focuses on ways clients function at present and on enabling them to find alternative choices to use in coping with their concerns in the present and future.

- Relearning is counseling that explores dysfunctional patterns of choices with clients; it enables them to "unlearn" those patterns and to learn new ones.

- The general level of counseling—spa, learning, or relearning—should fit the problem of the client, but all clients may advantageously be offered opportunities to experience themselves as positive human beings, to experience counseling as spa.

The Principle of Self-Interest and Social-Interest Balance

Effective counseling achieves a reasonable balance between self-interest and social-interest. Individuals need to believe that they are significant beings in their own world—that they make a difference. In addition, every person has the need to be involved with other people, to love and be loved, and to feel worthwhile to self and others (Glasser 1965).

- Client self-interest is an important consideration in counseling. Clients who learn to act more effectively in their own self-interest are able to make better personal decisions and choices.

- Client social-interest is an important consideration in effective counseling. Clients who learn to act more effectively in the interests of others gain a sense of personal satisfaction, and they may find that they meet higher order needs of their own, such as self-actualization, at the same time.

- Gains in self-interest and social-interest are more often complementary than mutually exclusive.

The basic principles enumerated above have been presented briefly as a way of introducing the Choice Awareness system and its application to the processes of counseling. The remainder of this chapter provides some background and an abbreviated overview of the concepts that undergird the system. The principles and the concepts presented in this overview are central to the theses of Choice Awareness and are developed throughout this source in a continuously expanding way.

Choice Awareness as a System and a Counseling Theory

As a system, Choice Awareness is founded on a specific definition of choice; that is, *choice is any action, response, or feeling over which the individual has some reasonable degree of control* (Nelson, 1976). Choice Awareness is designed to enable individuals to understand the choices they make so that they may take more effective control of their lives. As a counseling theory, Choice Awareness is designed to help you engage your clients in a process of growth toward more effective choices. This process of growth results in a sense of inner well-being for your clients, an outcome that is achieved both directly, and as a result of their learning to interact more effectively with others.

The process of growth toward *physical well-being* is never-ending; that is, it cannot be achieved and then effort ceased for all time. In the same sense, the process of growth toward *inner well-being* never ends. Choice Awareness is focused on helping you help your clients to find roadways that lead toward better choices and toward inner well-being.

Choice Awareness as a counseling theory is designed to assist you as a counselor: (1) to enable your clients to understand and appreciate their strengths more fully; (2) to help your clients explore how they make choices in their thoughts, feelings, words, and actions; (3) to assist your clients to consider how they might want to change the ways in which they have been choosing; and (4) to help your clients move in the direction of inner well-being.

If the phrase "inner well-being" sounds a bit mystical to you, that perception needs to be changed. Inner well-being, like physical well-being, results from exercising effective choices. Choices for inner well-being are as direct and logical as are choices designed to achieve or maintain physical well-being. This work is designed to clarify the choices that can help you set your clients on the road to better choices and to inner well-being—through Choice Awareness.

The purpose of this source is to help you to assist your clients. However, deep familiarity with the concepts of Choice Awareness and the ways in which you can engage your clients in considering their choices makes it most logical that you should participate actively in the process of exploring *your choices* and *your inner well-being* as a first step. We invite you to read this source first for your own benefit. This will help you prepare yourself to use the processes it suggests and its understandable language in your everyday work with your clients. The time you spend in this way will have a handsome payoff as it helps you make better personal choices, gain a greater sense of inner well-being for yourself, and work more effectively with your clients.

A suggestion: when you are invited to make a Self-Examination Journal Entry or a Counselor-Application Journal Entry, have a notebook at hand and take time to make an entry at the point it is called for. You will be better equipped to help your clients gain inner well-being through Choice Awareness if you do so. Here is the first opportunity. We invite you to take time now to locate a notebook you can continue to use, and a pen or pencil, and start your journal. Head your entry, date it, and begin. We encourage you to make each entry on a new page so that you will be able to add new, dated, observations when appropriate.

SELF-EXAMINATION—JOURNAL ENTRY: Based on your current level of understanding, explore and discuss the extent to which you have been aware of the constant opportunities you have to make choices in the moments of your life. Suggestion: head your entry CHOICE AS A CONSTANT. Date this entry and all future entries.

We see it as important for you to share these concepts with your clients, inviting their reactions and helping them see the relevance in their lives of the ideas presented. Most clients are unaware that they are making choices constantly. Explore this concept and others that follow with your clients as they are relevant for their needs. Consider especially how a lack of awareness of the ever-present nature of choices affects their lives.

The Beginnings of Choice Awareness

The term *Choice Awareness* in its first use was serendipitous. In 1972, John Bloom, a Purdue University doctoral student, developed a research proposal on the effectiveness of Transactional Analysis (TA), as presented by Berne (1964), Harris (1967), Freed (1971), and James and Jongeward (1971), with classes of upper-elementary school children. Bloom presented the proposal to administrative personnel in a local school district who denied his request, fearing the term Transactional Analysis might conjure images for parents of students as mental patients, of Freudian therapy as the antidote, and of school personnel as analysts. John Bloom and I wrung our hands briefly, then brainstormed until we found a term that appeared to be more acceptable—Choice Awareness. Bloom sought approval of the same proposal under the new title, and he completed his research (1973) on the effectiveness of TA in sixth-grade classrooms.

On the only variable in Bloom's research that showed a significant difference, personal acceptance of responsibility for failures, a placebo group—using an equivalent amount of time in an in-class industry—outstripped the Transactional Analysis-cum-Choice Awareness groups. We concluded that the non-significant outcomes resulted in large measure from the evident difficulties children experienced in accepting the idea of their having a Parent ego state of their own, and in assigning statements *of their own* to their Parent, Adult, or Child. That led us to an attempt to find other ways of expressing those concepts, and to the consideration of choices, rather than ego states, as the matter of consequence. Within a short period of time we had made so many modifications in transactional analysis as a result of focusing on the concept of choices, that we decided that we had evolved a new, workable system, and Choice Awareness was born (Nelson & Bloom, 1975).

The two theories, Choice Awareness and TA, differ in important ways. We question both the existence and the relevance of ego states as such. But whether or not we have three ego states, we clearly do make choices in our lives. We believe that is a far more relevant matter.

In Choice Awareness terms the inquiry, "There, there, you poor thing, how can I help you?" is an exaggerated (OD) caring choice; in TA terms that inquiry came from the Parent ego state. The difference is not just semantic. Making the assumption that the question came from an ego state could lead one to the conclusion that the behavior emerged uncontrolled from some well-spring within the individual over which he or she had little or no control. Making the assumption that the behavior is a choice makes it immediately clear that different responses are possible.

In his book, *What Do You Say After You Say Hello?* Berne (1972) pictured Jeder, every-person, as sitting before a player piano, following the movements of the keys in a programed design, playing out a life pattern that had been ordained, deluded with the idea of free choice in selecting and playing the tune. While Transactional Analysis offers some suggestions about "breaking spells" and "changing tunes," by contrast Choice Awareness focuses directly on taking control of choices and achieving inner well-being in the present and the future.

Dictionary definitions of *transaction* suggest the carrying out of an obligation or deal, for example, in business; while *analysis* suggests the separating of something into its component parts. In sum, TA suggests sorting into its component parts behavior that already exists—behavior that is somewhat obligatory in nature. The focus is on past, fixed behavior.

By contrast, *choice* is seen as the act of choosing or selection, and *awareness* is the state of being conscious, alive, awake, alert. Thus, Choice Awareness suggests making selections of behaviors—of words and actions (also thoughts and feelings)—while alert and conscious. The focus is on making effective choices in the present and in the future, rather than on analyzing the past.

Clearly patterns of *choices* can be changed. Choices made frequently become habits. What appear in TA as ego states and scripts are seen in Choice Awareness as clusters of thoroughly ingrained habits—developed through reinforcement, or as a result of the imitation of behaviors observed in others, or as reactions to those same behaviors. At any rate, it may be assumed that changes in behaviors, thoughts, and feelings can result in changes in habits or scripts.

While the initial impetus for Choice Awareness came from Transactional Analysis, no effort has been made to conform to the design of that theory. However, one of the original objectives of TA has been adhered to in Choice Awareness even more than it has been in TA. Transactional Analysis emerged from an effort on Eric Berne's part to simplify psychological theories and to construct one that might be understood and used readily by the general public. Somehow that worthy objective, simplicity, seems to have been lost, since the last book Berne wrote before he died, *What Do You Say After You Say Hello?* (1972) presented a glossary of well over a hundred items. Furthermore, Berne's followers seem to have engaged in a process of seeing how many terms they might cause to dance on the head of his theory. By contrast, Choice Awareness is, and will remain, simple in terminology, so that it can be used comfortably by both adults and children as a process for improving communication and enhancing personal and interpersonal choices.

Choice is seen in this theory as the major instrument for growth and change. In order to make changes in choices we need to know more about where we are than where we have been. We need to know more about what we want than what we have tried to get. We need to consider how we can achieve our goals in the present and the future more than we need to focus on the past.

Choice Awareness draws its strength from all of the theories of counseling that influence counselors today. My own background owes much to Carl Rogers and self theory. However, over the years I have seen much that is of benefit in several theories and I see great value in approaching counseling from an eclectic point of view. The systematic incorporation of a variety of approaches will be evident as this work unfolds.

Choice Awareness as an Antidote to Current Counseling Problems

The medical model. Counselors have often complained that the counseling systems they have to work with have been built on a medical model. Theoreticians have studied emotional problems and their cures, then used what they have learned to suggest how healthy people might stay healthy. The reality is that most counseling *and* medical theories have been built on the study of dysfunctional individuals, rather than on an understanding of healthy, normal people. Recently, more and more physicians have turned their attention to well-being, and have concerned themselves with how to keep their clients well. We in counseling also need to attend more directly to the question of well-being or wellness. We need to derive our practices more and more from an understanding of how healthy, normal people function. We need to consider how we might help those who have problems to model their behaviors on the behaviors of those who function effectively.

Choice Awareness theory evolved from efforts to help normal young people understand the choices they were making so that they might take more effective control in their lives. It has been broadened in its scope to reach a wider audience, but it has not deviated from that purpose. Choice Awareness is focused on how those who function effectively in our society manage to do so. It considers how they might maintain their effective functioning, and it suggests how persons who function less effectively might model the approaches used by more effective choosers.

Insufficient emphasis on choice. As you have contemplated the meaning of the phrase Choice Awareness, you may have wondered, "Don't all counseling theories emphasize effective choice-making as an objective of counseling in one way or another? If so, what is different here?" Many theories do indeed suggest that effective choice-making is a significant objective of the counseling process. The view is taken here, however, that current counseling theories miss the mark because they do not sufficiently acknowledge choice-making as the core activity of living—the central act in which human beings are engaged—nor do they give sufficient attention to exploring the processes of choice-making, or to considering ways in which the choice-making of clients might be improved.

Choice Awareness theory suggests that choices are the building-blocks of personal awareness and interpersonal behavior, that human beings are continuously engaged in a process of choice-making, and that enabling clients to make more effective choices is the central objective of all counseling.

Negative orientation. Perhaps you have been persuaded to the view most counselors take of their professional activity: that it must be focused on negatives. You may have come to view story-telling, even if the story reflects on some significant event or success in the life of the client, as interference or resistance. If so, after accepting the client's need to go off on a brief tangent, you redirect the dialogue into "more productive" channels. Also, in imitation of another aspect of the medical model, upon termination of a counseling process you may schedule check-ups at specified intervals—the equivalent of the physician's policy of promoting regular physical examinations. You may organize these followup activities in order to assure yourself and the client that no obvious problem exists, or, in the event that one appears, to get the client involved in further treatment as early as possible.

Neither your profession nor the medical profession has encouraged clients to share their joys and triumphs, to demonstrate their skills, or to explore their new views of themselves and their world. Perhaps you believe you are too overburdened to take on the chore of hearing clients when they have nothing but positive matters to report. There would seem to be something very appropriate in regular, reinforcing experiences that involve clients' sharing with physicians their exercise regimens, sleep schedules, and dietary habits, and describing their triumphs in maintaining weight or combating other health problems. Parallel experiences in counseling are even more justifiable.

Reinforcement of their triumphs and successes is very valuable for most people. It should prove highly worthwhile for you as a counselor to offer opportunities to your clients to participate in reinforcing experiences that go beyond problem-solving. Here we use the term *spa* or the phrases *spa-experiences* or *spa-like experiences*, in the contemporary sense of the word spa—denoting a place where people seek relaxation and engage in positive, self-sustaining activities—to refer to reinforcing experiences that go beyond immediate problem-solving.

There is greater urgency for you as a counselor to offer spa experiences to your clients than for the average physician to do so—if only because there are very few opportunities available otherwise for your clients to receive social-emotional support. In the physical realm, resources abound for spa or spa-like experiences—through camps, clubs, gymnasiums, and, logically enough, spas. On the other hand, individuals are left largely on their own to find opportunities to share their triumphs and joys or otherwise to engage in spa experiences in the social-emotional realm. Interactions with parents, marriage partners, and friends are the resources available to most individuals, but these people are neither always available, nor are they always open to your clients when they wish to share the excitement of their personal discoveries or to discuss hard-won gains they have made in their interpersonal relationships. Furthermore, one or more of these people may be involved in whatever problem is present. For many individuals that leaves as spa resources only bartenders, barbers, hairdressers or other persons who serve the public. Counselors are far better equipped to serve the need.

Choice Awareness theory makes it an important matter for you as a counselor to engage a significant proportion of your clients in spa experiences, and the following chapter develops that concept in some detail. The view is taken that such experiences are in a very real sense a primary objective of counseling. After all, what is a more appropriate objective of counseling than that of helping clients feel good about themselves, their lives, and their choices?

Choice Awareness as Systematic Eclecticism

In addition to the stress placed on negatives, another criticism made of current theories is that they encourage counselors to perform rather like the blind men and the elephant. That is, each theory tends to touch a different part of the client and to generalize to the whole. One blind man grasped the tail and declared the elephant to be like a rope, a second touched the side and said the beast was like a wall, and a third touched the ear and declared that the elephant was like a fan. Just so, behaviorally-oriented theories suggest that the problems of counseling clients are focused in the ways in which they act; affectively-oriented theories suggest that the problems of clients are centered in their misplaced negative feelings; and cognitively-oriented theories suggest that dysfunctional thoughts lead to the difficulties of clients.

Most of the theories counselors use to help their clients are not eclectic in design, but most counselors themselves are eclectic in their orientation. They borrow liberally from various theories. They hear of new departures, try them—not always in situations in which they fit best—and if they do not work well, they discard them or relegate them to infrequent use. They do not intend to be hit-or-miss in their efforts, but, because they lack a coherent theory within which they can fit various approaches, their efforts at eclectic counseling often appear to be more random than organized.

Choice Awareness is a cognitive-affective-behavioral system that is designed to enable you to work effectively and efficiently with a variety of clients. It uses concepts from existing theories, integrates them with choice concepts, and contributes simple language through which you can help your clients understand and change their choice patterns.

In the only complex phrase we offer, Choice Awareness is presented as the new *systematic eclecticism*. That is, Choice Awareness contributes a systematic way of thinking about counseling that allows counselors to incorporate a variety of existing theories, while focusing on choice-making as a central theme in human behavior.

Choice Awareness as Helping Clients to See Themselves as Choosers

For many clients to become more effective human beings they need to know they have choices and they need to believe in themselves as choosers. When they know they have choices and believe that they are choosers, and when they can live with these ideas comfortably day in and day out, they are in a good position to take more effective control within their world—at least of their own choices.

It seems a simple enough thing, and eminently reasonable within our free society, for clients to believe in themselves as choosers. Why then is there any need to explore this idea in any depth? Why should people, especially counselors, take their time to consider such an obvious matter?

Once again, we can use a parallel from the physical arena. In large measure it is obvious that physical health is a matter of choices. Individuals' chances for good physical health are substantial if they eat sensibly in terms of quality, quantity, calories, vitamins, and minerals; if they exercise reasonably; if they avoid tobacco and avoid or appropriately limit the use of such substances as alcohol and drugs; and if they get enough rest and experience enough challenge. Although new knowledge appears frequently in the media that supports and clarifies these rules for effective physical development, human beings have been aware of these ideas for decades or centuries, yet many people did not in the past and do not in the present act effectively on what they know.

Why?

The answer seems to be in part that people do not internalize information as applying to themselves. In the physical arena many people grow up believing that their youth protects them against disaster, almost no matter how self-destructive their choices may be. Similarly in the realm of personal and interpersonal choices people, do not seem to realize that their negative moves hurt others—and themselves. Some individuals make huge numbers of destructive personal and interpersonal choices without fully understanding that they themselves will be adversely affected by them. In both the physical and interpersonal realms negative choices are harmful.

Again we ask why people act in ways that are self-destructive? Why do they not act more often in their own self interest?

Although we live in a very free society, many individuals, and counseling clients in particular, do not perceive the power they have to act for themselves, or understand the effects of their actions on others. That is the root cause of many of their problems. They build habits of behavior, modeled largely on the behaviors of others around them, and they feel powerless to change patterns they have used for many years.

Part of the problem in helping clients see themselves as choosers is the matter of inertia. When they are in motion—whether the direction is appropriate or inappropriate—they tend to remain in motion. When they are at rest—whether their inactivity serves a useful purpose or none at all—they tend to remain at rest.

Inveterate smokers know that their habit is likely to shorten their lives by months, years, or even decades, but many believe they are powerless to quit, while others rationalize continuing, saying, "We've all got to go somehow." In similar ways your clients may know that their personal or interpersonal behaviors are likely to be ruinous to themselves or to their relationships. But, in this arena, too, they believe they are powerless to stop negative behaviors or to start more positive ones, or they find innumerable, illogical rationalizations for continuing their inappropriate behavior patterns, e.g., "I'd stop arguing with her all the time if she just wouldn't provoke me so often."

For most individuals the way to better physical well-being is through making great numbers of positive choices daily involving food selection, exercise, rest, and avoidance of harmful substances. Likewise for most individuals, the way to improved emotional well-being and better interpersonal relationships is making great numbers of positive personal and interpersonal choices daily, and avoiding making the kinds of choices that may be expected to create difficulties. It challenges inertia for individuals to truly accept the idea that they are choosers in nearly all of the events of their lives. But, after some time for adjustment of their thought patterns, nearly all clients welcome the revelation.

How Do We Make Our Choices?

In its everyday use the word *choice* most often denotes someone making a selection between two alternatives: "I could wear the red or the blue sweater; I'll choose the blue." Choice is used in interpersonal terms in similar ways: "My friend is asking me to go for coffee; I could say yes or no; I'll go along." The picture in our minds of what is happening is the classic S→R model. An external stimulus, a friend's request that I take a break for coffee, leads me to my response, agreeing to go. In that instance and others I may believe that the response is inherent in the stimulus: "We always break for coffee about now; therefore I have to do that."

Sc→ Cc→ Rc—is a more accurate picture of what actually happens.

Sc—we take in the stimulus and we make choices about it.

Cc—we choose, considering the relationship, alternative ways we could respond, and possible consequences.

Rc—we respond, at times modifying our response as we are making it, because of the reaction we perceive.

Let us look at each element in greater detail.

Sc. A stimulus confronts me. Using the example above, my friend suggests we break for coffee. At the same time there are likely to be several other stimuli present: the task I am involved with; the phone call I need to answer or make; another person who needs my attention; the arrival of a supervisor in the vicinity; a personal, biological, need. I choose which stimulus to attend to in the immediate moment. In this case we will assume it is my friend's request—but I make choices about that.

Cc. In the space of an eyeblink I consider what has gone on between us until now—I may want to avoid the person because of a problem that occurred a few moments ago, or I may be particularly eager for us to be together because of our positive relationship or because I have a story or a joke I want to share. I consider other realities—the pile of work ahead of me, for example. I scan an array of possible options: delay, respond eagerly, decline because of the work load, and so forth. In that same fraction of a second I consider the possible consequences of each of those choices, and I make an internal choice.

Rc. Consciously or otherwise, I choose my way of responding—matter-of-factly, with boredom in my voice, enthusiastically, and so forth—and I begin my response. My mind remains active as I implement my choice, and I may stop in mid-sentence and redirect my response because of a conflict I suddenly recall, or because I read disappointment or eagerness written on my friend's face.

We make choices about the stimulus and the response, and we process many choices in the brief interval between. It may seem overwhelming to think that any of us could consider so many factors in what initially appears to be a simple yes-no choice. But in point of fact, like the expert who reads many hundreds of words per minute, we process a great many ideas in the briefest instant and make what are really complex choices in many different circumstances every day of our lives.

When we use the word *decision* to describe an action, we most often think about someone making a conscious choice based on good information and awareness of alternatives and consequences. To make our immediate, everyday choices in more effective ways, we can bring many of them to consciousness and treat them as mini-decisions that deserve more attention than we are used to giving.

Choice Awareness shows you how to take advantage of the opportunities you have to make your choices in more effective ways, and to help your clients do the same.

Choice Awareness Concepts: Why We Choose as We Do

As we have indicated, ***Choice Awareness is a system designed to enable individuals to take more effective control of their choices.*** In spite of the great freedom individuals experience in our society, denial of choices seems to be characteristic of most individuals. Some of the common ways in which people verbalize their denials include: "I couldn't help it." "There was nothing else I could have done." "I was only following orders." "Look what you made me do." "Who me?" "That's just my personality." "That's just the way I am." "That was my Child" (in Transactional Analysis terms).

Most clients are only dimly aware of the choices they have, and they need help in making more effective choices, in acting responsibly, and in achieving inner well-being.

Choice Awareness is a system that considers the cognitive, affective, and behavioral domains. No one pulls a string in our backs and tells us what to say or do; *we choose our words and actions.* Further, even though we may not be able to control every thought we have, *we choose our thoughts*—in the sense that we can choose to focus on completing a tax form or any other task when we need to do so. Finally, because we are complex beings, in many circumstances *we choose our feelings*—in the sense that we select which feeling we act on from among the mix of feelings we have in the moment.

Your clients need help in understanding the implications of their choices. They need to realize that they make choices involving their words, actions, thoughts, and feelings.

Choice Awareness defines choice as any behavior over which we have some degree of control; thus, choice is the fundamental unit of behavior. Our behaviors, and most of our thoughts and feelings, result from patterns of choices we have learned to make.

Your clients need to understand that they can bring their words and actions and many of their thoughts and feelings under their control. Knowing that their behavior is within their control is an essential basis for change.

Choice Awareness suggests that our lives are a series of choices. From our first waking moment until our last glimmer of consciousness before sleep, we are making choices. We make hundreds of choices daily, especially when we are in close proximity to other persons. If we remain silent for many minutes, we have made many separate choices to do so, though we may or may not be aware of that. If we engage the other person in lively conversation, we have made many other choices.

Your clients need to understand the continuous nature of their choices. The alternative is that they feel powerless and "choiceless," and then act in ways that support that view. You may usefully focus on choice-making behaviors in counseling, bringing them to the awareness of your clients, and exploring with them ways that they may change their behaviors.

Choice Awareness suggests that in every choice we make we have many options. Nearly every choice we make we can exercise in a great many ways. We have come to think in either-or, with-against, yes-no, now-or-never terms that greatly oversimplify the choices available to us. When we have considered two choices, fight or flight for example, we may believe the task is done and that we are ready to make our selection.

Even in situations that genuinely seem to call for either-or responses—for example, accepting an invitation to go to dinner with a friend—we rarely respond with a simple yes or no. If the response we select is positive, we can express it in many ways: "OK." "I guess so." "Oh, sure." "Hey, great, I'd really love to." "You're the boss." "If you really want to." "I guess I don't have anything better to do." Our negative responses also can vary greatly: "Are you kidding?" "Hell, no."

"You've got to be out of your mind." "I'm too busy for such frivolity." "Sorry, no can do." "Aw, shucks, I just made another commitment." "Gee, I wish I could, but I can't." "I can't today, but what about tomorrow?" Furthermore, we can equivocate in a number of different ways: "Check with me later." "We'll see." "Let me see how far I get with my chores; if I get far enough I can't think of anything I'd rather do."

Open-ended situations such as entering a room or filling a vacuum in the conversation give us almost limitless opportunities to choose. We could, for example, introduce a controversial topic, tell the other person of our affection for him or her, share a deep personal conviction, mention an event that we observed, talk about something we have read, speak about a matter that is troubling us, inquire about a concern of the other person, stand on our hands, scratch, pick up a newspaper and begin to read, turn on the television, or leave the room.

How your clients have tried to take matters into their own hands is every bit as important as whether they have tried to do so, since the route they have taken may be symptomatic of their problems or it may suggest a solution. How blocked your clients perceive themselves to be is highly indicative of their perceptions of the choices they have available to them.

Is there always a choice a person can make? In answer to that question, Frankl (1959) suggested that we always have at least one choice available to us: we can always choose *how*—with what attitude— we will do what we believe we must do. In any given circumstance, then, there are likely to be many ways of choosing; this is something that many counseling clients need to understand.

Choice Awareness suggests that we make choices in large measure because of the habits we develop in our relationships. We develop habit patterns very readily and we tend to cling very strongly to those habits. We learn many of our patterns early in our lives, modifying them only minimally as circumstances and reactions seem to demand. "For example, we may make choices involving leadership with those who are younger or over whom we believe we exercise some control; on the other hand, we may even avoid making reasonable suggestions with those who are older or who have some control over us" (Nelson, 1980, p. 54).

We tend to build stereotypical patterns of behavior with the people who are important in our lives. We may learn to treat one parent with deference and respect; the other we may fear and avoid. One sibling we may act toward subserviently while another we may coddle and baby. When we encounter new relationships, whether as preschoolers or much later, we try to apply one of the basic patterns we have learned to use, depending on which of our existing relationships seems most like the one we have—or believe we want to have—with that individual. We adjust the pattern only minimally at first to see if it works with that person. Thus, as young persons we evolve patterns of behavior that are different, but nevertheless stereotypical, with father, mother, older sister, older brother, younger sister, younger brother, and various female and male peers. When we encounter teachers, neighbors, or distant relatives, we try one pattern or another with those individuals as well, making adjustments primarily as we believe we must. Subsequently, as we encounter teammates, roommates, boyfriends/girlfriends, spouses, supervisors, co-workers, subordinates, customers, and competitors, we attempt first to fit an existing stereotypical habit pattern to those relationships, again making adjustments only as we believe we must.

As a counselor you encounter clients who have evolved habit patterns with fathers, mothers, and others who have been of significance in their lives, and that they attempt to duplicate, often inappropriately, in other relationships. Even as they are contributing to the patterning of the relationship, they may feel discomfort and internally resist the direction they are taking; the result is that they send out mixed messages to the individuals involved. For example, to a new acquaintance they may imply at times: "You take charge." Yet other aspects of their behavior may send the message: "But I won't like it if you do."

Choice Awareness suggests that we have goals in our relationships. With the people who are important in our lives, we have both *immediate* and *long-term* goals. For example, we may have an immediate goal of convincing another person to join us for a party on the weekend, and we may cling tenaciously to that goal in spite of obvious resistance and our foreknowledge that the host of that party is seen by our friend as vulgar and boorish. Our long range goal with our friend may be that of maintaining the warm, friendly relationship we have, or even improving it, but we may doggedly pursue our immediate goal in spite of the likelihood that it will divert us from our long-term goal.

Like other people, the clients you see may have given very little attention to their own long-term goals with the people who are important in their lives. It can be a great service to help them to specify their long-term goals, and to enable them to realize that the pursuit of their immediate goals may be counterproductive if their long-term goals are really important to them.

SELF-EXAMINATION—JOURNAL ENTRY: Take several minutes and enter in your journal your reactions to the concepts discussed above. Begin with the third concept and consider the relevance of each of the following concepts for you in your life: that choice is any behavior over which you have some degree of control; that you are making choices all the time; that in every choice you have many options; that you make your choices in large measure because of the habits you develop in your relationships; and that you have goals in your relationships. Discuss the extent to which these concepts enlarge your thinking. Continue your journal entry by exploring the relevance of these concepts for particular clients you have encountered. Suggestion: head your entry CHOICE CONCEPTS.

We see it as important for you to share these concepts with your clients, inviting their reactions and helping them see the relevance of these concepts in their lives. Most clients feel powerless in their lives to some degree or other. Invite in-depth consideration of the concepts you and they see as most relevant for their needs. Give special emphasis to considering the relationship goals your clients have with others.

Choice Awareness Concepts: The Available Choices

Choice Awareness suggests that we make our choices on an OK to OD continuum. At one end of the continuum are OK choices, choices that are acceptable for the most part to all individuals involved. Major OK choices are those that affect the relationship in some very positive way: a hug, a heartfelt compliment, a genuinely helpful action. Minor OK choices are those that are positive, but are unlikely to have any profound effect on the relationship: a greeting, completing an agreed-on task such as telephoning at a particular time, contributing to a conversation. On the other end of the continuum are OD choices, with the term meaning overdone (as in cooking); overdose (as in drug/alcohol abuse); or an overdraft (as in banking). Minor OD choices are those that are seen as negative, but in no significant way: not listening, forgetting to call, criticizing, making a nagging comment. Major OD choices are more negative and are almost guaranteed to affect the relationship adversely: shouting, scolding, fighting, lying, and so forth.

Your counseling clients may be unaware of the need for OK choices in their important relationships. If they have not had good models for making OK choices, they make many OD choices, or they wait passively for others to react toward them and then they respond, often in ways others see as OD. They need to learn that they can initiate interactions and make choices that are OK, at least for themselves, if they want to improve their relationships and gain in self-respect.

Choice Awareness suggests the useful analogy that we have accounts in our important relationships. It is helpful to conceptualize that we have joint accounts in our important relationships. When either of us makes a major OK choice by offering an extremely positive statement or by doing a very thoughtful thing, it is as if we made a large deposit to the account; by the same token, any major OD choice we make acts as a large withdrawal. Similarly, minor OK and minor OD choices act as small deposits or withdrawals. Relationships that are on a very positive footing can tolerate some negatives—some withdrawals—without disastrous results, because the balance is sufficient to allow that; on the other hand, those relationships that are on a very tenuous or negative footing need positives if they are to thrive.

In our throwaway society it often seems as though people who enter counseling are seeking their own permission, and yours as counselor, to withdraw from particular relationships. "The balance is negative, so let's declare bankruptcy," they think, "and start over by opening a new business—that is, by building a substitute relationship." The trouble with that conclusion is the same people then seek new relationships to which they bring the same negative patterns of choices. They may be able to restrain their negative impulses during the establishment (courting) stage of a relationship, but once a commitment has occurred (long-term involvement, marriage) they are likely to revert to patterns of choices that are similar to those they used before. To say it another way, in the early stages of a relationship people tend to overlook minor negatives in the other person and to put their own best foot forward, because they are focusing in some measure on their long-term goal—building the relationship. Once the relationship is established, however, the long-term goal fades into oblivion and the focus becomes short-term—which often includes such actions as getting even for imagined or real slights or other perceived negatives. Habit is a powerful source of choices, and for most people, focusing on short-term goals is the more habitual mode.

No case is being made here that all long-term relationships should be maintained forever, but in many cases it would be beneficial for your clients to make strong attempts to contribute more positive patterns of choices to their existing relationships—to act in the social-interest. This is likely to be to their benefit—to serve their self-interest as well—since their own well-being depends in great measure on their liking their own choices.

Choice Awareness suggests that we make choices of five kinds: Caring, Ruling, Enjoying, Sorrowing, and Thinking/Working. The acronym CREST is used to sum up nearly all the choices human beings have available to them, and both the acronym and the choices represented can be used as keys to improving self-images and relationships. It should be noted that these choices have points of overlap, and that a given behavior may be classified in different ways under different circumstances. For example, a hug is a caring choice if it is given in response to a need; it is an enjoying choice if it is made spontaneously and freely.

Your clients need to understand the kinds of choices they are making and to consider the choices that might be more effective if they are to gain in self image and improve their relationships. Through exploration of CREST choices they may be helped to consider directions they might take in achieving these goals.

Caring choices. We make caring choices whenever we attempt to meet the needs we see—choices such as holding, assisting, helping, reflecting feelings, guarding, and defending. We may make these choices verbally: "How are you today?" "You sound really tired right now." Or we may make them non-verbally: an arm around the shoulder, passing someone the butter. We may make these choices for ourselves or for the other person. We may make them in OK or OD ways, the latter by babying others beyond their desires—characteristically OD caring is experienced as smothering. And we may make these choices in ways that are fresh or stereotypical in terms of sex, age, and role. For example, females, older persons, and teachers or nurses may be looked to for caring choices, while others may overlook the opportunities they have to meet the needs of others—or their own.

Many of your clients come to counseling because they need caring and do not experience it sufficiently within their relationships. Fewer of your clients seek help because someone in their environment makes caring choices too frequently for their needs. Your clients may have great difficulty in making caring choices with others because they put their self-interest before social-interest, perhaps because they feel so ill-cared-for themselves. They need to understand their own potential for caring for others and their need to care for themselves in OK ways.

Ruling choices. We make ruling choices whenever we exercise leadership—in fact, *leading* or *leadership* could be used as the designated term, except that CLEST is less memorable than is CREST. Furthermore, the term *ruling* can serve as a reminder that such choices are readily overdone. Ruling includes such choices as requesting, suggesting, asserting, ordering, scolding, and forbidding. We may make these choices verbally: "Please come over for dessert this evening." "I have to have this back on Tuesday." "Call me when you're back from your trip." "Cut it out!" Or we may make them non-verbally: beckoning, holding up a hand in a gesture that says STOP. We may make these choices for ourselves or for the other person. We may make them in OK or OD ways, the latter by giving too many orders or by using a tone of voice that is too strong—characteristically OD ruling is seen as dominating. And we may make these choices in ways that are fresh or stereotypical in terms of sex, age, and role. Males, older persons, and supervisors or elected officials are expected to make ruling choices, while others may overlook the opportunities they have to exercise leadership.

Many of your clients come to counseling because they feel powerless in their lives, or because both they and others with whom they interact see themselves as responders—with the result that no one exercises leadership and the relationship founders. Few of your clients come to counseling because they make too many ruling choices for the benefit of their relationships. Far more have difficulty making ruling choices with others because of their feelings of powerlessness and choicelessness. They need to understand their own potential for exercising leadership with others, and for themselves—in OK ways.

Enjoying choices. Enjoying includes all choices that primarily express positive feelings: acting in fun, playing, complimenting, loving, and creating. We may make these choices verbally: "Wow!" "That's great!" "I'm glad to see you." "I love being here with you." The old psychiatrist joke: "You don't have an inferiority complex, you are inferior." Or we may make them non-verbally: smiling, hugging an old friend, the "high five" after a fine play. We assign these choices to children: "Smile," we say, "these are the best years of your life." Or "Have fun while you can." But we provide poor models for young people to follow. We see these choices as events —a dinner out, a ball game, a vacation—and overlook the moment-to-moment chances we have to make a great many of these choices. We may make these choices in OK or OD ways—teasing is the characteristic example of OD enjoying. And we may make these choices in ways that are fresh or stereotypical in terms of sex, age and role. For example, boys are traditionally supposed to enjoy themselves through team sports, and girls through interpersonal pursuits. Younger people are expected to spend their time more than older persons in "frivolous" activities, and athletes and entertainers are looked to for enjoying choices. These choices are so highly stereotyped that we all may overlook many opportunities to make enjoying choices for ourselves or with others.

Many of your clients come to counseling because they do not experience much enjoyment in their lives, a few because they are the brunt of the OD enjoying choices of others. Your clients may have difficulty making enjoying choices for themselves and with others because they have overstressed the Biblical injunction, "put away childish things," without differentiating childish (foolish, unthinking, silly) from childlike (innocent, trusting, spontaneous).

Childlike usually suggests those qualities of childhood worthy of emulation or of admiration, such as innocence or straightforwardness; *childish* usually suggests less pleasing characteristics, such as peevishness or undeveloped mentality (*Webster's New Collegiate Dictionary*).

Your clients need to understand their own potential for enjoyment, and the need they and others have for OK enjoying choices.

Sorrowing choices. We make sorrowing choices whenever we express our negative feelings—such choices as being sad, feeling hurt, being angry, crying, pouting, and shouting. We may make these choices verbally: "I'm worried about Pat." "Oh, woe is me." "That's stupid!" Or we may express them non-verbally: A downcast look. Tears. Pounding on a table. We make these choices for ourselves. Even when others' negative feelings trigger sadness or anger in us, our sorrowing choices are our own. We may make these choices in OK or OD ways. It *should* be OK for us to express our negative feelings directly, although in our culture even reasonable statements of sadness may not be OK with others; certainly such statements are to be preferred over choices that are more clearly OD—choices that involve meanness or miserableness. And we may make these choices in ways that are fresh or stereotypical in terms of sex, age, and role. For example, females, young and old persons, and individuals (especially females) who are grieving, may be expected to express their sadness through tears. Others, especially adolescent through middle-aged males, may deny their needs to express negative feelings—even though they may be overwhelmed by those feelings—and they may not accept others' needs to express their negative feelings.

Some of your clients come to counseling because they have difficulty expressing their negative feelings because they see such expression as weak. Others have difficulty because they express their negative feelings too frequently and experience adverse reactions from others. Both groups of clients need to realize that others are affected by their negative feelings and choices. They need to understand that they and others have negative feelings that *will* be expressed; and they need to learn to find OK ways to express those feelings.

Thinking/Working choices. We make numerous thinking/working choices as we conduct the regular and special tasks of the day—choices such as wondering, contemplating, asking or answering questions, planning, doing, redoing, and procrastinating. We make some of these choices verbally: "How do you get the answer?" "First you divide, then add." "I ought to be finished with that tomorrow." However, we make even more of these choices non-verbally as we think about the matters we encounter, and as we take steps to complete our tasks. We may make these choices in OK or OD ways. The latter occurs most often when one person wants or needs enjoying or caring choices and the other keeps on working, or responds cognitively. And we may make these choices in ways that are fresh or stereotypical in terms of sex, age, and role. For example, males, younger persons, and entry-level employees may act without thinking sufficiently, while their opposite numbers may sometimes ponder longer than is necessary when action (work) is required.

Some of your clients come to counseling because they do not give themselves sufficient permission to think and to act effectively on their thoughts, and as a consequence feel powerless in their world. Other clients come because they enter into tasks too impulsively. Still others because they mull matters over in their minds *ad nauseum*, seldom getting their tasks completed. In each case they need to learn to use their potential for thinking and working effectively on their tasks and on their relationships.

SELF-EXAMINATION—JOURNAL ENTRY: Take several minutes and enter in your journal your reactions to the concepts discussed in this section. Consider the relevance of each of the concepts for you in your life. Discuss how you exercise each of the CREST choices in your life and whether you tend to make them in OK or OD ways. Continue your journal by considering the relevance of these concepts for particular clients you have encountered. Suggestion: head your entry CREST CHOICES.

We see it as vital for you to share these concepts with your clients, inviting their reactions and helping them see the relevance of these concepts in their lives. Most clients are unaware of the variety of choices they have open to them and act in habitual ways, often repeating inappropriate, OD patterns of behavior they have learned to use. Invite your clients' consideration of the concepts you see as most relevant for their needs and encourage them to apply to themselves any other concepts they see as appropriate. Help them explore which of the CREST choices they make in OK and OD ways, and encourage them to consider how they might implement new patterns of choices in their relationships with others.

Choice Awareness Concepts: Applications

Choice Awareness suggests that we influence, but do not cause, consequences to happen. It is helpful to realize that our behaviors have consequences, but not all the choices of others that follow our behaviors are consequences of what we have said or done. If to our "Good morning" another person replies "What's so good about it?" it is unlikely that our good words *caused* that response. What we did or said yesterday, the tone of voice we used, an earlier action of that person's spouse or child, the traffic that day, and the condition of that person's physical or mental health are some of the factors that may have *influenced* that response. The likely, but not guaranteed, consequence of a positive choice is a positive response; the likely, but not guaranteed, consequence of a negative choice is a negative response. Likely consequences serve to confirm our expectations; less likely consequences confirm the other person's freedom to choose. Though results cannot be guaranteed, at least from time to time we can influence consequences more positively than we do.

Your clients may do little to produce positive consequences and much to produce negative consequences because they follow habit patterns and are unaware of the impact of their behaviors. Whether their actions are passive or aggressive, if they believe they are not powerful people they may remain blithely unaware that their choices have impact on others. You can help them see that they have impact on others and that they can act in ways that may be more likely to produce the positive consequences they seek.

Choice Awareness suggests that we choose our feelings in the moment. Because we are complex creatures, in many situations we experience a mixture of feelings. Someone invites us to speak to a group about a matter of interest to us; we may simultaneously feel excited, concerned, inadequate, complimented, and downright frightened. Someone we care for is late and we feel love, anticipation, annoyance, eagerness, fear, anger, and, in the moment of that person's arrival, relief. In either situation we select from among the mix of feelings those we act upon. It may be our habit to act out of inadequacy in the former instance, and anger in the latter, but our reaction is our choice. Our feelings do not own us—we are the owners of our feelings and of the choices we make, based on those feelings.

Your clients are unlikely to have a clear sense that their feelings are in their control unless they have known people who act as though they have choices about their feelings. It is important to help your clients understand that they are in charge of their feelings, rather than the other way around, and to help them learn to select their positive feelings more often as a basis for their words and actions.

Choice Awareness suggests that we choose our feelings about ourselves and others. Most of us allow ourselves to be influenced by the labels others put on us when we were children. We take such labels as the shy one, a real pistol, good boy/girl, heart breaker, dummy, nuisance, and so forth, and we wear these as badges long after many of the adults or older children who pinned them on us have given them up. We may act on habits and labels even in the face of contrary information. For example, many people, at what seems like the last moment, scuttle their own chances for such attainments as promotions, earned degrees, or effective interpersonal relationships because succeeding in these matters does not fit their self-concepts. Similarly, we may continue to see others in terms of the labels we have put on them, not allowing them the space to change, or even scuttling their successes, because we have them conveniently pigeon-holed and find it difficult to change our views of them. We all need to understand, accept, and build upon our personal strengths, to continue to grow and develop, and to encourage others to do the same.

Your clients are likely to be among those people who, unaware, choose to focus on the negatives that exist among the various feelings they have about themselves. As Transactional Analysis suggests, they see themselves as Not OK. Persons who have not felt good about themselves or others have a long journey ahead and that journey must start with a single step. You can help your clients see that the journey toward better feelings about self and others may begin when they make a single, positive choice in a direction away from the one they have been taking.

SELF-EXAMINATION—JOURNAL ENTRY: Take several minutes and enter in your journal your reactions to the concepts discussed in this section. Consider the relevance of each of the concepts in your life. Be sure to discuss how you make choices involving your feelings about yourself and others. Suggestion: head your entry CREST CONCEPTS AND FEELINGS.

As with other choice concepts we see it as important for you to share these ideas with your clients, inviting their reactions and helping them see the relevance of these concepts in their lives. Most clients are unaware of the fact that they make choices based on their feelings in the moment, and that they choose their feelings about themselves and others. You may wish to encourage your clients to consider how they might make different choices of feelings and thereby implement new patterns in their relationships with others.

Choice Awareness Concepts: Counseling Implications

Choice Awareness theory supports minimum change in counseling as an objective. As a system designed to help individuals to take more effective control of their choices, Choice Awareness theory encourages you to conceptualize the mental health of your clients as if it were in a continuously-moving spiral. A few negative choices by others may move it downward. A few positive choices on their part and they may direct the spiral upward. Instead of the deeper level personality reconstruction objective that characterizes much counseling, then, Choice Awareness suggests a minimum change objective that is consistent with the ideas set forth a number of years ago by Leona Tyler (1960).

Most of your clients do not need to have their personalities reconstructed. They need to make more positive choices with others and for and about themselves, and to receive reinforcement from the changes they make. These objectives lend themselves to brief counseling processes and followup.

Choice Awareness theory supports inner well-being as an objective of counseling. Helping clients gain inner well-being is, in a very real sense, a primary objective of counseling. Choice Awareness theory suggests that this objective may be sought in much the same way that physical well-being is sought—by direct action that is designed to create well-being, rather than by waiting until something goes wrong, solving the problem, and hoping that well-being emerges as a result.

As your clients might seek to achieve physical well-being through exercise of muscles and suitable food and liquid intake, they may seek to achieve inner well-being through exercise of positive choices and suitable intake of feedback from the environment—if you let them know that is possible.

Choice Awareness suggests that clients need first to be listened to in counseling. The less is more counseling principle suggests that most clients need first to be listened to, both because few have had that opportunity and because for many that experience is a sufficient basis for taking needed action. Choice Awareness theory encourages counselors to use the skills of listening first, then more active approaches as they are needed.

Many of your clients need little more than to air their concerns. For others that airing may stimulate action that resolves the issue at hand; the rest need more active counseling approaches.

Choice Awareness suggests that clients be helped to learn and to use choice-making skills. Because of the perceived sense of choicelessness in most of your clients, despite the numerous opportunities they have available for making moment-to-moment choices, Choice Awareness theory encourages you as counselor to participate actively in enabling your clients to understand the choices available to them and to plan and rehearse making more effective choices.

Your clients have most of the choice-making skills they need. They may habitually restrict their caring and ruling choices to their interactions with children or others in their charge, and they may make relatively few enjoying choices in the moment, for example. Though choice-making skills may be dormant or applied in habitual ways by your clients, they are largely within their repertoires. Most often they need help in using skills they already possess.

Choice Awareness theory suggests that fundamental, traditional, aims of counseling are choice related. Though originally proposed by Cribbin (1955) many years ago, the following fundamental, traditional, choice-related aims of counseling are relevant today: (1) helping clients develop initiative, responsibility, self-direction, and self-guidance; (2) helping clients gain in the ability to choose their own goals wisely; (3) helping clients to know themselves and their environment in order to function more effectively in their world; (4) helping clients anticipate, avoid, and prevent crises from arising in their lives; (5) helping clients recognize, understand, meet, and solve problems they face; (6) helping clients make wise choices, plans, and interpretations at critical points in their lives; (7) helping clients acquire the insights and techniques necessary to enable them to solve their own future problems; and (8) helping clients become effective citizens who participate in and contribute to the democratic way of life.

Your clients make choices related to all of the above aims of counseling. Your task as a counselor can be more effectively handled when you see these aims as involving choices, and act accordingly. Certainly if you are to achieve the final aim, enabling clients to become effective participants and contributors in the democratic way of life, you must help them gain a sense of themselves as persons who are able to make effective choices.

COUNSELING APPLICATION—JOURNAL ENTRY: Take several minutes and enter in your journal your reactions to the concepts discussed above, indicating the extent to which you subscribe to these concepts and apply them in your counseling. Continue your entry by discussing the changes it would make in your approach to counseling if you subscribed fully to these concepts. Suggestion: head your entry MY CHOICES IN COUNSELING.

What is Choice Awareness?

Choice Awareness is a system designed to help individuals understand themselves and others, and to enable them to make more responsible choices in their lives. It is a comprehensible and comprehensive system that uses straightforward, understandable terms that may be shared by counselors and clients, adults and children. As a counseling theory, Choice Awareness helps clients see themselves as responsible choosers and assists them to combat the inertia that effects their lives.

From the point of view of Choice Awareness, one of your central tasks as a counselor is that of helping clients understand and incorporate relevant choice concepts effectively in their actions and interactions. For one client a key concept might be the reality that he or she is making choices all the time, for another it might be clarifying and acting on relationship goals, for a third it might be helping that person become an initiator in interpersonal interactions, and for a fourth it might be mastering the skills of making more effective self- and other-caring choices. Inner well-being depends on making effective choices, and you are challenged here to help your clients master choice-making skills as needed. A significant and worthwhile objective of counseling is that of enabling your clients to understand and find suitable ways to integrate relevant Choice Awareness concepts in their lives.

Choice Awareness is designed to counter some of the criticisms of current counseling practices: that counseling is too dependent on the medical model, that present counseling systems do not sufficiently emphasize choice behavior, and that counseling is too often focused on countering negatives. Choice Awareness involves bringing habitual ways of thinking, feeling, and acting to a conscious level, thus enabling clients to get beyond superficial S→R choice-making. Choice Awareness broadens the concept of counseling; it considers the cognitive, affective, and behavioral domains; it synthesizes current theories; and it incorporates them in a unified, systematic, eclectic approach in which the concept of choice is central.

Choice Awareness is the new *systematic eclecticism.*

References

Berne, E. (1964). *Principles of group treatment.* New York: Oxford University Press.

Berne, E. (1972). *What do you say after you say hello?* New York: Grove Press.

Bloom, J. W. (1973). The effects of transactional analysis on the self-concept, locus of control, and sociometric status of sixth-grade children. Unpublished doctoral thesis. Purdue University, Lafayette, Indiana.

Brammer, L. M. (1986). Needed: a paradigm shift in counseling theory. *The Counseling Psychologist, 14,* 443-447.

Cribbin, J. J. (1955). A critique of the philosophy of modern guidance. *The Catholic Educational Review, 53,* 73-91.

Frankl, V. E. (1959). *Man's search for meaning.* New York: Washington Square Press.

Freed, A. M. (1971). *TA for kids.* Sacramento: Alvyn M. Freed.

Glasser, W. (1965). *Reality therapy.* New York: Harper & Row.

Harris, T. A. (1967). *I'm OK, you're OK.* New York: Harper and Row.

James, M., & Jongeward, D. (1971). *Born to win.* Reading, MA: Addison-Wesley.

Nelson, R. C. (1976). Choice Awareness: An unlimited horizon. *Personnel & Guidance Journal, 54,* 462-467.

Nelson, R. C. (1980). Choice Awareness encourages effective citizenship. *Educational Leadership, 38,* 53-57.

Nelson, R. C. & Bloom, J. W. (1975). *Choice Awareness: An innovative guidance process.* Boston: Houghton Mifflin.

Stefflre, B. (1965). *Theories of counseling.* New York: McGraw Hill.

Tyler, L. E. (1960). Minimum change therapy. *Personnel and Guidance Journal, 38,* 475-479.

Chapter 2

Spa, Learning, and Relearning: Accenting Spa

Level I: Counseling as Spa

Choice Awareness posits three levels of counseling: *spa, learning,* and *relearning.* Counselors generally focus their efforts with individual clients at one of two levels: learning or relearning. Here we suggest that they also always incorporate Level I counseling, *counseling as spa.* The focus in counseling as spa is on encouraging clients to appreciate themselves, their strengths, their abilities, and their interests, and on helping them to re-create themselves through enjoyable experiences.

When people seek counseling, what do they really want? Assistance with a long or short term difficulty or help with a decision, certainly. But do they want more?

When people return for counseling some time after they have completed what appeared to be a successful counseling process, does that indicate that counseling was a failure? Are they recidivists? What do they really want? Could it be that the counseling process in itself was so rewarding to these people—because they were encouraged to find good things to think and feel about themselves—that their central, underlying purpose is to renew those positive thoughts and feelings?

Counseling as spa is needed because all clients—from healthy, normal people who have an immediate need, to those who experience extreme long-term difficulties—want to feel good about themselves and their world; and because clients enter counseling in part to gain these good feelings—even though their search is often overlooked because the focus of the effort is on problem-solving.

Many clients who return for counseling after a period of time do so because the counseling process itself felt good to them, because someone listened, and because someone helped them gain a sense that their problems were surmountable and that they could handle them. Rather than seeing the returns to counseling as recidivism and indications of failure, counselors should consider whether or not their returns are indications of success and efforts to regain the positive feelings that occurred as a result of the experience. For many clients the counseling experience may have been almost-joyful, almost-exhilarating, and they hope in the inner recesses of their minds that the next exposure to counseling will take them further on the road to gaining the natural high they sense might be just ahead. Still other clients fail to progress as rapidly as counselors would have them. It is likely that some do so because they believe they will be cut loose from the benefits of the relationship if they agree that the problem is solved. The rationale for counseling as spa is that clients in counseling want to experience the joy of a relationship in which they are valued for themselves, and a process in which they are encouraged to feel good about themselves. Those are legitimate and positive functions of counseling.

In counseling as spa clients see counselors during the high points and plateaus of their lives, and during those times when they need to rise above the mire of their difficulties. They share their joys and excitements, the everyday and the mundane, and they present themselves as coping with the nuisances and aggravations of their lives—or they shake off those aggravations for the present. No problems of any great depth are presumed to affect clients deeply during the moments in which they seek spa as the focus of counseling. However, it may be evident that they need to spend some time in the learning or the relearning level of counseling.

Spa focuses on such matters as strengths, skills, self-concepts, life scripts, feelings about self and others, thought patterns, behaviors, and the sense of purpose or meaning. The exploration is undertaken in the same spirit as the exploration in the physical domain is undertaken in a spa. Attention is given to tightness and flabbiness, but the overall objective is the renewal of existing strength.

Counselors listen as clients reflect on the joys and commonplace events of their lives, "stroke them" for their self reported gains, "warm them" by supporting their efforts and their goals, and "massage them" to renew their strength for the struggles they face. The accent is on the positive, and the strengths and capacities of the individual are reinforced. At the same time counselors remain alert for the tightness that suggests undue tension, and the flabbiness that suggests insufficient exercise of their capacities, either of which may suggest that counseling as learning or relearning is indicated.

Nearly all clients will benefit if they and their counselors spend some time at spa level during the process of counseling. And it is likely that they will want to return to "take the waters" periodically, to engage regularly in the renewal and growth process offered through Choice

Awareness. Either the counselor or the client may suggest counseling as spa, and either may suggest contracting for a deeper level of contact if that seems appropriate.

SELF-EXAMINATION—JOURNAL ENTRY: At this point, although your understanding of the concept of spa must obviously be limited, discuss the extent to which you believe you spend some of your time at spa level in your own personal life—feeling really good about yourself, appreciating your strengths, and enjoying your special skills—for example, your sensitivity to other people. Suggestion: head your entry SPA FOR ME.

Following a brief discussion of the learning and relearning levels of counseling, the emphasis in the remainder of this chapter is on counseling as spa. This is appropriate since the balance of this work focuses primarily on counseling as learning and relearning. Spa receives special attention early in this work in large measure because it emphasizes a new, foundational direction for the field of counseling.

Level II: Counseling as Learning

The focus in Level II counseling, *counseling as learning*, is on assisting clients to explore the concerns they have and on enabling them to learn new ways of confronting those concerns. The client who seeks counseling at the level of learning is expected to present problems that are within the normal range of difficulties faced from time to time by eighty to ninety per cent of the populace.

Content can be similar in all three levels of counseling. What varies is the depth of the content and the assumptions made about the duration of the process. When counselors function at Level II, counseling as learning, they emphasize ways in which the person functions at present, and they assist the client in generating new alternatives to evaluate and use in coping with concerns and frustrations. Clients who seek counseling at this level may also need to engage in relearning from time to time, and they are likely to gain greatly from periodic exploration at spa level as well.

In counseling as learning, clients see counselors during the confusing and frustrating times of their lives, when they face personal concerns or have need to make major or minor decisions that are difficult for them. They share their concerns and the problems they have in coping with the aggravations of life. The counselor helps them understand their own feelings and their patterns of behaviors and enables them to find alternative responses and develop new methods for achieving their goals. The emphasis is on developing approaches to confront new or persistent, minor to moderate level problems—rather than on relearning, but that emphasis is more a matter of degree than of kind. Assumptions are made that the degree of difficulty is not great, that the duration of counseling will be limited, and that extended counseling will require a new contract, or will become counseling as spa.

Level III: Counseling as Relearning

The focus in Level III counseling, *counseling as relearning,* is on enabling clients to understand the ways in which they have been functioning ineffectively; to "unlearn" patterns of thoughts, feelings, and behaviors that have served them poorly; and to "relearn" more effective patterns of choices. Problems of some depth are presumed to affect the client who engages in the relearning process. However, differences among the three levels of counseling are frequently more matters of degree than of kind.

The word *relearning* is seen here as applicable since in most instances clients have available to them the skills and patterns of behaviors they need. Frequently the problem is that they have narrowly restricted or discarded skills and patterns of choices that they could use in effective ways, and they need to be helped to activate or reactivate these skills and patterns. Counseling as relearning emphasizes the exploration of dysfunctional ways of acting, thinking, and feeling; unlearning existing patterns; and learning new modes of acting, thinking, and feeling.

Clients who engage in the relearning process see counselors because they are deeply involved with long term patterns of behaviors, thoughts, or feelings that no longer serve them well, even though those patterns may have served as effective defenses for them in the past. These clients may be self-referred, or others may have encouraged or mandated their receiving assistance. The counselor helps them understand the benefits and risks of making changes in their patterns of behaviors, thoughts, or feelings, and enables them to make changes that are indicated. Clients who need to engage in major relearning tasks are likely to gain from periodic exploration at spa and learning levels as well.

> COUNSELING APPLICATION—JOURNAL ENTRY: In terms of your present understanding, discuss the extent to which you believe you emphasize each of the three levels: spa, learning, and relearning, in your counseling. Continue your entry by considering whether you believe it would be appropriate for you to redistribute the time you give each of these levels, and if so, how. Suggestion: head your entry SPA, LEARNING, RELEARNING.

Spa

The emphasis on helping clients achieve spa experiences in the course of counseling is one of the unique aspects of Choice Awareness theory. We believe that in the course of counseling most clients need joyful, reinforcing experiences that go beyond problem-solving. We see such experiences as spa or spa-like, and suggest that the counseling office, like the spa, should be a place where clients can seek relaxation and engage in positive, self-sustaining activities. Beneath the obvious or not-so-obvious presenting problem for most clients is a wish to feel genuinely good about themselves and to experience the joy of life and inner well-being, perhaps even beyond their capacity to imagine.

Some clients, especially those who are met in such institutions as public schools, colleges, universities, and employment settings, want nothing more out of counseling than a confirmation that they are OK, or that the decision they have made seems to be effective. Both can be seen as spa objectives. Others have worked through their problems and would like to revel in the joy to which they feel entitled as a result of their progress. Even those who are in a continuing struggle with some kind of difficulty may benefit from pauses in their struggles, during which they may be helped to feel good about themselves and their efforts.

Perhaps you, like most counselors, have focused on problem-solving—on learning or relearning processes. If so, you tend to over-look the need your clients have to experience the fullness of the joy of self-discovery and growth. You may see the attempts clients make to reward themselves as resistance to continued effort, or as evidence that the counseling process has been completed. Rather than providing a vehicle for enjoyment of the gains made, then determining whether further counseling is needed, you may return to your own agenda or terminate the counseling process.

In Choice Awareness theory the need for spa experiences is readily acknowledged, and you as counselor are urged to offer such opportunities throughout the counseling process. The parallel to spa experiences in the physical domain remains relevant here. Physical spa experiences are rewarding because they feel good in themselves and because they are pleasurable and fun—even though they may clarify the need for developing additional skills, or for maintaining suitable body weight, for example. Similarly, counseling-as-spa experiences have their rewards because they feel good in themselves, and because the activities are pleasurable and fun—even though they may clarify the need for solving additional problems, for gaining interpersonal skills, or for achieving an improved self-view. Certainly, *work* ought to occur from the beginning of counseling, but as a counselor you may also wish to give attention to your clients' enjoyment of themselves, of the competencies they have, and of the gains they make—from the beginning of counseling.

In Chapter One we drew a parallel between the work of the counselor and the physician, suggesting that for you as a counselor, and for physicians as well, the offering of spa opportunities could be justified solely on the grounds of the occasional problem that would surface. A physician might learn that a client's nutritional habits involving a crash diet are counter-productive, or you might learn that one of your clients is relishing the extremes to which he or she has gone in assertiveness. Over and above the occasional problem that might emerge, however, we suggest that spa experiences are worthwhile on their own merit. Human beings have too few opportunities to receive reinforcement in their lives. Although both medical and counseling professionals might argue that using time solely for reinforcement would be a questionable practice, the potential contribution to the mental and/or physical health and well-being of clients clearly justifies the expenditure of some effort at achieving spa.

Achieving Spa

More than most other parts of this source, this chapter is experientially oriented. It suggests some points of discussion through which you may achieve counseling as spa with your clients, and offers you experiences through which you may achieve spa for yourself. One result of engaging in these experiences is that you should have a deeper understanding of your clients' reactions to the concept of spa, another is that you should find it easier to create counseling-as-spa experiences for your clients.

Take a moment now and reflect upon the extent to which you agree with the following statement: *I do many things well.* You will be asked to note this in a journal entry later:

If you are like most people, you may see your own worst side, dwell on the qualities you do not like in yourself, focus on what you *cannot* do or be, and in general express uncertainty about your good qualities. The same is likely to be even more true for your clients. In either case it is not a good way, as they say, to run a railroad. Certainly if you or your clients want to improve "your railroad's" business, you have to know what your liabilities are; but, your deficits are not what produce for you. It is more important to know your assets: what stock and how many miles of track you have, what your land holdings are, what your financial assets are, and what business contracts you have been awarded.

For you or your clients, focusing on assets should be like going to a spa, bathing in health-giving waters, engaging in pleasurable exercise, and feeling the warmth of a brisk massage. If you and your clients are like most people, you can use physical spa experiences to refresh you so that you can go on with your everyday tasks sustained by two things you may need badly—relaxed muscles and a new outlook. Similarly, you and your clients can achieve inner spa experiences and move toward inner well-being as a result of focusing on things you can do, releasing some of your inner tensions, and gaining a new internal outlook.

CONSIDER THE FOLLOWING:

Barbara was highly self-critical and negative about her capabilities. She compared herself to an older brother and sister and she always found herself wanting. A group exercise her counselor organized helped turn her thinking around. Group members were asked to take turns citing basic or complex things they were able to do: breathe, eat, walk, talk, sleep, think, play the ukulele, dance, and so forth. Barbara felt a rush of warmth each time her turn came and she responded: make friends, smile, cook. From the ideas she and other group members suggested, she could begin to see how many key behaviors she demonstrated every day. Even when another group member said he could fly a plane, something she had always wanted to do, the glow remained. Rather than focus on that deficit, she was inspired by the number of simple, everyday skills and abilities the experience reminded her that she had.

Many of your clients, like Barbara, lose sight of the simple, everyday things they can do, focusing instead on things they cannot do. It is important for them to come to the realization that they spend more time than is desirable in this negative pursuit. Perhaps you yourself are inclined to focus on negatives, rather than emphasizing the things you can do.

SELF-EXAMINATION—JOURNAL ENTRY: Take a few minutes, at least five to ten, and as the first part of your entry, write down the heading and discuss your immediate reaction to the statement that was highlighted earlier in this section: I DO MANY THINGS WELL. Next, under the heading THINGS I CAN DO, build a list of simple, everyday things you can do, perhaps beginning with the simplest of all—breathe. Savor each idea as you write it. Keep at it until you get a sense of joy, of spa, from the positiveness of the experience. Continue your journal entry by reflecting on your list of can-do's, and what you learned from making the list.

••••••••••

Be sure to take time out to reflect and to make note of your reflections as you are requested— especially in this chapter.

••••••••••

You cannot be just a spectator in gaining inner well-being through better choices any more than you can gain physical well-being by watching others exercise.

••••••••••

When you use this activity with your clients, be very reinforcing about their taking pleasure in the things they can do. Point out that their strengths provide a solid base on which they can build, while their weaknesses are like sand on which they cannot build—and dwelling on weaknesses unduly undermines their security.

Labels, Traits

Most of us put labels on ourselves that limit us and hold us in a kind of time warp that often reflects more on the past than the present. Our labels become I-can't-help-it's or I-have-to's that interfere with our freedom to choose. In some measure inner well-being comes from shucking off old labels that bind us too tightly. A trip to the spa may help us see that the labels we have that do not serve us well can be discarded, or at least modified.

If you say, "I'm a night person"; you may use that as an excuse for being rude or dull in the morning, and it is a self-fulfilling prophecy. That is, if you say it often enough you really *cannot* seem to function well early in the day. However, night person or not, you are not likely to miss the 7 a.m. flight for a week in Bermuda, or for an important business meeting or interview, even if it means getting up at 4:30 a.m. We each control our labels, our labels do not control us. Holding labels loosely or discarding them altogether can help us move toward inner well-being.

CONSIDER THE FOLLOWING:

Bob was a late maturer who had always been shy around women. He had begun to see himself as a failure there. A fleeting brush with homosexuality had caused him to begin to think of himself as gay, yet he strongly resisted that label for himself. His counselor pointed out his resistance and helped him see that if one ten/thousandth of his behavior had been homosexual, it was hardly a basis for taking on that label as a total description of himself. Bob began to work seriously on his shyness, and ultimately met and married a fine young woman. His experiences in that relationship led him to say to his counselor in a subsequent counseling-as-spa visit, "I may be one part in ten thousand homosexual, but I'm nine thousand, nine hundred and ninety-nine parts heterosexual."

Like Bob, you or your clients may describe yourselves with labels that limit you or affect you in negative ways. It may be valuable for you to take time to reflect on limiting or negative labels you use to describe yourself or your behavior.

SELF EXAMINATION—JOURNAL ENTRY: Take a few minutes to think, then enter in your journal a list of three or four of the *labels* you put on yourself. Use the heading: LABELS. Go beyond listing *roles* or *jobs* such as parent, child, spouse, student, mechanic, secretary, and so forth. Think of *labels* like night person, procrastinator, responder, optimist, Type A, and so forth. Continue your entry by reflecting on two or more of the labels you noted and their negative implications. Discuss the following: Are the labels you have been putting on yourself useful? How do you reinforce these labels? What *could* you do, what *would you want* to do, to change your labels?

When you use this activity with your clients, reinforce the idea that, whether they realize it or not, the labels they have been carrying are choices, and if they wish they can change their labels or discard them altogether, even though that may take considerable time and effort.

Traits

Here are several pairs of adjectives. Take some time to decide which trait in each pair describes you best. You will be asked to note these in a special way in the journal entry that follows. In some cases you will find that the other adjective also describes you, but less well; keep those adjectives in mind as well.

BRAVE	COWARDLY
SAD	HAPPY
FRIENDLY	ALOOF
PESSIMISTIC	OPTIMISTIC
ORGANIZED	DISORGANIZED
SLOPPY	NEAT
THOUGHTFUL	THOUGHTLESS
WITHHOLDING	GENEROUS
HONEST	DISHONEST

SELF-EXAMINATION—JOURNAL ENTRY: Take at least five minutes to make this journal entry. Under the heading TRAITS, in capital letters, jot down the traits above that describe you. Then, in small letters beside those traits, jot down any of the contrasting traits that also describe you. In the same way, add other relevant trait pairs that are not on the list. Next, recall contrasting events that might lead you to conclude that *both* traits in a pair describe you *in ways that are OK for you.* For example, for BRAVE and COWARDLY you may recall an event in which your avoidance of danger may have seemed cowardly. Perhaps you skirted around an angry crowd rather than take the shortest way across the middle, an action that you now see as clearly OK. Then recall another event in which you took what appeared to be a brave course, that you also see as OK. Do this for several traits, including those you added to the list. Discuss how your traits and labels relate to your sense of inner well-being.

When you use this activity with your clients, reinforce the idea that many of the traits they ascribe to themselves suggest both positive and negative behaviors. Help them accept two ideas: that few traits apply to anyone all the time, and that traits involve choices of behaviors.

One recurring theme of Choice Awareness is that all of us oversimplify issues by putting them in either-or terms. Are you happy or sad? Were you ever tempted to answer YES when you were asked such a question? Maybe that response would have been best.

Are you not really brave in some situations and cowardly in others?

Think about it. That is true for most of us.

Suppose you found yourself in a position in which you had to give a speech to a potentially hostile audience. Or pitch to a murderous hitter who aims at pitchers like you. Or ask about a raise you were supposed to receive, but have not. Or save a child from drowning. Or stop a driverless car that is beginning to drift away from a curb toward a crowd of people—and loud sounds from a nearby construction site prevent your being heard. Think of other situations you believe call for bravery.

In all likelihood you would act in a brave way in some of the situations some of the time, but not in all of the situations all of the time.

Are you brave or cowardly then?

YES.

The relevance of all this is that you need to see where you are in the balance between being brave and cowardly, happy and sad, sloppy and neat, and so forth, and accept yourself the way you are, at least for now. Otherwise you are likely to pick one adjective or another in a pair, take it as your label, and act in ways that fit the label even when it is not in your best interest.

Many young people and adults accept challenges from others that endanger their lives or their well-being because they see themselves as brave, and they believe they must accept any challenge to their bravery. An important part of bravery is being secure enough to say no when the risks are too high—even if others offer the taunt, "You're just chicken." For most of us it is a spa experience to accept ourselves and the breadth of our traits.

CONSIDER THE FOLLOWING:

Marisa saw herself as a "neatnik," both at work and at home. Her husband accepted her needs and helped maintain the household in accordance with Marisa's standards. When their twins were born Marisa took off six months from work, kept their home in order, and was a good wife and mother—even according to her high expectations. Once she resumed her career, however, she worked herself into a frenzy trying to compensate to the twins for the time she spent away from them during the day, maintain the household in "apple-pie-order," and make up for lost time on her job. Physical complaints ultimately forced her to reconsider her priorities. She put away some of the nice pieces of crystal and bric-a-brac that she found herself protecting from the twins, scheduled household chores on a less frequent basis, and modified her expectations for order and neatness—and decided she was still OK.

Like Marisa and many of your clients, you may have taken on a label—though not necessarily that of "neatnik"—and behaved in such a way that you make the label "come true." You made your behavior conform to your label. If the label is positive and within reach, you may wish to maintain it. If the label creates expectations that are unreasonable, you can modify it.

SELF-EXAMINATION—JOURNAL ENTRY: Take a few minutes to think, then enter in your journal your observations about any *positive* trait or label you put on yourself that tends to stress you unduly from time to time—under the heading; TRAITS OR LABELS AND STRESS. Discuss whether or not you might allow yourself some greater latitude in living up to that label. If you have no such trait or label, consider whether your standards for yourself on some trait might be upgraded somewhat—but not to the point where you stress yourself.

When you use this activity with your clients, reinforce the idea that many labels are self-fulfilling prophecies; change the label and the behavior can change as well. Help them see that it is their choice to maintain or change a given label, gradually, over time.

Positive Statements and Strengths

Here are some positive statements you might say to yourself. Circle the number before *all* of the statements you believe apply to you. You will be asked to note these traits in the journal entry that follows.

1. I'm a loyal friend.
2. I have a pleasant personality.
3. When I say I'll do something I do it.
4. I'm friendly toward others.
5. I'm often generous.
6. I know right from wrong and I act accordingly.
7. I can be trusted.
8. I have a good sense of humor.
9. I'm a good worker.
10. I'm not moody.
11. I'm likable.
12. I'm a good conversationalist.
13. I don't walk over other people.
14. I don't let others walk on me.

SELF-EXAMINATION—JOURNAL ENTRY: Take a few minutes to think about, then enter in your journal, the positive statements that apply to you. Use the heading POSITIVE STATEMENTS. Continue your entry by writing additional statements until you believe you have represented the most important and positive things you can say about yourself. Add observations about how you feel as a result of this activity.

When you use this activity with your clients, reinforce the quality and quantity of the positive statements marked and added to their lists. Help them find other statements they may add to their lists, and encourage them to make additions on their own in the future.

It is important for you to realize what your strengths are and to make positive statements about yourself. The alternative is likely to be that you spend time berating and criticizing yourself, thereby heaping gloom on yourself and making matters worse. The same goes for your clients.

While it would be objectionable if your clients were to brag about themselves frequently for all to hear, it is quite another matter if they silently recognize the kinds of strengths they have—or if they enter them in a private journal so they can reinforce themselves periodically for their positive qualities.

In our society there seems to be a tendency to value modesty over many other traits. We seem to be quite schizophrenic about this tendency, however, if we can judge by the attention we give to someone like Muhammed Ali, who often said boldly, "I'm the greatest." For those who give great credence to the Biblical injunction, "Blessed are the meek," it is important to reinforce the point that meekness can be an outward expression of great strength that "is not puffed up." To take this point one step further, a *New Testament* injunction is: "Love your neighbor as yourself." That puts self-love, or self-respect, on a very high level. It suggests that the amount individuals love themselves equals the amount they should love their neighbors—but the *first* criterion is love for self. Finally, it seems clear that those people who love themselves least in our society, and who in turn love others least, are among those who are most likely to turn up in counseling as clients. One key to inner well-being is knowing and appreciating our inner strengths

CONSIDER THE FOLLOWING:

Daucie was a student in a class of middle-school students with which I once worked. Although I saw him as a well-liked, effective student, and a genuinely polite and sociable youngster, I became somewhat concerned about him because he was so quiet in class. I had met his parents socially and felt very much at ease broaching the subject of Daucie's quietness with them. Subsequently, they talked to their son and he was very open and honest in his response: "There are enough kids who need all the attention they can get, so I just let *them* have it." I believe that it was Daucie's realization of his own strengths that allowed him to be comfortable receiving my attention when I gave it, and accepting of the need I had to give attention to others the rest of the time. That is the very essence of personal security.

Take a moment now and decide to what extent you believe the following statements apply to you:

"I am aware of my personal strengths."

"I feel a quiet comfort in myself."

"I feel a true and healthy affection for my self."

"My self concept allows me to enjoy inner well-being."

SELF-EXAMINATION—JOURNAL ENTRY: Take a few minutes to think about these statements. Discuss in your journal the extent to which they apply to you. Use the heading: POSITIVE STATEMENTS. Continue your entry by stating the thoughts you have at this time about how you might either sustain your self-concept (if it is positive), or change your self-concept (if it is negative), so that you might have a greater sense of inner well-being. What spa experiences might help you achieve greater inner well-being?

When you use this activity with your clients, give them support for any of the statements they can apply to themselves. If they contend that none of these statements fits them, encourage them to select one statement as a goal they might work toward over time. Be sure the goal selected is one they may be able to reach.

Games and Scripts

Games and scripts are two key elements in the Transactional Analysis lexicon (Berne, 1964). Games are ongoing series of transactions that may appear to be complementary, but that contain an ulterior transaction and a predictable payoff. We will use *Uproar* here as an example. Scripts are life roles that are predetermined once the players build particular patterns of behavior, and those patterns are most often encouraged or determined within the family. The life script we will use next as an example is *Losing My Mind*. Clients who evidence a game or script may be helped to deal with it on the level of learning or relearning. But, clients may also be helped to see its humorous side, or may be rewarded for any actions that suggest they are making better choices, thus achieving counseling as spa.

As we have suggested, in the game of *Uproar* as in other games, roles tend to be predetermined. In this case, one player is the accuser and the other the defendant. In our example, the accuser is the father and the defendant is his teenage daughter, Alicia, who has sought counseling. In a typical rendition of the game, Father sees Alicia putting on her sweater and yells, "Where in hell are you going? The dishes aren't done and you haven't cracked a book yet." Alicia begins to defend herself, an argument results, she runs off to her room in tears, and slams the door. Thus the game begins with Father sending an ulterior "You're not OK," message, in TA terms, and the payoff is that the two maintain interaction, but avoid any semblance of closeness (James and Jongeward, 1971).

If Alicia were your client, and you had helped to identify for her the game she and her father have played in the past, you might subsequently invite a spa experience by saying, "OK, you said a minute ago you had a good week with your dad. How about sharing with me the choices you made that foiled the game of *Uproar*. I'm sure he gave you the opportunity to play it this week." That experience would be at the spa level if you helped Alicia reward herself for any positive interactions she initiated: "I did one of the things we talked about last time. I asked Dad's advice about something—whether he thought Shirley was taking advantage of me when she asked to borrow my notes—rather than waiting for him to start his attack." Suppose she fell into his trap in another instance—"He lit into me when I was exactly one minute late and I let him get me all upset even though I'd practiced saying calmly, 'Thank you, Dad, for worrying about me.'" You might help Alicia see the humor in falling into the trap, thereby lessening the likelihood that she would make the same choice in the future.

Suppose over time you come to the conclusion that Hal is playing out a very serious and potentially deadly life script—when the term life script is taken to mean "...a person's ongoing program for his[her] life drama which dictates where he[she] is going with his[her] life and how he[she] is to get there" (James & Jongeward, 1971, p. 69). The script Hal is compulsively acting out can be called *Losing My Mind*. You discuss that possibility with him and he agrees that may be the case. He tells you there has been a history of mental illness in his family and that for brief moments he sometimes loses touch with reality. His parents often suggest he is just like his Uncle Charles—and Charles spent years in a mental institution. If you decide to work with Hal rather than referring him to another professional, your strategies for working with him will surely involve learning and relearning. But if you decide to take the counseling process to spa level, you might encourage him to list all the functional actions he has taken and the tasks he has performed successfully over the past week, encouraging him to revel in those evidences of his effectiveness and stability.

We have given but one sample of a game and a script in this brief discussion, but the process of counseling offers many possibilities for exploring these matters with clients. Despite any appearances to the contrary, all games and scripts involve choices. An important dimension of counseling can be that of enabling individuals to make effective choices rather than blindly playing out parts in games and scripts. Effective contributions to this goal can be made at the level of spa.

Creating Spa Moments
Throughout Counseling

There is every reason for counseling to be a spa experience for the counselor as well as for the client. In a genuine sense, Choice Awareness is a matter of freeing the counselor to work creatively and systematically with the client. Counselors who gives themselves permission to be creative can interweave spa moments within any of the levels of counseling through the use of graphics and everyday materials which help focus the attention of the client, present important ideas metaphorically, and lighten the atmosphere—bringing a momentary smile—while furthering the goals of counseling.

Using paper and a felt pen, for example—even if you are the least artistic counselor who ever trod the earth—you can draw a rudimentary sketch of a train headed toward a fork in the roadbed, where one side leads to trouble on a track labeled OD and the other leads to more positive outcomes on a track labeled OK. In such a way you can represent what is happening with many of your clients. You can draw a series of three ovals and mouths that represent a smiling face, a neutral face, and a frowning face, and label it WHICH FACE DO I SHOW?—thereby helping clients see that they are choosing a feeling response to a particular circumstance. You can draw a monstrous stick figure towering over a cringing, smaller stick figure, and label it HOW TOM SEES HIS BOSS. You can make a sketch in which two people say to the client, "You've got to choose between us," and label it WHICH WAY TO GO? You can boldly print lists of alternatives, where appropriate—with or without an accompanying grimacing face—for example, with a person who gets in arguments or fights all the time, and label it WHEN I FEEL LIKE FIGHTING.

Two significant advantages are likely to accrue from such graphics: first, they tend to focus discussion and encourage periodic return to the topic at hand; and second, they can be carried away by clients as tangible reminders of actions they had agreed to take (see Nelson, 1987 reference for a fuller explanation of these ideas and additional ways of using graphics in counseling).

In an ASCA Elementary/Middle School Guidance Conference session, Ed Jacobs (1988) offered several additional suggestions of creative techniques and props for use in counseling.

- Take a styrofoam cup and label it JOE'S SELF ESTEEM. Let Joe hold it for a moment, then have him put it on a chair and have that action represent his giving his self-esteem to his boss, mother, spouse, friend, or other person. Help Joe see that he keeps choosing to give his self-esteem away, but that he can take it back, with difficulty perhaps, whenever he really chooses to do so.

- As a metaphor for their relationship, have any two people who are tense with one another hold either side of a rubber band, and pull. Ask them what will happen if they each choose to relax, work together, and accept the other as he or she is.

- Use a worthless audio cassette tape, pull out a segment, and tear it up to simulate making the choice of tearing up old, useless internal tapes that keep a client from functioning effectively.

- Have the client record negative self-messages that interfere with progress—"I'm a worthless piece of nothing," and so forth, and play those messages over and over. Suggest, "You'll never make progress if you choose to listen to this 'crap' all day long"; then tape over the message with positive self-statements to be listened to repeatedly.

- Hold up a video cassette and label it JUDY'S LIFE. Add the previous year's date, and ask Judy if that part of her life is complete. [Jacobs did not allow for the possibility that the *interpretation* of the previous year's "video" could be changed. For example, a recent divorcee could be helped to view the previous year as a year of growth in self-sufficiency rather than one of tragedy.] Using another tape, add the coming year's date and ask Judy if that part of her life is complete. Challenge her to make new choices so that the negatives she can see ahead for herself do not come to pass.

- If a previous life event troubles Bob, print the date (1981) or a descriptive term or phrase (MY ACCIDENT) and tape it to a chair. Help Bob see that he is choosing to allow the event to dominate his life. Keep the sign in view as long as it is a continuing focus.

- Ask Sarah, who does not seem to be listening to something that is in her interest, to cover one ear; smile and say, "I don't want you to let this to go in one ear and out the other."

- Use a lump of clay to help Frank see how he diminishes himself. Pull off a portion that represents how he reacts to his father's criticism, another that stands for his problems with one of his co-workers, a third that simulates his own negative self-feelings, and so forth. Then put the lumps back to re-form the whole, representing the idea that he can make the choice to get himself together.

- An idea of Jacobs', for use with two people like Juan and Maria who are in poor communication, is modified here as follows: Write the letter L, for listening, on one end of an index card, and the letter T, for talking, on the other end. Place the card on the table between the two people. When Juan is talking, the T points in his direction and Maria is asked to really choose to listen. When Maria wants to talk, she gestures toward the card and waits for a nod from Juan before turning the card around and beginning to communicate verbally.

- Have Jenny hold out her hands; name each problem she has and pile on one book after another—telling her that each book represents one of the many problems that bother her—until she says she cannot hold any more. Use this to help her see that she can gain by choosing to focus on *one* difficulty rather than letting all of them weigh her down.

- Use 5—1 and 10—1 scales regularly for various purposes with particular clients. Use a 5-point scale to represent "How I feel about myself today"—where 5 means "tops" and 1 means "I hate myself." Use a 10-point scale to represent "How my marriage (or other relationship) feels to me right now." In either case if Wesley picks any number that is not at or near the maximum, help him examine what he can choose to do that might help movement to the next higher number.

- If Ted is uncomfortable with intimacy, pick up a chair and hold it between the two of you. Say, "Now let's hug." Tell him that the chair represents the barrier he puts between himself and others.

- Use movement in counseling. For example, walk around in a circle with Joyce to demonstrate her circular thinking or acting. When she says, "I don't want to do this anymore," suggest, "That's not the point. You can't just *want* to change; you have to *do* something to change."

Two points that Jacobs (1988) made are well worth stating here. First, counseling should not be boring. There are many ways in which the interest of the client can be piqued and the creativity of the counselor can serve the needs of both individuals. Second, counseling itself should have a sense of movement about it. "We're taught to dawdle," he suggested. "Instead, we ought to move the counseling process along." When we tie that idea with the concept of spa in counseling, it becomes apparent that movement can increase the sense of joy in the process of counseling, thereby contributing to the well-being of the client and of the counselor at the same time.

COUNSELING APPLICATION—JOURNAL ENTRY: Consider—to what extent do you feel comfortable about offering counseling-as-spa experiences to your clients. Discuss the changes that would have to occur in you before you would feel comfortable in offering such experiences. Continue your entry by beginning a list (or create a card file) of activities you see as appropriate for you to use to create a spa environment for your clients. Head your entry (or label your file): SPA FOR MY CLIENTS.

All of the concepts of Choice Awareness can be used to create spa-activities. Use your creative powers and consider the potential for developing activities that are suggested by the following headings:

Habits and Choices

Relationships and Choices

Goals and Choices

OK/OD Choices

Caring Choices

Ruling Choices

Enjoying Choices

Sorrowing Choices

Thinking/Working Choices

Choices and Feelings in the Moment

Choices and Feelings About Self

Choices and Consequences

Gains Through Counseling

Developing spa experiences for clients offers you as counselor special opportunities to be creative and positive at the same time. The essence of spa is whatever is likely to generate positive feelings, joy, in

---

clients' lives. Tailor spa experiences in counseling to the special needs of your clients—in ways that reinforce them for gains they have made.

We suggest you save five minutes or so at the end of *any* interview to bring your clients to the level of spa in counseling; it will enable them to face the world with a more positive outlook, with greater strength to meet their daily challenges. You can do this by creating your own activities that fit the needs of your clients, or by extending lists or continuing with activities you have begun. Do not balk at repetition. Most clients can endure endless reiteration if it involves extending a list of positive traits, things I can do, or positive self-statements—in the same way they are able to endure hearing the statement "I love you" repeated endlessly, provided it is said sincerely. At the very least, consider creating spa moments throughout the counseling process.

Spa, Learning, and Relearning

Learning and relearning are familiar dimensions of counseling for experienced counselors. These dimensions involve assisting clients with major and minor choice points that affect their lives, or with explorations—at one or another of many possible levels of intensity—of the personal concerns that challenge them. On the other hand, spa in counseling includes helping clients to consider the everyday things they can do, to examine and challenge their labels, to consider their positive traits, to explore their strengths, and to savor the gains that result from counseling. We challenge you to go beyond the traditional and vital aspects of counseling—learning and relearning—and do what you can to create spa opportunities with those you counsel. Achieving those special moments with your clients may help you experience spa for yourself.

References

Berne, E. (1964). Games people play. New York: Grove Press.

Jacobs, E. (1988). Use of creative techniques and props in individual and group counseling. ASCA Elementary/Middle School Guidance Conference, Colorado.

James, M. & Jongeward, D. (1971). *Born to win*. Reading, MA: Addison-Wesley.

Nelson, R. C. (1987). Graphics in counseling. *Elementary School Guidance and Counseling, 22,* 17-29.

Chapter 3

Counselor Choices

Degree of Lead

Acceptance of the principles and philosophy of Choice Awareness should influence your choices as a counselor in working with clients in a number of ways. Depending on your personal theory of counseling, the influence may be major, leading you to reconstruct your philosophy of counseling, or minor, perhaps contributing primarily to the language you use to communicate with your clients about their choices. This chapter should help you determine where you might fall on that continuum.

Regardless of your counseling assignment, suppose you have a friend and co-worker who is one of the parents of an eighteen-year-old named Brad. You stop by to return an item you borrowed and agree to stay for a while and visit. Then you find that your friend has been trying to console Brad.

"You're a counselor," your friend blurts out. "You've got to help us."

Crying copious tears, Brad immediately begins to pour his heart out. He has given up high school and the allure of future college scholarships so that he might work and support his new wife and their coming baby. He wanted to do that and thought it was right since he was the father of the unborn child. He had even been happy to do it. Now Gail, his wife, has asked him to leave the apartment. She has told him she cannot forgive him for getting her pregnant, she hates being tied down, and she wants to return to school and have a future, and she cannot stand being married to him. The note of despair in Brad's voice seems to be very genuine, and when he suddenly turns to you and says, "Will you help me?" you find yourself nodding and responding positively to his appeal.

If you take the perspective of Choice Awareness, your assistance will focus on enabling Brad to take more effective control of his choices. You will consider his feelings, thoughts, and behaviors as you do so; you will try to implement in your counseling the concepts and the language you have learned; and you will help Brad see how those concepts and that language may work for him. But what does that mean you will say and do?

The choices you make may be explored in terms of the degree of lead you give Brad—the extent to which your remarks follow the lead he gives or lead him in the direction in which you want the discussion to go.

The Degree of Lead Table and the discussion that follows show the sequence of non-verbal and verbal choices that are available to you as you listen to Brad or any other client. Counselor choices that come from near the top of the non-verbal and verbal portions of the table tend to lead the client less, relatively speaking, than do those choices that are near the bottom of the table. It should be noted that to some extent the ordering of the items in the table is arbitrary, and that any choice may be expressed in a variety of ways and under a variety of circumstances. These matters clearly affect where the particular choice belongs on this Degree of Lead Table.

Less is More:
Economy in Counseling

In the situation described above, with all the possible counselor choices available to you, what will be your initial focus when Brad presents a variety of stimuli? Do you pay particular attention to his emotions; do you focus on the ways in which he puts his thoughts together; or do you consider first the possible behavioral changes that are suggested by the ideas he shares with you? Do you explore the details and realities of the situation involving him and his new wife primarily through listening or through asking questions; do you move early to the process of considering alternatives and making suggestions?

One fundamental question you might ask yourself in any given moment of counseling is whether the needs of the client call for *economy* or *impact* in movement and verbalization. The communication triangle below presents the issue:

Degree of Lead Table
(Read vertically in columns)

Non-Verbal Behavior

Minimum	to	Maximum

Silence
  Eye contact
    Attending behavior
      Comfortable body position
    Slight nods
      Minimum facial responses
     Minimal gestures

Vigorous nods
  Changes of position or tension
  Frowns, broad smiles (congruent)
  Dubious, disapproving looks
  Head shaking (disagreement)
  Frowns, smiles (incongruent)

Verbal Behavior

Minimum	to	Maximum

Minimum verbal response
  Reflection of feeling
   Reflection of content
    Restatement
     Summarization
    Clarification
     Assertions, statements

Direct questions
  Topic initiation
   Alternative exploration
  Role play
    Suggestions, advice
   Interpretation
    Confrontation
    Planning

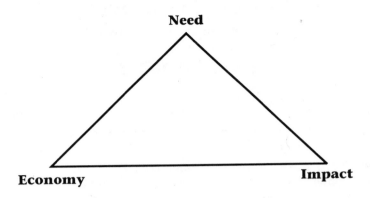

In Choice Awareness theory the position is taken that communication by the counselor is designed primarily to be economical or to have impact. When you make responses that keep the focus on the matter at hand and that enable the client to maintain or secure control of the dialogue, you are being economical in the moment. When you change focus or maintain or secure control of the dialogue, you are having impact on the counseling process. The triangle is used because it suggests that in meeting the needs of the client, you need to achieve a reasonable balance between economy and impact. An important consideration, however, is that economical and impactful responses do not "weigh" the same in counseling. Responses that reach toward economy are "light in weight" because they direct the process of counseling less than those that reach for impact. Thus, if you are to achieve balance in counseling, you will want to make more economical than impactful responses to your client over the process of counseling.

In Chapter One we introduced the *less is more* counseling principle, suggesting that the amount of support and direction should not exceed the client's needs. Consistent with that point, we do not suggest that you avoid making responses that have impact, only that you should not become overly dependent on impactful responses, especially early in counseling. The principle of economy is best achieved when you listen—if that will do the work that needs to be done—and when you confront—if the client needs to be challenged about a way of looking at the world—especially when it is unlikely that the client will make that discovery without your assistance. In most effective counseling processes the number of economical responses clearly exceeds the number of impactful responses.

Choice Awareness as a theory puts emphasis on enabling individuals to take more effective control of their own choices, and supports minimum change as an objective in counseling. In the situation involving Brad, the initial focus of your counseling ought to be that of listening—and certainly listening responses are economical. Brad is so caught up in the emotionality of the moment that if you ask him many questions, point out the choices he has been making, or propose possible solutions, you may block his achievement of his most immediate goal: that of obtaining an outlet for citing the frustrations and the injustices he believes he has experienced. Further, despite Brad's appearance of uncertainty, he may already have made a decision he wants to validate before making it operational, and a listening approach should help determine whether or not that is the case.

Listening involves the use of such non-verbal leads as: silence, eye contact, attending behaviors, relaxed body position, slight nods, minimum hand gestures and facial movements; and such verbal leads as minimum verbal responses, reflection of feeling, reflection of content, restatement, summarization, and clarification. Listening uses counselor skills that involve accepting and clarifying the concerns and feelings of the client. Counselor leads that emphasize listening concentrate the focus of counseling in the hands of the client to the greatest extent possible.

In Choice Awareness terms, listening is a caring choice. If you focus initially on the depth of feeling Brad has, if you accept his need to share those feelings, and if you convey your concern and your interest in helping him, you are making caring choices. You can do this with a variety of verbal responses, including especially reflection of feeling. In those instances when Brad or other clients are pained by the experiences they face in life, your listening responses are likely to be highly therapeutic.

There is something very heartening for your clients when they learn that they have found a direction in which they wish to go. It is even more heartening if they can sense that they themselves have worked out the problem with minimal assistance from you. You show more caring for your clients if you give them enough room to work out matters on their own than if you move immediately into the process of controlling the interview by asking questions, offering suggestions, or proposing behavior modifications. This is not meant to suggest that you act in a way that could be characterized as withholding, rather that you restrain your impulses long enough so that your clients can present or discover solutions of their own if they are available to them, or if they emerge as a result of the opportunity you have given them to hear themselves and to work out their own concerns.

Economy in responding, especially the use of good listening behavior, can be an ideal stimulus for growth on the part of your clients—regardless of whether the level of your counseling contract is seen as spa, learning, or relearning. When you offer your clients support in this way, you are conveying your trust that they can eventually solve their own problems.

Non-Verbal Behaviors: Accepting

Silence. Comfortable, attentive periods of silence can be productive opportunities for your clients to feel the closeness of your caring, for both of you to engage in thoughtful internal processing about the matter under discussion, and for your clients to find ways to resolve their own concerns. When Brad is fairly flowing with dialogue in the initial stages of counseling and expressing his concerns easily and openly, silence and a slight head nod on your part may be sufficient to encourage him to continue the dialogue unimpeded. On the other hand, the same behavior, silence and a head nod, may be totally insufficient, almost punitive, if Brad blurts out, after he has been thoughtful for some time, that he sometimes thinks of suicide. The effective use of silence involves reading the behavior of the client and allowing non-verbal to supplant verbal behavior when that seems to be sufficient.

Eye contact. In the mainstream culture in our society, maintaining reasonably steady eye contact is highly valued; thus, with many clients, good eye contact on your part is essential if you are to be perceived as helpful. Provided he is part of the mainstream culture, then, Brad might well develop a greater sense of trust more rapidly with you if your eye contact with him is strong. Eye contact is a two-way matter. Although you may not have a precise grasp of the implications of Brad's eye contact, you will make some interpretation of his behaviors—seeing directness and strength of purpose when he seeks eye contact with you, and avoidance and discomfort when he does not maintain eye contact.

The amount and intensity of your eye contact and your expectations for the eye contact of your clients should take into consideration a variety of factors, including ethnic-cultural background. There are clear differences in the acceptability of eye contact and other non-verbal behavior patterns among such cultural groups as Black inner city populations, rural Blacks, Hispanics, native American Indians, Asian-Americans, refugee groups from various parts of the world, and the mainstream White population. The important thing to note is that problems are likely to arise if you generalize your own cultural expectations concerning eye contact and other non-verbal behavior patterns, and remain insensitive to the patterns of your client's group.

In addition to cultural patterns, the amount and intensity of your eye contact should be related to the topic at hand and to the needs of your clients as well. It is likely that your clients will vary their eye contact, and expect the same from you, when they are introducing difficult topics or dealing with matters of great personal sensitivity. Ivy (1980) pointed out that clients tend to talk most about topics in which counselors show the greatest interest, and that some beginning counselors maintain their strongest eye contact when the discussion turns to the topic of sex, while other counselors look away. Short of exploring the idea of eye contact and its relationship to cultural and situational needs in great detail, it may be sufficient here to suggest that you give careful consideration and remain alert to your own personal patterns of eye contact, to how they seem to affect your clients, and to ways in which you might wish to adjust your own personal patterns of choices to achieve maximum effectiveness in counseling with individual clients.

Attending behavior. An important part of listening may be called attending behavior. Are you among the counselors who convey that you are giving attention with every fiber of your being? Are you among those who yield to every distraction and try to accomplish other things while listening; or do you fall between these extremes? You can convey your attentiveness by facing not quite squarely toward your client and leaning forward slightly, avoiding both extraneous movement that conveys nervousness and such closed body positions as folding your arms. In such matters as answering telephone calls or knocks at the door, you can convey your attentiveness by putting the needs of your client above all but urgent calls for help. Good attending behavior is therapeutic for your client, who is likely to have received only partial or limited attention in most interactions with others. Your successful efforts to make good attending choices can do much to set the counseling interview apart from other interactions.

Attending behavior is acknowledged as important in most theories of counseling, yet somehow the message does not seem to get across well to some counselors, perhaps because they have known few if any individuals who have used such behaviors skillfully. Perhaps if the choices of one counselor who seems to have developed this behavior to a humane science are described, the requisite skills may become more apparent.

This counselor, a Purdue University staff member, has conveyed the message politely and effectively to secretaries, students, and administrators alike that she dislikes being interrupted for anything but emergencies. Her telephone calls are held until she has completed her interviews. When she is talking with someone even in the lobby outside her office, she is virtually indistractible; should someone attempt to interrupt, she intensifies her eye contact with the individual with whom she is speaking. She is willing to accept that her behavior is an irritation to others at times, but since she subsequently gives the same intensity and courtesy to the individual who has had to wait, the level of her involvement is well accepted. She is one of the best-loved and most appreciated counselors at the university, and her skill in listening had to be part of the reason she was named Dean of Students. (Her name is Betty Mitchell Nelson, and she is related to me by marriage.)

Whether you are counseling with Brad in his parents' home, or with clients in your office, your attending behavior and the ways you choose to respond are important determinants of your counseling effectiveness.

Comfortable body position. The process of counseling itself is tension-producing for many people who seek assistance. It is helpful to the client to see you maintaining a comfortable body position, since it conveys effectively that the topic and content of the interview are not shocking or distasteful to you. At the same time, an overly-relaxed posture, slouching, for example, should be avoided because it may suggest disinterest on your part. A comfortable body position and good attending behavior convey genuine interest and help to assure the client that you are listening.

Slight nods. Slight, periodic head nods are important aids in conveying that you understand the client and that you see the focus of the dialogue as relevant. While this action can be overdone in frequency or intensity, the natural use of head nods is reassuring to most clients and it is vital for some.

Minimum facial responses. As with other non-verbal behaviors, facial responses that are attuned to the dialogue clarify to the client that you are listening. If the dialogue includes a report of a happy event or an exciting gain, your smile is taken as important evidence that you share in the positive feeling. By the same token, for example in your communication with Brad, your natural use of a slight scowl, an arched eyebrow, and other relevant minimum facial responses, when he shares negative experiences, may be taken as evidence that you understand his present feelings. The effective use of minimum facial responses sends the message to your clients that you empathize with them in their struggles and support them in their gains.

Minimal gestures. Since part of the dialogue belongs to you as counselor, you have the opportunity to convey both verbally and non-verbally that you are listening. Natural hand movements used for emphasis, and other gestures that are not overdrawn or wooden, can do much to reinforce your responses and offer evidence that you are listening.

SELF-EXAMINATION—JOURNAL ENTRY: Take stock of yourself openly and honestly by assessing your own use of non-verbal behaviors in counseling. What are your special strengths and weaknesses in showing acceptance to your clients through your non-verbal behaviors. Discuss any specific plans you have for making more effective use of these non-verbal choices in counseling. Suggestion: head your entry NON-VERBAL ACCEPTING CHOICES.

We believe that it is important for you to share your knowledge of effective non-verbal choices with your clients, in effect giving away your skills by helping your clients acquire them. You can enable your clients to see that the accepting behaviors they use with others—listening, silence, eye contact, nods, and minimal facial responses and gestures—affect their relationships, and that they can implement more effective patterns of choices if they need to do so.

Verbal Behaviors:
Accepting and Clarifying

Minimum verbal responses. Responses that use a word or two to call for continuation of the present focus may be referred to as minimum verbal responses. Examples are: "Mm hm." "Yes." "I see." "Go on." "I understand." In spite of the tendency of many counselors to string three or four minimum verbal responses together, one of these comments is generally sufficient. When Brad is active verbally he is likely to need little more than the assurance that you are listening and that what he is saying is understandable and acceptable to you. Minimum verbal responses keep you as counselor in contact with your clients, keep the focus on the matter under discussion, and convey your acceptance of your clients as capable persons in need. In the spirit of seeking minimum change and enabling clients to develop their own solutions to problems, minimum verbal responses are often both economical and sufficient.

Reflection of feeling: Among the most important counselor choices is reflection of feeling. These are responses that mirror the client's feelings, along with some of its content. Example: CL (client): "I don't see how she could ask me to leave like that when I've been trying so hard." CO (counselor): "You're really upset because her actions seem to be so unjustified."

It is likely that Brad, both as a product of our culture and as a maturing male, has had little or no experience in which he has sensed acceptance of his feelings of vulnerability and upset; likewise, he may have had little or no experience with reflection of feeling. Reflecting his feelings is a way of conveying your acceptance of those feelings, and it simultaneously builds his own acceptance of those responses.

There is need for client comfort with reflection of feeling; perhaps even more important is a deep level of counselor comfort with these choices. If you are like most counselors, you have had little or no experience with reflection of feeling yourself in your everyday life. If that is the case, you may have tried these responses and rejected them as "not me." You are more likely to be a vehicle for encouraging clients to understand their own choices and to choose more effectively if you use reflection of feeling generously, particularly in the initial stages of counseling.

After some trust has developed in the relationship and you have explored the idea with your clients that they have choices about feelings (see the following discussions of assertions/statements, topic initiation, and interpretation), from time to time you may want to modify your use of reflection of feeling—incorporating choice-focused language to achieve greater impact. For example, in the instance above you might say: "So out of the mix of feelings you have, you've chosen to be upset." As compared to a traditional reflection of feeling, your response would be likely to encourage Brad to rethink what he has said, and he is likely to react directly to your statement—so the response reaches well beyond simple acceptance. Such a statement, if delivered gently and discussed openly, should help Brad understand that being upset may be a very reasonable response, but that he could respond to the event in question with another genuine feeling: concern for Gail, for example.

Choice Awareness, as a system that seeks greater client control of choices and minimum change, strongly supports the value of reflection of feelings as more than technique; reflection of feeling is seen as one of the preferred choices in counseling whenever clients are expressing or evidencing strong emotions. The move into choice-focused reflections of feeling should be made carefully, and only when it makes sense in the relationship.

Reflection of content. Reflection of content choices mirror the client's remarks in somewhat different words. CL: "The last time I heard her say anything positive to me was before we got married." CO: "It's been a long time since you're heard anything positive out of her."

As with reflection of feeling, reflections of content afford clients opportunities to hear what they are saying, to obtain feedback, and to gain awareness of how their complaints sound to themselves and others. Reflection of content and reflection of feeling have often been parodied (CL: "I'm going to jump out of the window." CO: "You feel you're going to jump out of the window." CL: "Yes, I'm going to climb on the ledge right now." CO: "You're about to climb on the ledge now.") These techniques have been parodied for two primary reasons: because they represent ways of responding that are not part of the common vocabulary of our culture, and because they can be used both artificially and inappropriately. Providing a sounding board is sufficient for some clients and helpful for most others, but when it is evident that more is needed, other ways of responding should be used.

Reflection of feeling and reflection of content share the common advantage that they help clients attend to what they themselves are saying and how they are saying it—both of which they may overlook to their detriment. Choice Awareness theory reinforces the use of reflection of feeling and reflection of content—especially the former and particularly in the early stages of counseling—as vehicles for encouraging self discovery and for facilitating decision-making and action-taking on the part of the client.

Restatement: Restatement involves repeating the client's comment with minimal changes of content—often only changing nouns or pronouns. CL: "I'm feeling desperate right now." CO: "You're feeling desperate right now." It seems likely that restatement is the real and suitable target of many counseling parodies. However, when it is used very sparingly and for emphasis, restatement may be a valuable counselor choice that encourages client awareness.

Summarization: Summarization involves statements on the part of the counselor that pull together two or more remarks of the client or integrate an extended dialogue into a single response. CO: "So what you've been telling me is that you two were doing OK until Gail's father got in the act."

Summarizing is an extremely useful tool of the counselor. In many instances when you might be tempted to initiate a new topic, thus taking more active control of the process before it is needed, it would be more appropriate first to summarize so that you can see if that generates further dialogue on the topic under discussion. If it does so it has proven its worth; if not, it is likely to close the topic and act as an invitation to the client to introduce the next matter for consideration, or provide you an effective opening for doing so.

Clarification: When you feel the need to check out client statements or behaviors that seem to be in conflict, or that show a mixture of emotions, the technique of clarification may be useful. CO: "It seems as though you can't decide whether to be pleased that Gail's dad has stopped acting as if she had died, or unhappy that he's interfering now, or a little bit of both."

Many counselors habitually put such clarifications in question form: "Are you pleased that Gail's dad has finally shown interest in her, or are you unhappy that he is interfering?" A question like that forces a choice and tends not to help clients appreciate their own mixed feelings; thus, using statements for clarification purposes is generally to be preferred over using questions. Choice Awareness theory supports the idea that clarification is an important and economical counselor skill.

Assertions, statements: It is inevitable that counselors will incorporate into their counseling simple assertions and statements of fact. CO—in answer to a question: "It's about five minutes to ten." CO—providing information: "The Welfare Department Office is located on Fifth Street, and their phone number is _____." CO—making an assertion: "Because of the holiday we won't meet next Monday." At times assertions and statements may advantageously be choice-focused: CO: "When you said you'd call the Welfare Department as soon as you get home you were making a self-ruling choice; you were planning to take control of things."

In counseling with Brad and other clients, you are likely to have occasion to make many statements and assertions designed to promote understanding and to help them cope with problems they face. Some of your assertions and statements may advantageously be choice-focused—integrating the language of choice in the counseling process.

COUNSELING APPLICATION—JOURNAL ENTRY: Assess the extent to which you make use in counseling of verbal behaviors that convey acceptance and seek clarification. What are your special strengths and weaknesses along these lines? Discuss any specific plan you have for making more effective use of these choices in counseling. Suggestion: head your entry VERBAL ACCEPTING CHOICES.

We believe that it is important for you to share with your clients your knowledge of effective verbal choices that show acceptance. You can help your clients learn to use minimum verbal responses—reflection of feeling and content, summarization, and clarification—as effective choices in their relationships with others.

Impact in Counseling

It is impossible to achieve all the goals of counseling through the economical choices of listening and clarifying, and even if it were possible, it would be quite inefficient. As a consequence, the counselor needs to be prepared to use more active procedures. Clients who cannot uncover their own problems and discover their own solutions after they have been afforded the opportunity of being listened to and having their ideas clarified, are likely to benefit from counseling procedures that are impact-oriented.

In a 1988 conference presentation, William Glasser commented that at one time he listened to everything his clients had to say for long periods of time and then went to work with them on their problems and concerns. In his recent counseling efforts, he reported, his average listening stage had been reduced to twenty minutes. It would be highly inappropriate for any counselor to have a predetermined counseling schedule—a kind of lesson plan—with specific time allotments for the various stages of the process, but it seems quite appropriate for the counselor to be committed to engaging clients in active dialogue and effort within the context of the first counseling session, and in many cases within the first fifteen or twenty minutes. Counselors who leap on the first verbalizations of their clients and immediately begin to offer solutions or build plans with them need to evidence more listening. Counselors who listen *ad nauseum* need to strive for greater impact in counseling.

Choice Awareness theory supports the appropriate use of counseling techniques that involve impact, while cautioning counselors to avoid making their efforts along this line heavy-handed. This suggests that counselors might well balance their use of such impactful techniques as asking direct questions, making suggestions, interpreting, and confronting, with the liberal incorporation of economical techniques as well. All counselors have had extensive experience in their lives with people who have made generous use of *ask* and *tell* techniques. It is natural to expect that these techniques will be comfortable and come almost automatically in counseling. Skillful counselors are able to avoid "getting on a roll" in which they continuously ask questions or engage in a "why don't you. . . , yes, but. . ." game with their clients. Instead they use impactful techniques, then provide the opportunity for the response to become a vehicle for client self-discovery.

Responses that reach toward impact weigh more heavily—that is, they influence the process of counseling more—than those that reach for economy. Certainly you want the process of counseling to have an impact on the lives of your clients, and you want to move the process of counseling along. At the same time it would be well to avoid the temptation to bombard clients with more impact than they can well tolerate, acting as frequently as possible as a facilitator of client self-discovery and growth.

Non-Verbal Behaviors: Exploring

Vigorous nods. Vigorous nods and the other non-verbal behaviors from the second column of the Degree of Lead Table are likely to have significant impact on the direction of counseling, and as such should be used judiciously. Should Brad turn out to be the kind of client who scatters his focus over a wide variety of relevant and irrelevant topics, your use of vigorous nods when he is focusing more suitably may help to reinforce that focus. The problem with this kind of response is that it may create focus to the exclusion of breadth or depth. For example, if you nod vigorously when Brad is telling of the worst of his experiences with his wife, he may generalize that this is the kind of content you want to hear about and he may continue to focus on the negatives. Conversely, if you nod vigorously when he is telling of the warmth and love he has sometimes felt in that relationship, he may generalize that you want to hear only about the positives. As compared to vigorous nodding, careful, balanced use of more moderate reinforcing behaviors on your part is less open to misinterpretation. At the same time there is a place in counseling for stronger, more personal participation as exemplified in the occasional use of a vigorous nod.

Changes of position or tension. While it is inevitable that you will find yourself weary of a given position after maintaining it for a while, you need to realize that your changes of position or tension are bound to be interpreted in some way by your clients. When it is clear that Brad has refocused, either by his changing the topic or his physical movement or both, a change in your body position would seem only to reinforce and accept the change. However, when the topic is an ongoing one and you make a significant physical move, Brad is likely to see your action as calling for a change of focus. He may take your move as an indication that you are bored or that you disapprove of the present focus. It seems appropriate to send this kind of non-verbal message very sparingly in counseling. When you make the judgment that the focus of the discussion needs to be altered, a direct, relevant verbal message—"Let's get back to what happened this morning"—is usually better than relying on a subtle non-verbal message.

Deep frowns, broad smiles. These behaviors are self-evident, and so, doubtless, is the disadvantage they have in counseling; that is, they are likely to send the message that *this* is what we ought to (or ought not) be talking about. However, if you use these behaviors infrequently and judiciously and support them with understandable statements, these choices may help you project a more human, personal image.

Dubious and disapproving looks. One of the problem behaviors exhibited by many beginning and experienced counselors is that of conveying doubt or disapproval of the client's statements through non-verbal behaviors that send an "oh-you-can't-mean-that message." Often this is reinforced with a skeptical verbal statement or a question such as, "She *never* listens to you, Brad?" While no counseling system proposes the use of such behaviors, their use is common enough to deserve further comment.

Likely these behaviors were learned early by all of us as imitations of cookie-jar inquisitions: "You're *sure* you don't know what happened to the cookies?" Although these responses may seem quite natural to use, clients in counseling deserve either more trust or more openness or both. The counselor who feels skeptical concerning a comment of a client might do one of two things: (1) Refrain from projecting doubt or disapproval into the situation and accept the client's statement, since an attitude of acceptance and trust might encourage him or her to be both more trusting and more trustworthy. In the situation with Brad, for example, rather than injecting any doubt you might feel, you could convey your non-verbal acceptance of his feeling that Gail *never* listens, and support that with a verbal statement that clarifies your understanding of what he really seems to be saying: "It seems as though she just never listens to you anymore." Or (2) State the doubt directly: "I know it seems as though she really hates you, Brad, but I suspect that's just one of many feelings she has and that she's really mixed up right now." Dubious looks or statements have little merit in counseling, in large measure because they merely imitate the skepticism some clients meet wherever they turn—outside counseling.

Head-shaking (disagreement). Head-shaking in disagreement seems to encourage many clients to cite dozens of events that justify such a conclusion as "she really hates me," and thus in most instances it is clearly counterproductive. In the Brad-Gail conflict, let us assume you have fallen into the trap of telling Brad through shaking your head that you disagree with his statement that Gail hates him, perhaps reinforcing that idea with a statement to that effect. He probably will either turn you off and remove himself from the situation with you as quickly as possible, or catalog for you all the justifications he has for his conclusion. Neither of these outcomes will help him see that Gail may have other feelings for him as well, nor enable him to move in the direction of resolving the conflict.

The kind of situation in which head shaking in disagreement seems most relevant is that in which the client has launched on an extensive dialogue that seems to you to be purposeless for the contract to which you have both agreed. In such a situation your head shaking might serve to stop the flow and make interrupting and redirecting the discussion easier.

Frowns, smiles (incongruent). Once again it may seem irrelevant to discuss a behavior that has limited merit in counseling, and, except for the fact that it appears to be a part of the choice pattern of many counselors, it would not be included here. Obviously, when the client is showing distress, a smile on the part of the counselor would be incongruent; similarly, when the client is showing positive emotion, a frown would be incongruent. As with the other non-verbal behaviors cited in this section, the most relevant use of incongruent smiles and frowns is that of interrupting the flow of the dialogue so that a new direction can be taken. There are almost always better means for achieving that goal.

Verbal Behaviors: Exploring, Directing, and Challenging

Direct questions. Direct questions range from simple requests for factual information to probes that search at deeper levels. CO—simple question of fact: "How did you answer when she asked you that?" CO—probe: "Could it be that you feel a hurt to your pride that bothers you more than the decision that Gail has made?"

Most adults and most counselors are far too dependent on *ask* and *tell* communication, and obviously questions are the front part of that pair. There is a place for effective open-ended questions to be asked by counselors. Two related open-ended questions that might help in communication with Brad and that are often appropriate relatively early in the counseling are: (1) "What have you tried so far to solve this problem?" (2) "What have you thought about, but have not yet tried?" The first of these questions, if followed by ample time for client responses and reflection upon those responses and related feelings, (CO: "I see, so those are two things you've tried so far without much success"), has the advantage of avoiding innumerable related probes or suggestions that would be irrelevant because they have already been tried (CO: "Have you talked to her about your feelings concerning . . . ?" CL: "Yes, and that didn't work. . . .") The second of those two questions is useful because clients often sense what they need to do, but they eliminate suitable options because they do not know how to implement them. A third question that is often appropriate at a later stage of counseling, one that places responsibility appropriately on the client, is: (Now that we have reviewed all these possibilities) "What are you going to do about that?"

Occasional use of choice-focused questions can be effective in counseling: "What kind of choice did you think you made when you said that?" "Why do you think her statement wasn't an OK choice for you?" "What kind of choice might have been more effective for you to make just then?" "And suppose she says no, what OK choice might you make?" "You always wait for her to get the conversation started. How could you begin things—how could you initiate?"

Questions that call for one word responses, especially yes-no questions, tend to be ineffective in counseling. While all questioning risks the possibility that a pattern of counselor-asking/client- answering will emerge, the risk is particularly great when brief answers are invited. Whether questions call for brief answers or are more open-ended, however, there are several problems with heavy reliance on questions of any kind. Questions and answers keep the control of the process in the counselor's hands. Questions and answers may readily become a pattern; this is particularly true with children, adolescents, and adults of lower status who tend often to abide by the speak-when-spoken-to injunction. Some clients may assume when questions are asked that "correct" answers are being elicited, since this is the pattern they have experienced with persons in power positions. When they in consequence respond as they believe the counselor wants them to, they may be contributing little to the process of counseling.

Once a question-answer pattern has emerged, it may be difficult to escape, and the counselor is placed in the unenviable position of having constantly to guess the direction probing should take. The impossibility of this clairvoyance was suggested by one young lad who had meekly followed the counselor's lead for three full sessions. As they were terminating their third session, he asked politely, "Some day could we talk about my bed-wetting problem?" It seems most unlikely that the counselor would have happened on that avenue of exploration as long as he retained the reins of control through a tight questioning pattern. Furthermore, question-answer patterns too readily degenerate into witness-stand performances that suggest Sergeant Friday's "Nothing but the facts, ma." One final problem occurs with extensive questioning in that it implicitly promises clients that when they have answered the counselor's questions, the counselor will be ready to diagnose the ailment and prescribe the remedy, following the model of the physician. Most counselors are wise enough not to promise successful outcomes; they need to be wise enough not to imply such promises through their questions.

Despite the problems we have enumerated, questions are so much a part of the fabric of our society that they have become a crutch for many counselors. The position is taken here that questioning should not be the consistent, primary choice of the counselor in communicating with clients. The effective Choice Awareness counselor encourages clients to become solvers of their own problems and rulers of their own destinies; the counselor occasionally uses open-ended and choice-focused questions and avoids too great dependence on questions in general.

Topic initiation. In topic initiation the counselor introduces or reintroduces a topic either in statement or question form. CO—in statement form: "I find myself wondering where *your* parents stand in all this, Brad." CO—in question form: "Where do *your* parents stand in all this, Brad?" While on the surface it may seem to be a matter of little importance which verbalization is used, the statement form is gentler and more invitational than the question form—which seems more demanding—and the use of the statement form decreases the likelihood that a question-answer pattern will emerge with Brad.

Clearly topic initiation is a technique in which the counselor takes the lead, and equally clearly it must be done with some frequency. One thing that is lacking in the efforts of many counselors is the matter of depth in exploring clients' concerns. The counselor introduces a topic, asks a question or two, runs out of ideas to explore on that topic, introduces another topic, and yet another, deals with them shallowly, then subsequently returns to one of the earlier topics to probe for further information. It is important for counselors, as they initiate a topic, to prepare themselves in advance to explore the topic in some depth; otherwise it might be better if they let it remain in reserve for later discussion.

The matter of transition is often handled poorly by counselors as they initiate topics with clients. Clients are less likely to feel batted about like tennis balls if their counselors provide effective transitions as they initiate new topics or return to topics that have been mentioned previously. For example, CO: "Brad, you've talked a great deal about how Gail's parents see things, especially her father, and I find myself wondering where your parents stand in all this." In contrast to a topic initiation such as, "Where do *your* parents stand in this?" a transitional statement makes it clear that you have found the discussion useful, it helps Brad understand the flow of your thoughts, and it makes the change of topic less abrupt.

Choice-focused topic initiation is essential in Choice Awareness counseling, and any of the concepts of Choice Awareness can be grist for the mill. If Brad sees himself as having no choices to make, it may be time to introduce the idea that the opportunity to choose is with him constantly: "You seem to believe there's nothing you can do, but in actual fact you're making choices all the time. One thing you're doing is talking about it with me, and you've tried to talk with Gail about what's bothering you. Even when you sit in your room and cry about it, you're doing something, you're making choices. And they're not all bad ones—I'm sure you can think of lots worse." Later, if Brad is still constantly worrying about the situation with Gail without taking action, it may be time to incorporate the concepts of sorrowing and thinking/working choices: "There's a label for what you're doing about your problem with Gail. All your choices seem to be sorrowing choices, and I see a lot of miserableness there. That was natural enough at first, but I think now it may be good for you to shift gears and get on to making some thinking/working choices about the situation." If Brad defers to Gail's father and then resents his own behavior, it may be time to focus on his initiating action: "You let Mr. Levering take the lead and he backs you into a corner right away. If you got the first words out— if you initiated with him the next time—what could your first words be?"

Choice Awareness theory supports the value of topic initiation as a means of exploring matters that seem relevant with clients in counseling. At the same time we counsel patience, since many topics that are truly relevant are likely to be initiated in due course by clients; we argue for gradual rather than abrupt transition to new topics. We suggest that topics be explored in some depth once they have been introduced; and we endorse choice-focused topic initiation in counseling.

Alternative exploration. Alternative exploration is a form of topic initiation in which the focus is either on generating alternatives or on exploring their costs, benefits, and consequences. CO—enumerating alternatives: "Since you agree it would be helpful for us to spend awhile considering the alternatives available to you, Brad, let's start by listing what you've tried and what you've thought about doing so far, then we'll see if we can expand that list." CO—exploring costs, benefits: "Since you believe it may be one possible solution, let's explore the possible consequences and the gains and losses, if your parents were to take on raising the baby as their own."

Enumerating alternatives and considering their costs, benefits, and consequences is seen in Choice Awareness theory as an important aspect of counseling. Informal data gathered from tapes in counseling suggest to us that when counselors and clients agree *orally* to consider the alternatives available for clients to use, two to four alternatives emerge, then the discussion moves on to other matters. However, when counselors formalize the activity by taking out paper and pen (or felt pen, which is the medium we suggest for its boldness and clarity), the number of alternatives often increases to more than six. Furthermore, when clients in paper-pen situations are asked to indicate which alternative they are most likely to implement, they generally choose a response from among the last three or four cited. The very presence of the notes on paper appears to increase the focus and enhance the likelihood that if the discussion strays, either the client or the counselor is likely to look at the list before them and return to the point at hand.

The paper-pen format for exploring alternatives offers a tangible product of counseling: a list that may guide the choices of the client in the time following the counseling interview. This visual representation is advantageous when costs, benefits, and consequences are explored, since it permits logical consideration of these matters. Likewise the physical presence of a list of alternatives helps counselors explore with clients what is likely to happen if they follow a given path *and* if they do not.

Gary, an aggressive teenager who faced suspension from school for getting in fist fights, was helped to see the consequences of both of his major alternatives, pummeling his opponent, or "chickening-out," as he called it. On his own he concluded that there had to be some other way for him to handle his negative feelings—"There's gotta be something else I can do when I get pissed off, so I don't get the deep six here at school." His counselor responded, "Let's take a look at the choices you have at a time like that." She pulled from her desk a pad of paper and a felt pen, boldly printed the words WHEN I FEEL LIKE FIGHTING on the top of the sheet, and, as she wrote the word *fight* beside the number one and *chicken-out* beside the number two, she said: "Let's see if we can build a longer list of things you could do." Eventually the list was expanded to include: *think about getting thrown out of school, talk my way out of it, laugh about whatever it is, make an appointment to talk, cool off in the gym.*

"You know," Gary said at the beginning of the next counseling session, "that list really helped. I almost punched Barry's lights out when he called me chicken the other day, then I could see our list in my mind. 'You're trying to get me thrown out of school,' I told him, 'but it's not going to work.' And then I *laughed* at him. I told you the other day I thought that'd be cool. It *was.*"

Many theories support the idea of listing, comparing, and contrasting the choices available to clients in counseling when they must make major decisions. Choice Awareness theory suggests that the counselor should not stop there. The counselor should pay attention to alternatives related to the major issues clients face *and* to the alternatives they can use in everyday, seemingly minor situations. Successes in making effective minor choices act as building blocks for new choice patterns. Rather than attending solely to major choice points and broad issues involved in examining alternatives, Choice Awareness theory supports the idea of considering specifics. To that end role play and related strategies are often useful.

Role play. In using role play, counselors invite clients to participate in a process that is designed to develop client insight or to help the client find alternative choices for solving problems. For example, you might introduce role play to Brad by making a statement like the following: "I think it would be useful if we tried rehearsing what you might say and how you might say it when you talk to Gail about your mother and father raising the baby." Actual role play would follow this invitation, and a variety of role play strategies could be used. You might initially play the part of Brad so he could hear how an approach might be worded, and what tone of voice and supporting non-verbal behaviors might be appropriate. Subsequently you might play the part of Gail so that Brad has the opportunity to try out and evaluate the strategy he has chosen for talking with her.

In using role play it is important to listen and watch for non-verbal clues that suggest that the planned strategy is well-suited to the need and to the people involved, or that there are problems with the strategy. Most role play approaches need modification before they fit the client. Furthermore, if role play is to be used at all, it is important to carry it beyond the first few comments so that a well-suited approach does not founder for lack of effective follow-through.

Choice Awareness suggests that we make choices because of the habit patterns we develop in our relationships. Helping Brad to initiate an approach that involves new choices is important, but his usual habit patterns are likely to reemerge once he has stated his case. If he is to follow through effectively, that needs to be rehearsed as well.

It is often necessary, but not often easy, for clients to learn to implement new patterns of choices. Choice Awareness theory supports the idea of role play as an important procedure for enabling clients to try out new choices in a safe environment, and for helping them to modify and polish them until they can use them effectively. The pianist Lauren Hollander in a PBS radio interview once lauded the virtues of practice; "Practice," he said, "until it becomes easy. Practice until it becomes habit. Practice until it becomes beautiful." New patterns of behavior, whether at the piano or in interaction with others, do not spring forth beautifully formed and ideally implemented. We struggle with them much as a pianist might with an advanced piece involving new fingering patterns, new rhythms, and a new interpretation; or as a golfer might with a new stance, a new grip, and a new swing. The function of role play in counseling is to enable clients to begin the difficult process of practicing more successful patterns of behavior. Often the process is not complete until those patterns become easy, habitual, and beautiful. The task, then, is: practice, practice, practice. And role playing new choice patterns can be a most significant step in that process.

Suggestions and advice. Suggestions and advice are forms of topic initiation in which specific alternatives are put forth by the counselor. These techniques differ from alternative exploration in that they imply less objectivity on the part of the counselor. That is, when a counselor invites the client to participate in enumerating alternatives, the implication of openness is greater than when the counselor makes a suggestion or gives advice. CO—offering a suggestion: "Maybe you ought to think about this from Gail's perspective for a while." CO—giving advice: "Once you make your suggestion, I think you should let Gail think about it for some time and hope that she might come to see things your way sooner or later." Suggestions and advice may also be implied in questions. CO: "Have you talked with your parents about this?" (This question infers: you should, if you have not.)

Choice Awareness theory proposes that counselors limit their use of suggestions and advice. Clients generally have greater ownership of problem-solving strategies and learn more about how they might solve problems in the future when they are helped to explore a variety of alternatives than when they are given suggestions or advice. We pointed out concerning the use of questions in counseling that most counselors are too dependent on *ask* and *tell* communication; suggestions and advice form the second part of that pair. Most people who seek assistance have been faced with innumerable questions and have been given even more generous portions of advice by lay persons. Counselors take advantage of a great opportunity they have to distinguish themselves from others when they limit their use of questions, suggestions, and advice in favor of counseling processes that do more to promote client self-growth.

Interpretation. In interpretation, counselors label or describe the clients' thoughts, feelings, or behaviors from a different point of view, with the purpose of increasing client understanding. CO: "You seem to want both Gail and the baby to be dependent on you and you alone."

Interpretation has been criticized in counseling literature primarily because unskilled counselors tend to take limited information and draw conclusions that are unsupported or that clients are not ready to hear, perhaps to demonstrate their insightfulness. Interpretation is a complex and useful skill that can have considerable impact on the counseling process. Because of that very potential, Choice Awareness theory cautions that it be used infrequently and judiciously. Generally speaking, the more closely interpretations follow the information and attitudes that have emerged in the counseling interview, the more likely they will contribute to the process.

You will occasionally or frequently have insights that your instincts and experience suggest might be appropriate to your clients' situations. Rather than injecting those insights immediately after you have formed them, it may often be better if you hold them as tentative hypotheses and move toward them gradually through the use of topic initiation, reflection of feeling and content, summarization, and clarification. If you pause, consider, and work toward them gradually, the interpretations you eventually make will seem more relevant and supported, or you will not offer them at all.

Confrontation. In confrontation the counselor points out discrepancies or otherwise challenges the client. CO—pointing out a discrepancy: "You say you want to do something about this, but you don't get around to carrying out the plans you make for the time between our interviews." CO—challenging the client who is doing little: "Why don't you call and schedule our next appointment *after* you've worked on your plan for a few weeks and have some progress to report?"

Since confrontation usually has considerable impact on the process of counseling, Choice Awareness theory suggests that counselors use confrontation sparingly and selectively and only after the relationship has been well established. It should not be used to force inappropriate choices on clients. For example: "You said last time that you were upset because Gail's father was ignoring her and treating her as if she were dead; now you say you're upset because he's interfering—which is it?" Confrontation should not be abruptly and harshly stated, particularly when the relationship is being developed. Confrontation produces tension in the way that all learning produces tension. Although it is not always easy to achieve the appropriate amount of tension so that progress is encouraged, many clients do need to have their ideas, their assumptions, and their behaviors confronted. Infrequent, selectively-applied confrontations can be highly growth-producing.

Planning. The counselor focuses on half-formed plans of the client and helps refine them, or specifically invites or encourages planning. CO—reinforcing half-formed client plans: "You said you've thought a lot about mentioning your feelings of loneliness and rejection to Gail; that seems like something useful for you to try this week. If you think so, maybe we could talk for a bit about how you might do that." CO—inviting planful behavior: "So, out of all the possibilities you've thought about and we've talked about today, what will you choose to work on between now and next Friday?"

Choice Awareness theory strongly supports the concept of planfulness in counseling, especially if the plan is one that the client has participated in developing. Too many intervals between counseling interviews that could be used to produce growth are, to all intents and purposes, wasted. Choice Awareness theory charges counselors with the responsibility to see that some kind of planful action occurs in nearly all intervals between counseling contacts. This can be done by reinforcing a half-formed plan offered or inferred by the client, or by proposing some kind of observation, action, or tallying behavior when no client plan emerges. If further suggestions are needed, the companion Choice Awareness source, *On the CREST: Journaling Your Way to Better Choices*, offers a number of possibilities for helping clients to take advantage of the intervals between counseling sessions.

Counselors have many choices available to them in nearly every moment of counseling. They meet some clients who are able to solve their own problems on the basis of little more than the opportunity to be heard. Other clients need assistance that goes much further, even to the point of confrontation, if progress is to be made. Choice Awareness theory suggests that counselors tailor their choices to the needs of their clients, emphasizing economy in their responses when it is feasible to do so, and making judicious and appropriate use of choices that have more impact on their clients when that is necessary.

SELF-EXAMINATION—JOURNAL ENTRY: Take stock of yourself openly and honestly by assessing your own use of nonverbal and verbal choices for impact in counseling. What are your special strengths and weaknesses along these lines? Discuss any specific plan you have for making more effective use of impactful behaviors in counseling. Suggestion: head your entry CHOICES FOR IMPACT.

We believe that it is important for you to share your knowledge of impactful choices with your clients, giving away your skills by helping your clients acquire them. You can enable your clients to see that there are impactful choices they might use sparingly with others—direct statements and questions, topic initiations, and so forth—that could affect their relationships, and that they can implement more effective patterns of choices if it is important for them to do so.

The Informal Counseling Contract

One of the ways the counselor can enhance the effectiveness of the counseling process is by developing a contract with the client. In this case the term is used informally, rather than in the behavioral sense of a precise agreement in which the client is expected to fulfill specific expectations and receive prescribed rewards. The informal contract may be stated in answer to the general question: what are we about or what ought we to be about here? The contract is checked out with the client, is modified as needed, and, when it is feasible, is stated in Choice Awareness terms.

The informal contract with Gary, the teenager who was facing suspension for fighting, can be used as an example. After a period of listening and discussing, the counselor stated her view of the informal contract with Gary: "I think what you want from me most is my help in keeping you from being expelled for fighting—but whatever choices we figure out, they have to be choices that don't make you feel like a sissy." A head nod and the words, "Right on," from Gary gave the counselor the go-ahead to focus the discussion. The counselor viewed the informal contract as flexible. After further dialogue with Gary and his teachers, it became evident that Gary's self-concept was another issue the two might focus on. The counselor adjusted the informal contract: "Besides keeping you from being expelled for fighting, there's another thing I think we ought to work on. I think we ought to try to help you feel better about yourself."

For a more complex example, let us consider your efforts with Brad. Early in your contact with him you might mentally sit back and reflect on the emerging process between the two of you, the extent to which you are willing to continue to work with him and under what conditions, and what direction you believe the process should take. Your statement of the contract will depend in part on whether or not your expertise and your job assignment make working with Brad in your office appropriate, and whether you are willing for your agreement to be brief or extensive.

If you plan to continue to work with Brad professionally, you might offer a contract in these terms: "What I think you need most right now is somebody to listen to you, really hear you express your frustration and anger, and help you sort out what choices you can make about Gail and the baby. And those choices are going to be affected a lot by her choices and those your parents and her parents make. That fits with the kind of thing I do, so I'll be glad to continue to talk with you for a while today and to continue in my office in the future."

If you do not plan to continue to work with Brad—because it does not fit within your job description, or because even the possibility of suicide suggests to you that you should refer him—you might offer an informal contract, for the moment, in these terms: "What I think you need most right now is somebody to listen to you, and I can do that, today. But you have so much frustration and anger, and you're not sure you can make it without more help than I'm able to give you, so I'm going to ask you to see (so I want to take you to see) _____ (referral source) after we finish talking today."

The informal contract is designed to move the counseling process along, to clarify the kinds of choices the client may expect from the counselor, and to create a greater sense of focus for the process involved. It is often possible and desirable for the contract to be stated in Choice Awareness terms: "...help you to plan more effective caring choices with Gail," "...help you to make more enjoying choices for yourself," or "...help you to initiate in your interactions with Gail's father."

Counselor Choices

Choice Awareness theory supports the judicious, selective use of a great variety of verbal and non-verbal choices by the counselor in communicating with clients. The counselor is encouraged initially to help clients discover their own ways of solving problems. However, when this process proves ineffective or inefficient, the counselor takes more vigorous action. The counselor is encouraged to meet the needs of clients by seeking a reasonable balance between strategies that are economical—those that encourage clients to take the lead in the dialogue, and strategies that have greater impact on the counseling process—those that place the counselor in the leading, controlling position. The position is taken that counseling is, to a large extent, good, intimate communication, and the counselor is invited to help clients adopt communication skills and make choices that can help them solve their personal dilemmas.

Reference

Ivy, A. E., with Simek-Downing, L. (1980). *Counseling and psychotherapy: Skills, theories, and practice.* Englewood Cliffs, NJ: Prentice-Hall.

Chapter 4

Habits, Goals, and Meaning

Habits

Despite the fact that we have great freedom to make large and small choices in our lives, our perceptions are often to the contrary. One of the main reasons for this is that we human beings are creatures of habit. When we drive the same roads on our daily route, we take advantage of the efficiency of habit. Instead of having to think through every move we make, we turn over to a kind of automatic pilot within us the tasks of selecting the route, and the chores of starting, shifting, signaling, and turning. As we make our moves over familiar territory, we alternate between automatic behavior and semi-alertness that allows us to hum the tune on the radio and contemplate dessert, even as we slow for an intersection, a traffic light, or a vehicle turning across our path. We function at an enhanced level of alertness when we have several errands to accomplish and we need to deviate from our usual route. And most of the time we remain ready to spring into full alertness at the first sign of danger.

We also function on a continuum of interpersonal alertness. Seldom do we give our relationships our full attention. Most of the time we are content to follow our automatic or habitual behavior patterns and to shift to greater alertness only when something jolts us out of our lethargy. As in driving we may change our level of awareness only after we have a near brush with disaster—with someone else's upset or angry feelings. By then the damage may already have been done.

There are relatively few costs involved in following the same route in driving everyday. The car may even seem to function better because our moves are well rehearsed. The road makes no objection if we maintain the route—although we receive jarring messages if we drive over new chuckholes we have not seen before, and we may overlook a new stop sign. Our interpersonal relationships, however, are not likely to work out so well if we follow the same route continually. "Chuckholes" appear when we take a relationship for granted and do not maintain it effectively.

Transactional analysts talk about our need for strokes, our need for acknowledgement by others of ourselves as human beings. In Choice Awareness we see our interpersonal accounts as needing regular deposits if the balances are to remain positive. The Choice Awareness analogy makes use of another characteristic of bank accounts: service charges. Our accounts with one another erode if we do not make regular deposits, or if our choices are too stereotypical and boring, because both inaction and repetitive action function as bank service charges do. They subtract small amounts from the balance, inexorably, but with a regularity unthinkable in banking.

You and your clients may be all too aware of the risks you take when you are tempted to engage in new patterns of behavior. However, you may lose sight of the fact that you take other serious risks when you act in dull, repetitive ways in your relationships. It is important that you and your clients see your interactions—especially in relationships with which you are not satisfied—as little windows of opportunity to make new choices. There is likely to be no damage done if you follow your usual habit patterns most of the time, but you need to take some of your opportunities and be deliberate about making better choices. "In most circumstances there is available a brief instant which we may use as we have in the past, or we may use it to make new choices" (Nelson, 1977, p. 26). Meaning and inner well-being in your life depend in part on taking risks and making the kinds of choices that go beyond your usual habit patterns into newer, more positive, avenues.

CONSIDER THE FOLLOWING:

Jackie sought help from a counselor at the personnel office where she worked. She had been married to Joe for only a few weeks, but she was upset about the dullness and sameness of their life together. Their choices had not been very exciting during their months of dating, but Jackie was not prepared for their shift into stereotypical behavior patterns. During the evenings, Joe sat around reading the newspaper and watching television like his dad, and was little or no help on the chores related to dinner or other matters around the house. Jackie could see in her own behavior a mirror image of her mother as a full-time drudge, continually attending to employment and household chores. As troublesome as those discoveries were for her, they were not what upset her most. Her real concern was that there was so little communication between Joe and her. Her counselor helped her focus on the small, habitual patterns of choices she and Joe were establishing in the household, especially those that involved verbal interaction. She came to realize that she had contributed to the development of contracts she did not like in the relationship, and that she would have to learn to make different choices and to ask for different choices from Joe if she wanted the relationship to change.

Contracts are Habits

In the discussion of relationship goals and choices that follows, we make the point that choices readily become habit patterns and habit patterns readily become contracts. Jackie needed to realize that after three evenings or so during which she came home from her job and headed to the kitchen to work on dinner, while Joe picked up the newspaper and turned on the television, a contract had evolved. It was unspoken, but it said: this is the way it has been and this is the way it will be.

From the perspective of many men the contract might have been fine, but once Jackie pointed it out to Joe calmly and kindly, he agreed that he did not want to play out his life as his father had. For his part, he told her, he would be glad to pour the two of them a glass of wine and to share the events of the day before getting absorbed in other things. Jackie agreed to have a small snack on hand "to keep the wolf away from the door"—to assuage the immediate hunger both felt. After a few days the two had a new contract, and both were more satisfied with the level of communication between them. Joe still did not provide as much help as Jackie wanted, "But at least," she commented, "we're talking some."

Many counseling clients need to take a look at the contracts they have created. More often than not it is their own choices, not just other people's choices, that need to be altered. A comment neatly printed on chart paper by someone who attended a personal-growth workshop at Purdue University captured the essential idea: "If you always do what you've always done, you'll always get what you always got." Clients may well find that they need to alter their patterns of choices, and that if they do so, reciprocal changes may occur in the choices of others.

An important tenet of Choice Awareness is that effective patterns of choices facilitate, and ineffective patterns of choices block, good interpersonal relationships. Many of the people who seek help through counseling repeatedly make choices that prevent them from achieving their goals. You can help your clients understand that habits of choice-making that are positive help them create a positive environment, while habits of choice-making that are negative create problems for them.

The point bears repeating that one of the problems many counseling clients have in their relationships is that they see themselves as powerless. With that kind of perspective they may believe that their caustic comments or thoughtless actions have no power to hurt or frustrate others. If you confront them with the impact of their behavior on another person, you may find that they are genuinely surprised. "Who me?" is their question. Your counseling may well focus at least in part on the habitual choice patterns of your clients, the impact of these choice patterns on their relationships, and the gains that may occur if they take greater responsibility for their choices.

People make choices habitually that adversely affect their relationships with others. They also make choices habitually for themselves and about themselves that adversely affect their self-concepts and their sense of inner well-being. They eat too much or too little, they get too little rest or indulge themselves in sleep orgies, they exercise insufficiently or OD on exercise, they engage in destructive self-talk or delude themselves in one way or another, and in general they do not act in their own best interests. Again, these less-than-positive behaviors are likely to have evolved gradually and become personal habits and contracts, despite their potential for harm. With many of your clients you may advantageously focus on habitual self-choice patterns and the impact of those choices on their self-concepts and their sense of inner well-being.

SELF-EXAMINATION—JOURNAL ENTRY: Take a few minutes to think, then discuss in your journal the habit patterns of choices you have developed in one of your most important relationships, and the extent to which your habit patterns of choices for yourself move you toward or away from a sense of inner well-being. Suggestion: head your entry MY HABITS.

We encourage you to share these ideas with your clients, helping them see the impact of their habit patterns on themselves and in their important relationships. Most clients are unaware of the impact of their choices, and as a result they act in habitual, ineffective ways. They need to be helped to change their habitual patterns of choices when those patterns stand in the way of effective relationships and inner well-being.

COUNSELING APPLICATION—JOURNAL ENTRY: To what extent do you believe it is important for you to help your clients deal directly with their habit patterns, for themselves and with others? Consider with at least one specific or hypothetical client how you might focus on habits and the choices that individual could make to improve that person's life situation. Suggestion: head your entry CLIENT HABITS.

Relationship Goals

Choice Awareness is an eclectic system that permits considerable latitude in the goals sought and the strategies used to achieve those goals. Clients' needs vary, and goals and strategies must also vary. A question you may want to ask yourself concerning each client is: Is this a person for whom the clarification of goals, and choices to achieve those goals, is central? The position is taken here that all effective counseling is goal- and choice-oriented. Choice Awareness theory supports the idea that in most counseling processes these matters may advantageously be given explicit attention.

All of us tend to fall into particular patterns of choices over time in our lives and in our relationships. We make enjoying choices most often with our friends, ruling choices most often with children or others who are younger than we, and thinking/working choices on the job. We use all five CREST choices, but we let our notions of societal expectations control with whom we make each kind of choice. Generally we fall into narrow habit patterns even with those we care about most.

CONSIDER THE FOLLOWING:

Marie came to counseling because, after her mother's death, she and her father had lost the buffer that existed between them. Because of her mother's illness, upon graduation from college, Marie had taken a job in her home community and returned home to live. All had gone reasonably well under the circumstances until some time after her mother's death. Marie planned to take an apartment by herself, but hesitated to do so until she believed her father could handle matters effectively on his own. Over time she and her counselor sorted out the pattern of CREST choices she had evolved with her father, and Marie learned that she had restricted each of her choices in some way with him. Though her father's grief was apparently still overwhelming for him, Marie realized that she had followed her habit of long standing. She had "respected his need to be strong," and had made few caring choices that could be construed as permission for him to express his emotions. Likewise, she gave no hint of her own need for his help. Thus, her caring choices were limited to traditional actions on her father's behalf—keeping the house in order and putting meals on the table. Although Marie had been a leader in many college activities, when it came to ruling choices, she deferred to her father, then she resented him for thwarting her leadership abilities. The only place she allowed herself to make enjoying choices with any sense of freedom was with her friends, away from home. She felt disloyal to her mother when she smiled or laughed in the house, yet her mother had been a joyful, positive individual. Marie made sorrowing choices continually. She anguished over the loss of her mother, was continually frustrated over what she saw as her father's dependency and moodiness; and felt concerned and lonely because her chances to meet people seemed limited by her father's need for her. She thought continually about her problem, but her thinking was more like wheel-spinning than problem-solving, more like reiterated miserableness than purposeful planning.

The limits of the choice pattern that Marie had created in her relationship with her father are no more restrictive than those that evolve in many parent-child and other relationships. Most of us fall into similarly narrow patterns of choices with those we encounter on a day-to-day basis. Our choices may be somewhat more positive than Marie's, but they may not cover a broader spectrum.

Many factors affect the choices your clients make. Your clients and the persons they are concerned about might be from feuding families, or they may be on very friendly terms. One of them may hope to establish a deeper relationship. The clients or the other persons may be annoyed about something that has happened between them. One of them may want to hurt the other as she or he has been hurt. They may love each other deeply. In their relationship they may be on a "high."

These kinds of factors come into play even if your client says so little a thing as "Good morning" to that other person. The responses each makes to the other reflect the history of their relationship. The situation and matters of timing also affect their choices, but relationship factors most often influence what they say and do.

Even though relationships are not what your clients might like them to be, they are likely to spend more time in maintaining them as they are than in changing them. The known is less threatening than the unknown, so it is easier to follow habit patterns than to take the risk of venturing into new territory. What clients forget in acting in blind obedience to their pattern of habits is that *not* changing is risky as well. Relationships do not remain static; they continue to spiral either upward or downward. *Not* making changes that are needed means that inertia rules, and relationships will probably deteriorate unless your clients act to move them in positive directions.

Relationship choices readily become habit patterns and patterns readily become contracts. You have probably had a similar experience to that of going out for coffee with a new colleague three days in a row, and found that on the fourth day you were unable to get together. What happened? Perhaps you apologized subsequently, "Sorry I was tied up yesterday. I just couldn't get away for coffee." Or your colleague said to you, "What happened to you yesterday? I waited for you and then went out on my own." Both of you built an expectation, even a contract, on three similar events. It happens to all of us. I have a friend whose relationship I enjoy. Somehow the relationship evolved with me making all the moves; I was the initiator. Now that role is cast in concrete. I could say to myself, "I won't reach out again until my friend calls me." But I know the outcome of that—I have given it a try. I have come to the conclusion that the relationship is important to me, that I do not want to deny its importance, and that I will just have to make all the first moves if the relationship is to continue.

In many ways relationships affect our choices, and our habits are choice patterns we have institutionalized with particular people. So how do we change patterns we find difficult to live with? The key is to focus clearly on our goals for the relationship, and make the choices that we believe will help us move toward those goals. With my friend I have decided that I simply want to maintain a good, if somewhat limited, relationship. For it to be really close I would have to have a more reciprocal pattern of initiation, but since I value the relationship I have decided that I will continue to make the choices that at least allow us to remain in contact. Further, I am committed to the idea that when we are together, I will send clear messages that I value the relationship, rather than focusing on the frustration I sometimes feel about the initiation imbalance. If you or I make changes in our choices, we change our relationships, and we can make more suitable changes in our choices if we first explore the goals we have with others. Needless to say, the same is true for your counseling clients.

If the concept of goals in relationships is something you have not considered, you may think, "If people have goals in their relationships, aren't they likely to be manipulative and calculating. Isn't it better if we leave matters a bit more to chance, to the unfolding of the relationship in the moment?" Clearly such notions as love at first sight, the importance of first impressions, and instant likes and dislikes seem to support the will-o-the-wisp nature of relationships, and if the alternative to allowing nature to take its course is manipulation, I would also prefer random outcomes.

I believe, however, that without any genuine awareness, all of us have global goals for our important relationships; that these goals tend to be important, positive, simple, and non-manipulative; and that examining these goals is likely to lead us in the direction of making more effective choices. With my wife, Betty, I want at minimum to maintain a good relationship or, better still, to make our relationship warmer and closer. If I make choices without awareness of this goal, I may act far too often in ways that could send the relationship in a direction that is opposite the warmth and closeness I want. If I keep my goal before me, I am more likely to make positive choices.

It is useful to conceptualize our goals and relationships in the shape of a pyramid. At the top for most of us are a few relationships that can be deep, close, and loving. The next tier down is formed by several relationships that are friendly and warm, involving trust and caring, but that do not achieve quite the depth and closeness of the first, small group of relationships. A third, larger tier is formed by many relationships that are more superficial than close, and more businesslike than truly friendly. The fourth tier includes hundreds of people we encounter incidentally while walking, driving, shopping, and attending various events. With those people we want limited, respectful encounters in which neither of us interferes with the other, and each of us keeps to the right, or does whatever is appropriate to avoid blocking the fulfillment of the needs of the other.

It is important for us to remain open to the possibility that the other persons may want to change their position on our pyramid of relationships, and it is likewise important that we find a way to express our desires if we want to change our position on others' pyramids. By and large, however, we are content to let most of our relationships remain at the level where they are, and to maintain the patterns of habits we have evolved.

Exploring the pyramidal structure of relationships may be especially useful with particular clients. Those who narrowly interpret the mandate to love one another may assume that means they should love all people equally—as I once did—and they are likely to feel guilty because they have failed to fully follow their interpretation of that

Pyramid of Relationships

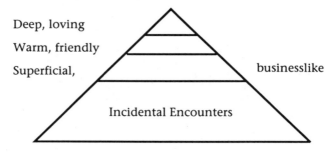

charge. I used to read that injunction that way; now I understand that it says simply that we should act in loving ways with others. In some relationships that means that we might encourage the other person to share deep personal thoughts in a loving relationship because that is what we want for ourselves; in other relationships we may prefer to respect each other's right to privacy.

If we are going to focus on a scriptural injunction as we think about our goals with others, we would do better to focus on: "Do unto others as you would have them do unto you." The superficial reading of that commandment is again that we should love all people equally. A deeper reading makes a different message clear: if we want a deep, loving relationship with another person, we must make deep, loving choices. On the other hand, if we are content with limited, respectful encounters, we should make choices that are consistent with that goal. The kinds of choices we want from others are the kinds of choices we should make toward them.

Some of your clients might be offended by this reading of the Golden Rule. If so, encourage them to take another look at its implications. Is it not possible that a significant source of the guilty, inadequate feelings they have is the expectations they have set for themselves that they cannot possibly achieve? My reading of the Golden Rule does not encourage destructive behaviors—I never want others to hurt me, therefore I should not hurt others. At worst it calls for neutrality; at best it challenges individuals to make positive choices with those people from whom they hope to receive positive choices.

All this suggests that we need to look carefully at the relationships we have, decide what our goals are, determine whether or not they are consistent with the kinds of choices we want to receive, then make choices that help us achieve those goals. This assessment should help us in three ways: to achieve greater depth in our most significant relationships; to be realistic about how many people we can give ourselves to in deep and loving ways; and, at the same time, to increase our capacity for deeper relationships over time.

Your best attempts to achieve your long-range goals with another person may be confounded because you let your short-range goals get in the way. If your friend did something thoughtless that troubled you yesterday, your goal today may be to get back at that person in some way. Such behavior has come to be seen as "natural," and people around you might even encourage you to act on your annoyance. However, whether the driving force behind the thoughtless action was something you did, or something external to the relationship that affected your friend, your action to get back at that person will probably escalate the difficulty and move you away from your long range goal for the relationship. An honest statement of the concern you feel is more likely to move you directly or indirectly toward your goal, it will more likely open the topic for discussion, and it will be seen as more positive than a vengeful action.

We all need to learn to distinguish between our immediate- and our long-range goals, and, because they are generally positive, act as often as possible on our long-range goals. It may be useful to think of actions on our long-range goals as investments in our relationships—especially when we act counter to our short-range, negative impulses. There is a risk in ignoring negatives, since it is possible that the other person will take advantage of our tolerance. But the greater risk is that our significant relationships will suffer because we do not think enough about our long-range goals, because we take those relationships for granted, and because we do not make the choices that can help us achieve our goals. We let relationships founder instead of giving them the positive attention they deserve.

To relate this concept directly to counseling, in large measure the view your clients hold of themselves is a key to their achieving their goals. Though it may be difficult, they may need to discard old tapes they play that say such things as: "I can't be an open person; it's just not me"—more open choices are within their reach if those choices will help them achieve their long-range goals. Or "The worst thing in relationships is to be taken advantage of"—the worst thing is to let the closeness they feel with some people deteriorate over time because they do not invest adequately in their relationships.

SELF-EXAMINATION—JOURNAL ENTRY: Take a few minutes to think, then discuss in your journal the goals you have in some of your most important relationships, and the habitual and spontaneous choices you make in those relationships that move you toward and away from your goals. Suggestion: head your entry RELATIONSHIP GOALS.

We encourage you to share these ideas with your clients, inviting their reactions and helping them see the importance of clarifying the goals they have for their important relationships. Most clients are unaware of their goals with others, and as a result they make too few choices that could move them toward their goals. They need to be challenged to make the kinds of choices that can help them achieve the positive goals they have for their relationships, and for their lives.

COUNSELING APPLICATION—JOURNAL ENTRY: To what extent do you believe it is important for you to help your clients deal directly with their goals with others and for themselves? In what ways, if any, might you counsel differently because you have explored this issue? Consider with at least one specific or hypothetical client how you might focus on goals and the choices that individual could make to bring more meaning into his or her life. Suggestion: head your entry CLIENT GOALS.

Meaning

The issue of meaning is important in the lives of many counseling clients. Though frequently they are not aware that is the case, an underlying cause of many clients' concerns may well be a sense that their lives lack meaning or that they themselves do not make a difference in their world. Counselors should ask themselves concerning their clients whether the issue of meaning might be significant in their lives. If the answer is affirmative, it seems highly appropriate that the counseling process give the matter of meaning direct or indirect attention. Our focus here is the clarification of the construct of meaning and its relevance in counseling.

To some extent all of us make our choices on the basis of the habit patterns we have developed in our relationships. For many of us the meaning in our lives would be enhanced if we made our choices more often on the basis of our goals than our habits. When our more elemental needs are met, we are able to consider larger matters. We do not often ask the question of what gives meaning to our lives, but the answer is central if we are to live lives that are deeply, personally satisfying. If we ask a related question of ourselves, it tends to be a superficial one: Am I happy? The happiness we seek is often an ephemeral, situational matter. Deeper happiness is likely to be a by-product of meaning, and for most people that meaning is likely to occur when their actions serve the social interest.

What does meaning mean? Raising that question is a first step in exploring the many genuine, deep abstractions that challenge existential thought. What is existence? Who am I? What is the purpose of life? Is it true that because I think, I am? These and other existential questions are intriguing and worthwhile; however, at this point we will respond to only one question, What is meaning? and follow that with some comments that are designed to clarify the answer and its relevance for Choice Awareness in counseling. Chapter Seven extends the discussion of existentialism as a counseling theory that emphasizes and demonstrates the skill of caring.

What is meaning? Meaning is whatever gives a person a sense of inner significance. It is the individual's purpose for being. Clearly there can be one overriding matter that gives an individual a sense of meaning. Frankl cited Nietzsche's statement, "He [she] who has a *why* to live for can bear almost any *how*" (1959, p. 157), and went on to suggest that people behave morally for the sake of a cause to which they commit themselves, or for a person whom they love, or for the sake of their God. For many people, then, the solution to gaining a sense of meaning or inner significance lies in committing themselves to a single objective: a cause, a person, or God; and clients who are lacking a sense of meaning may be helped most through a process of counseling that enables them to develop such a commitment.

Commitment to a consistent, single, overriding cause or person, or to God, however attractive and admirable that purpose may be, may remain somewhat out of reach for many people. What then? Are such individuals destined to wander through their lives in an existential, meaningless vacuum? In *Man's Search for Meaning*, Frankl suggested that the meaning of life for many individuals varies from day to day and hour to hour, and that what matters ". . . is not the meaning of life in general but rather the specific meaning of a person's life at a given moment" (1959 p. 171). Each person is questioned by life, and each person ". . . can only answer to life by *answering for* his [her] own life" (1959, p. 172), responsibly, and in the moment.

At least part of the process of counseling may be that of helping clients discover the meaning that exists in their lives or, lacking that, enabling them to create a sense of purpose and meaning for themselves. The sense of meaning we help our clients achieve does not have to be highly abstract and esoteric; it may be quite specific. It does not have to be singular; it may be multi-dimensional. It does not have to be external; it may also be internal.

Religion, God, is a source of great meaning for many people. There is something in most human beings that moves them to identify with a purpose in their lives that is larger than themselves. While it is often pointed out that many dastardly acts have occurred in the name of religion, doubtless far more positive acts have occurred in the name of a higher being, whether that being is called God, Jehovah, Buddha, Allah, or by any other name. Building a life in which meaning derives from a sense of service to God can be among the most admirable avenues an individual can take.

The television mini-series called *Wallenberg* was based on the life of the Swedish diplomat who helped many thousands of Jews escape extermination in the World War II holocaust, only to disappear behind what later became known as the Iron Curtain, in all likelihood as a prisoner. What gave Wallenberg's life a deep sense of meaning, perhaps for the first time, was *a cause*. He knew he meant something because he could see the living evidence of his efforts: more persons who survived the holocaust than would have otherwise. The opportunity for serving such a noble cause in the face of a constant life and death threat is not available to all of us, and if it were, most of us would be found wanting. Nonetheless, there are small and large causes to which each of us might dedicate ourselves, and the sense of purpose and meaning those causes could give us would enhance our lives.

Millions of individuals derive their sense of meaning from acting in the social interest through volunteer effort. They serve others through such organizations as the Red Cross, Big Brothers and Big Sisters, Meals on Wheels, the American Cancer Society, and so forth. Relatives of ours are among the many who gain a sense of meaning through their regular contributions to specific charities that serve people in impoverished countries, and they include in their daily prayers the names of several children they are helping financially. Many individuals gain a sense of meaning through participation in political action groups, through seeking the election of specific candidates, by raising money, or in other ways by helping to sponsor legislation. Although the Equal Rights Amendment failed, barely, to garner support by legislatures in three-fourths of the states, many women for the first time experienced the exhilaration of striving for a cause that went beyond themselves. One way in which I achieve a sense of meaning through service to others is as a singer with a small band. As we see it, we spread joy and gain much for ourselves as well through our visits to the county senior center and to various nursing and retirement homes in the area. Worthy causes abound. Many clients would do well to get beyond themselves and their own narrow needs and perspectives by reaching out in some way in *service to others*, and in that service find that their own sense of meaning is greatly enhanced.

In the theoretically-idyllic world of not-so-long-ago, young people gained a sense of meaning early in their lives. They may have been too busy to contemplate the issue of meaning, but in the deep recesses of their minds they knew that their contributions were needed. They churned butter, carried water, fed animals, and otherwise labored along with their parents—and they knew that they belonged. Few young people today know that what they do is of any value to anyone else. They labor, if they do so at all, in order to make their parents and themselves proud in a distant future. The sense of immediacy is gone. Parents are not aware that an immediate sense of meaning is lacking in the lives of their children, so they do little to encourage its development, but even the best efforts of parents who would like to help their children to gain a sense of meaning may have minimal effect. Chores often seem invented; gadgets do what children could do, or enable them to do whatever is asked of them in relatively little time. However, if there is one avenue through which young people can contribute, it is through *service to others*.

Space considerations here prohibit a lengthy discussion of youth service but, fortunately, that idea, youth service, is gaining currency (*Newsweek*, 1989). Creative young people and adults who work with children and adolescents should be able to come up with an almost-infinite variety of opportunities for them to serve others. Schools overlook young people as one of the most abundant resources they have available. Children and adolescents, and not just those who are outstanding students, can be mobilized to help younger children, their peers, and those who have physical disabilities or learning problems.

Outside the school setting, community-based programs can be created that direct and incorporate the energies of young people in working with older people and those who are less fortunate, and in meeting community needs. Name any current social problem and there is potential for youth to serve—drug abuse, alcoholism, vandalism, illiteracy, homelessness, and so forth—young people can be mobilized to help, and through helping they can achieve the sense of meaning their lives may currently lack.

A person can be a deep source of meaning in the life of another. Few people are ever so much alive and involved in life as when they are experiencing the love and excitement of a new relationship to a sweetheart or to a brand new offspring. The generous gifts of time and worldly goods people bestow on those loved ones may yield over time to a less dramatic, gentler pattern of choices, but love that is nurtured continues to bring meaning to both the giver and the receiver. Many clients need to learn to sustain such positive patterns of choices in their intimate relationships, and the reward for such learning is likely to be deeper meaning for all involved.

Friends who have a Down's Syndrome child have spent enormous amounts of time enabling their son to learn the significant and basic skills of life; he reads very well and has accomplished nearly all of the educational tasks expected of his age group. His parents became advocates for educational resources for handicapped children and did not allow traditional views of the limitations of Down's Syndrome children to discourage them from expecting significant learning from him. Call it a cause if you will, but it appears to me that the primary source of meaning they have felt has always been the love they have for a person, their child, rather than the cause they have espoused.

Most of us have the capacity to love and to give to more than one person. My mother-in-law achieved her sense of meaning and purpose in part through *family*; she took great delight in reaching out toward, remembering, and serving, a large extended family that included great aunts and uncles, first cousins and double first cousins, nieces and nephews, and of course her own brothers and sisters, her children, and their families. The death of her kin did not remove them from her recall and interest. Until she died she remained a font of family history and kept an active interest in all family ancestors and descendants; when she told their stories and anecdotes they were memorable and intriguing.

A second way in which my mother-in-law exhibited a sense of meaning was a more internal matter. She responded to the things she saw with a deep and abiding *interest in the world* around her. She marveled at the great expanses of corn and soy bean fields the train passed through when she came to visit us in Indiana, and she touched, smelled, and visually devoured the growing things she saw. There was no place we could go with her or take her where she was bored, because all the world was of interest to her. To walk with her in an antique store or a trash-and-treasures establishment was an especial delight, both because she knew the purpose of so many objects we could not identify, and because she was always interested in knowing about the objects she could not place. Perhaps in her own colorful way she was exhibiting the same kind of interest in the world that Thoreau demonstrated when he went to Walden Pond and survived more than adequately, and thought deeply, because everything was of interest to him—because he took the time to know and understand his world.

My wife, Betty, comes by honestly part of the sense of meaning in life she feels. She combines her mother's demonstrated interest in family and the world around her, and expresses it by demonstrating a deep *interest in people*. I have often thought that except for the difficulty she might have in keeping to time limits and breaking for advertisements—because she would be too interested in what the other person was saying—that she would make an ideal television or radio talk show host. Her capacity for helping other people feel comfortable, for drawing them out, for demonstrating genuine interest in them, and for recalling and following-up what they told her about in their last encounter is truly marvelous. I want at times to dismiss it as a gift, and thereby absolve myself of the obligation to demonstrate similar skill, but I know that I could, and others could, grow in that skill, if we would—and that it would give a greater sense of meaning to our lives and the lives of those we meet.

Most of us spend half of our waking life on a *job or task* that can be a source of meaning for us. Vocational theorists have suggested that people are judged by their work, and that the significance most individuals feel in this life depends in large measure on the work they do. Frankl (1959) suggested that he survived his experiences in a concentration camp in World War II in part because he had a manuscript he wanted to write, a task that let him get beyond himself, and that gave his life meaning, despite his circumstances.

Not every job or task people face can be fascinating, and some appear to be inherently meaningless. I recall seeing a television advertisement some years ago in which two adults were dressed as rabbits, cavorting about on carpeting to demonstrate how soft it was. I would not try to challenge anyone to derive any sense of deep meaning from such a compromise with human dignity, but I believe that *most* jobs can yield some sense of meaning to those who hold them—if they will allow themselves to see the possibilities. Some employers in recent years have become more sensitive to the needs of employees to see how their tasks fit into the larger scheme of things, at least within the company, and have involved employees in management issues through such means as organizing quality circles. Even in less enlightened companies, however, individuals can try to see for themselves how the product or service they help to produce contributes to the society, and in that way help themselves gain a sense of meaning through their work. Those of us who have what might be called careers instead of jobs can count our blessings because we are more likely to gain a sense of meaning through our tasks. Clearly we are likely to experience that sense of meaning more fully if we conduct ourselves professionally and in a dedicated manner, continuing to learn and grow in our expertise.

William Glasser (1976) suggested another route for gaining a sense of meaning in life; he encouraged individuals to develop a *positive addiction*, something that is so absorbing that they are able to transcend themselves and attain a deeper level of involvement than they have been able to achieve before. Glasser noticed that joggers, for example, sometimes get so absorbed in that activity that they lose a sense of time, go beyond what they have believed is their capacity, and free their minds to wander into avenues they had not thought possible. Jogging is not for everyone, and neither, probably, is a positive addiction, but thorough absorption in something to the point that we lose our time sense and free our minds to transcend our previous thought processes, may be available to people in a variety of ways. Such diverse activities as gardening, yoga, painting, sewing, crafts, woodworking, singing, playing a musical instrument, square dancing, walking, flying, snorkeling, skiing, and stamp or coin collecting, offer individuals possible outlets for such an addiction. As Glasser suggested, the activity should be positive—not harmful to the individual or others, as the use of tobacco products, hallucinatory drugs, or alcohol would be. One person's meat may be another person's poison, and what is meaningful and addictive in one individual's life may be harmful or non-addictive for another, so the design of a positive addiction must be an individual matter. If you as a counselor come to understand your clients well enough, you may be able to help them find something in which they can involve themselves that is absorbing enough to serve them as a positive addiction.

Meaning, in the several ways described above—through serving God, through a cause, through a person, through family, through interest in things or in people, through work or a task, or through a positive addiction—is available to your clients. Opportunities abound to serve; people everywhere are interesting; families or substitute families are available for all; the world contains a great many wonderful things to marvel about; and all clients work, or can become involved in a task, or can take on a positive addiction. Many clients rush by potential sources of meaning in every direction. The truth of the matter is that most of them have in their lives something or someone to which or to whom they are deeply dedicated, but they do not think in terms of finding meaning in life, so they remain insufficiently aware or involved.

One of the five guiding principles of Choice Awareness theory is that self-interest and social-interest need to be balanced. Many of the avenues available to your clients for achieving a sense of meaning in their lives would contribute to the social-interest dimension. But it should be noted that personal gain is almost inevitably a by-product when an individual gains a sense of meaning. As a counselor you serve your clients well when you help them see the possibilities for discovering or creating meaning in their lives, and when you encourage them to make choices that enable them to achieve a sense of meaning.

SELF-EXAMINATION—JOURNAL ENTRY: Take a few minutes to think, then discuss in your journal the things that bring meaning to your life. Discuss what you do to keep your life meaningful and what choices you could make to enhance the sense of meaning in your life. Suggestion: head your entry MEANING FOR ME.

We believe it is important for you to share these ideas with your clients, inviting their reactions and helping them see the relevance of the issue of meaning in their lives. Many counseling clients have a sense of meaninglessness in their lives and need to discover the significance their lives have, both for themselves and for others. If they see their lives as meaningless, they need to be challenged to make the kinds of choices that are likely to change that view.

COUNSELING APPLICATION—JOURNAL ENTRY: To what extent do you believe it is important for you to help your clients deal directly with the issue of meaning in their lives? In what ways, if any, might you counsel differently in the future as a result of thinking more deeply about this issue? Consider with at least one specific or hypothetical client how you might focus on the issue of meaning and the choices that individual could make to bring more meaning into his or her life. Suggestion: head your entry MEANING FOR MY CLIENT(S).

Habits, Goals, and Meaning

"Great gain toward goals can't be expected from minimal investments" (Nelson, 1977, p. 55), whether the domain is the financial world or the realm of human relationships. Choice Awareness theory encourages counselors to help their clients examine their long range goals, to invest time and energy so that they might achieve the kinds of relationships they want in their lives, and to discover the meaning their lives can have. Specifying goals so that they might be achieved, and discovering meaning, are two important steps in achieving inner well-being for both clients and counselors.

References

Frankl, V. E. (1959). *Man's search for meaning.* New York: Washington Square Press.

Glasser, W. (1976) *Positive addiction.* New York: Harper and Row.

Nelson, R. C. (1977). *Choosing: A better way to live.* North Palm Beach, FL: GuideLines Press.

Newsweek. (July 10, 1989). The new volunteers: Special report. Pp. 36-66.

Chapter 5

OK and OD Choices

The OK/OD Choice Continuum

In Chapter One we introduced OK and OD choices, defining the term OK as meaning positive choices that are at minimum acceptable in a relationship; and defining the term OD as those choices involving words and actions that are overdone (as in cooking), that act like an overdose (as in drug/alcohol abuse), or that overdraw (as in banking) in relation to an interpersonal account. Choices are also OD when they adversely affect the individual who is making them. This suggests that thoughts and feelings, as well as words and actions, can be OD choices. Choices exist on a continuum of major OK → minor OK → minor OD → major OD choices. For choices to be truly OK they must be acceptable to all individuals involved.

Each of the CREST choices may be made in OK or OD ways—for ourselves or for others. When we OD on caring we act in overprotective, smothering ways; when we OD on ruling our words or actions are dominating; when we OD on enjoying we use humor or teasing to a degree that is unacceptable; when we OD on sorrowing we either internalize and act in ways that show we are miserable, or externalize and act in ways that are seen by others as mean; and when we OD on thinking/working we simply think too much (perhaps working too little) or work too hard (perhaps thinking too little).

There are definite advantages in exploring all of the CREST choices and their OK and OD expressions with clients in counseling to help them figure out how to make better choices for themselves and with others both in the present and the future. However, in the interest of efficiency and brevity, any part of the Choice Awareness system may be explored by itself with clients in relation to the specific need they have. With some clients that may mean focusing on how they might make more OK enjoying choices with family members, with others that may mean focusing on how they might make fewer OD sorrowing choices for themselves. With most clients it is essential that the question of OK and OD choices be explored—whether the focus is on those choices that affect relationships with others primarily, or on self-choices.

CONSIDER THE FOLLOWING:

Rudy, a thirteen-year-old eighth grader, grudgingly sought the help of a counselor in his school, after agreeing to do so in the heat of an argument with his mother. The two had been having difficulty for some time, and each was deeply frustrated with the actions of the other. From his mother's perspective Rudy was too negative and uncommunicative. From Rudy's perspective his mother was always "on his case," nagging him about one thing or another. After a brief time span in which Mrs. Linkaus, the counselor, used mostly listening approaches, Rudy agreed, and his mother subsequently agreed as well, to the use of the family's tape recorder during mealtimes, when most arguments seemed to occur between the two. Mrs. Linkaus skipped the first four tapings and turned to the fifth, assuming that both protagonists might be guarded in their dialogue for the first few time blocks. The playback of the tape was very revealing to Rudy, especially in the context of the strategy Mrs. Linkaus suggested—looking for OK choices . Although he could rationalize his behaviors, Rudy admitted that it sounded as though he had chosen to eliminate positive choices altogether when he talked with his mother. By contrast, although what she had to say was peppered with negatives, Rudy's mother's communication included some choices that were clearly OK. Random passages from other tapes confirmed Rudy's continuous negativism. As a result he agreed to introduce positive topics and incorporate positive comments in his dialogue. The process of change was a genuine struggle for him, but Rudy saw clearly that when he brought up an item of news or an event from his day, he controlled the direction of the discussion, his mother was willing to hear from him, and the dialogue was more positive. The acid test for both was that their relationship improved.

Most people, like Rudy, are painfully aware of how the choices of others affect them, but they remain oblivious to the possibility that their choices affect others as well. Some make OD choices without any awareness that their choices hurt, believing they are powerless to hurt anyone.

There is a contemporary fairy tale, told in many versions, about a witch who persuades the people of a town that their supply of "warm fuzzies"—warm, positive statements and actions—will be exhausted unless they use them sparingly. Many of us act as if we believe that is the case, yet we may show great generosity with the "cold pricklies"— the negative choices—we send. We need to realize that our supply of major and minor OK choices (warm fuzzies in the parlance of that tale), *and* our supply of major and minor OD choices (cold pricklies), are both inexhaustible. Most of us need to learn to be more generous in making OK choices, especially major OK choices, freely and when asked, because we are all part of the human experience, and because we all need positive attention from others. And, "When we want to improve a relationship, we should be aware that all OK and OD choices are not equal; some choices. . . produce especially good feelings while others . . . produce deep hurt" (Nelson, 1977, p. 70). Your clients can benefit if you share these ideas in counseling at appropriate times.

Umbrella Language, Mixed Messages, and OK/OD Choices

Occasionally all of us use what we like to call "umbrella language," in which we send a message like "Don't forget your umbrella." We mean that to be an OK choice, but the other person may construe it as an OD choice. We may want the other person to hear "I love you, I care about you, I don't want anything bad to happen to you," but that person may hear instead, "You don't have enough sense to come in out of the rain—so I have to tell you what to do."

In working with your clients, there are at least two ways in which you can help them when they send or receive discrepant messages that cause problems for them. First, you can help them understand that it is possible for them to interpret others' umbrella language in positive ways—seeing the caring intention and making an active choice to ignore the implied negative. Second, you can help them find suitable ways to send their positive messages, encouraging them to make direct statements, such as "I love you," instead of relying on indirect messages that are likely to be interpreted negatively.

Choices involving umbrella language are problematic, but equally problematic for relationships are those choices that contain other mixed messages. For example: "You look really nice, but you shouldn't wear *that* outfit tonight." Or "I'm glad you called, but I'm too busy to talk right now." We will inevitably make such choices from time to time, but we need to realize that the OK portion of the statement is often overshadowed by the OD portion. We may want our positive intent to come through, but the negative element of our response is likely to be what is recalled.

Many of your clients have difficulty with long-term interpersonal relationships with their spouses, parents, or children, for example. If you have had the opportunity to listen to both sides of the issue with your clients and those with whom they have difficulty, you know that both individuals are likely to see their own behavior as more positive than that of the other person. both are unaware that the pattern of choices they have evolved includes the use of umbrella language, mixed messages, and OD choices. Your clients can use your help in coming to understand the OKness and ODness of many of their own choices, in counterbalancing the inevitable OD choices they will make with sufficient numbers of OK choices, in planning to make more effective choices, and in executing those plans.

We make OK and OD choices both with other people and with ourselves. The client who has been told, "You'll never amount to anything," may end up echoing that sentiment as a continual, internal, OD choice—a self-fulfilling prophecy. Persons who know that one more drink is likely to make them a hazard on the road make an OD choice for themselves by ordering another. The fact that choices are OD for self is no more of a guarantee that your clients will not make them than if they are OD choices involving other people. Your clients may act contrary to their own interests for various reasons. For example, it may be their habit to do so, or they may give priority to some other factor. In the case of drinking too much, clients may rationalize that they just want to be sociable with others, or they may decide that they want to forget their troubles.

Counseling processes have given little direct attention to supporting the OK choices clients make and encouraging them to reduce the frequency of their OD choices. If you choose to base your counseling on Choice Awareness theory, you need to do both of those things in the interests of helping your clients. For example, you may want to encourage some of your clients when they are in the heat of conflict to—"Take the instant you have, consider the relationship and your goals, and. . . wait. . . until you can find something OK to say" (Nelson, 1977, p. 73). As simple and obvious as that sounds, it is evident that such a thought process is lacking in the behavior of many counseling clients, and that is often just what they need to break a negative interaction cycle. Furthermore, it is just this kind of foundational process that can help your clients build the base they need for making their major life choices in more considered, more OK, ways.

SELF-EXAMINATION—JOURNAL ENTRY: Take a few minutes to think, then discuss in your journal the pattern of OK and OD choices you have developed in one of your most important relationships, and with yourself. Next, consider the extent to which your OK and OD choices in the relationship move you toward or away from your goals with that person, and the extent to which your OK and OD choices for yourself move you toward or away from a sense of inner well-being. Suggestion: head your entry MY OK/OD CHOICES.

We encourage you to share these ideas with your clients, inviting their reactions and helping them see the importance of clarifying the OK and OD choices they have been making in their important relationships and for themselves. Most clients are unaware of the impact of their choices on their relationships with others and for themselves, and as a result they make OD choices that move them away from their goals. They need to be challenged to make more OK choices if they are to achieve the positive goals they have for their relationships and for their lives.

COUNSELING APPLICATION—JOURNAL ENTRY: Discuss the extent to which you believe it is important for you to help your clients deal directly with their patterns of OK and OD choices, for themselves and with others. Consider with at least one specific or hypothetical client how you might focus on the OD choices that person now makes, and the OK choices that individual could make in the future to improve his or her life situation. Suggestion: head your entry OK/OD CLIENT CHOICES.

Habits and OK/OD Choices

Most of the problems clients face are not mysterious. They make too many OD choices and too few OK choices for themselves and with others. The patterns of choices they have learned include both habits and contracts, and some of these patterns serve them poorly in their relationships with others and contribute negatively to their own sense of well-being. Those persons who are dissatisfied with their lives need help in discarding old patterns of choices—habits—and in developing more effective, more OK, patterns of choices.

People do not set out to build patterns of negative choices; they evolve those patterns over time, in part because no one has helped them really, deeply understand that their positive choices need to overbalance those they make that are negative. They may believe sincerely that others make OD choices to which they must inevitably respond in OD ways. Clients who take this view may find it difficult to comprehend that they need to make choices they can like and respect, even if those toward whom they direct their choices do not respond positively. The venture will not always be successful. But the message many of your clients need is: *Do not hold on to your habit patterns; make choices you like and like the choices you make.*

CONSIDER THE FOLLOWING:

When I made a brief presentation to a class of college students, Eleanor, a class member, described a situation that troubled her. Jenny, one of her apartment mates, was a "couch potato." Much of the time she situated herself in the living room before the television, frequently watching one program while recording another for later viewing. In their early months together Jenny had turned down so many invitations to join the others in activities away from the apartment that Eleanor and her other apartment mate, Sue, had stopped asking her to do things with them. Jenny was ensconced in the living room so much of the time that Eleanor and Sue felt they had little freedom to entertain friends in the apartment. The two had stopped speaking to Jenny except when absolutely necessary and were waiting out the end of the school year, planning to take a two-person apartment in the fall. With some hesitation because of the class context in which the question was raised, I suggested that what I would like to do if I were Eleanor— despite the previous history, and if I could push myself to do so—is to return to the apartment daily with a statement of greeting, and occasionally invite Jenny to participate in an activity. My object would be to make choices I could like and respect myself for, in the full acknowledgement that I would merely be trying to make the best of a bad situation until it was over. We never got to the issue of confronting Jenny over the use of the living room because Eleanor immediately characterized that pattern of choices as self-righteous, and before long comments and questions by other class members moved us away from that issue. It was apparent that Eleanor had drawn the firm conclusion that she had made all the positive moves she intended to and any positive movement would have to be initiated by Jenny. Certainly there are relationships people believe are hopeless, but so long as they share the same household or otherwise have to face one another with some frequency, it seems essential that they maintain some kind of minimal, civilized contact—unless it is apparent that *any* contact aggravates the problem, as in a case of spouse abuse, for example. In effect Eleanor's underlying question was: How can I get Jenny to change her behavior without any further positive effort on my part? The inevitable answer to such a question is: You cannot.

If you face a client like Eleanor in counseling, it would be well to determine if she has drawn the conclusion that the pattern of choices she has evolved is the way she wants it to be—and she therefore seeks validation of her responses—or that she desires support for even more vigorous, negative action. However, if your client still retains some openness about making choices involving an equivalent to Eleanor's "couch potato" apartment mate, you may want to expend effort in helping her plan a pattern of choices that she can respect and like, choices that may maintain open lines of communication.

When we explore sorrowing choices in greater depth, we will discuss the idea of labeling. Suffice it to say at this point that we all take upon ourselves labels others have applied to us, and we may wear them forever as badges: the good kid, trouble-maker, lady-killer, and so forth.

Eleanor's use of the label, self-righteous, makes it clear that labeling can be used externally as well—to dismiss other people or their ideas. The danger in attaching a label such as self-righteous to a suggestion—in this case that Eleanor might think about making choices she could like—is that once verbalized it becomes difficult to let it go. What I called for on Eleanor's part, and what many clients need to consider, is summed up in the Biblical injunction, "Do unto others as you would have them do unto you." To that I would add: and continue to do so even if it does not produce the outcome you want—not because it is self-righteous, but because it is the humane thing to do, and because it can allow you to feel good about the choices you have made.

Spa, Feelings, and OK Choices

The groundwork has been laid for connecting OK choices, on the one hand, and spa, feelings, and accounts, on the other. In this section we make those connections specific.

The concept of spa has already been tied directly to the counseling process. An additional connection is valuable—to the concept of OK self-choices. That we need to care for ourselves is a self-evident proposition, but many of us act upon that need infrequently. Further-more, most of us could beneficially redesign part of our days—or at the very least, some part of our lives—in ways that could help us feel deeply and genuinely positive about ourselves. All people at one level or another seek confirmation that they are worthwhile human beings. All people at one level or another sense that they have a right to feel joy in their lives. All people need spa-like experiences in the emotional realm, and counselors may well help their clients gain those experiences.

Individuals come to counseling seeking confirmation of themselves; many of them return for counseling because they sense its promise in bringing them confirmation that they are worthwhile, and because the process hints of joy. Instead of viewing the return for counseling as recidivism, as failure, we need to determine whether or not it actually indicates a genuine success: a relationship, a process that is in itself salutary and warrants continuation.

In most counseling systems the confirmation that counseling gives the individual is not treated specifically; it is regarded as a by-product of the problem-solving that is considered to be the real focus of counseling. By contrast, the Choice Awareness system suggests that this confirmation, this joy, should neither be merely hinted at nor relegated to the status of an incidental by-product. Instead, the counselor should make it an explicit goal with the client and direct effort toward it regularly and specifically. Let us say that another way. As a counselor you are encouraged to spend part of the counseling time in helping your clients achieve spa, which they can do by making OK choices—especially OK enjoying choices—for and about themselves, and by feeling good about those choices.

Numerous ways of achieving spa in counseling are suggested in Chapter Two, and you are encouraged to design other, suitable ways of achieving spa that relate to the needs of your individual clients. Whatever you do to achieve spa you will do through your own choices and you will be providing a model that helps your clients make OK choices for and about themselves.

Just as there is a connection between spa and OK choices, there is also a connection between feelings and OK choices. In Chapter One we mentioned two Choice Awareness concepts that are feeling-related: we choose from among our feelings in the moment which ones we will act upon, and we choose our feelings about ourselves.

In those instances in which we have strong feelings, we tend to have many feelings. By and large it is those people we care about and value with whom we are inclined to have competing feelings. A given situation involving a close friend, our parent, or our spouse may seem to call from us a negative feeling—anger, for example—but in that moment we may also feel hurt, frustrated, troubled, and confused; at the same time we have a store of affectionate, valuing, caring feelings for that person. From among all those feelings it is our task to choose which ones we will act upon in the moment. If we remind ourselves of the long term goal we have with that person, we can more often choose to act on constructive feelings, and we can more often make an OK choice.

Our feelings about ourselves are not one-dimensional, and, if it serves our needs, we can choose to focus on different feelings about ourselves than we have focused on in the past. We know at some level that we are both weak and strong, brave and cowardly, intelligent and impractical, for example. A given situation may seem to call forth negative feelings about ourselves, but we can choose to focus on more positive feelings. We can label the action of moving away from some kind of trouble as cowardly, for example, and reinforce that label for ourselves; or we can feel good that we took the logical action in the moment, and see ourselves as intelligent. From time to time, then, we can see the same action as either an OK or an OD choice—depending on how we construe it. A counseling client, for example, may berate herself for not standing up to her father's criticism, yet overlook the reality that she subsequently acted on her own convictions.

One of the tasks you may take upon yourself in counseling is that of helping your clients choose appropriate feelings to act upon. If guilt is appropriate, that is what you may want to help them feel—enroute to taking appropriate action. If guilt is inappropriate, if the action they took is justifiable and sensible, you can help them feel good about that action.

SELF-EXAMINATION—JOURNAL ENTRY: Take a few minutes to think, then discuss in your journal ways in which your feelings about yourself and your resulting OK or OD choices help you to achieve, or prevent you from achieving, a sense of spa in your life. Suggestion: head your entry MY FEELINGS, MY CHOICES, AND SPA.

We encourage you to share these ideas with your clients, inviting their reactions and helping them see the importance of their feelings and the OK and OD choices they make in their important relationships as a result. Most clients need to be challenged to choose more positive feelings to act on so they might achieve the goals they have for their relationships and for their lives.

COUNSELING APPLICATION—JOURNAL ENTRY: Discuss in your journal the extent to which you believe it is important for you to help your clients deal directly with their feelings and their OK and OD choices. Consider with at least one specific or hypothetical client how you might help that person choose positive feelings to act upon that might improve his/her life situation. Suggestion: head your entry CLIENT FEELINGS & CHOICES.

Feelings, Accounts, and OK Choices

There are three key questions we can ask concerning each account we have with others who are important to us—and that the counselor can help clients ask concerning each of their accounts: Is the overall balance in this account positive? What OK choices am I making that contribute to this account in positive ways? Are there ways in which I am allowing this account to erode through inaction—through letting "service charges" deplete the account?

All people must expect that they, and others they relate to, will make OD choices from time to time, and any worthwhile relationship between people must tolerate that human failing. The criterion for a successful relationship should not be one of perfect responsiveness through continuous OK choices—that is an impossibility for human beings who live in this world. The criterion for a successful relationship should be that the balance in the account is positive. In most instances that is an attainable goal.

Your clients are likely to include people who see themselves as relatively powerless, as responders to others, as victims of the vicissitudes of life. From their perspectives they believe that those relationships in which their accounts are negative are in that condition because of the choices of the other person, not because of their own choices. In most cases your clients have evolved this perspective over many years. Despite that, many of your clients will find it refreshing and exciting to come to the understanding that they have choices—power they can exercise—in their relationships; that each choice they make contributes positively or negatively to the balance in their relationships; and that although negative choices by other persons seem to call for negative responses on their part, it is their choice how they will respond in the moment. Other clients may find these ideas difficult to comprehend or to accept. Even with these people, however, continuing consideration of their own choices and how those choices contribute to their interpersonal accounts is worthwhile, and should eventually make its point.

In our discussion of accounts we have focused our attention on relationships with others. Before we leave this topic, however, let us consider briefly self-accounts and OK choices. To a genuine extent our self-concepts and our accounts with ourselves may be seen as interchangeable ideas. While it is inevitable that long-ago events and labels and perceptions will enter into any self-concept, we can and do reinforce or modify our self-concepts through our choices in the moment. If our self-account is negative—that is, if we frequently think thoughts and do things that are harmful to ourselves—we maintain a negative balance in our self-account. Similarly, if our self-account is positive—if we think thoughts and do things frequently that are positive—we maintain a positive balance in our self-account. Negative actions and thoughts in the present have a negative impact on our self-concepts, and positive actions and thoughts in the present have a positive impact on our self-concepts. This concept may be important for many of your clients.

CONSIDER THE FOLLOWING:

When Rudy, the thirteen-year-old we introduced at the beginning of this chapter, began to work with his counselor, Mrs. Linkaus, to a great extent she focused her efforts on helping him understand the pattern of choices he had been making with his mother. Initially, Mrs. Linkaus was content when Rudy showed some understanding that his choices in that relationship were nearly all OD, while those his mother made were positive, OK, at least some of the time. Gradually Mrs. Linkaus introduced the concept of accounts in relationships; Rudy began to see that what he got with his mother tended to reflect what he gave, and that if he wanted the account with his mother to have a more positive balance, he shared the responsibility for helping it move in that direction. Eventually Mrs. Linkaus helped Rudy explore his account with himself. She helped him understand that he made few positive choices with anyone because his own self-concept was shaky; and she eventually helped him see that he may have been making many of his negative choices with his mother as a way of seeking the criticism and punishment he felt he deserved.

Whether the focus is the client or ourselves and whether the issue is negative accounts with others, with oneself, or with both others and oneself, the antidote is the same: more positive than negative choices, more OK than OD choices. We express our feelings about ourselves through our choices. If we feel good about ourselves, we tend to make OK choices; if we have negative feelings about ourselves, we tend to make OD choices. As with the chicken/egg question, there is a legitimate question about which comes first. Clearly, though, if we make OD choices, we enhance the chances of feeling bad about ourselves; by the same token, if we make OK choices, we enhance the chances of feeling good about ourselves.

OK and OD Choices

Choice Awareness theory helps counselors assist their clients to understand the OK and OD choices they have been making, and, where necessary, to modify their patterns of choices. Many counseling clients see themselves as incapable of affecting those around them; in many cases that becomes a license for them to make one OD choice after another.

Most clients can benefit from learning that they sometimes send negative choices when they intend to send positive choices—for example, through mixed messages and what we call "umbrella language." In the latter, the receiver perceives a message as negative—"Don't forget your umbrella" is read as "you don't have enough sense to come in out of the rain"—while the sender intends a positive message—"I care about you and I don't want anything bad to happen to you." In Choice Awareness counseling the individual is encouraged to send clear and direct positive messages through OK choices.

Many clients habitually make OD choices, and the OD choices they make result in their having problems. As a counselor you can assist your clients by exploring with them their OK and OD choices, by creating a spa environment for them, by helping them see that they can choose more often to act on their positive feelings, and by encouraging them to build their interpersonal accounts through making more, and more effective, OK choices.

Reference

Nelson, R. C. (1977). *Choosing: A better way to live.* North Palm Beach, FL: GuideLines Press.

Part II

The Five CREST Choices:

Caring

Ruling

Enjoying

Sorrowing

Thinking/Working

In the section that follows we explore in depth the five CREST choices of the Choice Awareness system. For many clients the key to more effective choices, and to greater inner well-being in turn, is sorting out which of the five choices they might make more often in OK ways, and which they might make less often in OD ways, in their interactions with others and for themselves. These matters are discussed, and attention is given to helping clients plan ahead to make more effective choices.

We expect that you will refer to this source as you work with clients, and we believe that it is important for each of the subsequent chapters to stand on its own; therefore, many dimensions of choosing are discussed and related to each of the five choices. We invite you to focus on both the similarities and the differences as we consider each choice.

Chapter 6

Caring Choices: Exploration

What is Caring?

C in the acronym CREST stands for caring. Clearly it is vital for individuals to have most of their needs met, either by themselves or by others—through caring choices. Effective interpersonal relationships depend on those involved making an adequate number of each of the CREST choices, more often in OK than in OD ways. Likewise, good self-concepts depend on individuals making an adequate number of each of the CREST choices for themselves, more often in OK than in OD ways.

In order to help your clients make more effective caring choices in their lives, you need to have a deep level of understanding of what these choices are about. This chapter is designed to expand that understanding; the following chapter considers directly the use of caring choices in counseling. Subsequent chapters are designed to expand your understanding of ruling, enjoying, sorrowing, and thinking/working choices, and to point out ways you can use those understandings in counseling.

"What's wrong?"

"I'll get you a drink of water."

"How can I help?"

"I'm on your side."

"I can see you're disappointed."

"I'd be glad to put the stamps on some of those letters to help you get finished."

"I care about you" (like you, love you—when the person needs support).

"Oh, you poor, poor thing."

The choices above are all caring choices. Caring choices are responses to our own needs and to the needs of others, and they are designed to be helpful. We make caring choices when we offer help, give it, or feed back the actions, the feelings, or the words of the other person: "The way you're crumpling that letter tells me you're really annoyed with the news you received." "I can see how disappointed you are. That's one rejection too many." We make caring choices without words when we see the need of another and gently put a hand on that person's shoulder or when we wordlessly pick up papers for a person who has dropped them.

Is the caring choice we have made OK? Four primary factors determine the answer. One factor is the extent to which our words and actions fit the *need* of the other person. A second factor is the *timing* of our words and actions in relation to the readiness of the other person to receive our caring. A third factor is the *situation*—hugging and holding a person who is disappointed may be an OK choice in one setting, not in another. The fourth important factor that affects whether our words and actions are OK is the *relationship* we have with the other person. On balance, the deeper the relationship we have, the more likely our caring will be seen as OK.

The now/later frame of reference is also important in determining the OKness of a choice. A great deal of solicitousness may feel good in the moment to a child, for example, but the long range effect of it may be to create dependency. In the same context it is important to note that children who are the recipients of very few caring choices in their lives are likely to become adults who neither give nor receive caring well. One key to developing an appropriate pattern of giving and receiving caring choices seems to be that of receiving and giving a reasonable number of appropriate caring choices during the formative years. However, the fact that growth along these lines has been stunted does not mean that it cannot occur in adolescence or adulthood.

To this point we have considered caring choices that are directed toward others. Of at least equal importance are the caring choices we direct toward ourselves. One way we take care of ourselves is by remaining alert to our surroundings so that we can anticipate problems. The analogy of driving a car is useful here. We see the traffic light to the left of us turn to yellow and we prepare to move forward. We notice a "yellow-bellied light-runner," a species of bird with which we are familiar, approaching from the left. Rather than asserting our right to move forward as soon as the light has turned green, we wait and let the creature vault past so that he or she might hurry along to feed the children, drink beer, or watch television. We have taken care of ourselves through anticipating another's actions. Many of us would do well to function in interpersonal relations as effectively as we do in driving—considering the likely outcomes of our choices and adjusting them accordingly—though the statistics on motor vehicle accidents suggest that our anticipation in this arena, too, is quite imperfect.

We take care of ourselves when we take the time to present ourselves well, when we exercise, eat properly, and get enough sleep. We need to take care of ourselves through the choices that involve both our bodies and our minds.

What is our self-talk like? Do we frequently say things like the following? "I can't do that." "That was a dumb thing I did." "No one will want to hear what I have to say." Or are our messages more positive? "I haven't figured out how to do that, but I'm sure I can." "It didn't turn out right, but at least I tried." "I think this is a group I'll enjoy."

A self-caring person could stand in front of a mirror and say such things as the following:

"I like the way I dress."

"I take care of myself well."

"I respect myself."

"I do what I set out to do."

"I have good relationships with several people."

"Some of my personal strengths are. . ." (and list a significant number of strengths).

Those of us who believe we are important enough to care for ourselves find it easier to accept caring from others and to make caring choices with others.

As with each of the other CREST choices, for a caring choice to be truly OK it must be OK with the sender *and* the receiver. When we feel good about ourselves we realize we are worth caring about, and we are more able to receive caring choices from others when we are in need. Likewise, when we feel good about ourselves, we realize that others need our caring choices and we are more able to make the choices others need.

Besides treating our bodies in healthy ways and talking to ourselves in positive ways when we are in need, we can make caring choices for ourselves by asking others for the caring we need:

"I need a hug."

"There's something I'd like to talk about with you when you have time."

"I need someone to let off steam with. Can you just listen for a while?"

We cannot be sufficient in giving caring to ourselves, but we can learn to ask for the caring we need. Certainly a sense of our own worth is an important basis for deciding that we can ask for something from another (Nelson, 1977, p. 92).

Caring and ruling merge in such comments as, "Don't forget your umbrella," an idea we developed when we considered OK and OD choices in the last chapter. The sender may see the statement as caring, since the intent is to help more than it is to lead; however, the receiver may hear it as a ruling choice. Umbrella language involves statements that are seen by the sender as helpful and positive, but that may be seen by the receiver as critical and negative. In urging the other person to take an umbrella the sender may believe she/he is sending the caring message, "I love you, I care about you, and I don't want anything bad to happen to you." However, the receiver may perceive the statement as ruling, believing it implies, "You don't have enough sense to come in out of the rain unless I tell you to do so."

Urging another to take an umbrella represents a kind of statement that will almost inevitably be made, and all good relationships can endure many such statements. But when a person wants to say, "I love you, I care about you, and I don't want anything bad to happen to you," that message should be delivered clearly, not commingled with a ruling choice. By the same token, it is important that the receiver of an umbrella choice tune in not only to the words sent and the resulting internal defensive feelings, but also to the meaning behind the statement. We can choose to love people even if they have no other way to show their love than by saying such things as, "Don't forget your umbrella."

Caring merges with enjoying when need and enjoyment come together. A hug or a smile given because it is needed by either person is a caring choice, while one that is given spontaneously out of joy and love is an enjoying choice. A helpful action may be given with little thought to need, and an action that seems spontaneous may be meeting a need of which the sender is unaware. The more clearly need is present, the more clearly the choice is caring; the more clearly appreciation and delight are present, the more clearly the choice is enjoying. Certainly there is overlap in such choices, however.

Caring choices are generally responses to sorrowing choices, and as a consequence, caring and sorrowing merge at many points. The need of one person may generate sadness in another. Asking for caring implies some kind of negative feeling. The primary difference between the two is that sorrowing expresses a negative feeling, whereas caring is an effort to meet the need behind that feeling.

Thinking/working and caring choices merge most often when we are planning to meet our needs or the needs of those around us, or when we are examining possible approaches to problems. Few choices, if any, occur without both thought and effort entering into them. Since this is the case, we assign caring and thinking/working labels somewhat arbitrarily. The considering and planning process we call thinking/working, while we asign the label caring to the process of meeting needs even though it clearly involves both thought and effort.

Caring merges with other choices at many points, however, caring choices can generally be differentiated from other choices on the basis of two variables: there is a need on the part of the individual who is the recipient of caring, and the action in response to that need is intended to be helpful.

Experiences that began in infancy and childhood affect the ways in which we all seek to meet our needs for caring choices. Very early in our lives, as babies, we began to learn what kinds of caring choices were OK for us to make. The caring we received when we were hungry, cold, wet, and tired formed our vague initial impressions of what caring was about. Eventually we were weaned of most of the services we received and we modified and developed our concepts of caring. If the weaning occurred as we were ready for it, and if loving, supportive messages accompanied our learnings, we came to the conclusion that caring can be a good thing when there is need. If the weaning was forced, if we gained the impression that our needs were inconvenient to others, we learned that needing care is bad, that care should be given only when need is strong, and that denial is a suitable policy. If our own require-ments for care remained unmet, we learned to take care of our needs in some way, whether direct or indirect, appropriate or inappropriate.

Most of us learned to make caring choices in stereotypical ways. Males in traditional settings received strong messages that told them caring is a female responsibility, so they learned to avoid, when possible, either being care-givers or receivers. They were socialized to be athletic, self-sufficient, and dominant. The playthings they received as gifts: footballs, toy soldiers, guns, and tractors, reinforced the verbal messages they received. Even those individuals whose parents took care to avoid obvious stereotyping, who experienced no ban on tears or hugs, encountered the expectations of peers, and the dreaded label "sissy" was given boys who did not live up to the stereotypical image of strength. Under those circumstances it is understandable that many males learned to deny their caring impulses and to wait for females to fill the caring void, whenever possible.

Females in traditional settings, by contrast, learned that they were to be both care-givers and the recipients of the caring choices of others. They were socialized to be gentle, pliant, warm, and caring. The playthings they received as gifts: dolls, cuddly toys, scaled-down household items, and nursing kits, set expectations for the kinds of behaviors adults wanted them to exhibit. Even those individuals whose parents took care to avoid obvious stereotyping, who received atypical toys and were encouraged to develop their own skills and powers, encountered peer expectations, and the less-dreaded label "tomboy" was given to girls who did not meet social expectations. As a result females expect to give care to others and receive it for themselves.

Age- and role-stereotypes are two other realities in our society that affect caring choices. The older person, up to a point, is deferred to for caring; and, despite the capability of others to make caring choices, in many circumstances the person who represents a particular occupation is also deferred to. This is obvious in school and hospital settings in which teachers, nurses, therapists, and doctors are expected to make caring choices. The expectation of caring is less obvious in business and industry settings, but employees tend to look to supervisors and other management personnel for the caring they have received in the past from those in charge of them. The fact that someone is looked to for caring is no guarantee that the person is suited to the task; however, the fact that someone is not looked to for caring is no guarantee that the person is unsuited to the task.

We receive sex-, age-, and role-stereotyped societal messages for making and receiving caring choices early in life, in the home, in the classroom, at play, and through television, books, and other media. Through all of these influences we learn how we are expected to act in all of our roles: son/daughter, brother/sister, spouse, parent, friend, co-worker, superior/subordinate, and community member. These inter-personal and occupational roles, our gender, and our age necessarily influence our caring choices, but they do not determine those choices.

Choice Awareness theory suggests that CREST choices are the essential options human beings have available to them in nearly all of the circumstances of life. It seems unwise to restrict or connect caring choices—since they are one cluster of only five significant options—to either sex, or on the basis of age or role. All of us encounter our own needs and the needs of others; all of us need to develop skill in responding to those needs with caring choices. Rather than being defined by our roles and responsibilities, we need to define them for ourselves. If we make most of our choices on the basis of sex, age, or role, we have canceled ourselves out as important and we have made many choices that are not truly OK for ourselves since they do not fit us as individuals.

Your clients are likely to be among those individuals who have not evolved satisfactory means for meeting their needs for caring, or who are not skilled in responding to the needs of others. One of your important tasks as a counselor is that of helping individuals find ways in which they might meet their own needs and respond to the needs of others through making more effective caring choices.

SELF-EXAMINATION—JOURNAL ENTRY: Take a few minutes to think, then discuss in your journal the caring choices you make in one of your most important personal relationships, and the extent to which the caring choices you make in that relationship move you toward or away from your goals with that person. Next, discuss the extent to which the caring choices you make for yourself move you toward a sense of inner well-being. Suggestion: head your entry MY CARING CHOICES.

We encourage you to share these ideas with your clients, inviting their reactions and helping them see the importance of the caring choices they make in their significant relationships and for themselves. Most clients need to be challenged to make more OK caring choices for themselves and with others if they are to achieve the goals they have for their relationships and their lives.

COUNSELING APPLICATION—JOURNAL ENTRY: Discuss the extent to which you believe it is important for you to help your clients deal directly with their patterns of caring choices, for themselves, and with others. Consider with at least one specific or hypothetical client how you might focus on the caring choices that person *now* makes, and the caring choices that individual *could* make, to improve his/her life situation. Suggestion: head your entry CARING CHOICES AND MY CLIENTS.

Making Effective Caring Choices

We all need to learn to initiate with caring choices and with requests for caring. Instead of relying on a hang-dog look it would be better if we stated our need directly. When we rely on non-verbal behaviors to send the message that we need care we take the risk that others will misinterpret our communication. They may not sense that we are offering an invitation for them to make caring choices; they may even interpret our non-verbal message as a call for privacy or as an accusation against them. Effective self caring requires direct requests for assistance from others.

Since most people do not feel free to admit their needs or ask for the caring they need, it would often be valuable for us to take the initiative when others appear to be upset or annoyed. Certainly it would be better from our perspective if others stated their concerns forthrightly, since we would then be assured that they want us to respond. However, our own hesitance to reveal our needs is evidence that such statements do not come easily.

It may be a quirk of our culture, though it seems to be true in other societies as well, that we learn to respond to verbal behavior and leave non-verbal behavior alone. We wait for words and tiptoe away if they do not come; or, if we give ourselves permission to become involved, we may fire off a series of questions: "What's wrong?" "Did I say something?" "What can I do to help?"

When another person appears to be having difficulty of some kind, it may be that he or she is doing very well thinking through a problem, making a decision, and planning an action; alternatively, he or she may be hurting and want assistance. A battery of questions is unnecessary in either instance. A more appropriate way for us to express our caring is through listening and reflecting feelings. Reflection of feelings is a desirable skill, even for the non-counselor, since it seems to invite statements rather than demand answers: "You look downhearted." "You seem to be troubled about something." "I can tell you're really disappointed right now." The individual who has matters well in hand is likely to assure us of that; the person who wants assistance may feel deep gratitude for the opening.

Reflection of feeling is a caring choice and a skill that can be applied in all situations in which feelings are evident, even including those that are positive: "You're really excited about that." "Happiness is written all over your face." "I can see how good you're feeling about that news." Whether the emotion is positive or negative, reflection of feeling supports the individual's right to have the feeling, rather than encouraging its denial.

One of the reasons even sensitive, experienced counselors hesitate to use reflection of feeling is that they have a strong need to be right; they prefer to ask questions rather than take the risk that the feelings they name might not be exactly on target. Counselors who ask questions rather than show caring to clients through listening and mirroring their feelings need to realize that the matter of correctness is frequently less important than the genuine demonstration of interest and concern offered through reflection of feeling.

"When we jump to the 'what's wrong' question, we are making an assumption, then asking about it. In our own minds we first assign some kind of feeling to the other person anyway. It would often be better if we gave an invitation to speak through stating that feeling" (Nelson, 1977, p. 96).

If you have reflected feelings and missed the mark, your clients are likely to correct you, and no harm will have been done. Your clients are likely to feel better if they sense that you are trying to understand their strong feelings than if they experience a barrage of questions from you. Reflections of feeling can be far more useful than asking questions or offering suggestions, and this is particularly so when the other person is evidencing strong feelings.

When we make caring choices toward other people, we expect certain CREST responses more frequently than others. These responses seem natural to the individual, and they are, but only because they are habitual, and because they have been learned as part of the socialization process.

Consider a situation in which you say to someone: "You look really upset; I'd like to help if I can." What are the options available to that person? In that event, and in most events, all of the CREST choices are available to him or her. Caring: "I'm OK, but I heard *your* mom has been sick and I was thinking about asking you how you're doing." Ruling: "I appreciate your interest, but just cool it—I'll take care of it myself." Enjoying: "I really appreciate your asking." Sorrowing: "I *am* worried; one of my neighbors is in for surgery today." Thinking/working: "Oh, I was just making a mental list of all the things I need to do today and I know I left something out."

Although it is clear that the response to your caring could be any of the five CREST choices, two of the choices seem more likely to follow—enjoying and sorrowing. Enjoying choices, especially statements of appreciation, are among the characteristic choices in response to caring. Here are several examples: "Thank you." "I appreciate your concern." A grateful smile. A pat on the hand. "I don't think you can do anything for me now, but it feels good that you want to try." "You can't do anything, but your offer to help gives me a lift."

Sorrowing choices are also characteristic responses to caring. The sorrow may be acknowledged as real or the source of the sorrow may be mentioned or inferred in such responses. For example: "Yes, I'm still under the weather from my cold." "I was just thinking about my neighbor who's in for surgery." "I need some help with a problem." "There's nothing anyone can do, but if you've got some time, it surely would help if I could cry on your shoulder."

Both sets of illustrations above emphasize OK choices, and in fact appreciative statements in response to caring choices may even be seen as *major* OK enjoying choices because they are so reinforcing. You and your clients need to develop OK response patterns in most circumstances, and responding positively to caring choices is essential. However, one of the problems both you and your clients face is that your efforts to show concern are not always responded to with OK choices.

If other persons are embarrassed to acknowledge their needs, their responses might be something like: "Don't fuss over me, there's nothing wrong." Or "I'll take care of things myself." Alternatively, individuals may immediately sink into despair and send OD choices that may prove useful in counseling, but that may seem overwhelming or even punitive to the lay person: "Nothing I ever do turns out right." Or "Nobody cares about me." A third possibility is that other people will go on the attack: "Get out of my life!" "It's people like you who are always making trouble for me." Or "Don't give me that crap—I know you don't give a damn."

When proffered help is declined, lay persons are likely to turn to habitual responses—generally OD ruling or sorrowing. To statements like "don't fuss over me" or "get out of my life" they may incline to such choices as: "If that's the way you feel about it, get lost!" Or "See if I ever try to help you again!" Certainly it is difficult for the lay person, or even the counselor, to maintain composure and offer an OK choice at such a time, but a further caring choice is possible: "Hey, you don't have to tell me what's wrong if you don't want to, I just want you to know I'm willing to help."

Whether we are offering to help a friend or a client, rejection can be devastating—if we let it be. We need to examine the original impulse. If we were genuinely reaching out to another person because we sensed a need we might fulfill, we should continue our actions in the same direction, or at least appreciate our own efforts. If we realize that we were trying to show superiority or that efforts from us could not have been expected to help for some clear reason, then we would do better not to pursue the issue further at the moment. It should be noted that what often appears to be rejection is a further call for help that says: "Prove to me you really are concerned about me." Or: "I don't like myself, so you can't possibly care enough about me to want to help me." While further efforts in caring are by no means guaranteed to reach the individual, those efforts are often more defensible than other alternatives. This is an important understanding for counselors and clients alike.

The individual we offer to help may sink into despair and make such OD statements as: "Nothing I ever do turns out right." Or "Nobody cares about me." As a counselor you may welcome such statements and believe that they indicate you are making progress in counseling. Because you are not caught up in that other person's life, such remarks may not disturb you. Rather than feel bad, you make another caring choice: "I can see you're really hurting now; if you'd like to share, I'd be glad to have you tell me more about that." That same response may also be perfectly suitable for clients to make to someone in their lives, but because they are involved and feel attacked, it is not easy for them to consider that alternative. Although such comments from another person may seem overwhelming or even punitive to clients, it is possible for them to learn to make further caring choices rather than become defensive. One of the tasks of counseling can be seen as that of helping clients find ways to make OK choices, even caring choices, in the face of rejection.

We have explored the kinds of choices that may be made in response to caring, and we have considered briefly what we might do when the response is OD. Before we end this discussion, let us consider what the options are in responding to caring that is OD. Such choices tend either to be ill-timed, that is, made when the individual is attending to other matters or trying to forget the difficulty, or they may be overstated. For example: "Oh, you poor, poor thing."

When an OD caring choice is offered, several possible responses may be triggered, including wallowing in sadness— OD sorrowing: "Yes, it is really awful and nobody knows how bad I feel." Or the statement may be rejected—OD ruling: "Knock it off." However, it is also possible to make any of the other eight OK or OD CREST choices. OK caring: "You really sound upset about my troubles." OD caring: "Oh, my, I can tell you're really very deeply concerned; what can I do to make it better?" OK ruling: "Please don't worry about me, I'm handling the problem just fine." OK enjoying: "Thank you for your concern." OD enjoying (teasing): "Wow, you're in seventh heaven— someone to fawn over." OK sorrowing: "Yes, the news on the home front is not good." OK thinking/working: "I've been listing some of the different things I can do and I'd like your reaction to my ideas. . . ." OD thinking/working (an internal choice): "Let's see, I could ask this guy to stow the pity, fuss at him, tell him I'm doing OK, or mull this over until I come up with the perfect response."

Making effective choices is easier, ultimately, when we realize we can make a great variety of responses. This is information both we and our clients need.

All of us need to love others and be loved by others and ourselves. In Choice Awareness theory spontaneous choices involving loving and liking are classified as enjoying. In many situations, however, no more loving choice can be made than caring for another who is in need. When we give a hug or receive one as reassurance in a time of trouble, we experience the duality of that choice; we sense both the joy and affection it expresses and the helpfulness it conveys. The five choices overlap, certainly. However, when the accent is on helping, on meeting a need, we count the choice as caring, rather than enjoying.

It is possible to OD on self-caring just as it is possible to OD on caring for others. Being too self-protective, spending great amounts of money on grooming aids and on time in grooming, or otherwise doing too much for oneself, is indicative of OD self-caring. Likewise it is possible out of a lack of positive self feeling and self love to be insufficiently self-protective or self-caring. In such cases the choices being made are likely to be a combination of OD self-ruling and OD sorrowing that send the message: "I can't spend time and effort on me because I'm not a worthy person."

Balance is an essential factor in caring for others. Effective relationships thrive on balance—in the leadership taken by both persons (OK ruling choices), in the sharing of happiness and of liking/loving choices from both persons (OK enjoying choices), in the sharing of sadnesses and frustrations (OK sorrowing choices), and in participation in the talk and the work within the relationship (OK thinking/working choices). But, relationships are insufficient if they lack reasonable balance in caring, with both persons contributing when the other has needs.

Balance in each of the five choices is important for self as well. We make reasonable ruling choices for ourselves if we are both demanding and fair in our expectations of ourselves, and tolerant of our failings. We make reasonable enjoying choices if we are involved vigorously in life and are appreciative of our strengths. We make reasonable sorrowing choices if we share our frustrations and sadnesses while exhibiting neither meanness nor miserableness. We make reasonable thinking/working choices when we allow ourselves to participate thoughtfully and effectively in chores and responsibilities. But we still cheat ourselves if we do not show adequate care for our health, safety, diet, and personal well-being, or if our self talk is not positive—especially when we are in need.

We and those people who come to counseling alike have been reared in a society that vacillates on the issue of self care. Most males and some females receive messages that suggest self care is a waste of time, while many females and some males receive messages that suggest that even self-indulgence is appropriate. You need to take seriously for yourself and convey to your clients the message that self care is important and that it needs to be balanced with other choices. It is important that you and your clients make caring choices for self and for others in balanced and responsible, or OK, ways.

The issue of caring choices reaches across the three levels of counseling: spa, learning, and relearning. Because caring choices are a major part of spa, when you help your clients become comfortable in making reasonable self-caring and other-caring choices, you are helping them create a sense of spa for themselves. Some of your clients may readily engage in the kinds of positive experiences that we characterize here as spa; in such cases you may need only to increase your tolerance for discussions in this direction. For many other clients, gaining permission to care for themselves, or to express their caring for others, requires learning or relearning.

SELF-EXAMINATION—JOURNAL ENTRY: Take a few minutes to think, then discuss in your journal ways in which you can make more effective caring choices in one of your most important personal relationships, and with yourself. Suggestion: head your entry MORE EFFECTIVE CARING CHOICES FOR ME.

We encourage you to share these ideas with your clients, inviting their reactions and helping them see the importance of making more effective caring choices in their important relationships and for themselves. Most clients need to be helped to consider how they can make more OK caring choices for themselves and with others if they are to achieve effective interpersonal relationships and inner well-being.

COUNSELING APPLICATION—JOURNAL ENTRY: Discuss how you might help your clients make caring choices that would improve their relationships and their sense of inner well-being. Suggestion: head your entry MORE EFFECTIVE CLIENT CARING CHOICES.

Caring Choices

From the point of view of Choice Awareness, one of the important tasks of counseling is that of helping clients learn to make caring choices in response to their own needs and the needs of others. Inner well-being depends in part on making effective caring choices, and the counselor here is challenged to help clients master the skills of making suitable and responsible caring choices for self and for others.

Reference

Nelson, R. C. (1977). *Choosing: A better way to live.* North Palm Beach, FL: GuideLines Press.

Chapter 7

Caring Choices: Application

Caring Choices and Your Clients

When you examine your clients' concerns through the filter of choices, you are likely to find that many of those concerns involve caring. Doubtless many of your clients feel a deficit in both the quality and quantity of the caring choices they receive. Minimal exploration is likely to lead to the conclusion that they also have a deficit in both the quality and quantity of the caring choices they send. You can contribute significantly to the lives of many of your clients if you explore with them who in their lives needs caring from them, how they might respond to the needs of those others, and the caring they want and need in return.

We can represent the mental health of most counseling clients as a downward-turning spiral that has been set in motion by a deficit in OK choices in general and perhaps in caring choices in particular. As they grow and mature, many people who become clients are frustrated and angry because their needs are inadequately met. In turn, both because of the frustration and anger they feel, and because their models offer little that is positive to imitate, they make few caring choices with others. Then, because people they meet are unlikely to give caring unless they sense they will receive it in return, these people receive little caring from those around them. The spiral continues in a downward course.

The downward-turning spiral of mental health, which stems from inadequate caring by others, is often fueled and accelerated by a pattern of inadequate self-caring choices. Those who are inadequately cared for by others see themselves as unworthy of caring, so they limit the quality and quantity of their self-caring choices. They let themselves go physically, engage in negative self-talk, and generally treat themselves poorly in a variety of ways. As a result they feel even more unworthy, and they make even fewer self-caring choices.

It is a genuine challenge to enable adults, adolescents, or even children who have had little experience with caring, to develop a repertoire of caring choices; and the less caring those individuals have received, and the longer they have lived without sufficient caring, the more difficult that task appears. However, two factors are on the side of those who need help in becoming more caring persons with others and for themselves. First, caring choices *are* choices, and therefore they remain within the range of accessible behaviors. Although the habit of caring for others and for self may be lacking, it can be learned. Second, even those people for whom caring choices seem least accessible are likely to have a dormant repertoire of caring choices available to them.

Few people grow to later childhood or beyond without having had experiences with caring—with parents, siblings, relatives, pets, cuddly toys, dolls, or imaginary friends. The skills needed to touch someone who is in need, or to ask "Where does it hurt?" and the like, may be rusty and cob-webbed, but they lie in reserve to be taken out and polished for current use. Even those whose caring experiences were sadly lacking are likely to have observed others around them receiving tender loving care or have seen it demonstrated via such media as motion pictures and television. And if those options were lacking, they doubtless have at least fantasized receiving and giving care. An important aspect of inner well-being for you and for your clients is that of making effective caring choices in the face of needs; and the resources for making such choices are available in nearly all people.

CONSIDER THE FOLLOWING:

Randy, a 16-year-old, had been institutionalized briefly as incorrigible, but had been released to a temporary foster home because of crowding in the juvenile facility. His experience with the Fishers, a caring, loving, exciting family, put him off briefly, then he began to warm to their gentle ways. More often than he had done in several years, he thought about the little pup that he had many years ago that had warmed his life for four months until it disappeared. He had enjoyed holding it so, and its sad eyes seemed to mirror his own feelings. Moon—that was the name he gave the puppy—seemed to understand him. The breakthrough with the Fisher family came because four-year-old Dawn took him on, sometimes as her helper, sometimes as his comforter. She wanted him to tie her shoes, read to her, and tuck her in at night; and when he looked sad, as he often did, she slipped her hand in his and smiled rather sadly back at him. Once as he helped Dawn, tears filled his eyes. "What's wrong?" she asked. When she pressed him for an answer Randy told her, "I was just thinking about Moon, a little pup I used to have."

In our society we send messages to young people as they are growing up, and to males especially, that they should neither need nor give care. Although our society needs and values adults who are caring and loving wives and husbands, mothers and fathers, intimates and friends, we socialize boys to a great extent in preadolescence and adolescence in ways that are antithetical to those outcomes. If we do not actually participate in labeling gentle, caring young males as sissies, we do little to counter those labels when they are applied by others.

Both males and females, but males particularly, need permission to make caring choices both for themselves and with those about them. All of us have known males who are strong and athletic, yet gentle and kind; but, the experience of young males too infrequently includes such models of mature adult behavior. The result is that many young males restrict their caring choices quite severely.

It is likely that a few of your clients had little experience in their lives with caring choices. Far more of your clients, however, had a reasonable amount of caring as children, but have accepted such adult messages as: be strong, be tough, do not show vulnerability, and do not be moved by the vulnerability of others. The penalty for violating those standards is to be called a sissy—the ultimate put-down for most males of any age, but particularly for insecure children and adolescents.

Moved by a combination of parental discomfort, societal modeling, and peer pressure, young males learn to shun tears and other evidences of strong feelings, and hugs and other demonstrations of caring, as "for sissies." They build walls around themselves to ward off feeling, loving, and caring. Although their needs for giving and receiving care have been discouraged, they find that when they threaten, pound tables, and give other evidence of being angry, they are generally tolerated and sometimes applauded. Secure, well-cared-for adolescents learn to play the macho game sufficiently to avoid being harassed by their peers; but many insecure adolescents either learn to play the game to the hilt or are frustrated by their inability to do so.

When people ignore their need for caring and withhold their feelings or rely on anger, instead of expressing their hurt, sad, or vulnerable feelings, at least three adverse outcomes occur. (1) They have no genuinely satisfactory ways of expressing their inevitable negative feelings. When they are not in command of the situation, or when tender and gentle responses are clearly more appropriate, their anger is useless or destructive, and their withholding behavior has negative effects as well. (2) They are evolving habit patterns that are likely to harm their interpersonal relationships. Whether with a spouse, offspring, other relatives, or friends, their reliance on anger or on withholding as primary responses to negatives is likely to undermine their most valued relationships. (3) They are setting themselves up for shallow relationships with others. In a series of interviews I held some years ago, more than half of the women volunteered their perceptions that the men in their lives, husbands included, seldom shared with them their deeper thoughts and feelings, nor did these men have other male friends with whom they shared such personal matters. If the perceptions of these women can be generalized to any reasonable degree, and my observations suggest that they can, the primary reason men lack a person with whom they share thoughts and feelings may well be that they learned early in life to place stringent limits on making caring choices with others and receiving caring for themselves.

All people need their own permission to make caring choices. In Choice Awareness theory we make the assumption that caring is one of only five basic choices we have available to us as human beings. Ultimately, those people, those males especially, who seldom demonstrate caring, need to give *themselves* permission to do so since it is unlikely that the adults and adolescent companions who have modeled contrary patterns will offer it to them. To severely limit or to eliminate the caring option is to minimize or exclude one of five key alternatives available.

Most females not only permit themselves to make caring choices, they feel obliged to do so. However, societal rules that demand caring choices out of a sense of ownership or obligation are no more appropriate for the individual than rules that require avoidance of those choices. Inner well-being for both males and females requires that all people give themselves permission to make and receive OK caring choices when appropriate—to meet their own needs and the needs of others.

CONSIDER THE FOLLOWING:

When Randy, the 16-year-old we were introduced to earlier, first met the students and faculty in the new school he was to attend as a result of his foster home placement, he literally shuddered several times. "Everyone's so fruity here," he told the counselor when she checked with him after two days. He said he did not know how to act around students who seemed to want to study and who did not always laugh at his little vulgarities. He said that he thought the host he had been assigned was "a good enough kid, but too straight for me." Pressed for clarification, he complained that people seemed too good to be true; no one had picked a fight with him, and the teachers even wanted to help him. He was waiting for the other shoe to drop. The counselor quickly realized that he had had little experience in receiving caring choices and suggested that to him in a number of ways. She was as surprised as he when he burst into tears after she reached over and touched his hand. When he recovered he assured her that caring was not something with which he had much experience. One of his comments near the end of their second session was, "I think I'm going to like it when I get used to all this."

COUNSELING APPLICATION—JOURNAL ENTRY: Take a few minutes, preferably at least five, and think about one or two clients of yours who have had some difficulty with caring. As the first part of your entry write about the extent to which you believe those clients possessed a dormant pattern of caring choices they might call upon and on what bases you draw your inferences. As the second part of your entry write about any ways you believe you tried to tap these dormant patterns, and the success of your efforts. SUGGESTION: head your entry DORMANT CLIENT CARING CHOICES

When you encourage your clients to become more effective in making caring choices with others, you are helping them act on the principle of social-interest. They "do unto others as they would have others do unto to them," and, when they in turn have needs, they are likely to experience caring from others. Thus, though their actions serve the social-interest first and foremost, they serve the principle of self-interest as well.

Two systems of counseling appear to focus more than others on caring choices: self theory and existentialism. Counselors who subscribe to those theories often model those choices.

Self Theory

While all counseling systems are characterized by caring for the client, in no system is that focus more straightforward than it is in self theory as developed primarily through the works of Carl Rogers (1957, 1961). Rogers' philosophy is essentially humanistic and existential in that it suggests that experience is reality for individuals. The effort of the counselor is essentially caring—understanding and empathizing with clients as they encounter their world in their own unique way.

Self theory epitomizes deep, empathic listening to clients as a means by which the essential positive, self-actualizing abilities of those individuals can be activated and realized. Belief in clients is seen as an essential basis for enabling them to grow and learn.

The self theorist believes that regardless of their problems and the ways in which they unintentionally distort reality through their perceptions, individuals have underlying goodness in them. If we, as counselors, understand our clients' perceptions and convey our belief in them and in their capabilities, we can activate the natural healing processes in them, and, where necessary, enable them to perceive reality differently and change their behaviors in ways that lead to more positive outcomes. Self theory counseling is based on the assumption that when people feel deeply that they are heard and understood, they can begin to move in positive directions.

One of the focal points of self theory in counseling is the discrepancy between the real self and the ideal self. People who do not see themselves as worthy often lose sight of who they really are and focus only on an idealized image of what they would like to be—and they fall short of that ideal. Often their picture of who they are is more negative than it needs to be; and where such distortions occur, individuals are not accepting of themselves.

Rogers (1957) offered six necessary and sufficient conditions for "therapeutic personality change" or growth; these are paraphrased below. He suggested that when those conditions are adequately met, positive forward movement will occur for the client.

1. A genuine, deepening relationship must exist between two human beings.

2. One of the two persons, the client, is in a state of incongruence, feeling both anxious and vulnerable. The incongruence may be seen as a discrepancy between the ideal and the real self, with the result being anxiety and behavior that is unsatisfactory to the client and others. Resolution of incongruities is a focus of the efforts of the counselor.

3. The second person, the counselor, is congruent in the relationship. Even though counselors are not always self-actualized, they must be genuine and authentic within the interview itself.

4. The counselor holds a positive view of the client regardless of his or her overt behavior. This view, characterized as unconditional positive regard, allows the client to feel safe, unjudged, and free to be him/herself. Warmth and respect are key elements in the development of unconditional positive regard.

5. The counselor feels empathic understanding for the client and his/her internal frame of reference and attempts to communicate this feeling to the client. In conveying understanding the counselor effectively uses the attending skills of paraphrasing, summarizing, and reflecting feelings.

6. The counselor's empathic understanding and unconditional positive regard are communicated to the client. That is, the client must perceive the five previous dimensions within the counseling interview.

CONSIDER THE FOLLOWING:

In Rogers & Wallen (1946), Rogers described his contact with a serviceman, we will call him David, who sought assistance, initially mentioning that he wished he knew how to pray, he was unable to sleep, and he had walked the streets most of the previous night. He felt responsible and guilty in the death of an army buddy who went for ammunition on his signal, and who was killed as he attempted to comply with David's request. Rogers used self theory skills, reflecting David's feelings of frustration, self-blame, responsibility, and his concern that an argument prior to the death of his friend had somehow precipitated the tragedy. The resulting exploration of the events and the counselor's acceptance of his feelings helped David to see his distorted perceptions for what they were.

Here is the essence of some of Rogers' statements—reflections of feeling primarily—along with enough of the context of the client's comments to make clear the flow of the discussion.

D: Tells of walking in the rain most of the night because he has been unable to sleep; he speaks of his inability to talk to his parents while he was on leave; and he mentions that it is difficult for him to get over the death of his buddy.

CR: That's been very upsetting to you.

D: Yes, he agrees, then shares the information that the buddy was his only real friend, mentions how they had met and some of the things they had gone through together, and how they had come to know one another so well that they did not have to tell the other what to do. In an enemy attack David gave a glance that told his buddy the ammunition was getting low, and he promptly went to get more. It was then that his friend was hit by a shell and killed. David shares his feeling that he caused his friend's death.

CR: You feel that you're to blame that he was killed.

D: Yes, but I am not sure why, he says. Then he shares the other complicating factor. He and his buddy had had their only argument ever the day before the tragedy. He tells the details of the argument, and he mentions that the two did not speak for several hours after the quarrel. He indicates that the argument leads him to feel that he is to blame for what happened.

CR: Your being angry, you feel, was somehow responsible for his death.

D: He agrees, suggests that maybe he had not thought that through before because he was scared to, reflects on the help he is getting just by talking about it, then considers that it is probably the fact that the argument came the day before the tragedy that hit him especially hard. He talks at length about his buddy, their relationship, things they had done together, then shifts into a discussion of other topics including his own family, and the fact that he had been very upset when he was home on leave. He ends this lengthy discussion with a statement that he has been helped a lot even though he does not know what Rogers did, adding that he does not see why he had felt as much to blame as he had.

CR: It seems to have helped you just to get it off your chest.

In this brief presentation it becomes clear that when there is a great need on the part of a client to express deep anguish and concern, the counselor does well to listen deeply, almost standing aside, yet staying in touch, reflecting the feelings and the perceptions of reality of the client—in short, making caring choices. Through his own warmth of expression, his genuine concern, and his brief reflections of the heart of David's comments, Rogers allowed the client to express his deep feelings and to see through his own concern as a result.

Beyond this kind of reflective posture, effective self theorists also encourage clients to talk about their difficulties with the interview itself, and they share their own perceptions of their clients with them. Once again, the focus is on the relationship, and the strategies involved are elegantly and deceptively simple: effective listening and honest sharing.

Self theory in counseling focuses on enabling the client to answer one of the most significant of existential questions, "Who am I?" The assumption is made that the answer to this question comes from the inner being of the client. The task is that of assisting clients to explore and find their real inner selves, to trust what they feel and see, to make their own decisions, and to see themselves as dynamic, changing beings who are in a continual process of becoming.

The process of self theory relies heavily on reflection of feeling, restatement, summarization, and clarification, which are designed to help clients realize that they are being heard fully and accurately. The belief is that they then will be able to gain a deeper sense of meaning from the experiences they are describing and move toward more effective action and toward inner well-being. "The client speaks; the therapist listens carefully and attempts to understand the client's perceptions of the world; the client, having been heard and understood, can move forward" (Ivey, 1980, p. 269). Self theorists follow the leads of their clients so that they will be free to be themselves and gradually come to explore their reality and their perceptions of that reality. Counselors, too, are free to be themselves, sharing perceptions of their clients and relevant personal experiences, but remaining focused on who the clients are, and communicating their belief in their clients' abilities to grow and progress.

In the key characteristics cited, self theory focuses on caring as the preeminent choice for the counselor, suggesting that effective caring is the essential dimension for growth. Choice Awareness theory suggests that the self theory approach should be used by all counselors, especially in the initial stage of counseling, on the basis of two assumptions: (1) that many clients need no more direct assistance than that approach offers, and (2) that most clients can benefit by experiencing the depth of listening and understanding that is characteristic of that process of counseling.

Choice Awareness theory suggests three questions that may be raised relative to the use of self theory in counseling. (1) Are there equally humane, but more efficient ways of helping the client? The discovery process involved in self theory is often very effective, but rather slow. This suggests that the integration of other processes may be suitable for use with many clients. (2) Is self theory adequate or sufficient to the task? Not all concerns seem fully amenable to assistance through a relationship process. (3) Might there be ways of teaching clients to use the skills of caring in their lives that go beyond the modeling of caring that is suggested by the actions of the self theory counselor? Few clients seem to be able to incorporate such communication skills as deep listening and reflection of feeling solely on the basis of modeling, yet if they learn to apply those skills in their everyday lives, many clients could function more adequately with others and care more effectively for themselves.

SELF-EXAMINATION—JOURNAL ENTRY: Take a few minutes, preferably at least five, and discuss the extent to which you believe you create the kind of environment that self theory suggests—involving both empathic understanding and unconditional positive regard, limiting the use of questions, and allowing clients to derive their own solutions— particularly in the early phase of counseling. Next, discuss the extent to which you believe greater use of that kind of approach on your part might be relevant for your clients in counseling. Suggestion: head your entry SELF THEORY IN MY COUNSELING.

We encourage you to share these ideas with your clients, inviting their reactions and helping them see that they might listen deeply and reflect the feelings of others they care about in their lives. Most clients experience great warmth when they are listened to deeply. They can be encouraged to extend the same generous behavior to others, as evidence of their caring.

Existentialism

The basic focus of existentialism is human *existence*; the individual's state of being-in-the-world, and questions of meaning are central to the practice of existentialism in counseling. In large measure existentialism seems to represent more an attitude on the part of the counselor than a system or set of procedures or techniques for helping another person. Existential counselors are *with* their clients, and they attend to their clients' needs, feelings, and perceptions, as fully and genuinely as they are able.

A key concept in existentialism is *alienation*. We are beings in the world, and while the world acts on us we are acting on it. Alienation results whenever we are separate from others or from the world, or when we believe we are unable to choose and to act in relationship to others. The counselor enables alienated clients to see their relationship to the world and facilitates their making choices to create harmony between the world and themselves. Alienation may occur between the person and his or her body (Eigenwelt), between the person and other people in the world (Mitwelt), or between the person and the biological and physical world (Umwelt).

A second key concept in this theory is *existential anxiety*. The individual may develop anxiety as a result of being alienated; likewise existential anxiety may occur as a result of indecision and inaction. "Choices and decisions are often difficult, because any time we choose, we must accept the fact that by choosing we deny other alternatives and possibilities" (Ivey, 1980, p. 272).

The process of existential counseling involves exploring the individual's relationship to the world and to others, the objective being that of freeing the individual to act, rather than being acted upon. Frankl (1959) suggested that individuals always have at least one choice available to them, the choice of their attitude in any given set of circumstances. This suggests that the antidote, so to speak, to alienation and existential anxiety, is an attitude of *existential commitment, deciding* to choose and to act. However, since the need to make choices is constantly present in our existence in the world, existential anxiety is often activated. This cycle of choice and anxiety can be seen either as burdensome or as a continuous opportunity for being-in-the-world more fully—a challenge to commitment.

Existentialism and Choice Awareness share in common, among other matters, the concepts of *intentionality, responsibility,* and *awareness.* Both views suggest that people choose their behaviors, that they are responsible for their behaviors, and that they can benefit by gaining awareness of the reality that they have behaved intentionally.

Greene (1973) summarized the existential issue of intentionality—or choice, and responsibility—or action, as follows:

> For the existentialist, the self is devoid of character or coloration before action is undertaken. When the individual begins devising projects and purposes he [she] begins creating an identity. . . . The only significant choices are those that involve him [her] totally and project his [her] existence into the future still unknown. The only meaningful choices are those for which he [she] takes full responsibility (p. 256).

Martin Buber's (1970) concept of I-Thou relationships—seeing others as people, rather than as objects, is also a focus of existential counseling. The evolving, genuine relationship between the counselor and client serves as a model for all relationships, with openness and involvement as significant characteristics of the interaction.

The development of I-Thou relationships may well demand such a high level of human functioning that it requires considerable civilizing and maturing if it is to occur at all. As possible evidence of this, it appears that a substantial proportion of young children view other children as objects, remaining quite unaware that others have needs and feelings. Another explanation, however, is that I-Thou relationships are rare enough that even young children model the non-genuine behavior of those about them. In either case it suggests that the genuineness of I-Thou relationships may occur infrequently, and that they cannot wisely be left to chance. Two resulting central themes of counseling for the client are: finding out "who I am" and considering "how I may authentically relate to others."

In contrast to many other systems of counseling, in existentialism the focus of the dialogue is on what is happening now, how we are in relationship to one another, how you are affecting me, and how I am affecting you. Honesty and openness in the relationship is an essential part of the therapeutic process, and self-disclosures by the counselor—

at least involving perceptions of the process and of the client—are viewed as part of that honesty and openness. Difficulties that arise in the counseling process are viewed as opportunities for exploring the two participants' experiencing of each other and as opportunities for growth of the relationship.

CONSIDER THE FOLLOWING:

Corey (1982) described an existential counseling process between Dr. Fred Rose and Ruth, a 39-year-old woman who saw herself as a housewife facing a mid-life crisis, lacking a deep relationship with her husband, feeling lonely, having earlier discarded a religious value system she had come to see as oppressive, and searching through counseling for new values to live by. Rose saw her as well as overweight and rather too concerned about being nice.

No transcript of the counseling process was presented by Corey, but through the discussion it is apparent that Fred Rose demonstrated caring for Ruth in some measure through confronting the issues she presented quite directly. The comments that follow have been constructed in the assumption that statements similar to these were incorporated over several interviews at relevant points in the dialogue, that they were appropriate for the context, and that they were followed with additional, caring dialogue.

FR: You seem to be living a very restricted existence. That leads me to wonder in what ways you are letting yourself live as fully as you might.

FR: Much of what you tell me suggests that you are living a life outlined by others, rather than living by your own choices.

FR: I'd like to know what choices you have made on your own so far, and how the outcomes of these choices have affected you.

FR: What do you see as some of the important choices you are facing now?

FR: So that is one of the important changes you think you ought to make. And you don't seem to see anything preventing you from making it.

FR: You're constantly creating yourself by the choices you are making, and also by the choices you are failing to make.

FR: One thing that is a barrier for me in feeling close to you is that you are just *so* nice. I'd find it very difficult to be around someone a great deal who continually tries to be as nice as you do.

FR: Your weight is another barrier in my relating to you. Somehow I can't seem to have as much respect as I'd like to feel for you because of it.

FR: Rather than seeking some kind of escape or easing of your anxiety through Valium or another drug, and getting rid of the symptom, you need to get to the root of your anxiety attacks.

FR: So when you continually put your own needs last and choose to be the giver you end up feeling even more anxious.

FR: I see an important connection between your feelings of anxiety and the choices you need to make. Certainly there's anxiety when you take your freedom in hand and make choices that thrust you into new territory, but if you can make some of those difficult choices that's also when you have the greatest chance to feel free.

FR: One choice that seems to be before you much of the time is that of following patterns of behavior that are deadening, or mastering the courage to act. And when you act you begin to change your own destiny.

And, finally, an actual statement from Ruth:

"I've spent years telling myself that I had no choices. Now I know that I do have choices. And that is making a huge difference in my life."

This presentation offers a brief demonstration of the existential value of openness and honesty on the part of the counselor with the client. There are times when the deepest caring is conveyed through honest feedback to individuals of the way they are seen and what appear to be their behaviors or reasoning patterns. In Rose's own words, "My central task as Ruth's therapist was to directly confront her with the ways in which she was living a restricted existence and to help her see her part in having created her own restricted world and her deadness as a person" (in Corey, 1982, pp 28-29). This is not to be construed as a blank check for verbal brutality toward the client on the part of the counselor, however. The relationship Fred Rose developed with Ruth was characterized by warmth, support, and honest feedback, with warmth and support emphasized in early interviews. As a result Ruth was helped to open doors so that she had more potential choices available to her. Choice Awareness theory supports the idea that it is the combination of acceptance *and* challenge, of economy *and* impact, that is the key to truly effective counseling.

The issue of meaning is vital in existentialism. Frankl (1959) saw the will to meaning as the underlying essence of the individual's existence, rather than the will to pleasure hypothesized by Freud, or the will to power hypothesized by Adler. Frankl pointed out that while Jean-Paul Sartre suggested that individuals "invent" themselves by designing their own essence, there is an alternative view—that the meaning of the existence of individuals is not invented, but discovered, by them. Frankl spent much of World War II in Auschwitz, a concentration camp. In that most basic, that most desperate circumstance, he came to the realization that survivors were individuals who knew that there were tasks waiting for them. Those tasks might involve a person, a relationship to God, or for Frankl, writing a book on logotherapy. As Frankl put it,

One should not search for an abstract meaning of life. Everyone has his [her] own specific vocation or mission in life; everyone must carry out a concrete assignment that demands fulfillment... everyone's task is as unique as is his [her] specific opportunity to implement it (Frankl, 1959, p.172).

Existentialism in counseling thus becomes in part a process of discovering the meaning that exists in the lives of the client and of the counselor. In the genuine, authentic encounter of counseling that discovery may lead to a deeper sense of self.

Whether the focus is on enabling clients to discover meaning in their lives, on helping them to work through their anxiety or loneliness, or on encouraging them to confront the choices they are making, existential counseling offers a strong caring dimension. Choice Awareness theory vigorously supports the attitude of openness and honesty, tempered with warmth and support, that existentialism offers to clients. However, Choice Awareness theory raises the same three questions concerning the use of existentialism in counseling that it raised with self theory. (1) Can we help clients in ways that demonstrate sufficient caring, but that are more efficient? (2) Is existentialism appropriate to all problems? (3) Might we teach clients to use the skills of caring in their lives in ways that go beyond the modeling of caring that is suggested by the actions of the existentially-oriented counselor? Counseling that is characterized by an existential attitude, that is, by openness and honesty, offers significant advantages over any system of counseling that is practiced as patterned behavior, as behavior that does not adequately take into account such matters as the relationship between the client and counselor, and meaning, in the lives of each.

SELF-EXAMINATION—JOURNAL ENTRY: Take a few minutes, preferably at least five, and discuss the extent to which you believe you create for yourself the kind of supportive and challenging environment that existentialism suggests. Consider such issues as alienation, existential anxiety, and meaning. Suggestion: head your entry EXISTENTIALISM IN MY LIFE.

We encourage you to consider the relevance of exploring existential questions with your clients. Alienation, existential anxiety, and meaning should be grist for the counseling mill. Further, we believe that it is important for you to model and encourage the intense in-the-moment awareness that characterizes existentialism in counseling.

COUNSELING APPLICATION—JOURNAL ENTRY: Discuss the extent to which you demonstrate an existential attitude in your counseling. Consider whether or not your more frequent use of an existential approach might be relevant for your clients in counseling. Suggestion: head your entry EXISTENTIALISM AND MY COUNSELING.

Caring Choices: Planning Ahead

A significant contribution of Choice Awareness theory is its focus on planning for better choices. Once clients have clarified that they make too few caring choices with particular individuals in their lives, or alternatively that they are smothering others with their caring choices, it becomes clear that they need to implement new patterns of choices. Some will be helped by developing more caring attitudes toward others—deciding that they will be alert to the needs of those others, and following through on that decision. Others can be even more planful—considering specific ways in which they might respond to events they know are likely to occur.

A planful approach must deviate to some extent from both self theory and existential approaches to counseling, since these counseling approaches focus primarily on in-the-moment and relationship processes. It is my observation that relatively few clients spontaneously incorporate the skills of communication in their own lives that are characteristic of self theory and existential counselors. Rather, they seem to compartmentalize, appreciating the skills of their counselors, but seeing those skills as out of reach for themselves. Even clients who attempt to use some of these skills may find them so far removed from their usual communication processes that they either give up the idea of acquiring them or find that it is too difficult a struggle for them to do so. As a system, Choice Awareness makes allowance for planfulness in acquiring better communication skills.

Planning for better choices appears at first blush to be antithetical to spontaneity, which is valued in both self theory and existential approaches. While the ultimate goal of Choice Awareness is effective, spontaneous behavior, we believe that there must be a process of transition for most clients that involves the acquisition of increased numbers and improved quality of choices. In other words, most clients cannot be truly spontaneous until they have broadened the spectrum of choices they have available to them. Once the spectrum of choices is enhanced and enlarged, they are more able to respond to events in the moment with a fuller, richer range of responses. Planfulness, then, is supported in Choice Awareness theory, not in opposition to the in-the-moment emphasis of self theory and existentialism, but as an essential process for increasing the range of choices available to the individual so that the relationship, in-the-moment interactions, and spontaneity, can be enhanced.

Client problems often involve relationships with people who are not direct participants in the counseling process. Effective counseling may beneficially assist the client in planning to make more OK caring choices with others, thereby acting in the social interest while gaining in self-interest as well.

CONSIDER THE FOLLOWING:

Julia consulted Laura Dee, the Resident Assistant assigned to her floor, concerning her roommate, because Maria seemed so constantly to focus her conversation on missing her family, her boyfriend, and her home town. Julia was an optimist and her own family was loose-knit; the creed of her family was independence and self-sufficiency. Therefore, it was difficult for her to understand anyone who could not relate to the wonderful, new, open university environment that was unfolding before her. Julia tried joking, distracting, and mini-mizing the problem with Maria, then began to shut her out when those strategies did not work. Laura agreed to contact Maria, then suggested that it might be equally important if Julia could show more caring toward Maria. Laura helped Julia rehearse some of the things she might do and say to respond more adequately to Maria's needs, and to set limits so that she did not become Maria's counselor. Julia's efforts met with success; it was not long until Maria's attitudes began to shift and she showed greater willingness to participate in activities on the campus and in the residence hall. Ultimately Maria's homesickness dissipated, and she seemed genuinely glad to be back in the residence hall after the Thanksgiving holiday.

Here are some of the kinds of things Julia reported to Laura that she said to Maria.

J: I can see you miss all of those people very much.

J: I understand that this is really a hard adjustment for you.

J: (At 9 p.m.) I've got to get in about an hour's reading tonight and then get a good night's sleep, but if you need to unload for a while now that's OK with me.

Julia also showed support for actions on Maria's part in a combi-nation of caring and enjoying choices.

J: Last night seemed like a real breakthrough. You really got into the conversation at dinner and I don't remember you even mentioning your boyfriend at all.

J: I'm so glad you signed up for U-Sing (University Sing, a competition among the residence halls and sororities and fraternities). You have a really nice voice, and it's good to see you get involved in that way.

Almost all of us are able to anticipate many of the circumstances we will face in which caring is the indicated choice: Julia can expect that her roommate's homesickness of yesterday will be there again today; a counselor can expect that a client's anguish over the perceived rejection of a parent will not suddenly have disappeared. It is not particularly difficult for us to anticipate the need for caring—at the very least it is reflected in the moment in the person's facial expression. The problem is that most people do not give themselves permission to express the caring they feel, often because they believe they do not know how to convey their caring adequately. People avoid others who have experienced a loss through death or divorce and explain it away by such statements as: "I just didn't know what to say. I can never find the right words," despite the fact that they know the person in such circumstances is likely to need caring. It is not an insignificant matter for you to spend time helping your clients extend their repertoire of caring choices, and rehearsing those choices with them, so that they can make them in suitable and comfortable ways with the people who are important in their lives.

Counselors themselves may feel inadequate in making caring choices. That may be part of the reason that little attention has been given to the issue of enabling clients to make more effective caring choices with others in their lives. At the risk of stating the obvious, here are a few responses that counselors can use, or that they can suggest that their clients use, when others around them are facing a genuine sadness.

"I feel deeply for you right now."

"I wish there were something I could do.".

"I can see the hurt in your eyes."

"I'm here for you when you need me."

"I'm ready to listen when you need me to, or to give you something else to think about when you need that."

"I wrote to her about what happened. I figured it'd be awhile 'til you'd get around to writing."

"I'm open for lunch three days next week and I'd really like to get together with you."

A hand on the shoulder.

A hug.

A gift of flowers.

A handwritten note.

A carefully selected card.

Certainly it is possible for an individual to make too many caring choices or to make a few that are too intense for the other person. What is more likely to happen, however, is that the individual will make one or two rather feeble caring choices, then move on to other matters.

Many months after the death of her husband, my sister was still frustrated by the reactions of some of the people she had considered her close friends. The husband of one friend made an offer to call and check in on her from time to time, to which his wife responded, "No, Rustie knows where we are. She'll let us know when she needs us." Rustie also mentioned that at her first social venture after Frank's death, no one seemed to sense her near-paralysis about entering the room where many of their couple-friends were gathered. She needed the reassurance that she was welcome for herself. If such insecurities come to as strong a person as my sister, it seems likely that they affect most people.

The expression of true caring involves more than one or two statements or actions. Deep hurt or grief requires understanding and caring over time. It also requires some kind of balance between allowing other persons space to make their own choices, and reaching out to them. Depth of understanding of the nature of caring is deeply needed by clients—who tend to focus on themselves—and by counselors as well.

Well-timed caring choices can be seen as spa experiences. When they match the need, caring choices are every bit as welcome as the self-concept-building experiences involved in well-timed enjoying choices. It is a great relief to know, at last, that someone cares, someone understands. Those who accept appropriate caring from others when they are hurting, experience a sense of inner peace. The sender of the caring choice, too, may experience a parallel sense of peace. Both may experience spa.

All people from time to time encounter others who have need for caring choices—and if they are not aware of that reality the counselor might well explore with them the question, "Who in your world would benefit from your caring choices?" All people from time to time have need for caring choices themselves. Few people are sufficiently skilled in making caring choices in response to their own or others' needs. The counselor needs skill in making caring choices which tend toward the listening and accepting end of the degree of lead continuum, *and* in making choices that are likely to have greater impact. Clients benefit when counselors help them understand the nature of caring, and develop the skills of caring for themselves and others.

Caring Choices

People need to learn effective ways to meet their own needs and the needs of others. Therefore, for a great many clients, developing the skills of caring for oneself and others can be an important component of counseling. Self theory, or Rogerian counseling, offers a model of caring through deep listening skills, reflection of feeling, and other accepting responses. Existentialism offers a related model in which caring is conveyed through heightened attention to what is happening in the moment, to the evolving relationship, and to the question of meaning in the life of the client.

Self theory and existentialism rely on self-discovery and self-exploration, and seldom in either counseling process are clients given direct input. Exploration of such concepts as caring, OK and OD choices, or the idea that we choose our feelings would not be characteristic of self theorists or of existential counselors. At the same time, many of the basic assumptions of Choice Awareness are congruent with assumptions made in those theories: e.g., that we choose our thoughts and feelings, that we are making choices all the time—often unawares, that our choices are largely habitual, and that we have goals in our relationships.

The position is taken in Choice Awareness that when self discovery and self-exploration are effective in helping clients become more self-directing, there is no need for the counselor to reach beyond the economical counseling approaches of self theory and existentialism; *the less is more principle* is well-served. However, Choice Awareness theory suggests that some desirable and humane efficiencies can be gained through a variety of more active procedures, for example, through engaging clients in the direct process of exploring communication skills and choices, through having clients consider their goals and how their choices serve those goals, and through rehearsal and role play. A sense of inner well-being for clients—even a sense of spa—can result from the warmth of a counseling relationship, or from the more direct processes of exploring and modifying choice patterns, or both.

References

Buber, M. (1970). *I and Thou*. New York: Scribner's.

Corey, G. (1982). *Case approach to counseling and psychotherapy*. Monterey, CA: Brooks/Cole.

Frankl, V. (1959). *Man's search for meaning*. New York: Washington Square Press.

Greene, M. (1973). *Teacher as stranger*. Belmont, CA: Wadsworth.

Ivey, A. E. with Simek-Downing, L. (1980). *Counseling and psychotherapy: Skills, theories, and practice*. Englewood Cliffs, NJ: Prentice-Hall.

Rogers, C. (1957). The necessary and sufficient conditions of therapeutic personality change, *Journal of Consulting Psychology, 21*, 95-103.

Rogers, C. (1961). *On becoming a person*. Boston: Houghton Mifflin.

Rogers, C. & Wallen, J. (1946). *Counseling with returned servicemen*. New York: McGraw-Hill.

Chapter 8

Ruling Choices: Exploration

What is Ruling?

The R in the acronym CREST stands for ruling. It may not seem possible to use ruling choices in significant ways to achieve more effective interpersonal relationships and inner well-being, but it is. The very sound of the word ruling may conjure up images of crowns and scepters, ermine robes, and absolute power over life and death; but the definition of ruling offered here is more moderate than that. The clear definition of ruling as an inclusive term is important both for you and your clients.

Simply stated, any choice that shows leadership is seen as a ruling choice. In fact, we could have used the label *leading* or *leadership* to designate these choices. The acronym CREST, however, is much more memorable than the alternative, CLEST. Another benefit of the word ruling is that it can serve as a reminder that it is easy to OD on this kind of choice—and when we overdo, our behavior is likely to be seen by others as dominating. This is not to suggest that all ruling choices are OD any more than all leadership is OD. Many ruling choices are OK, some are major OK choices, and OK ruling choices are important elements in any effective relationship. Good self-concepts, too, depend on individuals making an adequate number of OK ruling choices for themselves and with others.

"Come here, please."

"Listen to this."

"You better start taking care of yourself more."

"I'm beat, so let's eat out tonight."

"Let's go out for ice cream later."

"Pass the lemon slices, please."

"I'll finish reading one more page, then take a break."

"Watch what you're doing."

"Stop!"

"Leave me alone."

"Get out of here."

The choices above are all ruling choices. Each exercises some form of leadership and suggests or otherwise calls for some kind of behavior on the part of the person to whom the comment is directed, or for oneself. We make ruling choices when we suggest actions, when we control our own behavior, and when we make demands upon another. The examples given above are all verbal, but we may also make non-verbal ruling choices. Some examples are: pointing toward the door another person needs to enter, holding up a hand in a gesture that says STOP, touching a finger to our lips to signal silence, or crooking a finger and making a beckoning motion.

The question of OKness in ruling choices, as with each of the other choices, is a matter of several considerations. Do our words or actions fit the needs of the other person? A coach who sends team members running around the gym five times as a warmup activity has made an OK choice with most of the team members; an English teacher who uses the same ruling choice as punishment may have made an OD choice for all involved. Timing is a second factor of importance. The suggestion of a coffee break may be welcomed by individuals under many circumstances, but not if they have just gotten well started on a task that cannot readily be put aside. The situation is a third significant factor. To a person who is in tears, the statement, "I'll finish one more page and then I'll take a break and we can talk," is not likely to be an OK choice. The relationship with the other person is also important. "Let's go out for ice cream," may not be seen as an OK suggestion from a total stranger.

The OKness of ruling choices should also be viewed in a now/later frame of reference. Relationships may develop in such a way that ruling choices are made predominantly by one person, and that may be seen initially by both as appropriate—for example, parents with children, supervisors with employees, and, traditionally, male dating partners with females. For most relationships to grow and prosper, however, any significant disparity in ruling choices favoring one person must eventually yield to a more balanced pattern. The consequences of a continued imbalance are likely to be dependency or resentment—or both. Children who are allowed too much freedom in making ruling choices with others are likely to mature as dominating, demanding adults; conversely, children who are given too little freedom to make ruling choices even for themselves are likely to remain immature and dependent on others. The key to developing a responsible pattern of ruling choices is having the opportunity to be on the receiving and the giving end of a reasonable number of ruling choices throughout our lives. However, since these are choices, it remains possible, though not necessarily easy, to modify well-entrenched patterns of ruling choices.

Those of us who seldom take charge in particular relationships might find that our friends welcome ruling choices from us now and then. If we are inclined to engage in such a conversation as: "What do you want to do?" "Oh I don't care how about you?" "Anything you want to do is fine,"and so forth, we might find that a statement of our preference would be most welcome. Our suggestion may even be seen as a major OK choice. Example: "I'd really like to get a Chinese meal tonight then see the new movie downtown." The response might be: "Great, I was hoping you'd come up with a suggestion."

On the other hand, if we constantly take charge in a particular relationship we might find that our friend would be pleased if we were to modify *that* choice pattern. If we decide to hold back, we probably ought to allow time for the other person to break out of his or her habit pattern. For example, we might say, "Hey, we're always doing what I want to. How about if you make the decision for tomorrow night? I'll give you a call before I leave work, and whatever you say goes."

Ruling choices made for self are also important. When we state our expectations and plans for ourselves, or place demands upon ourselves, we are making ruling choices. In considering self-caring choices we used an example of waiting at a traffic light, seeing it turn yellow, and observing a "light runner" approaching from our left. Although caring for ourselves may be the predominant focus of our thoughts, we might let *self-ruling* predominate instead. "Just because that person is being an idiot is no reason for me to act the same way. I've got loved ones to consider, I'd better not demand the right of way just now." Or "Dammit, I've been waiting here long enough, and it's my turn, so I'm going to take my piece of the road NOW." The latter choice has two important overtones to it: the ruling overtone is: "I have to stand up for my rights, no matter what—my ego is at stake"; the sorrowing overtone is: "I have a right to be angry when someone stomps on my privileges— and when I'm angry I have a right to act." Placing one's life and property, or another's, in jeopardy because of an internal message that demands action at all costs, *is* self-ruling. In our view it makes a case for a balance between self-ruling that asserts our rights, and self-ruling or self-caring that protects us. Balance among the choices, whether for ourselves or others, is a wise and legitimate objective.

We rule ourselves well when we take ourselves in hand and do what we must to achieve our objectives; when we demand of ourselves that we continue our exercise regimen even when we have wearied of it; when we eat sensibly even if no one else is around to judge us harshly, and platters are piled high with tempting foods we genuinely enjoy; and when we get enough sleep to function well even when there are other things we might prefer to do.

What is our self-ruling talk like? Are we overly cautious or do we make demands on ourselves that place ourselves in jeopardy unnecessarily? Do we say to ourselves: "You can't do that, so don't try." "Children (even when the are my age) should be seen and not heard." "Don't get involved." "Don't take any lip from anybody." "I'd be a nobody if I let someone step on my toes." "Don't show the slightest weakness—and don't *have* any needs." Alternatively, are we able to find the middle ground that shows both strength and human vulnerability?

A reasonable self-ruling person could stand before a mirror and say such things as:

"I am a self-starter."

"I make good self-ruling choices."

"I take charge of my own life—reasonably."

"I can't do everything, but I can do something."

"I either work things out myself or ask for help when I need it."

"I don't have to dominate, but I see that my ideas are heard."

"I don't make too many or too few self-ruling choices."

When we feel good about ourselves we realize that for our relationships to have depth, others need reasonable ruling choices from us, and we ought to accept reasonable ruling choices made by others.

Besides taking charge of our bodies in healthy ways and talking to ourselves in ways that demonstrate effective self-ruling, we make positive ruling choices for ourselves when we ask others to make ruling choices with us:

"Let me know when you need to leave."

"Tell me when you think you understand the process and we'll try it."

"Say when I've served you enough."

"Stop me if I've told you about this before."

In our discussion of caring we pointed out that caring and ruling choices merge in such comments as, "Don't forget your umbrella." We use the term umbrella language to connote statements the sender intends as caring, but that the receiver may see as ruling—even as OD ruling. In Choice Awareness it is not seen as a matter of great importance that the five choices be discriminated precisely. There is often some overlap, and the intent of the sender cannot always be determined. A single choice that sends a caring message but is received as a ruling message is not likely to harm a good relationship. The more important consideration is that we learn to send unadulterated caring choices at least some of the time, when it is our intention to respond to the needs of others. Similarly, we need to learn to send unadulterated ruling choices at least some of the time when it is our intention to exercise leadership—and our positive, or OK, ruling choices are likely to be welcome.

Ruling and enjoying choices interact when the message includes both leadership and a response to positive feelings. "Let's go to the movies this evening," said openly and with exuberance, has elements of both choices. It clearly shows leadership, so it incorporates a ruling choice. The more insistence there is the more definitely the choice is tilted toward ruling.

Ruling and sorrowing choices overlap when leadership and sadness or other negative feelings are part of the message. "Sorry, we've got to close now." Or "You've *got* to be on my subcommittee. We just can't handle it without you." Ruling and sorrowing choices merge most often whenever a person handles sorrowing feelings by acting in a controlling or a domineering way.

Ruling and thinking/working choices overlap when logic and leadership come together. For example: "Now that we've looked at all the choices, I think we have to reverse the decision we made earlier." Thinking, whether of a deep or superficial nature, enters into all choices. We assign the ruling label whenever choices involve leadership; we use the label thinking/working choices for most planning and sorting processes.

Ruling and other choices cannot be discriminated precisely; however, ruling choices can generally be differentiated from other choices if there is leadership in the suggestion made or the action taken.

We learned important lessons in infancy concerning all of the CREST choices. The simple act of turning away from a food we disliked or holding tightly to an object an adult wanted to take away are examples of ruling choices we made early in life. The responses we received helped us understand which of our leadership choices would be accepted and which would not. If adults ruled over us arbitrarily and continuously, we learned to accede to, or thwart, the wills of those others. If we were allowed to assert our choices somewhat in matters of playing, eating, and sleeping, we learned that we could make some acceptable ruling choices. If adults set very few limits for us, we learned that no one cared much what we did, or that we had great power to make our own ruling choices. The ways in which we express ourselves through ruling choices are influenced by early life experiences.

We may have learned to make ruling choices stereotypically. Most females learned that males are to be deferred to in matters of leadership, while males learned that matters of leadership are their prerogative and obligation. The playthings traditionally given to girls have tended to reinforce caring, while boys have been given earth-moving, powerful, take-charge kinds of toys. Both sexes learned conflicting messages. Boys heard: "Be strong." "Take charge." "Don't cry." But also: "Drink your milk." "Don't sass your mother." "Go to bed." Girls heard: "Act like a lady." "Don't be a pushy female." "Do well in school." But also: "Don't threaten boys' egos." "It's OK to use feminine wiles to get your way."

Role and age stereotyping also influence the development of patterns of ruling choices. Parents, supervisors, and older persons in general are looked to for ruling choices. Workers follow supervisors' directions even when they see better ways of completing tasks. Whole armies follow leaders they are assigned even when the task is hopeless or there is a better direction to go. Clearly it would be inappropriate for employees or squads to cast off in new directions in many circumstances; the pity is that those individuals who could, may not offer suggestions when it would be easy to do so.

Sharing in leadership is appropriate for males, females, the young, the old, parents, children, supervisors, subordinates, elected officials, and community members. While more ruling choices may be expected from those who hold leadership positions, roles should not determine all ruling choices. Behaviors should be based on existing realities and the need of each person to develop a sense of responsibility for the success of the enterprise, whether it involves a family, a work setting, or a community endeavor. In the competitive world of business and industry an awareness of the potential of workers to contribute to the enterprise they are engaged in has led to the development of quality circles—opportunities for employees to share in the leadership. In all important areas of life people need to see themselves as participants, not as cancelled-out creatures who are acted on by others.

Your clients may be individuals who have not evolved satisfactory means for meeting their needs to exercise leadership. They may have learned to dominate, but more likely than not they feel powerless, choiceless. It is important in counseling for you to help your clients find ways to express their leadership abilities so that they can feel capable in their world; and you may be able to do this best with many clients by helping them directly to develop skill in making ruling choices.

SELF-EXAMINATION—JOURNAL ENTRY: Take a few minutes to think, then discuss in your journal the ruling choices you make in one of your important relationships, and with yourself. Discuss the extent to which the ruling choices you make in the relationship move you toward or away from the goals you have with that person, and toward or away from a sense of inner well-being. Suggestion: head your entry MY RULING CHOICES.

We encourage you to share these ideas with your clients, inviting their reactions and helping them see the importance of considering the ruling choices they make in their important relationships and for themselves. Many counseling clients need to learn to make more OK ruling choices for themselves and with others if they are to achieve the positive goals they have for their relationships and for their lives.

COUNSELING APPLICATION—JOURNAL ENTRY: Discuss the extent to which you believe it is important for you to help your clients deal directly with their patterns of ruling choices. Consider with at least one specific or hypothetical client how you might focus on the ruling choices that person *now* makes, and the ruling choices that individual *could* make to improve his or her life. Suggestion: head your entry CLIENT RULING CHOICES.

Making Effective Ruling Choices

Both you and your clients need to feel comfortable in initiating and responding to others with ruling choices. "Parents and teachers often wait for the misbehavior of children before they take action, responding after the fact. Behaviorists have helped people to see that they can figure out when some events are likely to take place" (Nelson, 1977, p. 112). Teachers or parents can learn when to change a pattern of activity once they observe that the attention span of a child for a particular task tends to be of a certain duration, say ten minutes. Good counselors tend to develop a keen sense of when the relationship would benefit by a well-placed suggestion.

In a personal relationship you may rationalize, "My friend won't want to be interrupted now," and then psychologically drum your fingers until you believe the time is right. Often that time never comes. You could devote that energy to considering *how* you might take the lead in an OK way. You may find that your leadership is most welcome and that it meets a need of the other person as well.

As we have suggested, most of us have experienced conversations like the following: "What do you want to do tonight?" "Oh, I don't care, you decide." "Well, I just want to do what you want to do." It is just such conversations that should convince us that most of us feel uncomfortable in the leadership role. The truth of the matter is that either individual may feel relief when the other person states clearly what he or she would like to do. In many relationships the most significant change that could be made would be that of learning to initiate more frequently with effective ruling choices.

When we make ruling choices toward other people, we expect certain CREST responses more than others. These responses tend to be habitual rather than well-considered. Suppose that a half hour before the agreed-upon time, you call someone with whom you have made a luncheon appointment and say: "I'm starved, can you go for lunch right now?" How might that person respond?

Any of the CREST choices is possible. Caring: (Reflecting the feeling) "You really sound ravenous." Ruling: "Let's go!" Enjoying: (With a chuckle) "I love it! I love it! We're right in tune." Sorrowing: (Regretfully, with overtones of self-ruling) "Oh, gee, I won't be able to get away for at least forty minutes yet." Thinking/Working: "Shall I meet you downstairs or at The Pink Penguin?"

If the other person sees your suggestion of moving up the time of lunch as OK, his or her response is likely to be a thinking/working choice or a complementary ruling choice, as in the examples cited above. If the other person sees your choice as OD the response is more likely to involve OD sorrowing or OD ruling. An internal sorrowing choice involving frustration might be heard as a long pause. An external sorrowing choice might be: "Nuts, I thought we agreed on the time yesterday." An OD ruling choice might be: "You'll just have to hold your horses a while; I said noon and I meant it."

Your call may be viewed as a major OK choice if the other person welcomes it as an opportunity to have more time for lunch, or more time with you, and he or she is likely to respond with an enjoying choice like the one above (I love it! I love it! ...)—another major OK choice.

When someone makes an OK ruling choice, it is generally easy for us to make an OK choice in response. However, when we view a ruling choice as OD, when someone says in a demanding tone, "Hand me that report," we may find it a challenge to make an OK response. If we see ourselves as equal or superior in power, we may come back with an even more OD ruling choice: "Get it yourself!" If we see ourselves as less powerful we may comply, but make internal sorrowing choices.

When someone makes an OD ruling choice, such as "Hand me that report," it is possible for us to make OK or OD choices of each of the five kinds. OK caring: "You don't usually say things in a tone of voice like that, are you feeling OK?" OD caring: "There, there, you poor thing; here's your lolly." OK ruling: (Gently) "Hey, take it easy." OD ruling: (Bristling) "Don't talk to me in that tone of voice." OK enjoying: (In jest) "Why sure, boss." OD enjoying: (Teasing) "Now don't be shy; just speak up whenever you need anything." OK sorrowing: "It bothers me when you order me around like that." OD sorrowing: Tears. OK thinking/working: Considering internally what might have brought on that choice. OD thinking/working: "I have several suggestions for you when you want a report. One. . . Two. . . and so forth." We are in a much better position to make effective choices when we realize that we can make a great variety of responses even to OD ruling choices.

If we are attempting to change a pattern of behavior and we make an OK ruling choice that is responded to poorly, it may shake our resolve to do anything further to improve the relationship. It should not. Suppose we suggest to a friend who has complained about all the chores he has to do: "I'll stop by and give you a hand on Saturday." And he responds: "Oh, no, don't bother." What we need to do is examine the choice, consider the circumstances, and determine if the suggestion was in fact appropriate or inappropriate. If we decide the choice was a good one in terms of the relationship, and that the other person is experiencing something unrelated to us that we do not understand, we should at minimum give ourselves credit for our generosity, and at maximum restate the offer. If we take a middle position, we may want to make a simple and honest observation: "I don't understand what's got you so upset." On the other hand, if we *do* understand what is affecting the other person, we need to take that into account when we decide what to say or do next.

Our ruling choices, even those that are most positive or have a helpful intent, may be rejected simply because other people do not see themselves as worthy of our time and effort, or because they have need to be in charge. We need to reinforce rather than criticize ourselves when we have made OK choices—even if they have not been responded to well—and resolve to continue to make such choices as long as we are in the relationship.

Not only is it possible for us to make OK or OD ruling choices with others, it is also possible for us to make OK or OD self-ruling choices. "Self-ruling can be vital and effective, absent and needed, or constant and oppressive" (Nelson, 1977, p. 108). Having too many shoulds or should nots is detrimental to inner well-being; likewise it is possible for us to set too few expectations for ourselves. In either case we convey a lack of positive self feeling and self love.

We need to achieve balance between allowing others to make ruling choices and taking the lead ourselves. Similarly, we need to achieve balance between setting reasonable expectations for our own behavior and allowing ourselves sufficient freedom to act.

We have been reared in a society that is inconsistent on the issue of self-ruling choices. On the one hand society seems to value tight controls, rigid personal standards, and highly moral behavior. On the other hand it seems to respect people who "grab all the gusto" they can, who exhibit rugged individualism, or even who exploit others—if they do it successfully. You need to set rules for yourself that are neither overly restrictive nor overly loose—and encourage your counselees to do the same. It is important that you and your clients learn to rule yourselves in OK ways and that you learn appropriate ways of taking the lead—of making ruling choices—with others.

Ruling choices reach across the three levels of counseling: spa, learning, and relearning. When you enable your clients to take charge of themselves and their relationships in appropriate ways, you may at times be helping them to create a spa environment for themselves. A significant proportion of your clients may gain through learning or relearning that enables them to make more effective self- and other-ruling choices.

SELF-EXAMINATION—JOURNAL ENTRY: Take a few minutes to think, then discuss in your journal ways in which you can make more effective ruling choices in one of your most important relationships, and with yourself. Suggestion: head your entry MORE EFFECTIVE RULING CHOICES FOR ME.

We encourage you to share these ideas with your clients, inviting their reactions and helping them see the importance of making more effective ruling choices in their important relationships and for themselves. Many clients need to be helped to consider how they can make more OK ruling choices for themselves and with others if they are to achieve effective interpersonal relationships and inner well-being.

COUNSELING APPLICATION—JOURNAL ENTRY: Discuss how you might help your clients make ruling choices that would improve their relationships and their sense of inner well-being. Suggestion: head your entry MORE EFFECTIVE CLIENT RULING CHOICES.

Ruling Choices

In Choice Awareness theory ruling choices are seen as those choices that involve leadership. We began to acquire our patterns of ruling choices very early in life, and we may remain tied unnecessarily to early learnings and stereotypical ruling choice patterns. Clients in counseling need to learn when and how to make more effective ruling choices, they need to understand their own responses to such choices, and they need to learn to take the initiative in making those choices for themselves and with others.

Reference

Nelson, R. C. (1977). *Choosing: A better way to live.* North Palm Beach, FL: GuideLines Press.

Chapter 9

Ruling Choices: Application

Ruling Choices and Your Clients

A great many of the concerns of your clients are related to ruling choices. Doubtless many of your clients believe that they are acted upon by others and they feel quite powerless to effect events in their own lives. If you analyze the problems your clients bring into counseling, you can see that many of them have a deficit in both the quality and quantity of the ruling choices they send. You can contribute significantly to the lives of many of your clients if you explore with them with whom they might beneficially exercise more positive leadership, and how they might respond in more effective ways to the leadership of others.

The downward-turning spiral of mental health that is experienced by many of your clients is activated by the sense of powerlessness they feel. They do not envision themselves as able to take charge in their lives, they defer to others, and in so doing they confirm their judgment that others are in control of them. Individuals who have exercised very few ruling choices in their lives offer a genuine challenge to you as a counselor. The longer they have lived and the less powerful they have felt, the greater the challenge.

As with caring choices, however, two factors are on your side in helping your clients become more effective in making ruling choices. First, ruling choices *are* choices, so they are accessible to the individual. The habit of deferring and feeling powerless may be strong, but, like the journey that begins with one step, the movement toward more effectiveness in exercising leadership begins with one choice. Second, even those people for whom ruling choices seem inaccessible are likely to have a repertoire of ruling choices, perhaps dormant from childhood.

Most children believe they are powerless to affect the world and that they make very few ruling choices. However, one need only observe them on a playground or in a pre-school play area to see that they make significant numbers of ruling choices, often in a kind of parody of the adults around them.

"Throw it here."

"I'm up next."

"You're out."

"I'm gonna play third base."

"Give me something to swing at."

"That's my crayon."

"Gimme a yellow one."

"Stop that!"

"C'm'ere."

"You be the one who's come to visit."

"I get to wear the big hat."

"Pretend you can't hear me."

"You can't play with us."

"Come on over to my house this afternoon."

"Let's play Crazy Eights."

"Wanna watch cartoons?"

"You want some crackers and peanut butter?"

As children, with other same-age and younger children, or with dolls, toy figures, or animals, we all had experiences in which we exercised leadership. As a result of these experiences we have a repertoire of leadership behaviors we are able to call upon once we determine that we need to upgrade our skills in that direction. Even if we have had few positive models for making OK ruling choices, even if we have been thwarted in many of our efforts to assert ourselves, we are not likely to be devoid of experience or ideas along these lines. An essential element of inner well-being for clients in counseling is that of making effective, OK, ruling choices both for themselves and with others.

CONSIDER THE FOLLOWING:

Laura, a soon-to-be seventh grader, sought help from a counselor during summer school. Her complaint was that her father, with whom she had previously had a good relationship, had begun to be accusatory toward her about her behavior involving boys. Laura was physically mature for a thirteen year old, but, she assured the counselor, her father had no reason for his accusations. After hearing her out the counselor suggested some positive ways in which she might take charge of the relationship—to preempt her father's focus on the negative. Laura was extremely skeptical, but agreed to try one thing that would *initiate* the contact each afternoon for the next three days. Her initial suggestion was, "Dad, we used to have fun playing checkers. How about a game this afternoon." Laura was pleased with the results even though her father lectured her at a number of points about her playing. "At least," she said afterwards, "he didn't ask me whether I'd been 'screwing around' with the boys." On the second day, before her father could speak, she commented favorably on his appearance—he was dressed-up for a church meeting—and once again she was gratified with the response. On the third day she did what she had told the counselor, "That's one thing I'll never, never, never, never, never be able to do." She began the contact with her father by saying, "Hey, Dad, I want a better relationship with you. We need to talk." The tears and hugs that followed her suggestion and punctuated their discussion gave Laura evidence of her father's genuine concern, and helped begin the process of turning the relationship around (Nelson, 1976).

As in the situation with Laura and her father, many relationships falter because one person is resentful of the choices made by the other person, feels powerless in the relationship, does little to change matters, and feels resentment even more deeply. Laura headed home each afternoon anticipating accusatory behavior, steeling herself to be frustrated and hurt, convinced she could do nothing to alter the situation. She learned that it was possible for her to take charge of the interaction by speaking first—and some of her choices were gentle, positive ruling choices. When she took charge of her part of the relationship, she was thrilled to find her father genuinely responsive.

As long as Laura felt powerless, she hung her head and responded in a sullen manner. In all probability her sullenness was misperceived by her father as evidence of guilty feelings on her part. People who feel powerless frequently send unclear non-verbal messages that result from their negative feelings, and those messages are subject to misinterpretation by others.

In our society we respect adults who demonstrate leadership in their interactions with others. Nevertheless, we socialize both sexes, especially girls, in ways that make that outcome unlikely—by telling them that they should do as they are told. We refer to assertive women as aggressive or pushy, and when we hear either label applied by others, we may be more likely to chuckle than to challenge the point, even if we have a contrary opinion.

Both females and males need their own permission to make ruling choices for themselves and with others. All of us have known females who are gentle and feminine, yet strong and assertive, but there are too few such women whom young people experience as models of mature adult behavior. As a result it does not occur to many girls and young women that they might exercise leadership in firm, yet gentle, ways. On the other hand, we expect boys to learn to take charge, and we send them messages that they have failed as males if they are unassertive. Since the models adults provide are often inadequate, boys may behave aggressively, rather than assertively, or believe that they have failed in their responsibility as males.

When males *or* females, workers or supervisors, older or younger people, ignore their need to demonstrate leadership, adverse outcomes occur in at least four areas. (1) They experience a power vacuum in many of their relationships. The great majority of people see themselves basically as responders, rather than initiators. This being the case, two responders often find themselves in the same place, each waiting for the other to take the lead, each assigning to the other the responsibility for initiating. (2) They develop shallow relationships. When two responders wait for one another to take the lead, the inevitable result is that little happens and each becomes frustrated with the lack of depth of the relationship. (3) They develop habit patterns and contracts in their relationships that do not serve them well. While it may suit a person initially if a dating partner or a spouse, for example, is willing to take the lead in most matters, people change, and what may have seemed to be attractive and helpful initially may be seen as annoying or galling over time. (4) They feel like failures. When supervisors, older persons, and males feel an obligation to demonstrate leadership, but hesitate to lead, they may believe that they have failed as persons.

All people need their own permission to exercise at least minimal leadership in their own lives and with their relatives and friends. Choice Awareness suggests that ruling is one of five basic choices human beings have available to them. To place severe limitations on the expression of that option is to severely limit one of the five basic alternatives people have for interacting in the world in which they find themselves. Most males obligate themselves to demonstrate leadership and power in at least some aspects of their lives, sometimes in ways that are not personally relevant or socially acceptable. Many females shy away from leading, even when they are well-suited to leadership. Members of both sexes need to give themselves permission to take the lead appropriately and reasonably in their own lives and with the people who are important to them. Many counseling clients, regardless of sex, age, or role, need to be encouraged to give themselves permission to make OK ruling choices for themselves and with others, and to take the responsibility and accept the consequences of their choices.

> SELF-EXAMINATION—JOURNAL ENTRY: Take at least five minutes and discuss the extent to which you believe you limit yourself in sex-, age-, and/or role-stereotypical ways in the

ruling choices you make—for yourself and with others. Discuss the extent to which you believe a new pattern of ruling choices might benefit you in your personal life. Suggestion: head your entry STEREOTYPING AND MY RULING CHOICES.

We encourage you to share these ideas with your clients, inviting their reactions and helping them see that they can exercise leadership in ways that go beyond sex-, age-, and role-stereotypes. Most clients can benefit by appraisal and a shift in the pattern of ruling choices they make for themselves and with others.

When you encourage your clients to make more effective, more OK, ruling choices with others you are helping them act on the principle of social-interest—and often as not they are serving their own self-interest as well. When they fill the power vacuum in positive ways their behaviors contribute positively to their relationships and afford them opportunities to meet their own needs as well.

Assertiveness

All counseling systems are designed in some way to encourage clients to take more effective control in their lives, but no true system of counseling focuses in a very direct way on ruling choices—by that name or any other. It is perhaps because of that omission that assertiveness training has evolved in recent years. As Gilliland, *et al.*, suggest,

The fundamental goals of assertive training are. . . (1) [to] empower clients to actively initiate and carry out desired choices and behaviors that do not harm other people physically or emotionally, and (2) to teach clients alternatives to emitting passive, helpless, dependent, and stifled ways of dealing with life situations (1984, p. 166).

Assertiveness training emerged as a result of the women's movement, since it was clear that women were especially inclined to be passive in situations that might more appropriately be met with active responses. However, it soon became apparent that both sexes were in need of education for assertiveness, since both males and females have difficulties in dealing with authority figures and in taking charge of their own lives in the face of problem situations involving others.

Most people grow up having heard such injunctions as: "Do as you're told." "Speak when you're spoken to." "Children should be seen and not heard." Thus it is understandable that many people find it difficult to change their behavior from childhood, and to learn to exercise more adult judgments. On two major grounds it can be argued that such messages should not be sent even to children: (1) because so many people are paralyzed by these injunctions in their adult lives; and (2) because authorities on the sexual abuse of children and on missing children suggest that we increase the vulnerability of young people by continually repeating such injunctions. Many individuals need help in developing assertive behaviors, and counselors have unique opportunities to respond to that need.

From the viewpoint of Choice Awareness theory, assertiveness involves both self- and other-ruling choices, and these may occur on at least four levels. We illustrate these levels here in relationship to three situations. In Situation A, your friend and you went to a party with the understanding that you needed to leave by 10:30 because of an important early morning obligation; it is now 10:30. In Situation B, you and your cousin are getting nowhere in a political discussion and you are ready to quit exploring the matter. In Situation C, you have entered a store at 5:20 fully aware that the sign on the door indicates that closing time is 5:30, but the clerk discourages you from coming in, saying, "It's almost closing time. Could you come back tomorrow?"

The simplest level of assertion infers or makes a matter-of-fact statement of a self-ruling choice. The examples that follow relate to the situations cited above. (A) "It's 10:30. I'm ready to go home now." (B) "I don't think either of us is going to convince the other, so I'd like to drop the discussion and talk about something else." (C) "The sign on the door says you're open until 5:30; I'll be sure to finish by then." Though gentle, these assertions go beyond the permission level many people give themselves. It is clear that those who do not allow themselves to make even these modest assertions are in need of assistance.

Sometimes the first assertion is not heeded or the urgency of the situation calls for skipping the first level. In either case, the second level of assertion might well be a moderately stated other-ruling choice. (A) "You said you would leave with me at this time." (B) "You keep baiting me to continue the argument; please stop." (C) "You're wasting the few minutes I need by arguing; please let me in."

Further assertion may incorporate a statement of empathy for the needs of the other along with a stronger self- or other-ruling choice. (A) "I know you're having a good time and hate to stop, but if you're not going to leave now I'll go on my own (or you/I will have to make other arrangements such as call a taxi)." (B) "I understand that you want to continue the argument because you think logic is on your side, but please drop the issue for now." (C) "I expect you want to clear your register so you can leave at closing, but this is the only place I can make this purchase. I'll write a check for the exact amount if I find what I want."

A fourth step is possible in an assertiveness escalation: a matter-of-fact, but stronger, self- or other-ruling choice. (A) "Goodbye." (B) (Firmly, but without anger) "Stop!" (C) "Let me speak to the manager."

Assertiveness ends and aggressiveness begins when either individual moves against the other person through abusive language, attacks on the character of the other person, or physical coercion. There may be instances in which such actions are justified, but too frequently aggressiveness is chosen before other more suitable options have been tried.

All of us encounter incidents in which we can beneficially assert ourselves because our desires or needs are unknown or because someone else is treading on them. It is sometimes appropriate, though unassertive, for us to ignore those desires or needs. It is not appropriate for us to do so repeatedly or as a pattern of behavior. Conversely, repeatedly and aggressively stating or acting upon our own needs or desires without regard to the needs or desires of others is also inappropriate.

One of the important functions of counseling is that of helping clients develop skill in asserting themselves, when necessary. Choice Awareness theory suggests that assertive behaviors are generally OK self- and other-ruling choices, unassertive behaviors are generally OD self-ruling choices, and aggressive behaviors are generally OD other-ruling choices. If you help those of your clients who have the need to learn to make assertive, OK ruling choices you enable them to alter some of their least effective behavior patterns.

CONSIDER THE FOLLOWING:

Delia Barnes, described by Sheehy (1981), encountered many opportunities to be assertive. Her life differed from the lives of many counseling clients primarily in the number of risks she took and the number of times she persevered in the face of resistance. Sheehy made it clear that Delia's determination was often shaken and there were many times when she was tempted to yield to pressures. Yet her life testifies to the value of remaining assertive, if only in making self-ruling choices.

Delia experienced a vague, continuing depression following the birth of her third daughter, in the main because in her own eyes she had failed to produce the son who would one day take over her husband's contracting business. When she sought counseling she was told that she had been trying too long to please others; it was time to begin doing things for herself. She returned to school to take advanced graduate work in education, her parents' dream for her, but she hated that choice. She stopped teaching and decided to find an identity of her own. Her pastor suggested she do God's work, and she saw that as a perfect fit for her. She asked to be admitted into the local seminary, and when denied permission, she dug in her heels. Despite having opted for non-family pursuits, she became pregnant and bore the son her husband had wanted, and stayed home with him until he was three. In the meantime one denomination within her religion agreed to ordain women. After throwing herself enthusiastically into her preparation for the ministry, she encountered many further difficulties. Community members shunned her for her decision. She was preached at from the pulpit in her home church as "the Devil. . . in the form of a woman." She played it safe for a year after her ordination and worked with a counseling service, then a minister agreed to try her as an assistant pastor in his church. Her first sermon, after several months, was a success, but the pastor felt threatened by the positive reaction, relegated her to minor tasks, and their relationship deteriorated. She asked what Sheehy called "the archetypical female response: What's wrong with me?" (p. 9).

When the Bishop, ultimately, asked her to resign as assistant pastor, for once Delia did not bottle up her feelings; she made his letter public. The congregation was supportive, members drew up petitions to keep her, but the bishop would not yield. A third of the congregation left when she resigned, but that was of little consolation to her. For a period of time she volunteered to work in a state hospital for the insane and the retarded, and after an initial period of depression she came to love her work, especially because of the other volunteers. Finally, the ideal job was offered to her in a statewide agency run by her denomination. She was to be a guest preacher and family life educator for all forty churches in the area, working as part of a teaching pair with another pastor who was a minister and family life educator, and who turned out to be an intelligent, supportive male. Almost twenty years from the time she received her first push to assert herself, she found the excitement, inner peace, and support she had sought.

Because most people travel well-trodden paths in living their lives, few encounter the number of bumps and bruises Delia Barnes experienced—but all are likely to encounter experiences that call for assertiveness, and difficulties may arise from time to time where they are least expected. As Sheehy wryly observed, in the case of Delia, "She had to become a rebel in order to live out the most traditional kind of moral and ethical existence" (p. 13).

Many people who seek support for new directions, or for casting off old expectations, find their way into counseling—although few have the determination to persevere in the face of constant resistances as Delia did. Helping clients to be assertive, enabling them to encounter everyday irritations (as in the three situations labeled A, B, and C above), and encouraging them to face the constant pressures of continuing frustrations, as in Delia's case, can be important facets of counseling.

Many counseling clients need to learn to use self- and other-ruling choices as a means of encountering the problems they face in life. Choice Awareness theory lends supports to counselors who choose to spend time helping clients develop and rehearse the skills of assertiveness. Not all client problems can be solved through their learning to be more assertive, less passive, or less aggressive. However, in those instances in which such changes are appropriate, the counselor might well spend time exploring assertiveness, in the form of self- and other-ruling choices, with the client.

SELF-EXAMINATION—JOURNAL ENTRY: Take a few minutes and discuss the extent to which you believe you are or are not effective in asserting yourself through the self- and other-ruling choices you make. Discuss the extent to which you believe becoming more or less assertive would benefit you in your view of yourself and in your personal life. Suggestion: head your entry SELF/OTHER-RULING CHOICES, ASSERTIVENESS AND ME.

We encourage you to share these ideas with your clients, inviting their reactions and helping them see that they can become more assertive, where appropriate, in situations they face. Many clients can benefit by exploring their need for assertiveness and by considering the ways in which they might become more suitably assertive—without being aggressive—in situations that call for self- and other-ruling choices.

COUNSELING APPLICATION—JOURNAL ENTRY: Discuss the extent to which you believe it is important for you to help your clients become more assertive than you typically have until now. Consider with at least one specific or hypothetical client how you might help that person become more assertive, indicating what kinds of behaviors you would like to see, and how you might work to help bring those changes about. Suggestion: head your entry SELF/OTHER- RULING CHOICES, ASSERTIVENESS AND MY CLIENTS.

Ruling Choices: Planning Ahead

Choice Awareness theory encourages planning for better choices. Those clients who come to see themselves as too unassertive or too aggressive, who realize that they make too few or too many ruling choices for their own benefit, are likely to be ready to implement new patterns of choices. Some will be helped if they decide to remain alert and take the lead with others in situations in which there is a power vacuum. Others can be more planful: thinking ahead and rehearsing specific ruling choices they might make in situations they expect will occur.

It is impossible for individuals to anticipate all the incidental situations that call for ruling choices that may occur in the grocery store, in the line at the movies, or with a sales person, but many of the situations that trouble us most are predictable. We may not know when, or over what issue, Dad will impose his judgment, but if it is his style, we know it will happen. In other instances we may be able to predict that sometime soon our spouse, friend, or roommate will play the stereo too loudly for our liking, toss clothes in a heap on the floor, or leave the cap off the toothpaste.

Life holds many mysteries, but in the area of interpersonal interaction it also holds many predictibilities. In any case, if we have thought through and rehearsed how we might initiate and respond with appropriate self- and other-ruling choices, we are less likely to be victimized and to berate ourselves later for being someone else's doormat.

Many of your clients would benefit if you explored with them the kinds of situations that call for ruling choices, if you helped them learn to take charge of their lives, and if you rehearsed appropriate actions and statements they might use to encounter the situations that face them. For some of your clients those actions would require counseling as relearning, since it might be very difficult for them to change an ingrained pattern of choices; for others the process might be that of learning; for still others the process may be entered into joyfully as a spa experience. In any event, planning for more effective ruling choices is supported in Choice Awareness theory as an essential component in enabling individuals to take more effective control in their own lives.

In our discussion of caring choices we made the observation that while planning appears at first blush to be antithetical to spontaneity, most clients cannot be truly spontaneous in making caring choices until they have broadened the spectrum of choices they have available to them; the same is true of ruling choices. Once their range of choices is enlarged, clients are more able to respond to events in the moment with a fuller, richer array of responses. Planfulness is supported in Choice Awareness theory as essential in increasing the range of choices that are genuinely available to the individual.

CONSIDER THE FOLLOWING:

In Chapter Seven we discussed the problem that Julia shared with the Resident Assistant assigned to her floor, Laura Dee, concerning her roommate, Maria, who continually complained that she missed her family, her boyfriend, and her home town. Julia had begun to withdraw from Maria, preferring the company of those who were more involved in school, but she felt guilty about that action. Laura suggested that Julia improve her relationship with Maria through making more effective caring choices. Once Julia's relationship was on a better footing with Maria, Laura encouraged her to expand the range of her behavior to include all the CREST choices, asserting that good relationships require the full color spectrum of OK choices. Once again, Laura helped Julia rehearse some of the things she might do and say to take the lead gently and positively with Maria. Again, Julia's efforts met with much success.

Here are some of the ruling choices Julia reported to Laura that she made with Maria over time.

J: I need to study now, but let's go out for ice cream later.

J: I'll wait for you if you want to have breakfast with me.

J: Please turn down the stereo; this problem is really tough and I need to concentrate.

Julia also invited Maria to make ruling choices.

J: Do you want to go out for the pizza now, or would you rather wait until I've done my laundry?

J: I'm free for the rest of the evening. Anything in particular you'd like to do?

Almost all of us are able to anticipate many of the circumstances we will face in which leadership is needed: Julia can expect that her roommate's dependency will not suddenly go away. A counselor can expect that a client's feeling of powerlessness, after his ex-wife gains custody of their children, will not suddenly disappear. The problem is that most people do not give themselves permission to take the lead in their interactions, or they do not believe they know how to do so adequately. It may contribute significantly to the well-being of your clients if you spend time helping them extend their repertoire of ruling choices, and rehearse those choices with them, so that they can make them in suitable and comfortable ways with the people who are important in their lives.

Counselors may feel inadequate in making ruling choices—in taking the lead—without dominating the process. That may be one small part of the reason that little attention has been given to the issue of enabling clients to make more effective ruling choices with others in their lives. Here are a few choices counselors can use, some of which they might help their clients also to use, to express or invite leadership in their interactions with others.

"I think now it would help if we talked about X."

"We've gone around and around on that topic; I'd like for us to leave it for a while."

"I'm going to suggest that we not see one another for three or four weeks; that ought to give you time to make some progress with your mother. You can call me for an appointment when you have something positive to report."

(A good beginning for many interviews) "There are some things I know we ought to talk about today, but I'd like to begin with whatever is on your mind."

"So—where do we go next?"

"I think it's time to choose one of the options we've talked about and put it into practice."

A nonverbal choice. Pointing to the list of ideas you have been building as a way of encouraging its further development.

Frequently ruling choices require reinforcement. A new assertion of self, especially for a person who has been unassertive, often calls for more than one or two statements or actions, and it is likely to require follow-up and continuous effort over time.

Appropriate ruling choices can enable clients to achieve the level of spa in their feelings about themselves and in their interactions with others. When clients realize that they have affected their world, they feel powerful and positive; they gain the same feelings when they make ruling choices that fill the vacuum that exists in some of their relationships—and filling the vacuum may be a spa experience for the other person as well.

All people from time to time have opportunities to exercise leadership, to make ruling choices—and if they are not aware of that reality, the counselor might well explore with them the question, "Who in your world would benefit if you exercised leadership more frequently?" All people from time to time have need for leadership from others. Few people are sufficiently skilled in making effective ruling choices day to day and in encouraging others around them to do the same. Clients benefit when counselors help them understand the nature of ruling choices, and enable them to develop the skills of ruling for themselves and others.

Ruling Choices

Many of your clients need to learn to make more effective ruling choices as they face everyday situations and those they encounter infrequently. Your counseling may well assist your clients to take more effective leadership action for themselves and with others. Assertiveness theory teaches individuals specific approaches by which they can meet their needs effectively—taking charge of themselves and the situation—without becoming aggressive. Choice Awareness theory conceptualizes assertive behaviors as ruling choices and suggests that you may beneficially encourage your clients to make effective ruling choices in the situations they encounter. The outcomes should be that many of your clients will cease feeling powerless and gain a greater sense of inner well-being.

References

Gilliland, B. E., James, R. K., Roberts, G. T., & Bowman, J. T. (1984). *Theories and strategies in counseling and psychotherapy.* Englewood Cliffs, NJ: Prentice-Hall.

Nelson, R. C. (1976). Choice Awareness: an unlimited horizon, *Personnel and Guidance Journal, 54,* 462-467.

Sheehy, G. (1981). *Pathfinders.* New York: William Morrow.

Chapter 10

Enjoying Choices: Exploration

What is Enjoying?

"Let's pretend we're on a desert island, with trees to climb, and lots of good things to eat.

Life is really great for me today!

It's really exciting being here with you.

You're one of my favorite people.

It's fun to do things with you.

I just thought of such a good thing to do for Mom.

Let's see how many things we can figure out to do with this plastic container.

I know who you love best.

Wiggle your ears again, maybe you can take off" (Nelson, 1977, p. 121).

E in the acronym CREST stands for enjoying, and the choices above are all enjoying choices. Through enjoying choices we let others know of our good feelings for ourselves and for them. We make enjoying choices with simple greeting statements, with thank-you's, with compliments, when we tell an amusing anecdote, when we share a feeling of excitement, and in a great variety of other ways. We make enjoying choices without words when we clap our hands, smile, laugh, pat someone on the back, create something, fantasize, meditate, and relax. Enjoying choices are the most important choices we have available to us for achieving a sense of inner well-being and spa in our lives, and as such they deserve considerable attention in counseling.

Through enjoying choices more than any of the other choices we express the positive aspects of our self-concepts. The converse is also true; good self-concepts depend on our making an adequate number of OK enjoying choices for ourselves and with others. When we feel good about ourselves, we may make many enjoying choices and we are likely to receive enjoying choices in return. When we do not feel good about ourselves, we may tend to make very few enjoying choices; and the likely outcome is that others will send few enjoying choices our way. "It is very important for us to understand that we can feel good and then make enjoying choices, or that we can make enjoying choices and then feel good" (Nelson, 1977, p. 122).

Is the enjoying choice we have made OK? The key related questions are similar to those we raised about other choices. Do our words and actions fit the wants or needs of the other person? A troubled friend or sad co-worker is not as likely to be receptive to an amusing anecdote as is a smiling, happy spouse or child. Is the timing suitable? Children often burst into home ready to share an experience from school and find mother or dad busy with supper preparations or deep in a project of some kind. While we might wish the parent would take the time to respond, it is certainly not the ideal moment for a deep, responsive sharing of the experience. Is the situation appropriate? The hug given "just because I love you" in some instances might best be saved for a little while if a friend is thoroughly immersed in solving a problem. Does the relationship support the suitability of the choice? A loving pat on the fanny suggests a deep level of intimacy, and may be seen as appropriate only in one direction in the relationship—parent to child, but not child to parent, for example.

OD enjoying includes choices that are unresponsive to the wants or needs of the other person, are inappropriate in timing, do not fit the situation, or are problematic in terms of the relationship. However, some enjoying choices are almost inherently OD: laughter that pours salt in the wounds of another, humor at the expense of a friend, a dangerous "practical" joke, or unacceptable teasing: "You don't have an inferiority complex, you *are* inferior."

Some of us allow ourselves only acid-tongued, sardonic or sarcastic humor as an outlet for our enjoying choices, perhaps fearing closeness, yet wanting some kind of contact with others, figuring acidity is better than nothing. The importance of the relationship should be under-scored here. The same teasing comment might be seen as amusing by one friend and hurtful by another—a relationship involving two acid-tongued participants may be the most intimate they can permit for themselves. Thus, helping your clients assess the OKness of their enjoying choices may be in part a question of helping them understand the perspective of the other person.

The OKness of enjoying choices can also be viewed in a now/later frame of reference. Two people who see themselves as deeply in love may feel that it is right in the moment for them to have sexual intercourse, but on further consideration they may restrain themselves because there are risks for the relationship —now or later. A conspira-torial action may seem right for now because it creates a bond between the two people involved, but it may be discarded as inappropriate because of the possible future effects on other people. The key to developing a responsible pattern of enjoying choices is having the opportunity to be on the receiving and the sending end of an enormous number of OK enjoying choices throughout our lives.

Self-enjoying choices are crucial in developing a sense of inner well-being. We may well ask ourselves: Do I enjoy myself inwardly? Do I respond well to the opportunity to spend time by myself? Do I fill that time with loud music and vigorous activity to shut out loneliness, or do I relish the opportunity for introspection and quiet contemplation?

A reasonable self-enjoying person could stand in front of a mirror and say such things as:

"I like the way I look."

"I enjoy my company."

"I appreciate the ways in which I relate to others."

"I see myself as a good person."

"I like my smile."

"Among the things I enjoy doing are. . . ."

If we believe we are worthy of enjoying and appreciating ourselves, we find it easier to enjoy others and make enjoying choices with them. How we feel toward others in part reflects how we feel about ourselves. How we feel about ourselves is in part a function of what we internally say to ourselves. Making positive, internal self-statements, and limit-ing the number of critical self-statements, is important in building a positive sense of self. Self-talk that emphasizes what we can do, what we have done, and our appreciation of ourselves, helps build that positive sense of self.

There is an important difference between self-enjoying choices and self-indulging choices, although it may not always be possible to draw a precise line between them. Self-indulging choices, which include eating or drinking to excess, for example, may appear to be enjoying choices, but they often result from negative feelings; thus, they may really be sorrowing choices, thinly disguised.

We will return subsequently to the issue of the stereotyping of enjoying choices, but it seems most appropriate to mention age-stereotyping of enjoying choices in this context. Most of us have grown up with what is often called the "Protestant work ethic," whether we are Protestants or not, because it is endemic in our society. That ethic is based on two injunctions: hard work is good for us, and we adults must put away childish things.

The effects of the two injunctions are that we come to adulthood believing that enjoying choices are childish and the lot of the adult is hard work. We entitle ourselves to build up credits, through our hard work, for a night on the town, a vacation, a life of leisure at retirement; but we do not believe we are entitled to enjoy life now just because we *are*. Perhaps in reaction to this kind of controlling injunction, there are people who kick over the traces and indulge themselves with the attitude: eat, drink, and be merry, for tomorrow we die.

A middle position between indulgence and an all-work-no-play philosophy seems desirable, and may be supported on religious grounds. First, as we suggested in our introduction to enjoying choices (Chapter Three, Choice Awareness Concepts), a distinction needs to be made between childish and childlike. Truly there are actions that are not worthy even of children, and that may be viewed as childish; we should put those away (I Corinthians 13:11). But some of the best things we can do in this life—the innocent, positive, trusting things—are childlike and need to be supported: ". . .receive the kingdom. . . as a little child. . . for of such is the kingdom of God" (Mark 10:14, 15).

This middle position allows us to seek the "natural highs" of life, to enjoy ourselves and others in wholesome, positive ways that produce no headaches the morning after. We can compliment our spouse, put an arm around a friend, smell the flowers, trudge up a steep hill and enjoy the view, notice the structure of a leaf, plant a garden, telephone a relative just to say hello, sing out joyously, watch a sunset, or revel in a cool breeze on a hot day. It is through such simple pleasures, pleasures we often overlook, that we can bring enjoyment into our own lives and into the lives of others.

We can do much for ourselves in making enjoying choices, but few of us could be totally sufficient in making enjoying choices for ourselves. We need to encourage others to participate with us in making enjoying choices, and we may need to develop skill in asking for the enjoying choices we want. When we feel good about ourselves, we are more likely to give ourselves permission to ask others to participate with us in making enjoying choices.

Enjoying and caring involve some of the same behaviors. A pat on the arm may be given because the other person is upset about something, then it is a caring choice. It may be given as a friendly gesture of outreach, then it is an enjoying choice. An attempt to be helpful and meet the need of another is caring, but the same action taken freely out of good feelings may be an enjoying choice. At times one choice may serve both purposes.

Enjoying and ruling choices come together when a positive suggestion involving leadership is made: "Oh, come here, you've got to see this!" Or "I'd love to have us go out for dinner together." In the first statement the leadership element appears stronger, so we would categorize it as a ruling choice. If the second statement is an initiation, a tentative feeler, we would see it as a ruling choice; if it is a response we would categorize it as enjoying—but an element of both choices is clearly present.

Enjoying and sorrowing choices result from very different feelings, so these choices do not often overlap. However, it is worth noting that those people who are most important in our lives also can be the source of our greatest despair. When we are upset with someone, our sorrow is likely to override our enjoyment of the person. However, if we have very deep feelings for the other person, we can reach back for our positive feelings and make caring or enjoying choices. We can make choices that produce joy in our important relationships, even during those times when we feel upset.

Enjoying and thinking/working choices overlap when we engage in creative activities, when we plan positive experiences, and when we choose an enjoyable outlet rather than choosing otherwise. When we are in the cognitive or laboring phase of these actions, we are making thinking/working choices; when our positive feelings predominate, our words and actions are enjoying choices.

Enjoying choices can usually be discriminated from the other choices because they are positive, they tend to have a quality of spontaneity, and they do not depend on need. Enjoying choices are ways in which we express our positive feelings; whether they are OK or OD depends on the choice itself, the situation, the timing, and the relationship.

The extent and kinds of enjoying choices we allow ourselves are related to our early life experiences. When we were babies and grasped the finger of a parent and tried to pull ourselves up, we were doing things that felt good in their own right. If Dad or Mom encouraged us, we learned something about OK enjoying choices; if not, we learned something quite different. If Mom and Dad showed great excitement over our random ma-ma-ma or da-da-da sound, we were encouraged in our language development and reinforced for ourselves. The teachable moment was lost for the time if we were ignored. If we grew up in an environment that was quite restrictive, we may ultimately have generalized: "There are lots of things I'm not supposed to do or enjoy." If the environment had few restrictions, we learned: "Anything goes; no one cares what I do." Most of us learned mixed lessons, that some of what we do gives others pleasure—so we keep doing those things, while other things we do irritate or anger others—so we had better take a different route to get what we want.

We learned to make each of the CREST choices in sex-, age-, and role-stereotypical ways, and this is clearly evident in enjoying choices. For most of us our learning of these choices was even more age-stereotypical than it was for the other CREST choices. Among the messages we may have heard that told us enjoying choices were more acceptable for children were: "Enjoy yourself while you have the chance." "These are the best years of your life." "Go out and play." However, when we acted childlike or childish as we grew older, we received clear messages that we should relinquish many of our enjoying choices. The words varied, but the essential message was: "Grow up!"

Some years ago during a talk at a conference I mentioned that we are socialized to assign enjoying choices to children. Afterwards I went out to lunch with a former student and friend who attended my session. I think a great deal of this fellow and his wife, they are both kind and warm people. My friend told me my point reminded him of an incident that occurred the previous evening. He had been clowning noisily with their two children, and his wife came along and said to him, "You're worse than the children." I wonder how many generations of parents in her family had socialized their children in ways that encouraged them to say the same thing; surely a person who is as gentle and friendly as she is was repeating a line she had heard before—mindlessly. At any rate, the message was clear: When children make a lot of noise while playing it is bad; when adults make a lot of noise while playing it is worse.

A group of counselors engaged in a consulting project were asked to make several observations of teachers, among them their facial expressions. In a feedback session one teacher was told that the observations taken each minute for thirty minutes showed the following: ten of her observed behaviors were negative—frowns, nineteen of her behaviors were neutral, and one was positive—a smile. The teacher's response was, "That's fine, I think of a smile as a very special reward to be given only when children have done an especially fine piece of work" (Nelson, 1977, p. 125). The counselor noted that the same teacher tolerated the enjoying choices of her students "reasonably well." The message was clear: It is all right for children to make enjoying choices, but adults, especially teachers, have to be far more selective in doing so.

If you are a golfer, a bridge player, or a sports enthusiast, you may question the idea that we relegate enjoying choices to children. Certainly, adults do engage in recreational activities, take vacations, and go to movies or sports events. That last is the key word: *events*. As adults we schedule events that allow us time to enjoy ourselves. We may even assist in programing events for children, e.g., Little League, or Boy or Girl Scouts. What is different in the activities of many adults from those of many children is that there is little spontaneous fun-time and many of the choices made are sex- or role-stereotyped. We do not walk or run because it feels good, we do it for exercise. We do not take long walks in the woods for pure pleasure, we carry along a fishing pole or a camera to legitimize our wanderings. We may engage in racket ball or tennis so competitively that an observer would be hard pressed to call it recreation. We *work* at playing, often in a deadly serious manner.

Our enjoying choice events are often sex-stereotyped. Men gather in clusters of two to four and attend or watch football or basketball games on television, often wordlessly, with grunted syllables, or with dialogue that focuses on the action on the field or the floor. Women gather in twos or larger groups at coffee klatches and talk about similarly predictable things. Men are permitted, and may feel obligated, to watch or engage in team sports. Women are permitted, and may feel obligated, to communicate about such topics as clothes and children.

We assign enjoying choices to children, but they see too few effective models for making OK enjoying choices, so they operate on a trial and error basis to see what will be allowed, or they imitate the behaviors of the adults around them. "What do the simple folk do?" is a song from Camelot in which the king and queen explore what "simple folk" do, when they are sorely pressed or blue. The two try whistling, singing, and dancing, then ask what else simple folk do. They come to the conclusion that simple folk sit around and wonder what royal folk do. Children are assigned enjoying choices, but have too few models for making them, so they sit around and wonder, and like Camelot's king and queen, imitate what others do, in their case—adults. Adults relinquish enjoying choices to children, and when they find they have time on their hands, they sometimes sit around and wonder what simple folk, in this case—children, do.

A good argument can be made that we restrict ourselves unnecessarily and unwisely in each of the five CREST choices; it is especially unfortunate that we do this so much in our enjoying choices. It is possible for each of us to be more friendly, more open, more exciting, and more involved in life than we are. For me, for you, and for most of your clients it would be both significant and positive if we all moved gradually and consistently in that direction. Instead of operating in the +10 to -10 choice rut when the range available to us is +100 to -100, we need to develop the positive side of our choices more fully. We let our sex and our roles define the limits of our enjoying choices, yet if we observe carefully we can see that it is people who move beyond these limits who are most interesting and worth knowing.

Your clients are likely to be among those who have not found good outlets for themselves for making enjoying choices. They see possibilities in the actions of others and wish they could allow themselves more freedom to be their greater possible selves. Michael Snyder, a minister friend of mine, fantasized in a sermon that many of us might appropriately be asked when we arrive in heaven, "Why didn't you *become* you—wonderful, made-in-My-image, you?" One of your important tasks as a counselor is that of helping individuals find ways in which they might *become* more of themselves, and they may be able to do that best through their enjoying choices.

SELF-EXAMINATION—JOURNAL ENTRY: Take a few minutes to think, then discuss in your journal the enjoying choices you make with one person who is important to you, and those you make by yourself. Consider the extent to which the enjoying choices you make in the relationship move you toward or away from your goals with that person, and the extent to which the enjoying choices you make for yourself help you achieve a sense of inner well-being. Suggestion: head your entry MY ENJOYING CHOICES.

We encourage you to share these ideas with your clients, inviting their reactions and helping them see the importance of considering the enjoying choices they make in their significant relationships and for themselves. Most clients need to be challenged to make more OK enjoying choices for themselves and with others if they are to achieve the positive goals they have for their relationships and for their lives.

COUNSELING APPLICATION—JOURNAL ENTRY: Discuss the extent to which you believe it is important for you to help your clients deal directly with their patterns of enjoying choices, for themselves and with others. Consider with at least one specific or hypothetical client how you might focus on the enjoying choices that person *does* make, and the enjoying choices that individual *could* make to improve his or her life situation. Suggestion: head your entry CLIENT ENJOYING CHOICES.

Making Effective Enjoying Choices

When you, your clients, or I, want enjoying choices—excitement, amusement, closeness, love, or creativity—we need to initiate with enjoying choices; and when we want the involvement of others, we need to invite them to make enjoying choices with us. If we wait, as responders, for others to make suggestions of something we might enjoy doing together, or for them to say something positive to us, we may find that other people initiate with choices that make returning enjoying choices quite difficult. We could instead make the first move—and that might best be an enjoying choice.

Perhaps it is our unwillingness to appear "pushy" or overly-assertive, but in our culture we tend not to state our own preferences clearly. Instead of saying, "I'd really like to have the two of us go out for dinner tonight," we create a trap for ourselves and the other person by asking what that person would like to do, or by saying something like, "How would you like to go out for dinner tonight?" The other person takes it as a free choice, because it is stated in those terms, and may respond positively, for example—"OK"; negatively—"Not to-night, dear, I have a headache"; or neutrally—"Oh, I don't care, I'll leave it up to you." If what we want is a positive response, we need to make a positive assertion. If we sound as if we are open to other possibilities or are lukewarm about the idea, the other person is likely to read that as permission to make a different choice.

A snare occurs in many relationships, but particularly in marriages, that O'Neill and O'Neill (1972) have called "the couple front." Essentially it involves a contract to do things together. In a marriage it may mean doing almost literally everything outside of work together. In a friendship it tends to be less overbearing. For example, it may mean attending a particular concert series or series of sporting events together, or being a regular bridge partner on Thursdays. If the couple front is tight and one person wants to go out to dinner, both must go or neither may go. One person or the other compromises. This is not altogether bad, of course. However, rather than compromise, it *is* possible for one person to go to dinner alone or to make arrangements to dine with a third person.

In couple fronts individuals ask the other to become all things to them, or at least more things than is realistic, and the unwritten contract is that each will invest most of his or her enjoying choices in the other. It is important that we all develop a wide enough range of relationships so that there are several persons with whom we can make a variety of enjoying choices.

When we make enjoying choices toward other people, we expect certain CREST responses more than others in response. Think about a particularly good friend of yours. Suppose that friend said to you: "Let's pretend we're two other people, maybe two famous people who would have known one another, or two characters from the same book. Who might we be and what would be exciting about being those people?"

Stop and think about that for a moment. What would you say to your friend?

Did you rush right on to read this next paragraph? Were you able to allow yourself to get into the spirit of such an activity? Did you resist making enjoying choices even in fantasy? Maybe that is a clue as to how you respond habitually to enjoying choice opportunities that come your way.

If your friend proposed that fantasy, you could make an OK choice from any of the CREST options. Caring: (Because you see the suggestion as unusual for your friend) "Are you feeling OK?" Ruling: "Wait a second, I'm trying to recall a name." Enjoying: "This should be fun." Sorrowing: "But if I couldn't be me I might not know you or any of my family." Thinking/working: "Let's see, I'm trying to decide whether it would be more fun to go back in history or pick a couple of people who are living today."

Clearly you could respond with any of the five choices, but generally speaking, another enjoying choice might be the most characteristic option, especially if you chose to appreciate your friend's suggestion. You could express your enjoying choice in a variety of ways: "I like games like this." "Gee, you have the best ideas." (Getting into the spirit of the activity) "I'd be like Huck Finn and you'd be Tom Sawyer (or a tomboy Becky Thatcher) and we'd never wear shoes; we'd chew tobacco and spit; we'd live on an island, and pole on down the Mississippi on a raft." That would tell your friend: "That's a major OK choice," and you would be making major OK choices by your response.

If for some reason you see the suggestion as OD, because of the timing or the work you have to do, for example, you might make one of a number of ruling choices. Two possible responses are: "Get serious." "We've got too much to do to get all tied up in an aimless game like that." Or, you might make a sorrowing choice: "Oh, Lord, I'm swamped! I can't get involved in that right now."

One reason we do not initiate often with enjoying choices, apart from the injunction against childishness, is that we fear ruling or sorrowing responses will be returned. A few "Get serious" or "I'm swamped" statements and we may put aside our own playfulness and follow the narrow, safer path. The problem is that we then like ourselves less and are less interesting to others.

I well recall my annoyance of a few years ago with a colleague. I came to resent his seriousness whenever we worked on a project together. Our interactions were not any fun—we made no enjoying choices with one another. After I had explored Choice Awareness for a time, it occurred to me that maybe I was mirroring his seriousness in my behavior whenever we got together, and I began to wonder whether or not I was the problem in the relationship rather than he. I planned ahead for my next encounter and went into his office with an anecdote to tell, and then I asked him about his wife. He actually smiled more than once, and we had a very pleasant interaction. I realized that the person I was resenting was me. I had met the enemy and "he is us." My colleague's behavior was not the issue. What I did not like was that I ceased letting myself be me when I crossed his threshold. That experience helped convince me that the important thing is for me to make my own choices—especially enjoying choices—and not merely reflect the choices of the others about me.

Enjoying choices may be rejected by others because they are upset about something, or because their self-images require continued solemnity. In the latter instance, making further enjoying choices is not likely to have a positive effect. Instead of letting others' expectations of our behaviors control us, however, it would better for us to be who we are, or become who we can become, and enter into life more fully through our enjoying choices. Perhaps in the long run others around us will come to mirror our behaviors and make more enjoying choices around us. In any event we will be true to ourselves.

It is vital for us to make self-enjoying choices. No one can enjoy life for us. If we are going to get that job done, we have to do it ourselves. Other people *can* make the caring choices for us that we do not make for ourselves. Other people *will* make the ruling choices for us that we do not make for ourselves. But other people cannot and will not make the enjoying choices that we do not make for ourselves. They just will not get made.

Some years ago Ann Landers reported in her column on some research into the amount of communication between married couples. Birdwhistle, the researcher, placed voice-activated tape recorders throughout the homes of a number of volunteer couples, and in their cars, and determined that couples who had been married for several years and who saw their marriages as positive, engaged in an average of twenty-five to thirty minutes of dialogue *per week!* A Newsweek (1990) brief supported that data, reporting that spouses converse four minutes a day and that parents converse only a half minute a day with their children. The messages we send one another about enjoying choices belonging to children clearly have lifelong impact—but we proved most inadequate models for them to imitate.

Our everyday enjoying choices can include such small, but important, items as sharing with others the excitement of our day, paying small compliments, thanking others for the tasks they complete, and verbalizing our positive feelings for them. Such choices are likely to be the best kinds of choices for extending and deepening the level of communication we have with all those whose lives we touch—including spouses.

You, I, your clients, all of us, have grown up believing that enjoying involves events, and that spontaneous, fun-filled actions belong to children. We need to change those expectations. We may hope that in another life we will have time to float among clouds, to play a harp, and to give up labor in favor of ethereal communing with God. But we have a world here we are part of that is crying out for smiles and laughter and compliments and communication. It is important that we learn not to rely on such OD enjoying choices as biting humor and sarcasm in our relationships. It is even more important for us to develop a repertoire and acquire skill in using the kind of warm, OK enjoying choices we want to have come our way.

SELF-EXAMINATION—JOURNAL ENTRY: Think for a few minutes, then discuss in your journal ways in which you can make more effective enjoying choices for yourself and with others. Head your entry MORE EFFECTIVE ENJOYING CHOICES FOR ME.

We encourage you to share these ideas with your clients, inviting their reactions and helping them see the importance of making more effective enjoying choices in their significant relationships and for themselves. Most clients need to be helped to consider how they can make more OK enjoying choices for themselves and with others if they are to achieve effective interpersonal relationships and inner well-being.

COUNSELING APPLICATION—JOURNAL ENTRY: Discuss what you can do in counseling that would help your clients make enjoying choices that might improve their relationships and their sense of inner well-being. Suggestion: head your entry MORE EFFECTIVE CLIENT ENJOYING CHOICES.

Enjoying Choices

In Choice Awareness theory enjoying choices are seen as the actions and words through which we express our positive feelings. We have learned the patterns and the limitations we put on those choices over our life span; as a result we may remain tied unnecessarily to old injunctions and to stereotypical enjoying choices. Many clients in counseling need to understand better their own patterns of enjoying choices, they need to learn when and how to make more effective enjoying choices, and they need to allow themselves to live their lives more fully and to achieve a greater sense of inner well-being, of spa, through their enjoying choices.

References

Nelson, R. C. (1977). *Choosing: A better way to live.* North Palm Beach, FL: GuideLines Press.

Newsweek. (March 26, 1990). Tempus fugit. P. 8.

O'Neill, N. & O'Neill, G. (1972). *Open marriage.* New York: Avon.

Chapter 11

Enjoying Choices: Application

Enjoying Choices and Your Clients

Relatively few of your clients' concerns relate directly to enjoying choices, yet underlying the complaints of those who feel powerless, uncared for, unaccountably depressed, or painted into some kind of a corner, is a joylessness about life that is often debilitating. Most of your clients believe there is little that is positive in their lives, but the concerns they express relate more often to gaining relief from the negatives. You can contribute significantly to the lives of many of your clients if you explore with them with whom they might make more enjoying choices, and how they might become more responsive to the enjoying choices of others.

In enjoying choices lies the greatest potential for helping clients feel good about themselves and others, which in turn leads to a sense of inner well-being—of spa. It is satisfying and meaningful to make or receive caring choices when there is a need or to send or receive OK ruling choices that contribute to a relationship, and sorrowing and thinking/working choices can make important contributions to well-being. However, the joy of life is not found in the absence of pain, it comes through positive action—through enjoying choices.

The downward-turning spiral of mental health that is experienced by many of your clients can be reversed more effectively through their own enjoying choices and the enjoying choices of others than through any or all of the other CREST choices. Many of your clients find it difficult to envision consistently-positive life experiences as being possible for them. If they have encountered relatively few enjoying choices in their lives, it is a challenge to you as a counselor to help them turn that around, and the longer they have lived and the less they have felt joy, the greater is the challenge.

Once again, enjoying choices *are* choices, thus they are accessible to the individual. The habit of not expecting to feel deep positives—

which is often armor against disappointment—may be strong, but the movement toward more positive experiences is still possible. Furthermore, even those people for whom enjoying choices seem inaccessible are likely to have had experiences, perhaps long forgotten, that they can build upon and thereby enlarge their repertoire of enjoying choices.

People who are immersed in hurtful relationships, or who are facing some other problem, may see joy and enjoying choices as beyond their reach, but in their childhood, and in some of their adult experiences, they have had experiences and relationships they may be able to reconstruct in some way.

The excitement of a fast bicycle ride.

The good tiredness after physical exertion.

The pleasure of a task well done.

The recall of a magnificent scene.

The smell of new-mown grass.

The sounds of birds in the spring.

A hug shared with a friend.

The warmth of an intimate relationship.

Staying up late into the night discussing dreams and plans.

A simple thank you.

The words, "Well done," or "I like you."

Giving or receiving a compliment.

All of us have had experiences like those and others that are pleasurable. As a result of those experiences, we have a repertoire of enjoying choices we can call on once we decide it would be beneficial for us to do so. Even if some of your clients have had few positive models for making OK enjoying choices, even if they are not responded to well by some of the people who are important in their lives, they still possess skills in making enjoying choices.

If your clients have those skills, then why are they not more fun-loving and involved with life? As we have suggested, it seems likely that many counseling clients have given up these skills for the seriousness of adulthood. An important aspect of inner well-being for many clients is learning once again to make effective, OK enjoying choices both for themselves and with others.

CONSIDER THE FOLLOWING:

Bradley came to counseling somewhat under protest, believing that needing counseling was an admission of weakness. He had tried prescription medicine for his lower back pain and his high blood pressure, but his doctors assured him that it was his life style that was the problem. He had destroyed his first marriage and his relationships with his children through his workaholic behavior, and he could see that he was in the process of destroying his second marriage, along with his health. His counselor helped him understand that he had substituted the pleasure of success in his work for all other pleasures, but at great personal cost. It took him awhile to begin to accept the reality that the key to his survival might well be giving himself permission to do something he had never allowed himself: enjoy life, smell the flowers, take pleasure in the moment. He saw himself as a carbon copy of his parents who were always busy at some task—too busy to smile. Ultimately he realized that he was still seeking their approval through keeping his proverbial nose to the proverbial grindstone, and he speculated that his health problems were likely to be previews of the health problems suffered by his parents. It seemed somewhat ludicrous to Bradley to have to take lessons in having fun and in responding more positively toward life, but gradually he accepted his need to do so. The spa assignments he received, and those he ultimately gave himself, included such actions as: List three ways in which you spend some time "smelling the flowers" each day for the next week. He had to work at accepting and completing such activities at first, but he gradually came to enjoy them, and eventually he was able to find greater joy in his life without having assignments. Over several months he was able to lower his blood pressure considerably, and he found that his back pain rarely bothered him anymore.

Bradley, and many other clients in counseling, learn narrow patterns of behavior that may serve them reasonably well for a time, but they find that problems eventually arise if they relegate enjoying choices to a minor role. For many, the best answer to such problems is regenerating dormant patterns and learning new enjoying choice patterns.

We have noted that in our society we emphasize a connection between youth and enjoying choices. Young people and adults, males and females, and people in all walks of life need permission to make enjoying choices both for themselves and with others. There are too few people of either sex or of any age or walk of life who provide good models of enjoying choices for others. Since the models are insufficient or inadequate, the outcome is that people learn to use OD patterns of choices or they follow stereotypical enjoying choice patterns.

When people, regardless of age, stifle their desires to make enjoying choices, adverse outcomes occur in at least three areas. (1) They develop poor habit patterns for their relationships. The most satisfying relationships are those in which each person contributes choices to the relationship from each of the five CREST options. Although people do not think in those terms, they feel cheated when a relationship omits any of the five choices, and this is especially true if the missing choice is enjoying. (2) They set themselves up for relationships that lack either warmth or depth. They may communicate in interesting ways during the shakedown phase of their relationships as they tell their stories, and they may be able to talk well, even excitedly, concerning their profession or a hobby or a special interest of theirs. However, they are likely to run out of things to say, and perhaps feel the need to move on to other relationships when their special topics have been exhausted. (3) They set themselves up to feel like failures. At least from time to time all people need to feel true joy in living. When individuals have inadequately practiced the skills of enjoying, they are likely to come to a time when they feel that life is passing them by. That is, unless they come to alter their pattern of choices.

Recently, I was at an awards ceremony at Purdue University and directly in my line of vision were a young man and his father. For part of the time the student, a leader in that honorary society, held the podium and distributed some of the awards. He spoke well and was well received by the audience, which included many of his peers. When he returned to the table nearby after his part of the program was over, I expected his father to respond enthusiastically, since I was certain I would have had I been in his place. "Dad" did not even turn his head. Later in the program the student was called back to the podium to receive a highly-valued scholarship for graduate school that obviously came as a surprise to him. I found myself thinking that surely his father would make some kind of acknowledgement of *that* special honor. "Dad" made some kind of sound as his son sat down, more like clearing his throat than anything else, and turned his head slightly in his son's direction. He did not make eye contact and his son saw more of his back than his face as he returned to the table. I found myself thinking that it was remarkable the son was doing anything of consequence since he seemed to receive so little reinforcement from his father. I wondered if the experience might be repeated twenty-five or thirty years from now as the son of the son one day appears on a similar program.

All people need their own permission to make enjoying choices in their own lives and with their relatives and friends. Choice Awareness theory suggests that enjoying is one of five basic choices available to us, and that enjoying choices can be the most important of those choices in many relationships. To place severe limitations on the expression of that option, to restrict enjoying choices to events, or to give them over to children, is to severely limit one of the five basic options for interacting successfully in the world in which we find ourselves. Young people seem to feel the obligation to make enjoying choices, and they do so often in ways that are not personally relevant or socially acceptable. Drinking to get drunk, or getting high on some other substance, are avenues they may take because they lack more positive models. Adults shun enjoying choices, limiting themselves to structured activities and events, even when they might benefit greatly by allowing themselves to become involved in more lighthearted, positive experiences. Inner well-being for you, for me, and for clients requires that we give ourselves permission to make OK enjoying choices for ourselves and with others.

SELF-EXAMINATION—JOURNAL ENTRY: Take a few minutes, preferably at least five, and discuss the extent to which you believe you limit yourself in age-, sex-, and/or role-stereotypical ways in the enjoying choices you make—for yourself and with others. Discuss the extent to which you believe movement toward a more extensive pattern of enjoying choices would benefit you in your personal life. Suggestion: head your entry STEREOTYPING AND MY ENJOYING CHOICES.

We encourage you to share these ideas with your clients, inviting their reactions and helping them see that they can make enjoying choices in ways that go beyond age-, sex-, and role-stereotypes. Many clients can benefit by appraisal and a shift in the pattern of enjoying choices they make for themselves and with others.

When you encourage your clients to make more effective, more OK, enjoying choices with others, you are helping them act on the principle of social-interest—and often as not they are serving their own self-interest as well. When they enter into life enthusiastically and fully, their behaviors contribute positively to their relationships and help them achieve a sense of spa within themselves.

Relaxation and Meditation

All counseling systems are designed in some way to help clients feel better about themselves and to make more enjoying choices in their lives, but no true system of counseling has focused directly or primarily on enjoying choices. In recent years, however, several techniques that essentially involve enjoying choices have been incorporated in various counseling approaches, and added to the repertoire of counselors. Relaxation training, meditation, positive addiction, exercise processes, biofeedback, laughter, and other enjoying choices are among these various techniques. The fundamental goals of each of these techniques are: (1) to help clients take direct control over at least a part of their lives while providing them with a model for doing so in other areas of living, (2) to make a positive impact on a client concern, and (3) to provide clients with positive experiences, which we view as enjoying choices. In this section we explore briefly the techniques of relaxation and meditation.

Relaxation training. The fundamental design of relaxation training is that of encouraging clients to learn systematically the process of *relaxing all major body muscle groups.* To learn the process of relaxation, the individual is taken through muscle groups in the body one at a time, perhaps starting with the hands and arms, then the feet and legs, the facial muscles and scalp, the neck and shoulders, the abdomen and stomach. Each muscle group is tensed in turn one or more times, then relaxed. Instructions are given in a soothing, reassuring voice tone and the individual either directly or indirectly is helped to clear other thoughts away. Tensing-relaxing actions with the eyes closed tend almost immediately to produce Alpha waves in the brain; these waves are characteristic of states of reduced stress. The mind and the body are both focused directly on the process of relaxation.

An important element of the relaxation training process, one that deserves specific attention, is the matter of *deep breathing*. Deep-breathing exercises may be done in conjunction with other relaxation training activities, or by themselves. The technique is somewhat similar to other relaxation training activities. The individual breathes deeply, briefly holds the breath, exhales slowly, then pushes a bit more when the lungs seem empty. This process is repeated numerous times, with the outcome being an apparent increase in the person's capacity for intake of air. This deeper intake of oxygen is beneficial since most people underuse their lung capacity, and like any other set of muscles, the lungs need exercise. Further, the increased intake of oxygen is beneficial for the entire cardiovascular system.

Once individuals have learned to relax all muscle groups, and to use deep breathing as a relaxation technique, their attention is often focused on *relaxing particular muscle groups* that bear the brunt of the stress they feel. Those who have lower back pain, headaches, or stiff necks, for example, are helped to concentrate on combating those problems through exercises related to those areas.

CONSIDER THE FOLLOWING:

Rowanda was enjoying her new job and its responsibilities as the first woman executive in her firm. She commented to her husband that she felt as if she were carrying the world of women on her back, however, and that on her level of success depended the fate of women executives in her company for the foreseeable future. Not surprisingly with such a load of responsibility, Rowanda began to develop stiffness in her shoulders. Once she determined that no medical problems existed, she sought the assistance of a counselor who helped her through relaxation training. She quickly mastered the skills she needed and came to realize that her shoulder stiffness was a good barometer of the tension she was feeling, as well as a signal for her to take time to unwind. A brief break and a few moments of back, shoulder, and neck tensing and relaxing and she was often able to take a fresh approach to the problems she was facing.

Relaxation training helps clients pay attention to their bodies, relax and, breathe more fully. Choice Awareness theory suggests that encouraging clients to take time out for such purposes is appropriate, that most clients need help in learning the processes of relaxation, and that clients often signal their need for assistance in this area, as Rowanda did, by using a physical simile. Rowanda's statement was, "I've got the weight of the world on my shoulders."

WARNING. Any physical symptom needs to be checked out by a physician to determine whether it is signaling a physiological problem, and even clients who assure you "the doctor says there's nothing wrong with me" should be questioned concerning the recency and depth of the exploration—or the physician should be contacted directly. In any case, clients should be cautioned to tense their muscles and expand their lungs only to the point that feels comfortable for them.

Relaxation processes are often combined with mind-clearing actions or activities involving fantasy. The separation is arbitrary, but we have incorporated these actions in the following discussion on meditation. The important consideration in both relaxation and meditation is that individuals learn to make more positive self-enjoying choices through their thoughts and their actions.

Meditation. The fundamental design of meditation is that of encouraging clients to focus their thoughts or clear their minds of mental images in ways that produce relief from bodily tension and stress. We are so accustomed to our minds being occupied and our thoughts flitting from one matter to another that it can be a real challenge either to focus thoughts or clear the mind of them.

In *meditation involving fantasy,* clients are encouraged to focus thoughts and recall images that are basically positive, and that produce feelings of relaxation. Individuals may be taken step-by-step through a process of guided imagery, perhaps on a magic carpet. Over many minutes they hear a soothing voice invite them to close their eyes and shut out all distractions, and that voice continues by describing the process of getting on a magic carpet, flying over the present setting, rolling all cares in a ball and tossing them over the side, gently flying through the clouds, arriving at a seashore or a beautiful mountain valley, cavorting and gamboling in that environment, enjoying the company of people who are really special, gaining a sense of peace and relaxation, and, ultimately, returning to the present time and place on the magic carpet, at ease with the world.

Meditation lifts individuals out of circumstances that may be troubling them and helps them move away from present realities so that they are able to gain perspective and think coolly about their actions. Fantasy, deep breathing, and relaxation, taken together, provide a model of enjoying choices.

One of the elements of meditation that is often thought of as crucial is the use of a *mantra,* which actually means a *hymn* or *calming sound.* The individual clears away other thoughts and focuses on repeating quietly or internally, and slowly, a word, usually of one syllable, that does not act as a distractor. Appropriate words in English, or constructed syllables, might include "one," "peace," "zum," and "O." The term mantra is foreign, and the "words" used may also sound foreign, "om," for example. As a consequence many people see meditation as shrouded in mystery, so they reject it. The objective is simple, however, to encourage the development of inner peace, and the mantra is a device that permits the individual to clear away distracting thoughts that block that peace.

Transcendental Meditation, or TM, is a specific form of meditation that was brought to the west by Maharishi Mahesh Yogi, who has refined the process and merchandised it in ways that enhance its mystique through secret mantras and specially trained TM instructors. However, TM advertisements make it clear that TM is a natural and simple process that takes only twenty minutes to learn because it is an essential aspect of the self.

Individuals can spend enormous amounts of money and time visiting the Far East and learning meditation processes and yogi, or they can be helped through far simpler processes that are more congruent with western philosophy, to clear away disturbing thoughts and learn to focus on pleasant and peaceful scenes. Whatever the form of meditation, *the objectives are: relaxation, concentration*—as on a mantra—and *contemplation*—perhaps through viewing or imagining a picture, a scene, a statue of a religious figure, or through repeating and reflecting upon religious passages or prayers.

CONSIDER THE FOLLOWING:

Roger was a successful businessman who felt a mild sense of stress resulting from his highly active life style. In many ways he saw no need for change, yet he envied the inner peace a colleague had achieved through meditation. Rather than expend many dollars on the process, Roger read extensively on the topic of meditation, chose his own simple mantra— "ah"—and decided to spend twenty minutes twice a day clearing his mind of distractions, taking a relaxed body position, and experiencing peace in his own way. He has been genuinely gratified with the sense of inner well-being meditation has helped him achieve.

Three of the primary purposes of meditation—peace, enlightenment, and spiritual growth—are unlikely to be obtained while the mind is in turmoil and the body is poised for action. Roger learned to relax his active mind and body and achieve peace. He commented, "Sometimes I'm sure I experience enlightenment, to the extent that I know what that means, and maybe some day I'll even achieve a sense of spiritual growth—that's exciting to contemplate. But whether I do or not, I know I'd never have achieved those objectives if I'd continued in my frantic way with my mind never at ease." Roger structured for himself *the four basic elements of meditation: a quiet environment*—so that he might shut out external distractions, *an object to dwell upon* (his mantra)—to clear his mind of internal distractions, *a positive attitude*, and *a comfortable position*—so that he might maintain concentration.

LeShan stated,

We meditate to find, to recover, to come back to something of ourselves we once dimly and unknowingly had and have lost without knowing what it was or where or when we lost it. We may call it access to more of our human potential or being closer to ourselves and to reality, or to more of our capacity for love and zest and enthusiasm, or our knowledge that we are a part of the universe and can never be alienated or separated from it, or our ability to see and function in reality more effectively (LeShan 1974, p. 4).

Meditation that helps people achieve some measure of any of those objectives is well worth the time expended.

One aid to meditation and relaxation, and also to biofeedback, which is discussed later, is *the use of tapes*. Tapes designed for meditation generally use simple musical strains, melodic but unfamiliar, that are designed to create a positive environment for meditation while screening out distracting sounds. Familiar music is not used because it invites too many associations and may not, as a consequence, assist in clearing the mind. As an alternative to music, some relaxation tapes have seaside, waterfall, or forest sounds. Tapes designed for relaxation, on the other hand, provide instruction in the process of relaxation. Generally a speaker with a pleasant, soothing voice, leads one through a specific relaxation regimen. While the content of these two aids differs greatly, each is useful in facilitating the process involved. The client may purchase commercial tapes. You may, as counselor, record material you believe would be suitable for the client, or the client may record suitable material.

Choice Awareness theory supports the idea of meditation as a process that allows individuals to clear their minds and spend time focusing on peaceful images. An attitude that Helleberg (1980) suggested may be useful in enabling clients to see that they have available a fundamental choice in relation to their state of mind: "So you've got a choice. You can either say, 'I can't relax because I'm so upset,' or you can flip that over and say, 'I can't be upset because I'm so relaxed.' You must consciously choose the second way or the first will win by default." Helleberg continued by suggesting that regular meditation, at least twice a day, ". . . is the only way I know to reverse the spiral" (Helleberg, 1980, p. 71-72).

Relaxation and contemplation are choices that are consistent with inner well-being and spa, key dimensions of Choice Awareness. Counselors need not fear the mystique of meditation. Nothing could be more appropriate than that the individual who feels stress be encouraged to find ways to relieve that stress. A mind at peace is an appropriate end in itself; and a mind that at times achieves that state may be more able to resolve its problems as well. As a counselor you are encouraged to facilitate the process of achieving peace of mind in your clients through both relaxation and meditation.

SELF-EXAMINATION—JOURNAL ENTRY: Take a few minutes, preferably at least five, and discuss the extent to which you engage in relaxation and meditation processes, and the extent to which you believe in the efficacy of these processes for yourself. If appropriate, design a relaxation or meditation regimen and commit yourself to a schedule for your regimen. Suggestion: head your entry RELAXATION FOR ME.

We encourage you to share these ideas with your clients, inviting their reactions and helping them see that relaxation and meditation may help them achieve some of their most important personal goals. Most clients can benefit by the use of these processes.

COUNSELING APPLICATION—JOURNAL ENTRY: Discuss the extent to which you believe it is important for you to enable your clients to engage in relaxation and/or meditation. Consider with at least one specific or hypothetical client how you might work with that person in designing and evaluating a relaxation or meditation process. Suggestion: head your entry RELAXATION FOR MY CLIENTS.

Activity Processes

Meditation and relaxation are at one end of the active-passive continuum of techniques designed to help clients take direct control of their lives through enjoying choices. Moving toward the other end of the continuum are such varied approaches as biofeedback, positive addiction, laughter, exercise, and other enjoying choices. The potential for growth in these activity processes is often overlooked by counselors, but since Choice Awareness is a systematic, eclectic theory, we explore each of these approaches here in brief.

Exercise processes. Dusek-Girdano (1979) made a strong case that the body gears up for physical activity whenever stress comes its way, and that the stress response is intended to end in physical activity. While we do not undertake here to explore the physiology of the stress response in any depth, the following quote builds the case for physical activity for all of us, but particularly when we have encountered stress.

> The outpouring of sugar and fats into the blood are (sic) meant to feed the muscles and the brain so that they might contend actively with the stressor which has provoked the system. The dilation of pupils occurs to give better visual acuity, to take in apparent threats visually. The increased heart and respiration rates are to pump blood and oxygen to active muscles and stimulated control centers in the brain. This is not a time to sit and feel all of these sensations tearing away at the body's systems and eroding good health. This is the time to *move*, to use up the body's products, to relieve the body of the destructive forces of stress on a sedentary system (Dusek-Girdano, 1979, p. 222).

The stress response in human beings helped early people to respond effectively to the very real dangers they faced. We have redesigned our world in large measure so that we encounter few physical threats, and we let our minds do much of our work for us. The body was designed to encounter physical dangers and meet challenges, then return to a state of equilibrium, having expended the energy necessary to meet the emergency. In redesigning our world we have substituted stress in the psychological realm for that in the physical realm. The body responds to psychological stress and physical stress in similar ways. The difference is that in the event of physical stress we expend physical energy to meet the challenge, while in the event of psychological stress we often emphasize maintaining control. The adrenalin and other physiological products we generate are not dissipated, and many are toxic or otherwise harmful unless absorbed by the body as a result of action.

We do not encounter the wild animals of the forest on a daily basis, either pursuing or being pursued by them—thereby gaining exercise and expending energy as nature intended, and most of us do not engage in vigorous physical activity on a daily basis in farming or other activities that are a part of our employment. The best substitute for most of us is a regimen of regular exercise that both dissipates the energy required to meet the stresses of living and enhances our sense of well-being.

A consensus has formed that suggests it is best for us to engage in regular, vigorous physical activity that stimulates the entire cardiovascular system, including the heart and lungs, for at least twenty minutes per day, from three to five days per week. And, as might be expected, recent information has suggested that *some* exercise is clearly better than *none*. Many individuals avoid energetic exercise because of their fear of heart attacks, not realizing that they may be increasing the odds of just such a problem. The heart is a muscle, and like other muscles it becomes stronger when it is used appropriately. Those who engage in regular exercise find that the strength of the heart increases, with the outcome being that it takes fewer beats to supply the body with blood, and the heart gets more rest and relaxation time. The lungs act in a similar manner. Most of us underuse the capacity of our lungs, but with exercise the respiratory system increases its capacity to take in air and exchange oxygen for carbon dioxide in the capillaries. This greater efficiency also carries over into the resting state.

Before engaging in vigorous physical activity of any kind, those of us who have lived sedentary lives should seek the advice of a physician to determine whether such a regimen would be advisable, and in any case, we should move cautiously and gradually toward our exercise goal. It should be noted that the muscles involved require both warm-up and cool-down time; that is, gradual increase in speed and intensity of movement to a peak level which is then sustained, then gradual decrease in speed and intensity of movement over several minutes—rather than a sudden cessation of activity.

Many Americans in recent years have become jogging or running enthusiasts, while others have found those activities to be unsatisfying or have experienced a variety of ailments that may be attributed to stress on the body from them. Those who enjoy such activities and can engage in them without harm to knees or ankles should be encouraged to continue. For others a variety of alternative activities can accomplish the same goals, though not necessarily in the same amount of time. Activities that may serve many other individuals are listed below, along with a multiplier that indicates how much more time might be needed to equal running as an exercise regimen. These figures are estimates that should be adjusted if the activity level is particularly vigorous or languid, and other activities may be compared to these for an approximation of the time needed to equal the exercise from running.

Cross country skiing x 1 (equal to running)

Swimming, bicycling, fast walking and aerobics x 1 ¹/₂ (once and a half as much time needed)

Calisthenics, weight lifting, golf (walking), other recreational sports x 2

Housework and light physical work x 2 1/2 to 3 (Adapted from Girdano & Everly, 1979).

CONSIDER THE FOLLOWING:

Mrs. Barlow was concerned that her teen-aged daughter had become rather listless and uninvolved. A physical examination turned up no problems, but the physician supported Mrs. Barlow's suggestion that Jody talk to her school counselor. Fortunately for Jody, Mr. Peters, the counselor for the ninth grade, was something of an exercise enthusiast. He listened and explored and ultimately concluded that the problem was one of insufficient activity. Jody had been active in sports throughout her elementary and middle school years, but when she entered the four-year high school, she was soon convinced that there was no place for her on the school volleyball or basketball teams, and she did not view herself as "the cheerleader type." As a result she had not developed any alternative exercise program. At Mrs. Barlow's suggestion Jody started a gym and swim program, and she soon came to realize that was exactly what she needed. The void left by her withdrawal from athletics was now filled, and a sense of involvement and self-acceptance began to replace her listlessness and self-criticism.

While some counselors may not see a regular pattern of exercise as a prescription they are comfortable in offering, it is likely that many counseling clients are adversely affected by their sedentary existence. We should not undervalue the high that can come from a vigorous use of muscles and the subsequent and gradual cooling-off period. When we do not pay attention to our physical nature, we receive a variety of physical and psychological signals that tell us we should refocus.

What are the advantages and disadvantages of competition or self-competition in an exercise process? If the objective is to exercise the body as a means of relieving stress, then competition, whether with another person or with self, is likely to be counterproductive. When the mind is wrought up over beating a rival, running faster or farther, or getting a better score, the amount of stress may be increased rather than decreased. For most people, individual activities such as walking or bicycling or running, if they are engaged in without the need to go farther or faster or longer, have greater benefits in creating peace of mind and inner well-being than any amount of competitive activity. Self-criticism, an emphasis on winning, and frustration when losing, characterize most competitive sports and many individual activities. Girdano and Everly (1979) referred to the "terrible athlete, therefore terrible person" syndrome. Unless activities are engaged in non-critically, because they feel good, and because the body needs them, more, rather than less, stress, and a diminished, rather than an increased, sense of inner well-being, may result.

The relaxation that follows exercise, and even the exercise itself, should ultimately bring a greater sense of peace and a lower level of stress to the individual. Persons who engage in regular exercise may quickly sense that they are able to react more appropriately to whatever comes along. People seek peace of mind in many ways, including counseling; too few see that exercise may be essential to experiencing that peace. Counselors need to be alert to the needs of their clients to alleviate their stresses and to attain a state of inner well-being—of spa—through exercise.

Biofeedback. When we become frightened, tense, upset, angry, or have any other strong feeling, our bodies react in ways that are designed to take care of us. Our heart rate speeds up to the point where we may feel its beat thumping in our chest. Our hands may begin to sweat or turn cold and our skin may either flush or the color may drain away. The pupils of our eyes dilate to take in the stimulus. Our mouths may become dry or salivation may increase. Muscles may tense, the stomach may appear to stop its action, we may feel nauseated, and our breathing rate may increase. If we are able to act vigorously on the danger or problem, our bodies quickly dissipate the energy that has been generated. If we cannot or do not act strongly, the energy remains to be dissipated over time, and the effects on the body have been negative.

The source of the problem may be clear—a sound in the basement, or a critical comment from a supervisor, or it may be subtle—a caustic comment that might have been intended as humor, or a vague threat to job security. Whether the source is clear or not, the bodily changes are similar. Those bodily changes *are* biofeedback; *biofeedback equals signals of stress from the body.*

Biofeedback has always been available to us. In recent years, however, technological advances have allowed us to measure small changes in bodily processes, and we are able to verify in greater detail what the body has been telling us all along in a rather gross way. An electrical instrument can measure heart rate, for example, and transform the signal instantly into light or sound, so that we are able to interpret the information easily, beyond our usual level of awareness. In a real sense biofeedback devices may be seen as educational tools that provide information about performance in a way that is analogous to the feedback of a bathroom scale.

Our bodies are sending signals to us all the time. We do not pay attention to most signals because we are busily engaged in coping with environmental stimuli. Biofeedback mechanisms can help us monitor those signals and increase our awareness of ourselves. Even more important they can help us gain in self-control .

Biofeedback has been used to help individuals monitor and control heart rate, blood pressure, brain waves, and muscular activity. As with meditation and many other phenomena that were not part of our heritage, it may seem as though biofeedback is mysterious and magical, in part because complex electronic instruments are used. The only magic is that technology has advanced to the point at which the equipment used can let us know when we are feeling stress, and how much. The consequence is that we are then able to send more tranquil, relaxing messages to the brain, which in turn relays those messages to the appropriate parts of the body. Ultimately we learn to become more tranquil persons, more self-aware, more in control. We learn how to bring to awareness clues we might otherwise have ignored. The equipment sensitizes us to messages the body has been sending us all along.

Every change that occurs in our bodies involves a physical release of energy that is signaled through changes in body chemistry (hormones, electrolytes, metabolizes, and so forth), electrical impulses, and physical movements of cell structure (in the case of muscles—which result in friction and the release of heat). When individuals are faced with stressful situations involving fears and worries, for example, their bodies, primarily their autonomic nervous systems, react in a number of ways to encounter those situations. Through biofeedback individuals are enabled to turn the process around. They learn that they can develop more tranquil states of mind that in turn reduce the activity of the autonomic nervous system. The final link is made when individuals learn to monitor their own signs of stress and produce changes, whether measured or unmeasured, that bring them greater tranquility in the face of stress.

Some of the gains that occur as a result of biofeedback come simply from the attention of the individual being diverted from the stressor to the production of a more relaxed state of mind, thus defusing the effect of the stressor. Other gains occur because the individual makes more effective choices in coping with stress. As Girdano and Everly (1979) suggested, biofeedback is noninvasive and has almost no side effects. It allows the body to heal itself, to correct chemical or electrical imbalance, simply by giving the individual information about the imbalance and about the success of the action the individual takes to correct the imbalance.

CONSIDER THE FOLLOWING:

Adam was a university student in a beginning class in psychology in which one requirement was participating in one or more of several research studies. He volunteered for a study on biofeedback because it sounded most interesting and because he wondered if it might help relieve his feelings of anxiety about his studies, his career, and his response to university life in general. The experiment involved the use of the electromyograph or EMG, which measures muscular contractions. He found it fascinating to learn that changes measured by the EMG were almost as great when he thought through how he might respond to a variety of stimuli as when he acted on the stimuli directly. In the process of learning to relax and screen out anxiety-producing thoughts Adam learned about the theory of Edmund Jacobson: that anxiety and muscle relaxation are incompatible, and that an effective way of reducing anxiety is to reduce muscle tension. Adam proved to be an excellent student of relaxation, which helped him greatly to gain a sense of internal peace; and he appreciated learning to control and focus his thoughts on his studies for time intervals that continued to increased in length.

Although the situation is changing, much of the equipment for use in biofeedback is quite expensive, much of the inexpensive equipment is less than precise, and any good equipment is likely to require extensive training in its use. As a consequence, we are not suggesting that you as a counselor obtain biofeedback equipment and training. What we are suggesting is that you should become alert to the likelihood that some clients may benefit greatly from learning to control the bodily systems that feed back signals of stress to them. If your informal efforts with your clients in the direction of relaxation, meditation, exercise, or other approaches assist them to change their choices and combat their stresses more adequately, fine. If not, it would be well for you to refer your clients to those agencies in your vicinity that offer reliable professional resources for biofeedback training. You should expect to continue to work on a cooperative basis with at least some of the clients whom you refer for assistance through biofeedback.

Choice Awareness theory supports the use of biofeedback and training as educational tools that can enhance the learning of self-control and enable clients to make better choices in response to the stresses of life. You need to be open to the potential for your clients to gain inner well-being— to make enjoying choices—through a variety of approaches, including biofeedback.

Positive addiction. William Glasser (1976) suggested yet another realm in which clients might attain enjoying choices; he called for positive addictions for all of us. Essentially, he said we all need to choose an area for growth that is important to us in itself and that can help us for the rest of our lives. He argued that clients can overcome weaknesses, inadequacies, depression, and other physical and psychological problems by becoming involved in, and addicted to, a positive activity. Two of the most common and successful activities he cited are running and meditation, but he listed a great many other possibilities including: baths, bird watching, chanting, composing, diary-keeping, exercising, gardening, hiking, knitting, needlepoint, religious faith, sewing, singing, weight lifting, and yoga.

For the positive addiction to be of greatest benefit, Glasser suggested it should be engaged in until an addictive state is achieved, that is, until discomfort is experienced if the activity is omitted. He offered six criteria for positive addictions: (1) the activity must be something noncompetitive that the person chooses to do and that can be done about an hour each day; (2) the activity must ultimately be done with a minimum of mental effort; (3) the activity may be done with others, but preferably alone, so that it is not necessary to depend on others; (4) the activity is seen to have physical, mental, or spiritual value to the individual; (5) the activity is seen by the individual as contributing to his or her personal improvement; and (6) the activity is engaged in without self-criticism—the individual must feel self-acceptance while it is being done.

Glasser cautioned that positive addiction must be a personal strategy; that is, the activity must be chosen and engaged in because the individual wishes to do it, not because it is promoted by the counselor or anyone else. That caution should be observed. At the same time it seems most appropriate for the counselor to encourage clients who lack a sense of direction, or who need to develop an area of personal growth or a feeling of self-acceptance, to consider whether a positive addiction might be of personal benefit.

CONSIDER THE FOLLOWING:

Shirley, a bright twelve-year-old, was encouraged to seek counseling following the death of her twin sister in an auto-mobile accident. Her counselor believed that she was han-dling the tragedy quite reasonably, under the circumstances, but there seemed to be such a void in her life that Mrs. Jacobs eventually asked her if she would like to read a brief, adult book entitled, *Positive Addiction*. Shirley borrowed the book, intrigued that any addiction could be positive, and returned it the next week even more intrigued with the possibility that she might find an activity that required skill, and that she could engage in for the rest of her life. She cast about for a number of weeks and finally settled on embroidery. Once she mastered more of the basics it fit the criteria of a positive addiction for her. To her parents and her closest friends she was willing to say, without a trace of morbidity, "I do this because it keeps my hands busy, it gives me a chance to do something that's quiet, and it helps me feel close to Sally."

If television has helped us become a nation of passive people letting others make enjoying (and other) choices while we watch, the concept of positive addiction might help us become active once again, taking charge of our lives and finding things to do that have physical, mental, or spiritual value. It is in that spirit that we support the concept of positive addictions as a relevant part of counseling based on Choice Awareness theory. Glasser's book is brief and readable. As a counselor you might consider obtaining a few copies to use as reading material for clients. It seems likely that those who might benefit most from a positive addiction would readily see the potential for finding an activity that suits their needs and enables them to make more and better enjoying choices in their lives.

Laughter and other enjoying choices. In his book, *Anatomy of an Illness*, Norman Cousins (1979) argued the case for laughter as an antidote, or partial antidote, in many illnesses. Here we consider laughter as a model for many positive attitudes and actions, as did Cousins: ". . . I became convinced that creativity, the will to live, hope, faith, and love have biochemical significance and contribute strongly to healing and well-being. The positive emotions are life-giving expe-riences" (1979, p. 109). One strong, supportive justification Cousins cited appeared in Proverbs (17:22): "A merry heart does good like a medicine; but a broken spirit dries the bones."

Through laughter and other positive actions, endorphins, nature's own healing chemicals, are released in the body. Except in extraordinary circumstances involving illness, there are no negative side effects to laughter, or the will to live, or creativity, as Cousins contended; and to which we add listening to music, playing a musical instrument, singing, reading, and following most positive addictions, as suggested by Glasser (1976). By contrast it is clear that negative emotions, which result in stress responses in the body, have numerous side effects that are harmful to the individual's well-being.

Cousins faced a life-threatening illness and wanted to reduce his dependency on pain-killers and other medications that might in some ways be counterproductive. He decided he would become a significant participant in the process of getting well. He knew that pain could be affected by attitudes, and postulated that affirmative attitudes might enhance body chemistry, so he undertook a regimen of laughter as part of his treatment. He used *Candid Camera* episodes and Marx Brothers films as therapy. He reported that ten minutes of genuine belly laughter had an anesthetic effect and often resulted in at least two hours of pain-free sleep. (Since reading Cousins' conclusions, I have made the request that the Donald O'Connor mannequin-dancing sequence in *Singing in the Rain* be used as therapy for me, along with reading and light classical music, if I am ever severely ill.)

Cousins' actions, though admittedly unscientific, have been given support by many in the medical community, and assuredly been laughed at by others—though perhaps they gained therapeutically from the experience. Whether his conclusions can be proven beyond a shadow of a doubt, it seems to me, does not matter. What matters is the reality that we can bring far greater joy into our lives through making a wide range of enjoying choices, and we can encourage clients to do the same. It is likely to be far easier for us to stay well through positive experiences than to become well; and, as we have suggested, too many of us have yielded our rights to enjoying choices to children.

CONSIDER THE FOLLOWING:

Mark, a skilled tradesman, sought counseling because of his feelings of depression. "I'm facing my midlife crisis, I guess," he said to Mrs. Reynolds, a counselor in private practice. Mark's story was an old one. He had been encouraged by his parents to get a college degree, and had started at a state university because of his parents' encouragement. Lacking motivation of his own, he had failed miserably at his studies. Now, years later, he felt depressed and troubled and convinced that he had failed in his life. This, despite the fact that he and his wife still loved one another, despite the three delightful children they had raised, and despite the extensive church and community involvement he had achieved. At fifty-two he did not want to commit himself to obtaining a degree. As a matter of fact he was considering early retirement within five years to start a small business related to one of his hobbies, tying fishing flies. Over long hours of discussion with Mrs. Reynolds, Mark decided that what he was lacking in his life was joy and laughter on the one hand, and intellectual challenge on the other. His enjoyment of his children, which came in part from working with them in athletic and school-related activities, had faded. They had matured and gone away to school and jobs. At the same time, his need to be better informed, to be more widely read, had increased as he realized his children had surpassed him in educational attainment. One result of counseling was that Mark dusted off an old hobby of his—magic—spiced it with humor since some of his tricks never seemed to come off, and began to experience great joy in entertaining in schools, hospitals, and nursing and retirement homes. To take care of his other need, he wrote to each of his children and asked them to recommend books for him to read that they might then discuss. He told them he had let his brain get rusty and that he wanted to grow along with them. It gave him great satisfaction to write long letters and mail tapes to his children with his reactions to literature and other challenging reading they suggested for him. In a comparatively short time he believed he had successfully bridged the gap he had allowed to grow between himself and his children. Once again his cup was overflowing, both because of that outcome and because of the joy he was experiencing through entertaining others with his magic and humor.

Most of your counseling clients, like Mark, have responded to problematic events in their lives by choosing to feel depressed, resigned, or angry. There are alternatives for them. Cousins' (1979) first serious bout with illness was at the age of ten when he was sent to a tuberculosis sanitarium. Even at that youthful age he was able to see that some patients were confident they would overcome the disease and resume normal lives, while others were resigned to prolonged and perhaps fatal illnesses. He joined the optimistic group of patients who actively recruited newcomers before they joined what his cohorts called "the bleak brigade." An important task you can take on as a counselor is that of encouraging your clients to take out membership in the order of the optimists, rather than joining the bleak brigade. When you assist your clients who have the need to learn to make more OK enjoying choices, you enable them to become more effective agents in making their own lives more positive.

Before we leave this topic we would like to point out that there is a risk in overemphasizing the curative potential of laughter and other enjoying choices. Not everyone survives an illness that could be fatal. Death as an outcome could be taken to mean that the individual did not laugh enough or show enough fight. Such a point of view might well ruin the last weeks or days of the dying person and generate life-long let-down feelings in those who survive. What should be crystal clear is that some illnesses for some individuals *can* be overcome, and laughter may help. In other instances, with other individuals, the same or different illnesses *cannot* be overcome. But even in those instances, laughter and other enjoying choices can brighten the time individuals have remaining to them.

SELF-EXAMINATION—JOURNAL ENTRY: Take ten minutes and discuss the extent to which you engage in activity processes, pay attention to the feedback from your body (either informally or through biofeedback), engage in a positive addiction, and participate in laughter and other enjoying choices. Discuss the extent to which you believe in the efficacy of these processes for yourself. If it seems suitable, design a regimen for making new choices for yourself in one or more of these areas. Head your entry ACTIVITY PROCESSES AND ME.

We encourage you to share these ideas with your clients, inviting their reactions and helping them see that activity processes, paying attention to the feedback from their bodies, a positive addiction, and laughter and other enjoying choices, may help them achieve some of their most important personal goals. Most clients can benefit from one or more of these processes.

COUNSELING APPLICATION—JOURNAL ENTRY: Discuss the extent to which you believe it is important for you to enable your clients to engage in activity processes, to encourage them to pay attention to the feedback from their bodies, to develop positive addictions, and to engage in laughter and other enjoying choices. Consider with at least one specific or hypothetical client how you might work with that person in designing and evaluating an activity process involving one or more of these components. Suggestion: head your entry ACTIVITY PROCESSES AND MY CLIENTS.

Enjoying Choices: Planning

Choice Awareness theory encourages planning for better choices. Clients who have limited the joy they have allowed in their lives may be helped to implement new patterns of choices and engage in activities that bring them genuine joy and pleasure. Some clients will gain if they merely decide to remain alert and take advantage of the numerous opportunities they meet every day for making enjoying choices. Others will need to be more planful: thinking ahead and rehearsing specific enjoying choices they might make in situations they expect will occur.

It is impossible for us to anticipate all the opportunities that might come our way to respond positively, but at least some of what pleases us is predictable. We know that clean, well-ironed clothes or a delicious meal or a neatly-mowed lawn will appear before us and we can express our appreciation. We can expect that a person we care about will smile warmly or will wear something that looks especially nice, and we can pay a compliment. Life holds many mysteries, but in the area of interpersonal interaction we know of many possibilities in advance. If we have planned and rehearsed how we might initiate and respond with appropriate self- and other-enjoying choices, we can contribute positively to the good feelings of others—which is in the social-interest—and increase the likelihood that the positive behavior of those others will be reciprocated—which is in our own self-interest.

For many of your clients it would be appropriate for you to engage in a direct and simple process of education for more effective enjoying choices, exploring the kinds of situations that call for new behaviors, and rehearsing appropriate actions and statements. Some clients may find it very difficult for them to change ingrained patterns of choices, and counseling as relearning is likely to be necessary, while for others the process might be that of learning. For most clients, at least from time to time, expanding the range of enjoying choices may be a spa experience.

In our discussion of caring and ruling choices, we noted that while planning first appears to be antithetical to spontaneity, the reality is that most clients cannot be truly spontaneous in making any of the CREST choices until they have broadened the spectrum of choices they have available to them; this is especially true of enjoying choices. Once their range of choices is expanded, clients are more able to respond more positively to events in the moment when they occur. Planning for more effective enjoying choices is supported in Choice Awareness theory as an essential component in enabling individuals to make their lives more positive.

CONSIDER THE FOLLOWING:

In Chapters Seven and Nine we discussed the problem that Julia shared with the Resident Assistant, Laura Dee, concerning Maria, her roommate, who missed her family, her boyfriend, and her home town. Laura encouraged Julia to expand the range of her behavior to include all the CREST choices, most particularly enjoying choices. Julia rehearsed some of the things she could say to Maria. Once again her efforts met with much success.

Here are some of the enjoying choices Julia made with Maria.

J: That color looks really nice on you.

J: Thank you for telling me again to get up—I *must* get to that class today.

J: I'm glad we've been able to work out things together.

J: OK, now, if you had to be an animal, what kind would you be—and why?

All of us are able to anticipate circumstances we will encounter in which we can make enjoying choices: Julia can expect that her roommate will look especially nice from time to time, or that the two will engage in a creative experience together. You can expect that clients of yours will experience positive feelings after they have made constructive choices. Encouraging your clients to expand their repertoire of enjoying choices, and rehearsing those choices with them so that they can make them in suitable and comfortable ways with those who are important in their lives, should contribute to their feelings of well-being.

As with other choices, you may feel inadequate in making enjoying choices, and that may make it difficult for you to encourage your clients to make more effective enjoying choices—to enable them to experience spa—for themselves and with others in their lives. Here are a few enjoying choices you might make with your clients or teach them to use in their interactions.

"You did a really good job on that."

"I can tell you're really pleased with the way that worked out."

"Fantasize with me for a moment. What would your relationship with your dad be like if it could be just the way you want it to be?"

"I've thought a lot about the progress you've made. You have a right to be thrilled—I am."

"That's one thing you can add to your list of positive traits—you're enthusiastic."

When you model enjoying choices for your clients, you make it easier for them to enter the circumstances of their lives ready to make statements and behave in non-verbal ways that convey their positive feelings to others. If you have helped your clients think through and rehearse how they might initiate and respond positively, with appropriate self- and other-enjoying choices, they are more likely to have the positive experiences they desire. In Choice Awareness theory, planning for enjoying choices is seen as fundamental if individuals are to have more positive experiences in their lives.

A case may be made that there is a relationship between irresponsibility and enjoying choices. Certainly it is possible for individuals to make enjoying choices at the expense of others. Although we see such choices as almost inevitable on an occasional basis, we hold no brief for enjoying choices that harm others—they are clearly OD. As with the other choices we have considered, we affirm the reality that choices have consequences and that individuals go against both the social interest and their own self interest when they act in ways that are not responsible.

Enjoying choices can be misused. Enjoying choices also hold the greatest potential for helping counseling clients develop their relationships with others—through giving compliments, smiling, and sharing positive feelings with others. They also hold the greatest potential for helping clients develop inner well-being—through internal, self-supportive statements and through relaxation, meditation, activity processes, positive addictions, and laughter.

Appropriate enjoying choices are most effective in enabling clients to achieve the level of spa in their feelings about themselves and in their interactions with others. It is important for clients to realize that they can affect their world in positive ways. Those who make generous numbers of enjoying choices and who respond positively to the enjoying choices of others help to create a spa environment for themselves and others.

If your clients are not aware of the reality that they have opportunities to make enjoying choices with others, you might well explore with them the question, "Who in your world would benefit if you made enjoying choices more frequently?" Furthermore, all people from time to time have opportunities to respond to the enjoying choices of others. Few people are sufficiently skilled in making effective enjoying choices day to day and in encouraging others around them to do the same. Your clients will benefit if you help them understand the nature of enjoying choices, and enable them to develop the skills of enjoying for themselves and with others.

Enjoying Choices

Most of your clients need to learn to make more effective enjoying choices. Counseling can be of great benefit to your clients if it encourages them to make self-enjoying choices—through relaxation, meditation, exercise processes, biofeedback, positive addiction, or humor—and through positive self-statements, or spa. It is equally important that your clients make other-enjoying choices—through smiles, compliments, thank you's, and pats on the back. Inner well-being and physical well-being are enhanced for your clients when they learn to do all they can to counter depression and other negative feelings, rather than succumbing meekly to them. You can help your clients to be significant participants in the process of achieving inner well-being—deeply, totally, and joyfully—and they can best achieve this goal through making more effective enjoying choices.

References

Cousins, N. (1979). *Anatomy of an illness.* New York: W. W. Norton.

Dusek-Girdano, D. (1979). In Girdano, D. A. & Everly, G. S. *Controlling stress and tension: A holistic approach.* Englewood Cliffs, New Jersey: Prentice-Hall. Chapter 15.

Glasser, W. (1976). *Positive addiction.* New York: Harper and Row.

Girdano, D. A. & Everly, G. S. (1979). *Controlling stress and tension: A holistic approach.* Englewood Cliffs, New Jersey: Prentice-Hall.

Helleberg, M. (1980). *Beyond TM.* Ramsey, New Jersey: Paulist Press.

LeShan, L. (1974) *How to meditate.* Boston: Little, Brown and Company.

Chapter 12
Sorrowing Choices:
Exploration

What is Sorrowing?

The S in the acronym CREST stands for sorrowing. Any choice that expresses negative emotions is seen here as a sorrowing choice. Through OK and OD sorrowing choices we handle the frustrations and worries that inevitably come to us in the process of living. We make sorrowing choices in a great variety of ways, ranging from straightforward statements of what is troubling us, to blaming others, to wallowing in our own negative feelings, to engaging in substitute or compensatory behaviors such as fighting, lying, cheating, and stealing. Many of our sorrowing choices are seen as OD, often even when we try to make them otherwise, and it is unlikely that any will be seen as major OK choices. As with ruling choices it may seem unlikely that we might use sorrowing choices to achieve inner well-being and spa-like experiences, but it is possible.

"I'm sorry about your bad news."

"My shoulder muscles hurt today."

"The story on the front page is really terrible."

"Everything is going wrong for me now."

(Sadly) "I wasn't selected for the committee"(team, job, role...)

"I'm concerned about your drinking."

"I don't have anybody to do things with now that Terry has left town."

"I'm overwhelmed with the pile of work ahead of me."

"That's just dumb!"

"You wops (limeys, blacks, honkies) are all alike."

"I'll get you for this."

The choices above are all sorrowing choices. They tell of hurts and negative feelings involving both ourselves and others. We make sorrowing choices when we respond to the negatives we face in our lives.

The examples cited are all verbal, but we also make non-verbal sorrowing choices through tears, fingernail-biting, angry or hostile moves, lying, cheating, and stealing.

The keys to OK sorrowing are complex. Some of us may not accept that we can ever be ill, upset, or frustrated; in such cases, we are likely to see all of our sorrowing choices as OD, and deny any problems we encounter. Likewise, others in our lives may not ever be accepting of our negative feelings. They see all of our sorrowing choices as OD and may attempt to distract us, amuse us, or shut us out when we have such feelings. Because most sorrowing choices are made for self, but affect others, the issue of OKness is both an internal and an external one. We ourselves, and those who are affected, *may* accept our sorrowing choice as OK if we express it directly and straightforwardly, if it is based on recent events and does not suggest that we are nurturing a hurt or harboring a grudge, and if we do not engage in self-pitying or blaming behaviors.

It is a matter of great importance that we see our own sorrowing choices, at least those that we state openly and straightforwardly, as OK. We need to allow ourselves that kind of margin since we inevitably encounter matters that generate sorrowing choices. It is through sorrowing choices that we respond to the negative matters we encounter and express important aspects of our self-concepts.

If we see ourselves as powerless in relation to others, we are likely to express our negative feelings internally—becoming miserable. The words we say, even to ourselves, project a negative self-image: "Nobody likes me anyway." "Anybody can do that better than I can." "I should have known better than to speak up about that." "What did I do to deserve this?"

If we see ourselves as more powerful than the other person, a child for example, or if we believe we have endured all we can tolerate, we may express our negative feelings externally—becoming mean. Often our actions go beyond assertiveness to aggressiveness and are directed against a person who may or may not be involved in our grief.

Both miserableness and meanness as ways of expressing sorrow suggest a poor self-view and they are likely to contribute to a poor self-view in others. It is only when we are willing to share openly the matter that concerns us that we project the kind of self-acceptance that says we can allow ourselves the humanness of frustration or upset. A positive self-concept enables us to accept that we will have "down times" occasionally, and allows us to let others in on what is troubling us.

We may not permit ourselves to express our sadnesses and frustrations openly because we fear being vulnerable and do not trust the responses we may receive. Since we *will* do something with our negative feelings, we are then likely to resort to meanness or miserableness or vacillate between the two. Rather than viewing withholding behavior as evidence of macho strength and control, we need to see it for what it is: fear of vulnerability, and of how others will treat us when we are vulnerable.

In most cases our negative feelings are evident to all who see us. What is not evident is where those feelings come from. Those with whom we live and work are likely to welcome our direct statements of concern, rather than take advantage of them.

Let us assume Mr. Blake, an employee in a box factory, is criticized at work. He returns home with nostrils flared, a scowl on his forehead, and slams his brief case or lunch box on the kitchen counter. Internally he may be saying, "I'm not going to burden my loved ones with the disaster at work. I'll be strong and macho and keep it to myself." Externally everyone else sees ANGER! If Mrs. Blake prepared the lunch, she may wonder if she put too much mustard in the sandwich. Junior may say to himself, "Oh, oh, I bet I left a roller skate on the stairs." Sis may be sure that Dad sat in paste she left on the dining room chair. Even Bowser and Tabby slink away, vaguely concerned that they might have caused the wrath they see oozing from every pore of their master. What may look like strength and control is really abuse of every living creature in the household. What passes for strength is actually weakness. Strength in such a circumstance comes in the form of sharing concerns so others need not take blame for something that is not their fault.

The OKness of sorrowing choices, as with other choices, may be viewed in a now/later frame of reference. Relationships may develop in which one person acts primarily as care-receiver, expressing his/her need through sorrowing choices, while the other acts as care-giver, making such choices with great frequency. For a limited period of time such a symbiotic relationship may serve the needs and fulfill the egos of each of the persons. In the long run, however, that kind of imbalance is likely to cause problems. Imbalances of this sort may evolve in any relationship, but they are most likely to develop between spouses or between parents and their children. Inadvertently a parent may reinforce a negative, sorrowful dependency on the part of a child by being willing, almost eager, to pity, to soothe, and perhaps even to fight for the needs of the child. From the point of view of the child, the protective, womb-like cocoon spun by a parent may seem initially to be both secure and desirable; but ultimately the child must venture into the world and contend on his or her own. Dependency may feel right *now*, but in the *later* frame of reference it may be a genuine disservice.

The key to developing a responsible pattern of sorrowing choices is that of responding relevantly in the present to the hurts and frustrations we inevitably encounter; "getting on" subsequently with the business of living; and returning with less and less pain, less and less frequently, to the matter that caused the frustration or hurt. We need to accept our own humanity, our own need to suffer when there is pain, and to realize that we will move on, despite occasional backward steps. Furthermore, we must learn to accept that others also have the same needs.

We cannot really sorrow for anyone else. Seeing another person in pain may lead us to feel some of that person's hurt, but basically, our sorrowing choices are self-choices. When we respond to another's need, we make caring choices. We make sorrowing choices when we express our own negative feelings in one way or another. When we express those feelings straightforwardly and allow others to know what is troubling us, we gain relief, and other people do not needlessly question what they might have done to cause us pain. When we attempt to stifle our own negative feelings, we risk hurting ourselves by creating internal stress, and we risk hurting others.

We may well ask ourselves: "Am I effective in responding to my inevitable negative feelings?" A person who handles sorrow reasonably could stand in front of a mirror and say:

"I know what troubles me from time to time in my life, at work, at home, and with others."

"I don't run away from, or wallow in, my inevitable negative feelings."

"I make and carry out plans that directly respond to some of the things that trouble me."

"I take appropriate action to alleviate my sorrows and take care of my needs."

"I allow myself suitable outlets when I face problems about which I can do nothing."

If we let ourselves respond appropriately to the sadnesses and frustrations we encounter, we may more readily allow others to do the same. Accepting our sadnesses, genuinely facing our feelings, and taking action when we can, are three important aspects of building a positive sense of self.

If your self-concept permits you the right to feel sadness, you take a giant step toward OK sorrowing. If you neither wallow in sadness, milking it for self pity and the concern of others, nor deny or misdirect it, you have taken the second major step. If you learn to own and state your sorrows straightfor- wardly and without blaming, you have taken the third step (Nelson, 1977, p. 140).

Sorrowing and caring choices overlap when we attempt to meet the needs of others while feeling sad because of their sadnesses, and when we ask for caring or make self-caring choices because of our own negative feelings. Sadness and other negative feelings lead to the needs that are served by caring choices.

Sometimes we want to unload our troubles and the only caring choice we desire is that of listening. Since we live in a very instrumental world, and others may feel obliged to make suggestions to help us, we may want to specify the kind of caring we prefer: "Just listen to me and let me tell you what's bothering me; I know there's nothing I can do about this—I only want you to hear me out." That kind of statement should help the other person understand the caring we desire.

Sorrowing and ruling choices overlap when we make requests or give orders because we feel angry or hurt, for example, or when we handle any negative feeling by acting in a controlling or dominating way. Sorrowing and enjoying choices merge rarely, but we need to realize that the same people who bring us our greatest joys are those who can also produce our saddest feelings. Sorrowing and thinking/working choices overlap when we try to think through what we might do to alleviate our negative feelings, and when we take action to improve matters. Basically sorrowing choices can be differentiated from other CREST choices because they are expressions of negative feelings such as anger, hurt, or sadness.

When we were very young we began to learn what was acceptable concerning all of the CREST choices. We learned to use our sorrowing choices, at first primarily by crying, to get what we needed or wanted, and we learned to repress some of our sorrowing choices eventually for the same reason. The responses we received helped us understand which sorrowing choices were and were not acceptable for us to express. The adults around us may have modeled either denial of negative emotions or wallowing in self pity—since few adults are skilled in understanding, stating, and taking action on the matters that trouble them, then going on with their lives. Our parents and others may have encouraged us inadvertently to get attention through being hurt or feeling inadequate, and we may have learned that angry explosions were more accepted than other expressions of feeling. As a result of poor modeling and lack of acceptance by others of our negative feelings, we may have become persons who deny or control emotions overmuch, who blame or act out toward others, who are not able to live up to external standards of judgment, or who develop poor self-concepts.

Rejection of our own sorrows often results in greater sorrow. Our sad feelings *will* find an outlet. We are indeed fortunate if we have learned to accept and express our sorrows effectively. If we have not, we can learn to change the patterns of choices we have developed, although that process will not necessarily be easy.

It is very likely that we learned to make sorrowing choices in stereotypical ways. Males are given the message that they are to deny sorrows and take action in time of need. As a consequence they are more likely to make external, rather than internal, sorrowing choices. If they do not find OK outlets, they are likely to resort to OD outlets of expression that involve meanness. Our current concern for spouse and child abuse are two pieces of evidence of that kind of expression. By contrast, females are more accepted when they complain and do little, and they are expected to be sensitive to the needs of others. If they do not find OK outlets for their negative feelings, they are likely to resort to OD outlets that involve miserableness. Men who follow sex-stereotypical patterns may get drunk, pick fights, or shout, while women may cry, complain, and wring their hands. Both are following models and acting in ways that have traditionally been considered more acceptable for members of their sex. There is no biological basis for such differences and in neither case are they useful patterns.

Stereotyping also extends to age. The younger the person, and ultimately the older the person, the more acceptance is given their sorrowing choices; in the years from middle childhood to later middle age, less acceptance is given to sorrowing. Messages are sent such as: "It's OK for her to cry, she's just a little girl." "Old folks are like that—anyway, think of all the friends and relatives they've lost." By contrast, a middle-aged man whose wife had recently died, scolded his young adult son, saying, "Don't let everybody see you crying like that. You've got to be strong, son." It seems likely that the father's lack of acceptance for his son's tears came from his fear that he himself might "break down and cry" if his son lost control—and that would be totally unacceptable for him. It is in such ways that we convey our expectations of adult behavior for males and females.

Your clients are likely to be among those who limit their expressions of sorrow because of sex or age; if so, they are not allowing themselves sufficient latitude for being fully human. As a counselor it is important for you to help your clients understand their sadnesses and frustrations, to encourage them to develop outlets for expressing those feelings, to enable them to find means to cope with them, and to help them go on with life.

SELF-EXAMINATION—JOURNAL ENTRY: Take a few minutes to think, then discuss in your journal the sorrowing choices you make in one of your important relationships, and with yourself. Discuss the extent to which the sorrowing choices you make in the relationship move you toward or away from the goals you have with that person, then discuss the extent to which the sorrowing choices you make for yourself move you toward or away from a sense of inner well-being. Suggestion: head your entry MY SORROWING CHOICES.

We encourage you to share these ideas with your clients, inviting their reactions and helping them see the importance of considering the sorrowing choices they make in their important relationships and for themselves. Most clients need to be challenged to make more OK sorrowing choices for themselves and with others if they are to achieve the positive goals they have for their relationships and their lives.

COUNSELING APPLICATION—JOURNAL ENTRY: Discuss the extent to which you believe it is important for you to help your clients deal directly with their patterns of sorrowing choices, both for themselves and with others. Consider with at least one specific or hypothetical client how you might focus on the sorrowing choices that person makes, and how his/her life might be improved as a result of more effective sharing of his/her sorrows. Suggestion: head your entry CLIENT SORROWING CHOICES.

Making Effective Sorrowing Choices

As with each of the other choices, when we feel sorrow or frustration we need to initiate—in this case with sorrowing choices and with requests for caring. If we are like many others, we may mope around and wait, as responders, hoping the other person will ask us, "What's wrong?" If we believe we cannot allow our vulnerability to show, we may then reply, "Oh, nothing," and lose the opportunity the other person has provided.

When we wait for another to observe and respond to our non-verbal sorrowing choices, we are likely to be disappointed in the outcome. A few years ago a teacher came to see me about her graduate program, and we talked at length. Two or three weeks later she came back and shared with me how disappointed she had been that I had not noticed that she was upset and I had not encouraged her to talk about her concern. I could not remember observing her signals and initially I felt bad because I had been so unobservant. It did not take me long, however, to realize that the responsibility was hers, not mine. She knew she wanted help, but she did not give herself permission to ask for it. There would have been nothing wrong in my making an observation concerning what I saw, and offering my assistance. However, if I had observed her signals, I might have concluded that she wanted the freedom to handle the problem on her own, and that my role with her at the time was that of advisor, not counselor.

Our culture does not encourage straightforward statements of concern. Rather, it seems to support a ritual in which we observe another's negative behavior, we ask what is wrong, we receive an "Oh nothing" response, and then we must guess whether or not the reply represents closure or is an invitation to probe further. If we incorrectly interpret the reply as closure, we may be seen as disinterested; if we incorrectly interpret the reply as an invitation to probe further, we may be seen as snoopy and interfering. In healthy relationships the person who has the need is the person who is in the controlling position; he or she has the opportunity to decide whether or not to share that need and ask for assistance. Clients in counseling can and should be encouraged to develop relationships with others in which they share their concerns openly.

There is a danger that those who have many sadnesses in their lives will build narrow relationships in which they define their role as the sorrower and the other person as the care-giver. Or if they tend to deny their sadnesses and frustrations, they may keep others at arm's length to avoid admitting their needs. In either case their relationships will suffer. What all of us really need from others is the full color spectrum of choices, the chance to care and be cared for, the chance to lead and be led, the chance to enjoy and be enjoyed, the chance to share our sorrows and the sorrows of others, and the chance to think about and work on the relationship with others who are important to us.

When we make sorrowing choices in the presence of other people, we expect certain CREST responses more than others. Suppose you say to a friend: "I'm really beat tonight; the work load today was unbelievable." How might that person respond?

Any of the CREST choices would be possible. Caring: "I can see you're really weary." Ruling: "You've got to do something about that; you can't go on at the pace you've been working." Enjoying: "Well, I'm pleased to announce that tomorrow is Friday!" Sorrowing: "You think you've got it bad, wait'll you hear what happened to me today." Thinking/Working: "Are you still working on that AMR project?"

It is clear that your friend could respond with any of the five choices, depending in large measure on that person's habit patterns and on the pattern of interaction you have already established. The person who leans toward ruling choices might feel obligated to tell you what to do: "Talk to your boss about that." "For goodness sake, don't let yourself get worn out for that old job." "You'll just *have* to figure out how to take a break now and then."

The person who emphasizes thinking/working choices may want to help you find a logical way to solve your problem, or to accept it for the time being: "I think you said that AMR project deadline is tomorrow—so it looks like you'll be coming to the end of the crisis soon." "Maybe you can get some help on your end of things." "Have you told your supervisor that you're overburdened?"

The person who empathizes deeply, and the person who is reminded of his/her own troubles, will make sorrowing choices in return, but the nature of those choices will differ greatly: "Oh, gee, I feel really upset, too; I can't stand for you to be taken advantage of so often." "Last year the same thing happened to me; I was working with Pat, and the pressure was really great because. . . ."

And the close friend, the person in a relationship that is developing, or the loved one, might be more likely than others to do what would be most welcome—make genuine caring choices: "If you like, I'll make you a cup of coffee and we can sit and relax awhile right now." "Let me know if there's anything I can do to help you. I can see you're really tired tonight."

When we make sorrowing choices or encounter the sorrowing choices of another, the responses we receive and those we send back speak volumes about the value and the stage of the relationship, and the habits that have evolved. Sometimes what we encounter or send is diametrically opposed to the long-range goals we have for the relationship. If so, that is a strong argument for making those goals specific and for acting upon them more often than we do.

In the course of a lifetime we encounter many sorrowing choices we see as OD. Perhaps someone calls us stupid or otherwise gets angry at us, appropriately or inappropriately. Unless we learn to respond in an accepting way to OK sorrowing choices—that is, through making straightforward expressions of our frustration, grief, or sadness—it is likely to be even more difficult for us to make OK responses when we see the choice as OD sorrowing.

Here are possible examples of each of the choices, both OK and OD, we might make if we were called stupid. OK caring: "You seem really angry and upset right now." OD caring: "Oh, my, you poor child, you must be under a terrific strain these days." OK ruling: "Why don't you come and sit down and we'll talk about what's troubling you." OD ruling: "Don't give me that kind of nonsense!" OK enjoying: (Chuckling) "Oh, wow, that *was* a pretty dumb thing I did." OD enjoying: "It takes one to know one." OK sorrowing: "That hurts." OD sorrowing: (Woefully, internally) "Somebody else has found me out." OK thinking/working: "Did I make a mistake?" OD thinking/working: "If you check you'll find the mistake was yours; I went over your work and found it, and now I've corrected it. Look there on column 23 and see how you carried it through all your calculations. . . ." We are in a much better position to make effective choices when we realize that we can make a great variety of responses to OD sorrowing choices, which tend to be the most difficult of all the OD CREST options to respond to effectively.

If we have as a goal attempting to improve a particular relationship, we may make a straightforward statement about what is troubling us. If the response we receive is critical or otherwise OD, it may shake our resolve to allow ourselves to be vulnerable and to share our feelings. It should not. Suppose we want our friend Paul to understand that our worried looks have nothing to do with him, so we say: "I'm really shook up today, one of my favorite relatives was in a bad car crash." And he responds: "So?" What we need to do is to examine the choice, consider the circumstances, and determine if what we said was appropriate. If we decide that it was, but that Paul does indeed have his own troubles right now, we should give ourselves credit for our openness, and decide whether we want now to respond to Paul's need or our own. Alternatively, we may decide that Paul's flip attitude is a defensive posture, and a barrier we might try to remove. If so, we might press the issue: "Come on, Paul, lighten up a bit; I'm really worried because Jan is one of my favorite cousins. Besides, I knew you'd see I was worried and I didn't want you to have to guess what was wrong." The second statement of the concern may penetrate, just as the second invitation to share a concern may penetrate after a person has responded: "Oh, nothing."

As we have suggested, our society seems to give inordinate value to macho, withholding behavior, so sorrowing choices may be rejected by those around us who do not believe they have permission to share similar concerns or otherwise express their vulnerability. If those others hold strongly to that point of view, further sorrowing choices on our part are not likely to be accepted. Rather than be controlled by others' expectations, however, we need to accept ourselves as feeling persons and find someone with whom we can share our concerns. It is just possible that if we share what is troubling us, others will learn that there is an advantage in sharing frustrations rather than withholding them.

As with enjoying choices, no one can express our sadness or frustration for us. No one can alleviate the stress we feel and take action that dissipates the energy we generate when we feel stressed. If that job is going to be done, we have to do it ourselves. We can dissipate those energies we generate through physical activity, through problem-solving behavior, or through owning and sharing our feelings. Those persons who achieve the most positive levels of inner well-being use each of those options when they are stressed or saddened.

You, I, and your clients have been reared in a society that vacillates on the issue of sorrowing choices. The message for males is a mixed one: withhold expressions of negative feelings and do not let anyone know how vulnerable you feel, but be a tender, loving husband and father. The message for females is more consistent, but it can be more debilitating when life demands strength: be submissive and loving and share your feelings with others. It is important that your clients learn not merely to echo stereotypical patterns for responding to the sadnesses and frustrations of life, but to develop a repertoire and acquire skill in making a variety of sorrowing choices that allow them to respond effectively to the realities they face.

SELF-EXAMINATION—JOURNAL ENTRY: Take a few minutes to think, then discuss in your journal ways in which you can respond more effectively through sorrowing choices to the sadnesses and frustrations you encounter. Suggestion: head your entry MORE EFFECTIVE SORROWING CHOICES FOR ME.

We encourage you to share these ideas with your clients, inviting their reactions and helping them see the importance of making more effective sorrowing choices for themselves, and sharing their sadnesses in their important relationships. Most clients need to be helped to develop more skill in making OK sorrowing choices if they are to achieve effective interpersonal relationships and inner well-being.

COUNSELING APPLICATION—JOURNAL ENTRY: Discuss what you can do in counseling that would help your clients make more effective sorrowing choices for themselves, and how you might help them share their sadnesses and frustrations effectively with others. Suggestion: head your entry MORE EFFECTIVE CLIENT SORROWING CHOICES.

Sorrowing Choices

In Choice Awareness theory sorrowing choices are seen as those choices that primarily involve negative emotions. We have learned the patterns and limitations on our sorrowing choices over our life span; we may remain tied unnecessarily to old injunctions and stereotypical sorrowing choice patterns. Many clients in counseling need to understand their own patterns of choices, they need to learn when and how to make more effective sorrowing choices, and they need to allow themselves to be more responsive to the sadnesses and frustrations experienced by those around them.

Reference

Nelson, R. C. (1977). *Choosing: A better way to live.* North Palm Beach, FL: GuideLines Press.

Chapter 13

Sorrowing Choices: Application

Sorrowing Choices and Your Clients

Many of your clients' concerns relate directly to the choices they make when they are upset, frustrated, worried, or angry. When they have these feelings, they make sorrowing choices. They are likely to see themselves as having no control over their choices at such times—indeed, they are unlikely to see choice as any part of the situation. You can contribute positively to your clients if you explore with them how they might make OK sorrowing choices that would take care of their inevitable negative feelings, and how they might respond more effectively to the sorrowing choices of others.

The case has been made that in enjoying choices lies the greatest potential for your clients to achieve a sense of inner well-being and for feeling good about themselves and others. Often the most important preliminary, however, is that of learning to make sorrowing choices that respond adequately to the negative feelings that are an inevitable part of living in this world. The downward-turning spiral of mental health that is experienced by many counseling clients could be alleviated if they learned more suitable choices to make when they experience negative feelings.

Many clients huddle in their own misery, feeling helpless and inadequate to do anything to alleviate their pain; others accumulate injustices over time, then lash out in a way that may be inappropriate in their present circumstances; still others see the world as a hostile place and respond to it continuously in angry, combative ways. Your clients may find it difficult to develop new ways of responding to their negative feelings since they have built their habits of reacting over a lifetime—in large measure because they have had few models for handling negative feelings in suitable ways.

Since sorrowing choices *are* choices, however, they are accessible to the individual. Habits may be strong, but movement toward more positive choices is possible. As with the other CREST choices, even those people who act in habitual, negative ways, are likely to have a repertoire of OK sorrowing choices that may be dormant, but that is available for them to use and to enlarge.

Most people follow well-established habit patterns when they meet circumstances that trouble them. They respond with choices that are basically either internal or external. If they choose the internal route, they act in ways that may be described as miserable; if they choose the external route, they act in ways that may be described as mean. Both of these patterns of choices are OD.

Some examples of internal choices that project miserableness are:

"Nothing I ever do turns out right."

"They won't pay any attention to me, anyway."

"Everything is going wrong."

"Why was I born?"

"What did I do to deserve this?"

Some examples of external choices that project meanness are:

"I'll go give them a piece of my mind."

"You're stupid."

"Can't you ever do anything right?"

"I've had it up to here with you."

"I'll punch your lights out."

What is missing in the array of sorrowing choices for many people is an honest admission of what is hurting or frustrating them.

"I got some bad news from my family today."

"Wow, things were a mess at work this afternoon."

"I just can't keep up with the workload right now."

"When you call me that it really bothers me."

"Orders are really slow right now. I'm worried that we'll all be laid off."

If we consider carefully what is going on inside ourselves, we can usually figure out what is bothering us. We may not be used to sharing our frustrations, and we may even believe that strength lies in withholding our feelings, but it is possible for us to learn to state clearly what is troubling us. What we need is our own permission to do what we need to do.

The clearest exception to the notion that we know what is troubling us is when our feelings are negative, general, and directed toward ourselves—when we are affected by a negative self-concept. We have suggested that WHY questions are often poor because the person may not know why he or she has acted in a particular way, and because such questions invite rationalization. Often a negative self-concept is the real explanation. When we ask a child who has bullied another why he or she took that action, one of the first words from the bully is likely to be a pronoun or a noun that indicates the other person: "He. . . ." "She. . . ." "They. . . ." "Paul. . . ." "Paula. . . ." The genuine reason is almost impossible for the child to verbalize. Few children could say, "I'm no good. I hate myself, and I hate everybody else. I did that because I deserve to be punished. Maybe if somebody beats me I'll feel better afterward. . . , but I doubt it."

Most of us have an extensive repertoire of responses to negative feelings that we use under specific circumstances, and most of us can articulate internally what is troubling us—except, as has been suggested, when we cannot face our own negative feelings about ourselves. What we may lack is permission to share our negative feelings straightforwardly and directly. One important task of the counselor is that of enabling clients to give themselves this permission.

CONSIDER THE FOLLOWING:

Brent was an eight-year-old who always seemed to be wound up like a top. For a period of time he had been under a physician's care and medicated as hyperactive. Dr. Reynolds, his new physician, took a dim view of long periods of medication for children unless that treatment was inescapable, and he gradually weaned Brent of the medication. The hyperactivity level, though somewhat moderated, returned. Brent's parents had divorced just prior to the time his hyperactivity had its onset, and his doctor theorized that Brent needed counseling rather than more medication. In a telephone conversation Dr. Reynolds encouraged Mrs. Sargent, the elementary counselor in Brent's school, to help Brent gain an outlet for his feelings, saying: "Mainly, he seems to be like his dad, withholding and denying. Now that he's away from his father's influence, maybe you can help him to find more direct outlets for his feelings."

Mrs. Sargent gave Brent some time to explore on his own, then helped him to see that when he tried to be strong and silent like his dad, his feelings often came out in inappropriate ways. She helped him to find more direct ways to express his feelings, first to her, then to the empty chair that he sometimes let represent his father, his mother, his teacher, or one of his classmates. Ultimately he became somewhat more direct in his expressions of feelings. As he shared his negative feelings more openly, he seemed less wound-up, more relaxed.

Brent's negative feelings about his parents' divorce had left him tense and brooding, and he held in nearly all his expressions of feeling. Like the proverbial lidded kettle simmering on the stove, he was steaming with frustration and resentment. He needed help in sorting out what he really felt negative about. So long as he lacked his own permission to express his feelings openly, he tended to deny them internally as well. Receiving permission to express his negative feelings helped him to clarify what was bothering him and to share that with others. The result was less misplaced anger and frustration on his part, and less scolding by others, in particular his mother.

Many counseling clients have developed inappropriate, unsuitable, and often sex-stereotyped habits of responding to the negatives in their lives. Members of both sexes need their own permission to express feelings in ways that are more open and direct. Typically males learn to withhold their feelings or, when cornered or overburdened, to react in hostile or angry ways. Typically females learn to express their feelings through tears and complaints, and they may share their feelings with a third party rather than with the individual who is involved. Both sexes tend to accumulate injustices until they feel entitled to act out in some more extreme way. For many males the extreme means include aggressive behavior; for many females the extreme means include bouts of depression. Transactional analysts refer to such behaviors as collecting brown stamps, suggesting that when enough stamps are collected they may be exchanged for a major explosion or breakdown.

When males or females withhold from themselves permission to express their negative feelings openly and straightforwardly, adverse outcomes occur in at least three areas. (1) They develop unsatisfactory habit patterns in their relationships. Deep, satisfying relationships do not require withholding; on the contrary, they thrive on honesty and openness—perhaps not of every detail of a person's life, but at least of the positive and negative matters of everyday life that are affecting the individual in the present. When people share their sorrows without resorting to miserableness or meanness, they confirm their trust in the relationship. (2) Withholding of sorrowing choices results in shallow relationships. Most people experience periods in their lives when negatives abound; if they cannot allow themselves to be open at such times, they are likely to find little else to share because they are unable to concentrate on other matters. (3) Withholding of sorrowing choices often leads to failed relationships. Others can sense the individual's negative feelings; they may blame themselves unnecessarily or feel frustrated that they are not allowed to help. Ultimately this may have a strong negative effect on the relationship.

Males and females alike need to be helped to find effective ways to express the inevitable negative feelings they have. Choice Awareness theory takes the position that sorrowing is one of five basic choices we have available to us. Severely limiting even OK expressions of that option renders ineffective one of the five basic options we have for functioning in the world in which we find ourselves—and it increases the likelihood that we will express ourselves in OD ways. Most males ultimately resort to external, OD expressions of frustration and anger, and most females ultimately resort to internal, OD expressions of upset or anguish, if they have not learned to use OK outlets for their negative feelings. Members of both sexes need to give themselves permission to make open, OK expressions of their negative feelings both for themselves and with others. Many of your clients will find it easier to give *themselves* permission to express their negative feelings openly with others if you give them permission to do so first. Ultimately, inner well-being for your clients depends on their giving themselves permission to make OK sorrowing choices both for themselves and with others.

SELF-EXAMINATION—JOURNAL ENTRY: Take a few minutes, preferably at least five, and discuss the extent to which you believe you limit yourself in sex-stereotypical ways in the sorrowing choices you make for yourself and with others. Discuss the extent to which you believe movement toward more open sharing of your sorrowing choices might benefit your personal life. Head your entry STEREOTYPING AND MY SORROWING CHOICES.

We encourage you to share these ideas with your clients, inviting their reactions and helping them see that they can make sorrowing choices in ways that go beyond sex-stereotypes. Most clients can benefit by changing their pattern of sorrowing choices—for themselves and with others.

When you encourage your clients to make more effective, more open, more OK, sorrowing choices, you are helping them act on the principle of social-interest, and at the same time serving their self-interest. When they share their concerns, others do not have to guess whether or not they have caused those negative feelings, they are not accumulating hurts that are potentially explosive—like a steam kettle, and the chances increase substantially that others will respond to them with caring choices.

The Gestalt Approach

All counseling systems are designed to encourage clients to cope more effectively with the sadnesses and frustrations that inevitably affect their lives. In terms of focus, however, the Gestalt approach to counseling appears to be the contemporary system that has encouraged the counselor to work most directly with the sorrowing choices of the client.

The Gestalt approach is phenomenological; it takes the view that understanding of the self and others is based on the totality of experiences, and those experiences are expressed through breathing, voice, gestures, and posture. Individuals strive to maintain equilibrium, which is constantly being disturbed by needs and events, and gratification or elimination of needs results in return to equilibrium.

Perls (1973) suggested that responsibility depends on response-ability—the ability to respond. Whenever a person acts, decides, or chooses, the person is exercising *response*-ability. The individual is accountable. He or she is always the person doing the acting, deciding, or choosing. Response-ability means owning, rather than blaming others or conditions, for one's thoughts, feelings, impulses, and behaviors.

"The role of the therapist involves devising and having the individual try experiments designed to increase awareness of habitual behavior that inhibits awareness" (Gilliland, *et al*, 1984, p. 95). The Gestalt view is that clients come to counseling with unmet needs and a set of behaviors that prevent satisfaction of those needs. The unmet needs lead to negative feelings and sorrowing choices. Often the individuals cling to behaviors that do not serve them well. People may hurt and want help, and at the same time be afraid of and resistant to change.

All aspects of the behavior of the individual are observed and used directly in the process of counseling. The individual may be asked to become the part of his or her body that is conveying discomfort, to verbalize what his or her swinging leg or tapping finger is saying. Or he or she may be asked to become some of the forbidden things in his or her life—cigarettes, whiskey, sex—and let those things speak and say aloud what they are telling the individual every day of his or her life.

The counseling process focuses on the unfinished business of the individual that tends to show up as guilt, resentment, and inadequacy. In many cases the client is not helped to get rid of feelings, but is enabled to live with them, and to see the other side of them—to understand that the other side of the feeling of hate is a feeling of love, that the other side of toughness is tenderness.

The empty chair technique is used frequently in Gestalt counseling. In that technique the individual is invited to take care of unfinished business by addressing another person who is visualized as present in the empty chair. For example, a daughter might tell her father of her hurt feelings, what actions of his led to resentment on her part, and what he said that generated unnecessary guilt or poor self-feelings.

This Gestalt technique and others may be seen in Choice Awareness terms as allowing the individual to state unexpressed sorrowing choices. Often these choices are stated initially in OD ways. Ultimately the result tends to be a greater understanding of the weaknesses and foibles of the person with whom there is unfinished business, as a result resentment decreases and the individual becomes willing to express to the person directly more genuine positive feelings, and some negative feelings, in more effective, more OK, ways.

Other Gestalt techniques that are often used with clients include: (1) inviting them to speak out loud the thoughts that are racing within them; (2) trying on new behaviors to see what can be learned; (3) dialoguing between parts of the person—my conservative self and my daring self, for example; (4) speaking alternately in the voice of the little child and the mature adult that is within; and (5) paying attention to the body—becoming the knot in the stomach, the doubled fist, or the tears.

CONSIDER THE FOLLOWING;

Lois, a forty-three-year-old working woman, had been involved in counseling previously, and had gained from an accepting, Rogerian approach. Her more recent complaint was a kind of generalized malaise, a state of mild depression that she thought of as evidence of a mid-life crisis. Her initial reaction to Mr. Lewis's active, demanding, Gestalt approach included both surprise and resentment. Talking to an empty chair that represented her deceased father, who had often abused her physically and psychologically, struck her as irrelevant, and she doubted that her relationship to her father was in any genuine way related to her current depressed state.

Mr. Lewis urged her on, arguing briefly, but convincingly, that what was depressing her was not so much in her present life as in her unfinished business with her father. Once she overcame her resistance to the "game-playing," as she saw it, she began to feel great relief in unburdening herself of the many negative feelings she had never shared with anyone. Ultimately the words expressing her deep frustration, resentment, hatred, and powerlessness came pouring out in torrents. Then, miraculously, what she had hidden from herself for so long also began to spring forth. She had not understood that even with all the brow-beating and physical abuse she had received, as a little girl she had felt a deep concern and at times a genuine love for her father. He had given her life, challenge, and a frightening, disquieting kind of love. For all those years, she realized, despite her feelings of powerlessness, she had in some moments been stronger than he, for she had understood his incapacity to express love, and she had pitied him. Now she could express to him as if he were present, the pity and the anger she had felt, and the love she had forgotten. Finally, a strange wave of positive feelings, including love, peace, and a sense of maturity, newly-acquired, washed over her.

The Gestalt approach was ideally suited to Lois' needs. She could not hope to face her deceased father directly and work through her feelings, in this life anyway, but the empty chair approach afforded her the chance to work through them in a relevant, alternative way. Lois, in common with most clients, had turned her resentment toward her father inward and had felt guilt because she knew she *should* love her father; she saw that as a value held in our society and as a cornerstone of her religious creed. Counseling helped her realize that she had turned her anger on herself instead of directing it toward her father. Some of the resentment she felt toward herself because she did not take action—because she continued to follow her submissive pattern with her father even when she became an adult. So long as she harbored all of those negative feelings, she was not able to see that they covered a hidden, but important, aggregation of positive feelings as well.

Perls (1969) suggested that we start life totally together, but we encounter splits that must be regained. The various techniques are designed to help the individual reintegrate parts of the self and become whole once again. "Gestalt therapy is centrally concerned with integrating our split-off parts into a whole person" (p. 276).

The Gestalt approach focuses on the individual's wants and values. Wants are seen as linking present experience and future gratification. Building awareness of wants helps the individual to make more effective choices for present and future action. The view is taken that many of the frustrations individuals face result from value patterns that are significant, often internally-conflicting, and generally unexamined, but they influence behaviors nonetheless. Making wants and values explicit can enable the individual to modify these influences and, subsequently, implement new patterns of choices.

The Gestalt approach accords homework an important place in counseling—we prefer the term *assigned tasks*. These tasks are used to increase insights and meanings; they also provide clients with opportunities to try out new and more creative behaviors. Assigned tasks are tailored to the willingness and ability of clients to try out the new behavior as a means of reducing their dependency on less functional behaviors. The nature of the tasks often parallels successive approximation—a traditional behavioral technique. An example might be encouraging a shy person to undertake one small action daily that belies shyness, perhaps such a simple action as being the first to speak on encountering a friend, and eventually initiating conversations with strangers in circumstances that appear to be safe. The effectiveness of the tasks depends on the extent of understanding between the counselor and the client, and requires some creativity on the part of each. Clients can be challenged to try out new, more effective choices that are within their potential for taking risks.

The Gestalt approach to counseling assists individuals to use internal messages to face what has been avoided, and thereby to gain closure in some of the person's unfinished business. Choice Awareness theory supports the use of this approach as appropriate for many clients because of its efficiency and relevance.

A cautious approach is appropriate, however. Whereas some counseling approaches rely on listening, attending, warmth, and the relationship, the Gestalt approach supports more remoteness and demanding behavior on the part of the counselor, thus allowing less opportunity for discovery on the part of the client. Because of these characteristics, it may invite genuine and would-be charismatic personalities. There is potential for destructiveness in any counseling process when it is misused, but the Gestalt approach appears to have more of this kind of potential than many other approaches. Because of these potential drawbacks, and because we believe in self-discovery as essential to self-control, it is our position that Gestalt approaches are best used after the relationship between the counselor and client is rather fully developed, and after it is determined that other approaches have resulted in insufficient gain. The Gestalt approach may cut through years of a client's dependency and self denial, only to result in dependency on a new figure—the counselor. For these reasons, we view Gestalt experiments not as last resorts, but as later resorts, in counseling.

Structured Sorrowing Choices

We have made the point that our negative feelings *will* be expressed, and that it is important for them to be expressed openly, if not to others, at least to ourselves. Otherwise we are likely to resort to external or internal OD expressions of those feelings—to meanness or miserableness. There is skill required both in sorting out what negative feelings actually signify, and in finding OK ways to express those feelings. In this brief section we suggest a three or four step approach we call *structured sorrowing choices* as a method for expressing negative feelings, especially when others are involved. Several years ago, Betty McComb, a Florida counselor, introduced this process to elementary school counselors in a conference; she referred to it as *the semi-magic sentence.*

Step 1	State the person's name.	"Pat,
Step 2	Say, "When you. . ." and specify what the person has said or done that troubles you.	when you yell at me for a little thing like dropping that piece of paper,
Step 3	Say, "I feel. . ." or "I felt. . ." and specify your feelings. Then, if you choose, add -	I feel really lousy,
Step 4	"And as a result I want to. . . and complete the statement.	"and as a result I want to go bury my head in the sand."

We encourage you to work directly with your clients on practicing structured sorrowing choices, both as ways they might have responded to recent events they have faced, and in anticipation of similar events occurring in the future. Three cautions should be noted. First, in Step 3, encourage the use of feeling words after "I feel. . ." or "I felt. . ." and discourage blaming behaviors and threats. Not: "I *feel like* hitting you," or "I *feel that* you don't care about me" (which is a belief not a feeling).

Instead: "I feel troubled," or "I felt annoyed." Second, in Step 4, encourage the sharing of internal wants rather than threats to the other person. Not: "As a result I want to punch your lights out." But: "As a result I want to go off somewhere and lick my wounds." Or: "As a result I want to stay out of your territory." Third, and probably most important, is to avoid the use of *that makes me feel* in Step 3 and *that makes me want to* in Step 4. We have choices about our feelings, and such language can lead us to act as though we do not. If we say, "That **makes me** feel rotten," we are implying that we could not be amused or feel concern for the other person. If we say, "That makes me want to get back at you," we invite the other person to escalate the difficulty by saying, "Just you try it!" Step 4 should simply be omitted if the individual cannot find some personal expression that would be appropriate.

A portion of Chapter Fifteen is devoted to a consideration of Rational-Emotive Therapy, but one contribution of Ellis (1979) is particularly relevant here: the concept that there is frequently (Ellis suggested that there is always) a feeling that is antecedent to anger. Individuals feel hurt, left out, discounted, ignored, or disappointed, for example, and turn to anger because they want to avoid admitting that others' words or actions have power over them, and because they see the expression of anger as somehow more potent in our culture. The problem is that anger escalates the level of difficulty and builds higher barriers without ameliorating the original feeling. Thus, when structured sorrowing choices are explored, the individual's attention ought to be drawn to the immediate feeling—the feeling that came before anger, when anger is experienced—in Step 3 above. Whether structured sorrowing choices *per se* are used or not, the client in counseling is likely to benefit by being helped to express a variety of feelings, rather than withholding, or expressing anger to the exclusion of other feelings.

Structured sorrowing choices, once learned and practiced to the point where the individual is skillful with them, may be modified to fit comfortably in personal dialogue. Eight-year-old Brent, whom we introduced earlier in this chapter, eventually said to his father, "It really bothers me when I ask you what's wrong and you clam up instead of telling me, Dad; and when that happens I don't want to ask you any more." The essence of the process, which is the important thing, may be preserved even if the language is modified.

Parenthetically, note that the same process may be modified in terms of its content and used to present *structured enjoying choices.* For example, if you were sitting beside me in a meeting and you offered me a pen when you saw that mine had run out of ink, I might say to you quietly, "_____, I really felt good when you saw my need and lent me that pen before I could even ask. I'd like to take you out for coffee later, because I like rewarding kindness."

Setting the Stage

One of the problems clients have in sharing their sadnesses and frustrations with others is that they want to focus on them in the moment, while the other person may not be able to listen just then. It seems a bit odd for individuals to have to put in reservations or make appointments to share something with a friend or relative, but the risk they take when they blurt out their needs is that they do not receive the kinds of responses they desire. A second problem clients have is that they may be more than willing to talk about their troubles, but they do not want to receive a barrage of possible solutions.

You can make two important suggestions to your clients that involve these two matters; both involve setting the stage for more effective responses. First, you can encourage your clients to pique the curiosity of the friend, spouse, or relative by saying something like this: "I can see you're really busy right now, so I don't want to interrupt you, but there's something important I'd like us to talk about. Let me know when we can have twenty minutes (other time interval) together and we'll talk." Adults, adolescents, and young children who have asked for time in this way generally find that the curiosity of the other person is considerable, other matters are soon put aside, and a level of attention is given the issue that is deeper than would otherwise have occurred.

Second, you can encourage your clients at times to state to the people who are important in their lives that they want nothing more than to be listened to and to share their concerns. In our culture most of us have learned to be very instrumental. Every question requires an answer and every problem demands a solution. As a result, when someone presents us a problem we may stop listening to the anguish and frustration, and begin a search for possible resolutions. We want to meet the needs of those who seek our help. It can be extremely valuable to us as listeners when someone relieves us of the responsibility to search for solutions by saying, "Please just listen to me. There's nothing I can do about this problem," (or: "I've already decided what I'm going to do"), "but I need to blow off steam and let someone know how frustrated (angry, upset) I feel."

You can help your clients to think through what it is they really want or need and to tell others that they need time to talk or to specify that they only want to be heard. These are two important stage-setting choices that can do much to relieve stress and create inner well-being for your clients when they want to talk with others about matters that are of concern to them.

SELF-EXAMINATION—JOURNAL ENTRY: Take a few minutes, preferably at least five, and discuss the extent to which you believe you are or are not effective in using such measures as Gestalt approaches and structured sorrowing choices to relieve your own sadnesses and frustrations. Discuss the extent to which you believe these approaches would have value for you. If it seems relevant, specify how you might employ

---

either of these approaches for yourself. Suggestion: head your entry ACTIVE SORROWING CHOICES FOR ME.

We encourage you to share these ideas with your clients, inviting their reactions and helping them see that structured sorrowing choices and carefully-selected Gestalt approaches may help them alleviate their sadnesses and frustrations.

COUNSELING APPLICATION—JOURNAL ENTRY: Discuss the extent to which you believe it is important for you to engage your clients in Gestalt processes or to teach them to use structured sorrowing choices or other means by which to express their negative feelings. Consider with at least one specific or hypothetical client how you might use either process. Suggestion: head your entry ACTIVE SORROWING CHOICES FOR MY CLIENTS.

Sorrowing Choices: Planning Ahead

Choice Awareness theory suggests that planfulness is appropriate in the realm of sorrowing choices. Clients who have become dependent on OD sorrowing choices—whether they express them internally or externally—can learn to make different patterns of choices. Some clients will gain if they merely decide to remain alert and to be more open in sharing their negative feelings with others as they occur. Others will need to be more planful, thinking ahead and rehearsing specific sorrowing choices they might make in situations they expect to encounter.

It is impossible for us to anticipate all the negatives that might come our way that will require our responses, but at least some of the negatives we encounter are predictable. We can expect that the illness of someone we care about will enter our thoughts and affect our outlook, or that a behavior that troubles us—arguing children, clothes on the floor—will be repeated. Although life holds many mysteries, in the area of interpersonal interaction we know of many possibilities in advance. If we have thought through and rehearsed how we might initiate and respond with appropriate sorrowing choices, we can express those feelings more openly, and often more acceptably, than we might otherwise have done. Saying, "I'm disappointed that you two are continuing to argue," or "It still frustrates me when I find clothes on the floor," may not be OK choices in the view of those involved, but they are likely to be taken as more positive than either pouting or flying into a rage.

Sharing our frustrations or other negative feelings with others, at least as compared to the alternatives, are choices that serve the social-interest. These choices also increase the likelihood that the responses we will receive will be more beneficial to us than might have occurred otherwise. Thus our actions also serve our self-interest.

Many of your clients would gain if you engaged them in a process of education toward more open and effective sorrowing choices. Some clients may find it difficult to change ingrained patterns of choices, and counseling as relearning is likely to be necessary, while for others the process might be that of learning. For some clients, at least from time to time, expanding the range of sorrowing choices may even achieve the level of a spa experience; the individual might be able to say, happily, "At last I know what to do so anger doesn't always boil inside of me."

In our discussions of other choices, we noted that planning may appear to be antithetical to spontaneity, but most clients cannot be truly spontaneous in making any of the CREST choices until they have broadened the spectrum of their choices. This is particularly true of sorrowing choices. Once their range of choices is expanded, clients are able to respond more effectively to events in the moment. Planning for more open and effective sorrowing choices is supported in Choice Awareness theory as an essential component in enabling individuals to take more effective control in their lives.

CONSIDER THE FOLLOWING:

In prior chapters we discussed the problem that Julia shared with her Resident Assistant, Laura Dee, concerning her room-mate, Maria, who was homesick for her family, her boyfriend, and her home town. Laura encouraged Julia to expand the range of her behavior to include all the CREST choices, even including sorrowing choices. Julia rehearsed some of the things she could say to Maria when they were relevant, and Maria responded well to Julia's statements.

Here are three of the sorrowing choices Julia shared with Maria.

J: I get worn out when you bring up the same problem over and over again.

J: Today let *me* dump on *you*. My chem class is really getting me down.

J: I'm really tired. Adding an element of ruling: Let's talk about that tomorrow.

Encouraging your clients to expand their repertoire of sorrowing choices, and rehearsing those choices with them so that they can make them in suitable and comfortable ways with others, should contribute to their feelings of well-being. As with other choices, it may be helpful from time to time if you model effective sorrowing choices for your clients. Here are two examples:

"We've talked about your whining behavior and how it blocks your relationships with others; let me tell you that it frustrates me when you whine like you were doing just then." A ruling choice followup: "Say that again, but tell it to me straight and I'll be able to listen much better."

"I had a somewhat similar experience after a car accident. Once I was sure nobody was hurt, the first thing I said was, 'I just spent hours washing and waxing this car.' It wasn't all that helpful, but I said what I was thinking, and it was better than lashing out."

Modeling sorrowing choices for your clients can be risky, but if the model is effective you make it easier for your clients to convey their negative feelings to others in acceptable ways. If you help your clients think through and rehearse how they might initiate and respond with appropriate sorrowing choices, they should be able to encounter their negative experiences so that they less often escalate into larger problems.

A case may be made that there is a relationship between irresponsibility and sorrowing choices. Some sorrowing choices are by nature irresponsible, e.g., name-calling or laughing at the expense of others, or feeling miserable at the expense of self. Such choices are almost inevitable from time to time, but they are clearly OD. As with other OD choices, these choices have consequences, and individuals ultimately hurt themselves as well as others when they act in ways that are irresponsible.

Clients who learn to make sorrowing choices effectively achieve greater intimacy in their relationships with others; they express their negative feelings so that others feel closer to them and are willing to help them or at least listen to them. Clients who learn to make effective sorrowing choices also achieve a greater sense of inner well-being—the burden is lighter when it is shared.

Can sorrowing choices ever be spa experiences? Yes. Think of the relief that comes when you finally get off your chest what it is that is bothering you, or when the tears you have held back for a long time go coursing down your cheeks. Physical spa experiences can be wearing, even exhausting, and emotional spa experience may be similarly exhausting. Not all spa experiences are joyful in the moment; often the joy comes afterward; but through sorrowing choices spa can be achieved.

Many of your clients would benefit if you explored with them the question, "Who in your world would benefit if you shared the things that trouble you from time to time—rather than holding in your negative feelings and leaving them to guess what's wrong?" Your clients will benefit if you help them understand the nature of sorrowing choices, and if you enable them to develop the skills involved in expressing their sadnesses and frustrations effectively.

Sorrowing Choices

Most people need to learn to make more effective sorrowing choices. Your counseling can be of great benefit if it helps your clients cope more effectively with the predictable, recurring sadnesses and hurts they encounter over time, and if it enables them to think through and rehearse how they might respond to those realities. The Gestalt approach uses a variety of small experiments that relate especially to non-verbal messages clients send, and to the "unfinished business" they have with others and for themselves. Gestalt techniques are viewed here as most appropriate for use with clients after the relationship is well developed, and when other approaches have proven ineffective. Choice Awareness theory suggests that clients may be taught the use of structured sorrowing choices, they may be given assistance with matters of timing in the expression of those choices, and they may be encouraged to ask directly for listening when that is what they want or need. Helping clients to make effective sorrowing choices is valuable in enabling them to achieve a greater sense of personal responsibility, take more effective control in their lives, and gain a greater sense of inner well-being.

References

Ellis, A. (1979). Rational-emotive therapy. In R. Corsini (Ed.), *Current Psychotherapies* (2nd ed.). Itasca, IL: F. E. Peacock.

Gilliland, B. E., James, R. K., Roberts, G. T., & Bowman, J. T. (1984). *Theories and strategies in counseling and psychotherapy*. Englewood Cliffs, N. J.: Prentice-Hall.

Perls, F. (1969). *Gestalt therapy verbatim*. Moab, Utah: Real People Press.

Perls, F. (1973). *The Gestalt approach and eyewitness to therapy*. New York: Bantam.

Chapter 14

Thinking/Working Choices: Exploration

What is Thinking/Working?

"What time is it?"

"Twelve fifteen."

"We're due at the Union in fifteen minutes."

"I called for reservations."

"Let's see, after lunch we may have time to work on the Warren project."

"We can probably solve that problem through brainstorming."

"Will you have your part done by Friday?"

"If we take another week we'll have it almost perfect."

Looking up a telephone number.

Reading directions, blueprints, plans.

Deciding which task to complete next.

Gathering necessary materials.

Figuring out how to correct an error.

Typing, hammering, measuring, inspecting, forging, inserting, and so forth.

The T (or T/W) in the acronym CREST (or CREST/W) stands for thinking/working, and all of the above are thinking/working choices. Through the hundreds of thinking/working choices we make daily, we conduct the ordinary and special business of life and respond to the realities we encounter. We make thinking/working choices when we consider our options, plan activities, ask and answer informational questions, and take care of our tasks. While we may verbalize many of our thinking/working choices, we make even more of these choices without words.

We have pointed out that thinking/working enters into all choices—since we cannot show caring, lead others, enjoy ourselves, or even express sorrow without our minds, and often our bodies, being moved to action. In a sense, then, we can consider thinking/working choices as "all other choices"—that is, all choices that do not emphasize meeting needs, showing leadership, or acting basically on positive or negative feelings.

The question often arises whether some choices are underdone, or UD, as opposed to OK or OD. For the most part, when we feel the absence of a choice in a relationship with another person, caring or enjoying, for example, that person is not merely withholding the choice from us, he or she is actively engaged in making some choice or other. Frequently that choice is thinking/working, and it may well be that the choice he or she is making is OD for us in the moment.

The key to OK thinking/working is whether or not the other person needs or wants a different choice from us. Often the question is one of balance. If you and a friend are working on a task and you are pressed for time, you may enjoy a quip or your friend may appreciate a brief anecdote of yours that lightens the atmosphere, but you may both prefer that most of the energy be devoted to the task. In another circumstance, one in which you and your friend each have tasks you must accomplish, each of you may make thinking/working choices that omit the other and be fully accepted in that action. On the other hand, if you have a deep need or are wanting your friend and you to have a pleasurable moment together, your friend's thinking/working choices may be OD for you.

Most of the behaviors that fall into the thinking/working category are seen as minor OK or minor OD choices. The occasional superlative breakthrough in a business, problem solving, or game context may be seen as a major OK choice. The extremely insensitive absorption of one person in an activity in the face of another's obvious need for assistance may be seen as a major OD choice. For the most part, though, we do not move relationships very far forward or backward through our thinking/working choices.

Your clients need to understand that they can contribute to their relationships in positive, cumulative ways through thinking/working choices. At the same time they need to realize that they cannot build truly effective relationships on thinking/working choices alone—they need to balance these choices with others.

In thinking/working choices, in addition to the OK/OD continuum, the dimension of depth needs to be considered. A great deal of our thinking and working is habitual and shallow. We follow old tapes that tell us what we should do, and we rerun old familiar patterns of behavior. In many areas of living it is suitable for us to run on automatic pilot. We can walk through the house at night without turning on lights; we can drive home only partly attentive to the route, turning corners, shifting gears, and braking as we have so often done before. We can even proceed through some of our relationships in rehearsed, prescribed ways. If the other person is as content to keep the relationship on the same footing as we are, the old patterns of behavior may be sufficient—at least for the present.

Difficulties may arise in driving *or* in relating to others, however, if we follow old tapes or rerun old patterns of behavior in situations that call for other choices. A new person appears on the scene. We compare that person to others we have known and attempt to build this new relationship on similar terms. We search through our repertoire of behaviors for getting acquainted with young female co-workers, for example, and we prepare ourselves to tell our favorite personal and family stories, and otherwise get ready to build a relationship that parallels others we believe might be similar.

Now, let us suppose the new person announces that she is a militant women's rights advocate and is sensitive to any gesture that stereotypes her as female. Once we know that, if we have had experience with such individuals before, the responses we make are likely to follow a pattern of behavior we have become comfortable using with "women's righters." We may enter the relationship enthusiastically, activate a walking-on-eggs style, or decide the effort is not worth it and write off the person—following our prior pattern. If we have reservations about the views that person represents, but see ourselves as responders, we may act in an accommodating way or avoid the new colleague until she approaches us. If we see ourselves as initiators, we may listen briefly, then attempt to sway the new colleague to our way of thinking. On the other hand, if we can be truly open to new experiences and to greater depth of thinking/working choices, we could say to ourselves: "This is an opportunity to encounter someone who represents a unique point of view; I want to get to know her and see what her values are and why she holds them."

The simplest level of thinking at times is merely using labels as excuses. If we feel inadequate in social conversation and have labeled ourselves as responders, we may let our negative self-concepts limit our choices, saying to ourselves at times: "I'm the responder here; I can't be expected to carry on a good conversation; why doesn't she say something to me?" The labels we give ourselves can be excuses for not venturing into new choice patterns.

The point has often been made that we use only a small fraction of our intellectual capacity. For most of us, much of the time, even when we are not following injunctions or habits, the thinking/working choices we make tend to be shallow—we underuse our choice capacity. Our depth of thought may be a frustration for ourselves and those around us.

Daily at thousands, perhaps millions of households, one spouse, usually the male, comes in the door after work, tired and hot, unfolds the paper, and flops back in an easy chair for a renewing, non-challenging exploration into the lightest level thinking/working choices available. The other spouse, usually the female, perhaps underchallenged and in need of stimulation, caring, or an enjoyable encounter, begins a slow burn at the perceived OD thinking/working choice.

The home-from-work moment is the classic example of OD thinking/working from the point of view of one member of a pair, but discrepancies between what is given and what is desired occur in many relationships (Nelson, 1977, 151-152)

Genuine, non-stereotypical relationships grow best in soil that has not been worn out by being cultivated in the same way all of the time. You can help your clients consider the habitual nature of their thought patterns and their responses to others, both those they have known for a long time and new acquaintances. You can encourage them to become more their own persons by reaching beyond such parental injunctions as: "Keep clear of strangers." Or: "Old ways are the best ways." You can help them see the advantages of thinking/working choices that go beyond old habits and labels, and you can encourage them to think more deeply and work more assiduously on their relationships.

As with the other CREST choices, the now/later frame of reference is important in thinking/working choices. Relationships can evolve nicely for a time with these choices as the primary focus. Likewise, for a period of time within any relationship there can be a continuing focus on such choices without necessarily causing difficulty. But what may happen in either situation is that one individual or both may look back on the period of time involved and feel quite unsatisfied. The work was completed, but the satisfaction level might have been much greater if the two had incorporated other choices in the interaction as well. By the same token, the absence of thinking/working choices of any depth is likely to leave one or both of the individuals involved feeling dissatisfied.

One key to developing a responsible pattern of thinking/working choices is giving strong and deep attention to those choices when the need is present, and sometimes even when it is not—for the pure joy of the challenge, and for the exercise of the brain cells. A second key is remaining alert to one's own needs and wants, and the needs and wants of others, for any of the *other* CREST choices.

Self-thinking/working choices are also important. Continuous self exploration is counter- productive, but some thinking about self is important in effective choice-making. Many choices that appear to be self-thinking/working choices are either superficial or more a matter of worrying (sorrowing) than thinking or working. When we feel concerned about something it may seem to occupy our thoughts constantly. However, there is a considerable difference between quality thinking time, in which we consider possible alternatives and the likely and unlikely consequences of each, and incessant rerunning in our minds of the event that triggered the worry.

Our self-concepts are implemented in part through our thinking/working choices. If our self-feelings are positive, we know we have good ideas and are capable of resolving issues effectively. The reverse can also be true. If we make good thinking/working choices and see the effects of those choices as positive, we are likely to feel positive about ourselves, at least in the moment.

We can do much for ourselves in making thinking/working choices, but not all of our problems can be worked out without assistance from others. One demonstration of a positive self-concept is the willingness to seek out others when we need their help. We project a positive self-concept when we admit our need for help and believe that others are willing to assist us.

Thinking/working and caring choices overlap when we explore our own needs or the needs of others and when we consider how we might respond. Thinking/working and ruling choices merge when we channel our own energies in order to complete activities or tasks, when we consider how we might obtain the assistance or involvement of others, and when we engage with others in activities or tasks for which we have sought their participation. Thinking/working and enjoying choices overlap when we are creatively engaged, and when we plan and carry out positive experiences. Thinking/ working and sorrowing choices come together when we plan and carry through our plans for alleviating our negative feelings.

Thinking and working enter all choices, but whenever the choice meets a need, we assign the label caring; whenever the choice involves leadership, we assign the label ruling; whenever the choice involves an expression of positive or negative feeling, we assign the label enjoying or sorrowing. It is when thought processes or effort predominates that we assign the label thinking/working choices.

We began to build our patterns of thinking/working choices in infancy. When our needs were not met, or when we wanted to reach something outside our grasp, we eventually learned to go beyond crying; we used trial and error choices to meet our needs. We may have conveyed the messages: "I'd rather do it myself" and "I want to think for myself." The responses we received helped us shape our sense of ourselves as thinkers and doers. If we were "helped" a great deal and protected from even minimal dangers, or if we were not given sufficient stimulation or encouragement to explore, we learned to follow injunctions, repeat patterns of behavior, assume labels, and limit our own permission to think. Any tendencies we may have had along those lines as young children were exacerbated if we saw few models for deeper thinking among the adults around us.

Even with thinking/working choices we are likely to have developed sex-, age-, and role-stereotyped patterns. Traditionally, females are assigned thinking/working choices in the interpersonal and domestic areas, and males in realms beyond the home environment. Older people are looked to for wisdom as well as leadership, and young children learn to do as they are told—in other words, not to think. Parents, teachers, and supervisory personnel are assumed to be the keepers of knowledge, and others defer to their thinking/working choices.

As a result of the models your clients have seen, the experiences they have had, and the stereotypes they have acquired, they are likely to have become shallow thinkers. They may believe, for example, that their relationships just happen and that the way the wind blows is the way they must go. It is important for you to help your clients to understand the kinds of thinking/working choices they have been making in their relationships, and to encourage them to consider whether deeper levels of thought and action might serve their purposes more effectively.

SELF-EXAMINATION—JOURNAL ENTRY: Take a few minutes to think, then discuss in your journal the thinking/working choices you make in one of your important relationships, and for yourself. Discuss the extent to which your thinking/working choices move you toward or away from the goals you have with that person. Then explore the extent to which the thinking/working choices you make for yourself move you toward or away from a sense of inner well-being. Suggestion: head your entry MY THINKING/WORKING CHOICES.

We encourage you to share these ideas with your clients, inviting their reactions and helping them see the importance of considering the thinking/working choices they make in their significant relationships and for themselves. Most clients need to be challenged to make deeper thinking/working choices for themselves and with others if they are to achieve their goals.

COUNSELING APPLICATION—JOURNAL ENTRY: Discuss the extent to which you believe it is important for you to help your clients deal directly with their patterns of thinking/working choices, both for themselves and with others. Consider with at least one specific or hypothetical client how you might focus on the thinking/working choices that person makes, and how more effective use of these choices might improve his/her life. Suggestion: head your entry CLIENT THINKING/WORKING CHOICES.

Making Effective Thinking/Working Choices

As with each of the other choices, when we have a problem we want to solve, or when we merely crave some kind of intellectual challenge or absorbing activity, we need to initiate with thinking/

working choices and ask others to participate with us, if that is appropriate. If we take the part of the responder and wait for an offer of assistance, a challenging idea, or a suggestion from another person, we may well be disappointed. Others may not interpret our anticipatory look as an invitation to engage in problem-solving, idea-sharing, or an activity. Further, if those others also see themselves as responders, they are likely to wait for us to initiate. In effective relationships the person who has the idea or the need is the person who has the best opportunity to open the door to some kind of dialogue or action. As a counselor you need to encourage your clients to initiate with thinking/working choices.

When we make thinking/working choices in the presence of other people, we expect particular CREST choices more often than others in response. Suppose you say to colleagues: "I need some ideas for publicizing our new program." How might they respond?

Any of the CREST choices would be possible. Caring: "I'll help you with that." Ruling: "Let's build a list of possibilities." Enjoying: "That sounds like a fun thing for us to do together." Sorrowing: "Oh, gee, my mind's a blank right now." Thinking/working: "What ideas have you thought about so far?" Your colleagues' choices will depend in part on the pattern of communication you have developed. In all likelihood they will see your invitation as a minor OK choice and begin to offer suggestions—other thinking/working choices: "Have you thought about a newspaper ad?" Or: "We might want to form a committee to look at that question."

If for some reason others see your inquiry as OD, perhaps because of the timing or their workloads, the responses you receive might be one of a number of ruling or sorrowing choices: "You'll have to figure that out for yourself." "Can't you see I'm up to my ears in things to do already?" "Now, where am I going to get the time to help you with that?"

In thinking/working choices, as with the other CREST choices, the twin issues of permission and power are important. Persons who feel powerful have permission to come up with suggestions or to insist that you solve the problem on your own. They may be inclined to make ruling or thinking/working choices similar to either the OK or OD choices in the second paragraph above. Persons who perceives themselves as less powerful do not have their own permission to make assertive responses or to think deeply, and are more likely to avoid the situation: "Oh, dear, I'm not sure I can come up with any idea that will help. What do *you* think?" Those same persons may be willing to make the working choices that move the process along—"Just tell me what to do and I'll do it"—but be uncomfortable about making suggestions when they are needed.

Your clients' patterns of thinking/working choices can tell you a great deal about their self-concepts, the habits they have developed, and the depth of their relationships. Some have no interpersonal relationships in which the trust level has developed to the point where they can even share a thought about how to solve a problem. Some clients who are parents or teachers may compartmentalize, give themselves license in their relationships with children, and bombard them with large numbers of thinking/working and ruling choices, but limit themselves sharply in other relationships. It would be beneficial to many of your clients if you helped them consider the important relationships in their lives to determine in which ones they might be making thinking/working choices that are OD, and in which ones they need to give themselves permission to make thinking/working choices more often and in greater depth.

In the course of all of our lives we encounter occasions in which we experience a thinking/working choice as OD because we want or need a different choice. Perhaps someone who is important to us cannot spend time with us because she or he is continually involved in Important Activities. In the moment of refusal it would be possible for us to make choices from anywhere among the ten OK and OD CREST choices. It may be important for us to give ourselves permission to make a choice that is more positive than is our usual habit.

To the Busy Person Involved in Important Activities we might offer any of the following choices. OK caring: "I can tell you feel really overwhelmed with work right now." OD caring: "There, there, it must really be tough that you can't even take a few minutes for yourself or for me." OK ruling: "I think it would do you some good to get away from that project for at least a few minutes." OD ruling: "You've worked at that long enough tonight; c'mon, put it away now!" OK enjoying: (gently teasing) "All work and no play, you know." OD enjoying: (sarcastically) "Let's see if we can get you paroled from this prison you've got yourself in." OK sorrowing: "When you work continually on your projects, I feel left out." OD sorrowing: "You're such an infernal drudge!" OK thinking/working: "How long more do you think you'll be tonight?" OD thinking/working: (internally—with strong overtones of sorrowing and self-ruling) "I'll start a major housecleaning, then I won't be available when that old workaholic is ready to take a break."

If we have as a goal improving a particular relationship, a variety of thinking/working choices may be of value to us. We may want to build a list of the alternative approaches we might use in improving matters. We may need to think through a strategy in which we increase the use of one of the CREST choices and decrease the use of another, then work hard to implement our plan.

Your clients have been reared in a society that appears to value "shooting from the hip" more than it does well-considered action. The males among them may have learned to act without giving sufficient thought to the implications of the actions; the females may have learned to think shallowly—without necessarily acting upon their thoughts. It is important that your clients learn not merely to let injunctions and habits substitute for thought and action, but to develop skill in making the kinds of thinking/working choices that allow them to encounter their problems and to build good relationships.

SELF-EXAMINATION—JOURNAL ENTRY: Take a few minutes to think, then discuss in your journal ways in which you can respond more effectively through thinking/working choices to the realities you encounter. Suggestion: head your entry MORE EFFECTIVE THINKING/WORKING CHOICES FOR ME.

We encourage you to share these ideas with your clients, inviting their reactions and helping them see the importance of making more effective thinking/working choices for themselves and in their important relationships. Most clients need to be helped to develop more skill in making OK thinking/working choices, and in supplementing those choices with others—particularly caring and enjoying—if they are to achieve effective interpersonal relationships and inner well-being.

COUNSELING APPLICATION—JOURNAL ENTRY: Discuss what you can do in counseling that would help your clients make more effective thinking/working choices for themselves. Consider how you might help them solve their problems and build their relationships with others more effectively through thinking/working choices. Suggestion: head your entry MORE EFFECTIVE CLIENT THINKING/WORKING CHOICES.

Thinking/Working Choices

In Choice Awareness theory thinking/working choices are seen as those choices that primarily involve cognition and working on tasks. All of us have learned our patterns of thinking/working choices over our life span, and we may remain tied to habits, labels, and injunctions, rather than approaching old and new relationships and old and new problems with fresh attitudes and a broad range of skills. Many counseling clients need to understand better their own patterns of thinking/working choices; they need to allow themselves to think more deeply and work more effectively in response to the situations they face; and they need to gain a greater sense of inner well-being through their thinking/working choices.

Reference

Nelson, R. C. (1977). *Choosing: A better way to live.* North Palm Beach, FL: GuideLines Press.

Chapter 15

Thinking/Working Choices: Application

Thinking/Working Choices and Your Clients

Many of your clients' concerns result from the ways in which they behave; many of their behaviors result from the ways in which they think. Your clients make many shallow thinking/ working choices on the bases of habits, the labels they put on themselves, and old injunctions. You can contribute positively to your clients if you explore with them how they might make OK thinking/working choices and balance those choices with the other CREST options.

The downward-turning spiral of mental health experienced by many clients could be tilted upward if they learned to make more effective thinking/working choices. Although random thoughts occur to your clients and some of their behaviors are reflex actions, they can bring most of their thoughts and behaviors into conscious awareness and make choices that are more functional than they may have made in the past. New patterns may not come easily, but since most thoughts and actions are in fact choices, they can be changed.

Permission to think other than superficially, and power to behave other than traditionally, may seem to be beyond the reach of some clients. They may rerun old thoughts and behavior patterns in familiar and unfamiliar situations and in old and new relationships, but most have a wellspring of thinking/working choices available to use. An important aspect of inner well-being for clients is learning to mobilize their thoughts and actions more effectively to meet the challenges they face.

People who are involved in relationships that trouble them may believe that they are thinking deeply and working on their concerns when they may actually be spending the time in worrying and in rerunning the hurts and slights they have felt. When individuals think shallowly or substitute worry for thought or action, they are building poor habits for solving their problems, they are setting themselves up for relationships that lack depth, and they are increasing the chance that they will feel like failures. When they develop breadth and depth in their thinking/working choices, they increase the chances that they will resolve their concerns and feel confident in their abilities.

Choice Awareness theory takes the position that a great proportion of the choices people make in their lives are thinking/working choices. To the extent that they restrict their choices in this area and make them superficially, they are using only a limited portion of their power to think and to act.

Most people have developed limited and stereotypical habits of thought and action. Males and females, the young and the old, and those in supervisory and subordinate roles alike, need permission to think on deeper levels and to act in ways that are consistent with those deeper thoughts. It is inappropriate for many to think and act as superficially as they do. Typically males learn to be very instrumental—they may therefore act hastily without sufficient thought. Typically females learn to be less instrumental—they may therefore think about and worry about matters that are of concern to them, but not feel empowered to take action. Similarly more mature persons and people in positions of leadership may feel obliged to be instrumental, and young people and those in subordinate positions may feel obliged to await the leadership of others.

Males and females, younger and older persons, and leaders and subordinates, need to be helped to approach the various tasks and concerns of life on the basis of thoughtful consideration, not shallow thinking or knee-jerk reactions. One of the challenges you can accept as a counselor is to help your clients explore and expand the limited permission they give themselves to make effective thinking/working choices. Inner well-being for clients depends in part on their giving themselves permission to make more effective thinking/working choices for themselves and with others.

SELF-EXAMINATION—JOURNAL ENTRY: Take a few minutes, preferably at least five, and discuss the extent to which you believe you limit yourself in sex-stereotypical ways in the thinking/working choices you make. Further, discuss the extent to which you believe giving yourself permission to think at deeper levels might benefit you and others. Suggestion: head your entry STEREOTYPING AND MY THINKING/ WORKING CHOICES.

We encourage you to share these ideas with your clients, inviting their reactions and helping them see that they can make thinking/working choices in ways that go beyond sex-stereotypes. Most clients can benefit by changing their thinking/working choice patterns.

When you encourage your clients to make more effective, more OK, thinking/working choices, you are helping them act on the dual principles of social-interest and self-interest. When they consider their words and actions thoughtfully, they are likely to interact more effectively with others, and the chances increase that others will respond to them more often with a variety of OK choices.

Reality Therapy

Reality Therapy, developed by William Glasser (1965), helps people behave differently as a result of helping them to think differently— thus it is directed to both thinking and working choices. Reality Therapy is based on the assumption that individuals have a deep need for identity—they need to know they are loved and they need to feel worthwhile to themselves and others. People often select ineffective behaviors to meet their needs, and that virtually assures failure. They deny the reality of the world around them. They break laws, disobey society's rules, claim neighbors are plotting, fear crowded places or close quarters, drink, and attempt suicide—all of these behaviors deny reality. Reality Therapy helps people learn who they are, consider how they interact and behave, and determine how they can be more accepted by themselves and others. The theory focuses on conscious, planned behavior in the present; the past is not considered; feelings and attitudes are not important; behavior is.

In Reality Therapy the counselor and client examine the client's life to see how his or her specific behaviors are destructive, so that the individual can take responsibility for his or her actions. As O. H. Mowrer said in the foreword to Glasser's *Reality Therapy* (1965), ". . . human beings get into emotional binds, not because their standards are too high, but because their performance has been, and is, too low. . . the objective of this (radically non-Freudian) type of therapy is not to lower the aim, but to increase the accomplishment" (p. xiii).

Glasser advocates that counselors find out what people want and need, examine their failures and their present assets, and consider how they must cope with the factors in their environments if their needs are to be satisfied. He stresses that clients have to meet their needs in a real world that is imperfect, that does not meet their specifications. If they are to fulfill these needs, they must act positively. Individuals can do something about their "fate" if they consider themselves and their environment realistically.

Reality Therapy focuses on taking responsibility, which Glasser sees as ". . . the ability to fulfill one's own needs and to do so in a way that does not deprive others of the ability to fulfill their needs" (1965 p. 13). The counselor explores the issue of responsibility with clients who must decide for themselves whether their behaviors are irresponsible and whether they should change them. Instead of seeking to change behavior directly, the reality therapist works on changing clients' awareness of their responsibilities, expecting behavior change to follow.

In Reality Therapy the person of the counselor becomes an important consideration. "The qualities of warmth, respect and caring for others, positive regard, and interpersonal openness are crucial" (Ivey, 1980, p. 310). Counselors are encouraged to use their natural self, humor, confrontation, even sarcasm, in very personal ways to assist clients to understand behavioral patterns and develop new action styles. Reality therapists feel free to confront their clients, to allow them no excuses, and to challenge the ambivalence they feel.

Reality Therapy focuses on learning and relearning. The counselor teaches the client new, more responsible, and more intentional, ways of behaving through modeling, instructing, and dialoguing. Planning is seen as important; clients are helped to develop strategies for meeting their needs in their world.

CONSIDER THE FOLLOWING:

Connie J., a college student at a small eastern school, had learned well the skills of procrastination, blaming, and making up stories, and had found that they worked with counselors and administrators during her high school years and in her first year of college. She had partied a great deal and had been dropped by her college for academic reasons, but she was sure she would be able to do enough to get by when she was readmitted. As one of the conditions of readmission, she had to see a college counselor every other week during her semester out. Mr. Lamont was assigned to work with Connie and her earliest impressions of him were that she would be able to "snow" him easily. However, she soon learned that he meant business. She was prepared to share her feelings and to rationalize her lapses as inevitable results of her poor upbringing—a pure fabrication—but almost immediately Mr. Lamont wanted to know what evidence she could give that she was taking responsibility for her behaviors. When she attempted to sidetrack the issue, Mr. Lamont pressed her again and again for evidence of her progress. It soon became clear to him that there was none, whereupon he asked her to specify what she was going to do. She tried to put him off by saying she thought she might see about her old job at a hometown drugstore and maybe she would take a correspondence course that would take care of one of her deficiencies; he quickly moved to the exploration of when and how she would achieve those objectives.

When Connie came back the next time without having taken any action, Mr. Lamont asked her to make a value judgment about what she was doing and whether her procrastination was accomplishing what she wanted. She agreed that it was not. Mr. Lamont made it clear that he would brook no excuses. He terminated the interview quickly, indicating that he expected her to use the time to accomplish one of the goals she had specified, and clarified that he expected to see her with evidence of progress, not rationalization, the next week. Further, he indicated that his recommendation for readmission would depend on clear evidence of her following through on her commitments and taking responsibility for her own life.

Connie made another attempt or two to ease her way through her problems, and she canceled two appointments. Mr. Lamont simply restated his expectations and indicated that he would under no circumstances recommend readmission until she had met with him eight more times on a weekly basis, and had given clear evidence of growth toward maturity in each of the eight sessions. He consulted his calendar and pointed out that on the present schedule their eighth meeting would take place two days before the committee would act on her readmission application. Connie attended all subsequent appointments; she had already followed through on the drugstore job; and she quickly completed and had in hand a "B" grade for her correspondence course when the committee acted favorably on her request for readmission.

The Reality Therapy approach was well-suited to Connie's needs; in point of fact it was no accident that she was assigned Mr. Lamont as a counselor. The very size of her file, the bills she had procrastinated about, her unkept appointments, and the absence reports filed by faculty members relating to her own and family illnesses and tragedies, had called for a confrontive approach. College counseling personnel saw the readmission issue as their last great hope for helping Connie learn to function more responsibly.

Reality Therapy requires that the counselor be skilled at ascertaining what the client really wants to do and developing with the client a realistic plan for achieving that goal. Connie wanted readmission, but she wanted someone else to take the responsibility for her achievement of that goal. Mr. Lamont insisted that the responsibility remain Connie's despite all postponements and excuses. The plan for Connie was not committed to paper. However, Glasser (1965) argued for a written plan that lists the specific actions the client must take in order to achieve the specified goal. He indicated that the client must own the plan—it must be the client's rather than the counselor's—and it must be relevant and realistic.

Eight fundamental principles undergird the work of the Reality Therapist. (1) Become involved with the client in a personal, caring way. (2) Emphasize present behavior and the here and now rather than feelings and the past. (3) Help the client to make a value judgment about what he or she is now doing and whether or not it is accomplishing desired objectives. (4) Help the client develop a workable, realistic plan of action. (5) Obtain a commitment from the client concerning when and how he or she will carry out the plan. (6) Accept no excuses for the client's nonperformance. (7) Do not punish, but allow reasonable consequences to follow. (8) Never give up.

The Reality Therapy approach to counseling assists individuals to examine the realities of their world and modify their behaviors so that they can live more effectively within those realities. The approach has been used in street clinics, schools, and various institutional settings where no automatic, immediate trust exists. It has been used by prison guards and others who simply state that they are in a position of control, then go on to challenge the irresponsible actions of their charges.

Reality Therapy has been criticized on the grounds that it assumes that client problems, even to the point of mental illness, can be equated with irresponsibility on the part of the client. While many clients may be helped on the basis of that assumption, it is not appropriate for all. This approach focuses on the here and now and avoids exploring client histories. While in many cases history is less relevant than living and working in the present, we may on occasion lose much that is relevant if we ignore the client's past. Finally, many counselors are tempted to use quick-fix, symptom-oriented methods that give them a sense of accomplishment; the very directness that is an attraction of Reality Therapy for many counselors may leave deeper problems unexplored.

Choice Awareness theory supports the use of the Reality Therapy approach for many clients, particularly those who are inclined to rationalize, blame, and procrastinate. In its emphasis on client responsibility and planfulness, Reality Therapy clearly assumes that the behaviors of the client are choices, and that they can be helped to take better control in their lives. We believe the directness and frankness of Reality Therapy, which has high impact, is most relevant with clients who are handling their world unrealistically, but we think it is best used after clients have been given the opportunity for self-discovery through more economical approaches.

SELF-EXAMINATION—JOURNAL ENTRY: Take a few minutes, preferably at least five, and discuss the extent to which you confront reality directly through your thinking/working choices. Discuss the extent to which you allow yourself excuses and procrastinate, or act responsibly. Head your entry REALITY AND MY THINKING/WORKING CHOICES.

We encourage you to share these ideas with your clients, inviting their reactions and helping them see that focusing on reality and making effective thinking/working choices may help them achieve some of their most important personal goals.

COUNSELING APPLICATION—JOURNAL ENTRY: Discuss the extent to which you believe it is important for you to use the Reality Therapy approach with your clients. Consider with at least one specific or hypothetical client how you might incorporate elements of the Reality Therapy approach in your counseling. Head your entry REALITY THERAPY AND CLIENT THINKING/WORKING CHOICES.

Rational-Emotive Therapy

Rational-Emotive Therapy, developed by Albert Ellis (1971), is a counseling system that focuses on helping people to use their thoughts to control their feelings. Ellis reasoned that people make themselves victims in this world due to their own incorrect, irrational thinking patterns.

Rational-Emotive theory suggests that people have a tendency to want to insist that everything happens for the best in their lives, and they severely criticize themselves, others, and the world when they do not get what they want. In many instances in which people's needs are not met they go from an objective event to a catastrophic view of the event.

Ellis and Grieger (1977) summarized the Rational-Emotive view of the way thinking affects emotions—the *A-B-C* Theory. *A* is an *Activating Event*, a fact, occurrence, or behavior the person encounters. *B* is the person's *Beliefs* about A. *C* is the emotional *Consequence*, how a person feels about A. Rational-Emotive Therapy contends that it is not the objective, Activating Event, A, that causes consequences. Rather, it is the person's Beliefs, B, about the event that trigger the Consequence, C, how the person feels.

The counseling process in Rational-Emotive Therapy is highly confrontive; it supports the idea that counselors should actively point out and dispute the irrational thought patterns of clients and teach them to dispute their own irrational beliefs. While Rational-Emotive counselors accept the self-theory concept that individuals have powerful tendencies toward growth and self-actualization, they take the view that humanistic approaches are too soft, since they fail to cope with the fact that people can hurt themselves greatly by their irrational thoughts.

The emphasis of the therapy in many instances is on changing the ways in which people think about their behavior, rather than on changing the behavior itself. According to Ellis and Harper (1979), most clients are seen as making irrational statements through their behavior. "If I don't pass this course, it'll be a tragedy." "I have nothing because the rich have taken it all." "My parents were cruel, so there's nothing I can do to help myself." "I have no job, so there can be no meaning in my life." Several generalizations guide these irrational thoughts.

1. It is necessary for me to be loved and approved by all the important people who come into my life, otherwise everything is awful.

2. For me to be worthwhile, I must be totally competent, adequate, and achieving. If I do not achieve that goal, it is all my fault and I am no good.

3. Some people are bad and should be punished. I will get even because that person slighted me.

4. It is better to avoid some difficulties and responsibilities. No one will care if I do not follow through on this task.

5. It is awful or catastrophic if things are not the way they should be. If the house is not picked up, it is a tragedy.

CONSIDER THE FOLLOWING:

Jack arranged a counseling contact with Albert Ellis and quickly came to the point. He was concerned that he might become a homosexual. Ellis asked Jack what that would make him. "A real shit," was Jack's eventual answer. Ellis used a parallel illustration. "Suppose you thought of stealing something and concluded that if you stole it you'd be a real shit. How much would you think about stealing?" Jack admitted that he would think of it often, that he might become obsessed with the idea. Ellis pointed out that stealing the object would have real disadvantages, but then he asked whether or not that would make Jack a total shit in all respects. Jack said no, and that helped him gain greater perspective on his problem.

Over time and through many statements and questions, Ellis directed Jack's attention to the A-B-C's of his concern. The essence of his comments was as follows: The objective reality is that you feel some attraction toward homosexual activity; that is A, the Activating Event. Your Belief, or B, is that homosexuality is a tragedy, whereas the reality is that although it has some disadvantages, some people see it as a legitimate alternative lifestyle. The Consequence, C, is that you have an irrational fear of being homosexual and you are hurting yourself with your irrational thought. Your obsession with the question may drive you in the very direction you fear you might go (adapted from Ivey, 1980).

As Albert Ellis did with Jack, Rational-Emotive Therapists tend to make generous use in counseling of open and closed questions, directives, interpretations, advice, and opinion. They look for patterns of thinking that they might attack; they use the past to discover patterns, and look to the future to change thinking patterns. At the same time, they are concerned with what the client is thinking right now. They offer an instructional model that lets clients know how they have been thinking and suggests how they might better think about their problems.

Clients are taught to substitute more constructive language for language they have been using that is destructive. To use: "it would be preferable" or "it would be very desirable" instead of saying "I must" or "I should." To use: "I can, but I find it difficult" or "so far I haven't, but that doesn't mean it's impossible" instead of saying "I can't" or "it's impossible." To use: "I have done poorly in the past" instead of saying "I always do poorly." To use: "it would be disadvantageous or inconvenient if . . ." instead of saying "it would be terrible or awful if . . ." To use: "I did that poorly" instead of saying "I am a bad or worthless person because . . ." The assumption is made that when clients change the language in their thought processes they find it easier to think and behave differently.

Rational-Emotive therapists use homework assignments in which clients try out new behaviors, then report on their success. As with Reality Therapy, excuses are actively discouraged; the Rational-Emotive therapist investigates the irrational thought patterns behind excuses involving such behaviors as procrastination and rationalization.

Rational-Emotive Therapy has contributed to the counseling literature by emphasizing the relationship between thinking and emotion and encouraging counselors to confront directly the inappropriate thought processes that lead so many clients down destructive pathways. The approach has also contributed to the literature by its citation of the irrational beliefs of clients as a basis for their emotional disturbances.

Rational-Emotive Therapy has been criticized on several grounds (Gilliland, et al, 1984). One criticism is based on the de-emphasis of the therapeutic relationship and the lack of concern about empathy and rapport. Clients who do not feel understood or adequately listened to may terminate counseling before they can obtain the benefits they might derive. A second criticism is that the theory suggests that it is effective for the counselor to be highly active and persuasive even in the initial phases of the counseling process. There is a danger that the counselor will be off target because of moving too quickly or impulsively to a definition of the problem. A third criticism is that the theory emphasizes changing emotion by changing thought patterns. Gestalt therapists conclude the opposite, and behaviorists take another tack altogether. It appears evident that the needs of different clients can be met by exploring emotions, thoughts, *or* behaviors. Finally, because the approach is persuasive and directive, it is possible that more psychological harm may result than with approaches that are less directive.

Choice Awareness theory supports the use of the Rational-Emotive approach with many clients, particularly those who most clearly have drawn harmful or erroneous conclusions from reality, and those for whom gentler, more economical approaches have not seemed to work.

It is important for clients to be helped to consider what they have been telling themselves and to explore to what extent unsuitable conclusions they have drawn may be leading them further into difficulties. In Choice Awareness, when we suggest that clients be helped to see that they have omitted caring choices in some of their relationships, for example, and that they might generate such choices, we are directing clients in a way that is similar to the Rational-Emotive approach. We continue in that direction when we help clients see that they have avoided making caring responses to the needs of another because they have over-generalized that the other person's criticism or punitive action is saying that they are incompetent or worthless—and caring choices are unwelcome from incompetents and the worthless.

We see genuine advantages in approaching some clients by challenging the ways in which they think about the problems they face, but, as with other highly active counseling processes, we take the position that individuals should first be allowed some room to discover the nature of their problem and to come up with solutions on their own.

> SELF-EXAMINATION—JOURNAL ENTRY: Take a few minutes, preferably at least five, and recall examples of times in which you used "awfulizing" overstatements—statements that show you ballooned out of proportion mere inconveniences—in your thinking/working choices involving the person and events you encounter. Discuss the extent to which you permit yourself to use internally the irrational thoughts enumerated in Rational-Emotive Therapy. Head your entry MY IRRATIONAL THOUGHTS.

> *We encourage you to share these ideas with your clients, inviting their reactions and helping them see that some of the thinking/working choices they make may be distortions of reality and may block them from achieving some of their most important personal goals*

> COUNSELING APPLICATION—JOURNAL ENTRY: Discuss the extent to which you believe the Rational-Emotive Therapy approach is or would be useful with your clients. Consider with at least one specific or hypothetical client how you might incorporate elements of this approach in your counseling. Head your entry RATIONAL-EMOTIVE THERAPY AND CLIENT THINKING/WORKING CHOICES.

Transactional Analysis

Transactional Analysis is a rational approach to understanding behavior; it is based on the assumption that all individuals can learn to trust themselves, think, make decisions, and express feelings (James & Jongeward, 1971). The work of Transactional Analysis was initiated by Eric Berne (1961, 1964, 1972) and popularized by James and Jongeward (1971) and Harris (1967).

Transactional Analysis presents a "language system which communicates with people rather than hid[ing] behind vague theoretical constructs" (Ivey, 1980, p. 301). It posits three basic ego states, Parent—the shoulds and oughts, Adult—the data processor, and Child—the spontaneous and free aspects of the individual. Although the writing on the point is not always clear since the Adult ego state is often emphasized, the basic posture of TA is that no ego state should predominate; Parent behavior is needed at times, Adult and Child behavior at other times.

Transactional Analysis proposes four life positions: I'm OK, you're OK. I'm OK, you're not OK. I'm not OK, you're OK. I'm not OK, you're not OK. Children are seen as initially OK (princes and princesses), who are made not OK (turned into frogs) by those around them. The assumption is made that the people who seek counseling are frogs, that is, they have evolved a sense of not-OKness and need assistance in accepting themselves.

The transactions analyzed in this theory are the moment by moment nonverbal and verbal interactions that exist between individuals. Transactions may be complementary—for example, an individual asks for help Child to Parent and the other person responds Parent to Child. Transactions may be crossed—for example, an individual may make an Adult to Adult statement and the other person responds Child to Parent. Transactions may be ulterior—for example, a male ski instructor may give special assistance to an attractive female student. Those who hear the conversation may assume the interaction is Adult to Adult or Parent to Child, but the ulterior communication may be Child to Child.

Transactions tend to follow patterns, and even life patterns, or life scripts, may be observed (Berne, 1972). Life scripts may have their beginning in infancy (pretty baby), in early childhood (don't do that—it's dirty), in school (pay attention, you'll get ahead), with peers (you're stupid), or at work (be on time, be neat). Many people play games that lead to or are part of stereotyped life scripts that they repeat over and over again.

TA theory suggests that strokes, evidences of verbal or nonverbal attention, are needed by people, and that negative strokes are preferred over no strokes at all. As a population we are seen to be externally motivated, hungry for strokes from others, and a large number of enterprises are in the business of selling strokes or implying that their products will help us obtain strokes: e. g., Esalen, Transcendental Meditation, the tobacco companies, General Motors (Ivey, 1980).

The structuring of time is an important consideration in Transactional Analysis. People structure their time to avoid boredom in various ways. *Withdrawal* in the form of fantasy, meditation, or dreaming is healthy to a point, but continual withdrawing may lead to depression and loneliness. *Rituals* are predictable exchanges of strokes—everyday greeting behaviors, church ceremonies, even compulsive behaviors. *Pastimes* are socially acceptable, meaningless, often prescribed, ways of spending time—discussing the weather, sports, women/men/babies, inflation, the youth of today. *Activities* comprise work, chores, and hobbies—our involvement with tasks, ideas, and objects; the activities we engage in effectively generally produce positive strokes for us. *Games* and *rackets* are interactions that lead ultimately to a predetermined payoff that is often negative for at least one of the persons involved. *Intimacy* is the most rewarding way in which we may structure time. Because it involves the open sharing of feelings, experiences, and thoughts in a trusting relationship, however, intimacy may be viewed as too risky, and therefore may be avoided.

As with Rational-Emotive Therapy, the counseling process in Transactional Analysis is highly confrontive, and the counselor is active and directive. The counselor pays attention to the language of the client and interprets client behaviors in terms of ego states, games, strokes, life scripts, and the time structure of the individual. The role of the counselor often involves direct teaching which may include revealing discrepancies and incongruities or other issues that seem relevant to the needs of the client.

CONSIDER THE FOLLOWING:

Thompson and Rudolph (1988) presented a transcription in which the counselor, in working with a 10-year-old-boy, focused on a single aspect of Transactional Analysis: stroking. In this excerpt the counselor (CO) was teaching Christopher (C), the client, to seek and give positive strokes. This passage exemplifies the counselor's active and instructive role in TA.

CO: Can you think of a positive stroke you've given someone today?"

C: Not really.

CO: How about when I came in, and you looked up and smiled?"

C: I guess. I smiled at most everybody in the class today.

CO: You have to remember that they don't have to be verbal; just a smile is a positive stroke. Can you think of any negative strokes you've given anyone today?

C: No.

CO: That's good. Of course, the same holds true for negative strokes. If, without realizing it, you looked at someone and gave that person a hard frown or something, that could be a negative stroke that you didn't realize you gave.

C: I don't see why I would have given any, even by accident. There wasn't any reason to give any.

CO: Well, good. Can you think of any positive strokes anyone gave you today?

C: When I got 100 on our test today. Mrs. Kincaid said that that was very good.

CO: I'm glad. Any negative strokes?

C: No. (Thompson & Rudolph, 1988, p. 186, reprinted by permission).

The instructive thrust of TA allows counselors wide latitude in examining the client's behavior, and teaching, as in the instance above, whenever the counselor believes there is need. In addition to their instructional role, transaction analysts often challenge the patterns of behavior their clients have evolved. They analyze and interpret and make efforts to convince their clients that some of the games and ego states they rely on to meet their needs are counterproductive, and they may use Gestalt experiments (James & Jongeward, 1971) to encourage their clients to consider adopting new behaviors.

The evolution of Choice Awareness, as noted in Chapter 3, was originally an attempt to make TA more comprehensible for children, but we moved continuously away from the constructs of that system. The ego states, Parent—Adult — Child, while in some genuine ways more comprehensible than their predecessors, superego—ego—id, still leave at least one significant question to be answered. Do we have within us three ego states? Whether we do or not, we clearly do have choices. While sophisticated clients may state, "That was my Child," as if they are not responsible for the functioning of that part of themselves, it is far more difficult for them to escape responsibility for their behaviors when they say, "That was my choice."

There is an elegance in helping people see that their behaviors are choices, since such an interpretation cries out for change when it is needed. By contrast, seeing behaviors as resulting from ego states and scripts can become another way of excusing oneself, and is therefore less elegant. The five CREST choices and the OK/OD expressions of those choices in the Choice Awareness system are less mystical than the complex of subcategories that have derived from the original, simple concept of Parent—Adult—Child. In his final book, Berne (1972) cited the Parent, the Influencing Parent, and the Active Parent; the Adult; the Child, The Adapted Child, The Natural Child, the Little Professor, the Ogre Father, and the Jolly Giant. To these James and Jongeward (1971) added the Constant Parent, Adult and Child; while Harris (1967) contributed the concept of the Archaic Parent, Adult, and Child. Dealing with these various concepts and the numerous games and other structures of Transactional Analysis is more abstract and less available for recall than OK and OD CREST choices. As Gilliland, *et al.* (1984) suggested, there is some danger that counselors may emphasize the jargon of TA and analysis of behaviors without giving sufficient emphasis to changing behaviors or to the affective or relationship aspects of counseling. To this we would add that there is danger that possibilities for change may be lost in the very acts of labeling and analyzing.

Although Berne's (1961) original goal of presenting a simple, readily comprehensible system for general use was admirable, the continual evolution of more complex games and sub-ego states has resulted in the need for the counselor to be the keeper of the faith, the interpreter, as it were, of a new mystique. By contrast, a purpose in the Choice Awareness system is to maintain simplicity of language and keep the focus on choice so that counseling is demystified for individuals, and so that they are enabled to take more effective control over their own lives through making better choices.

The concept of life scripts (Berne, 1972) suggests a kind of inexorable playing out of a role predetermined in infancy, childhood, or adolescence; and while there is an inference that life scripts can be altered, the literature of TA does not offer great encouragement in that regard. Although some individuals do seem to follow such patterns with little likelihood of deviation, the inevitable nature of life scripts as represented in Transactional Analysis literature seems more pessimistic than is necessary. Once again, we offer the concept of choice as an alternative, suggesting that life patterns of choices that evolve or are imitated may indeed have powerful effects on individuals. Nonetheless, it is more optimistic and helpful to see these patterns as well-developed, highly-structured choices rather than as life scripts, since patterns involving choices are seen more readily as amenable to modification.

Choice Awareness theory supports the use of Transactional Analysis with many adult clients, particularly those who seem likely to be intrigued by the analytical structure of the system. For many such individuals, guided exploration in the literature and concepts of TA would appear to have an advantage over other systems. Transactional Analysis places emphasis on helping clients explore the ways they have been behaving and interacting, and the assumption is made that this will lead to more functional future behaviors. Choice Awareness places its emphasis on helping clients see their behaviors and interactions as choices and emphasizes the planning of more effective choices if change is needed. We believe that the basic objectives of Transactional Analysis for clients are highly desirable, but we support a less complex approach, used in ways that place more control in the hands of clients.

SELF-EXAMINATION—JOURNAL ENTRY: Take a few minutes, preferably at least five, and discuss the extent to which you keep a reasonable balance in your use of Parent-Adult-Child transactions involving the persons and events you encounter. Consider how this balance relates to the balance you maintain among your CREST choices. Head your entry MY TRANSACTIONS.

We encourage you to share these ideas with your clients, inviting their reactions and helping them see that the patterns of transactions they have with others come from their patterns of choices, and that they can change the kinds of choices they make with others.

COUNSELING APPLICATION—JOURNAL ENTRY: Discuss the extent to which you believe it is important for you to use Transactional Analysis approaches with your clients. Consider with at least one specific or hypothetical client how you might incorporate elements of this approach in your counseling. Head your entry TA AND MY CLIENTS.

Behaviorism

The four therapies explored in this chapter focus on thinking/ working choices. Transactional Analysis and Rational-Emotive Therapy are seen as focusing on thinking choices, and Reality Therapy is seen as giving somewhat greater emphasis to thinking choices than to working choices. Behaviorism, behavior therapy, or behavior modification, is the counseling process that gives the greatest emphasis to the words and actions, the *working* choices, of the individual.

Behavior therapy is a counseling system that focuses on helping people learn to behave in ways that better serve their needs. Two basic postulates are: that the behavior of organisms, rather than cognitive or affective phenomena, determine the limits of learning, as well as attitudes and habits; and that environment and experiences determine how the personality of the individual develops.

The behaviorist takes the position that human beings can be studied objectively, their behaviors can be predicted, and the success of interventions can be measured. The behaviorist focuses on what is observable and measurable—stimuli, events, and actions, rather than on feelings or attitudes, or what the behaviorist considers to be vague, meaningless terms used by the client. "The intentional behavioral therapist can take vague descriptions of client problems, make them more specific and operational, and then show the client how these behaviors are related systematically to environmental sequences in cause-and-effect relationships" (Ivey, 1980, p. 221).

The A-B-C's of behavioral counseling involve Antecedent events, resultant Behaviors, and Consequences. *A—Antecedent events.* If an individual complains of depression, the counselor explores the antecedents: What were you doing when this feeling began? What was the time? The place? Who were the persons present at the onset of the depression? What happened step by step that led up to that feeling— so I can see what was going on? Have we missed anything important? *B—resultant Behaviors.* The counselor explores how the individual responded to the feeling of depression: What was the sequence of events? To statements such as, "I felt bad," tell me specifically what you did and said. Where did you feel the depression? Role play with me what happened; tell me what I should be doing as your mother (friend, other). *C—Consequences.* The counselor examines with the client the responses that ensued: What was the upshot of the event? What were the results? How did you feel when it was over? As the A-B-C model suggests, in the early stages of counseling the behaviorist usually asks a great many questions, but Ivey (1980) has indicated that it is possible to achieve the same ends less intrusively through incorporating reflection of feeling, paraphrasing, and summarization.

The behaviorist puts responsibility on clients for determining the goals of counseling though exploring such matters as what clients would like to change in their behaviors, how they would like their relationships to be different, what they would like the other person to do, how relationships would be if they were ideal. These explorations lead to selection of the behaviors clients need to change.

The behaviorist concludes that whatever follows a particular piece of behavior affects the probability of its happening again. Let us assume that John acts depressed and others avoid him. If John sees avoidance as a desirable outcome, his behavior is reinforced, if he does not see it as desirable, his behavior is less likely to be repeated. If Julia acts depressed and others attend to her, a similar phenomenon occurs. If she sees attention as a desirable outcome, her behavior is reinforced, if she does not see attention as desirable, her behavior is less likely to be repeated.

The issue of reinforcement is vital to behavioral theory. Indeed the claim is made (Lundin, 1977) that one's personality is acquired through the use of reinforcers—first and foremost are the essential reinforcers of food, water, air, and shelter. Beyond those essentials, determining what makes sense for the individual or the counselor to use as reinforcement for a particular behavior is a key to success in counseling. Some people respond well to social reinforcers: smiles, affection, recognition, time, attention, and approval. Others seem at least at first to require more tangible rewards: money, grades, certificates, and tokens. For many clients even negative attention is preferable to being ignored.

One reinforcer that is often used by behaviorists, food—most often candy—may be challenged on the grounds of suitability. In some cases, for example to induce such behaviors as proper toileting with retarded individuals, the benefits would seem to outweigh the potential costs. With more fully-functioning individuals, even though candy may elicit the desired behavior more quickly than other means, the question may be asked whether the benefits outweigh the costs in terms of tooth decay, eventual weight problems, and the possible connection of sugar intake to hyperactivity.

Behaviorists use a variety of strategies for reinforcing clients. Some of these strategies involve the client actively in the process and place the counselor in a mentoring role, while other strategies place more of the responsibility for action on the counselor as expert. Behavioral strategies may be placed along a mentor-to-expert continuum that includes self-management; behavioral contracting; behavioral rehearsal and role play; thought stopping, cognitive restructuring, and reframing; systematic desensitization; and satiation, flooding, and implosive therapy.

Self-management strategies clearly ask the client to take significant responsibility for the process of change and in so doing help the individual gain control over at least some elements in the environment. At one level self-management may involve only self-monitoring. For example, an eleven-year-old girl who saw herself as "crying all the time" agreed to keep a chart on the times she cried, noting when, where, with whom, and under what circumstances she cried. This simple action on her part had a salutary effect—she discovered that she cried far less often than she had suspected.

Self-management, at another level, involves modification of choices, a process that may include several steps, such as those outlined by Cormier and Cormier (1985, p. 523).

CONSIDER THE FOLLOWING:

Paul was a student who had difficulty managing his time and resisting opportunities to party with his residence hall buddies, and who consequently found his college career at risk. He was referred to Jerry Solarian, a college counselor. Jerry used steps similar to those outlined by the Cormiers with Paul.

Step 1. *Client identifies and records target behavior and controlling antecedents and consequences.* Without trying to change his behavior, Paul kept a log for three days, recording how he spent his time and under what circumstances. Then he added up his eating, sleeping, exercise, class, study, and social time. He was appalled when he realized how little study time he spent, and noted that he, more than others, seemed to be the stimulus for fooling around, tossing a ball, going out for food or drinks.

Step 2. *Client identifies desired behavior and direction of change (goals).* Paul specified that he needed to increase his study and class preparation time to at least one and a half hours a day.

Steps 3, 4, and 5. *Counselor explains possible self-management strategies, the client selects one or more, and makes a verbal commitment to a strategy.* Jerry suggested several possible ways Paul might organize and keep track of his study time. Paul chose to concentrate his study time in the morning after breakfast—since his first class was at 9:00 a.m. three days a week—and in the late afternoon, when he seemed most to be cajoling and distracting others. He chose the option of putting a small piece of paper tape on his wrist daily and making a tally for each fifteen minutes he actually studied. He committed himself verbally to the time frame and even more firmly to logging six blocks of fifteen minutes at some time during each day or evening. Jerry gave him several strips of adhesive-backed paper that remained from mailing-label pages.

Steps 6 and 7. *Counselor instructs and models selected strategies and client rehearses those strategies.* Jerry demonstrated how a shy client had used the tape-tally process to record instances in which he initiated contact with others. Paul tried a piece of paper tape under his watch band, and practiced moving the band to record a tally. He found that workable.

Steps 8 and 9. *Client uses selected strategies "in vivo" and records the frequency and level of the target behavior.* Paul kept tallies for his fifteen minute intervals of study over four days.

Step 10. *Client's data are reviewed by counselor and client; client continues or revises the program.* Paul reported that he was able to equal or exceed his target of six tallies on each day, and he enthusiastically agreed that he should continue the program.

Step 11. *Charting or posting of data for self- and environmental-reinforcement of client progress.* Paul posted a chart near the light switch to his residence hall room on which he kept a total of the number of fifteen-minute time blocks he studied. As a reward for himself, since he was a self-styled "fitness freak," he decided that any time he accumulated thirty points or more he was entitled to an extra half hour of lifting weights or playing handball. For him that was a genuine motivator and his success with the program continued throughout the semester.

Behavioral contracting is a related, more formal, self-management strategy in which the client enters into an agreement to perform specified tasks or attain particular goals. The contract usually contains specific consequences for performance or nonperformance. Contracting has been used in individual and group situations in weight management, drug and alcohol treatment, cigarette smoking, and monitoring physical fitness (Gilliland, *et al.*, 1984). The contract may serve as the primary strategy for behavior change, or it may be used as an evaluative tool. The contract pledge may be the individual's signature alone, or a reward or penalty system may be used. In the latter instances a trip, a purchase, or a specific sum of money may be arranged as a reward, or the individual may post an amount of money or a valuable object he or she will lose if the contract is not kept.

For a contract to be effective the terms need to be clear to all involved and the behavioral goals must be specific. Rewards and penalties should be clear and appropriate. The contract should be written in positive terms and any bonus(es) should be specified. Another person (or more than one) may be enlisted for support; if others are included, their roles should be detailed. Signatures indicating commitment should be obtained from all persons involved. A progress chart, a log, or some other means of monitoring progress should be developed and some means of verification, such as day-to-day checking by a teacher or supervisor, should be specified (Cormier & Cormier, 1985).

Behavioral rehearsal and role play techniques based on the strategy of modeling, are additional approaches that enlist clients actively in the counseling process. Many clients have difficulty emitting desired behaviors until they see and hear them demonstrated by others. The purpose of behavioral rehearsal and role play is to overcome that difficulty.

Once the desired behavior has been selected by the counselor and client, the counselor serves as mentor and coach and helps the client practice, adjust, and improve responses in situations that are similar to those that concern him or her. Alternatively, the counselor may take the client role and model behaviors that might more effectively respond to the situation that troubles the client; the client then takes his or her own part and rehearses the behavior the counselor has modeled.

The goal of role play is that of expanding client awareness and helping the client consider alternative behaviors (choices). The goal of behavior rehearsal is that of helping the client develop patterns of behavior (choice patterns) that may serve beyond the confines of the counseling office. The counselor who is skilled in the use of behavior rehearsal and role play affords clients an excellent resource for encountering their concerns through making better choices.

Thought stopping, cognitive restructuring, and reframing are among the cognitive strategies used by behaviorists. *Thought stopping* involves teaching clients to actively interrupt their own thought patterns—literally to say STOP internally every time the recurring destructive thought occurs. The rationale is that if unwanted thoughts are constantly interrupted they are almost certain to decrease in frequency. An extreme example would be that of a client who constantly returns to the thought that more alertness in the middle of the night would have prevented the crib death of his/her child. A more frequent example is the individual who obsesses over a "road not taken," or an opportunity declined.

Cognitive restructuring (Meichenbaum, 1977) involves changing self-defeating thoughts to self-enhancing or coping thoughts. When they face new situations many clients tell themselves in advance they will not come across well; while they are in the situation they tell themselves they are not making good impressions on those present; and after the experience they tell themselves, "I blew it again." Such thoughts almost always block the achievement of objectives. In cognitive restructuring clients are encouraged to acknowledge in advance that they often feel uncomfortable in new situations, but their task is only to do the best they can; during the experience they are encouraged to use the coping mechanisms of focusing on the task—what I want to say, do, or accomplish right now, or to take a deep breath or otherwise induce some form of relaxation; and following the experience they are encouraged to give themselves credit for each and every evidence of growth or positive outcome.

In simplest terms, *reframing* involves changing destructive thoughts to constructive thoughts. The mother who is frustrated with her son, who at the moment is acting in a very dependent way, may attend to the behavior and think, "I can't stand this child, I wish I were rid of him." In reframing, she might be encouraged to notice her son's tired eyes, his pleading look, and his voice tone. Her consequent response could be expected to change dramatically if she concludes that her son is tired and wants help. In reframing, the questions become: is there a larger or different "frame" which can help the client see the child's behavior as positive, or at least less negative; is there a different label that the client could put on her own behavior or that of her child; or is there another aspect of this situation that the client can look at that would give it a different meaning? (Bandler & Grinder, 1982)

Systematic desensitization is a strategy that Wolpe (1973) developed and refined to counter a wide range of problems, including stress, anxiety, phobias, and similarly problematic conditions. Systematic desensitization begins with relaxation training involving both muscles and mind, and with analyzing the client's problem. The counselor uses the client's description of whatever it is that causes stress or anxiety to develop a hierarchy of similar and related events that range from least to most anxiety-producing for the client. The second step in systematic desensitization is that of teaching the client to relax all muscle groups while imagining being in places that he or she sees as beautiful, safe, and serene. The client is given homework in relaxation training, often facilitated through the use of tape recordings of the relaxation training conducted by the counselor. The third step, which occurs once the client has learned to relax effectively, is the actual process of systematic desensitization. The counselor begins to present the nonthreatening or least threatening aspects of the situation, then gradually proceeds to progressively more threatening examples. Each threatening scene is paired with relaxation and visual imagery that the client has practiced. Whenever the client feels threatened by the situation being described, he or she gives a predetermined nonverbal signal, and the counselor immediately presents a scene of calmness or beauty accompanied by relaxation cues, and later works up to presenting the threatening scene again. The process is continued until the client can imagine the most threatening aspects of the situation without undue anxiety or stress.

An example of the strategy might be that of clients who experience severe test anxiety. Paired with calm images and relaxation techniques, the clients are helped progressively to imagine that a test is to occur three months hence, and ultimately to imagine sitting in the test room with the questions before them. Progressive increases in the threat level, and simultaneous positive images, have helped many individuals learn to cope with situations that cause extreme anxiety (Gilliland, *et al.*,1984).

Satiation, flooding, and *implosion* are related behavior modification techniques. In *satiation* individuals are generally "flooded" with the material goods that they crave, asked to smoke constantly or eat copiously and continually, invited to exaggerate their acting-out behaviors, or helped to hoard the goods (towels, and so forth) they have been squirreling away. In *flooding*, clients are asked to face their problems verbally through a kind of reverse systematic desensitization—they are bombarded with exaggerated visual images of the person/event/object they fear most. In *implosion*, clients are helped to face their fears, such as elevator riding, in an exaggerated way, often at first in the company of the counselor. Many people who experience satiation find that the object of their craving becomes repulsive. Many who experience flooding or implosive therapy find that they are able to overcome their unrealistic fears.

Choice Awareness theory supports the use of behavior modification procedures for many clients despite the fact that all of the strategies used in behavior modification have been criticized on three major grounds. (1) They may induce short term changes in overt behaviors without getting to the core of more deep-seated emotions and feelings. (2) They fail to provide clients with deep understanding and insights into the problems they face. (3) They rob individuals of their autonomy and freedom of choice—people may be manipulated into doing things they do not really want to do or that are not appropriate for them to do—in a form of brainwashing.

We are convinced that the procedures of behavior modification can and ought to be applied humanely and openly, and that the choices of clients ought to be considered crucial even in behavioral counseling procedures. We take this position despite statements of the kind made by a major character conceived by Skinner (1948—also cited in our preface), "Our members are practically always doing what they want to do—what they 'choose' to do—but we see to it that they will want to do precisely the things which are best for themselves and the community. Their behavior is determined, yet they're free" (p. 197). Our view is that individuals are far freer than Skinner suggested, and that counselors need not be put off in using behavioral approaches by inferences of mind control and manipulation.

Many counseling clients need to be helped to consider the frame of reference with which they view reality; many others need to be helped to learn or relearn patterns of thinking/working choices that may enable them to confront that reality more effectively. Behaviorists have contributed to the counseling field in at least two primary ways: (1) through demanding greater specificity on the part of counselors concerning their objectives, their procedures, and the measurability of outcomes; and (2) through the development of numerous specific techniques that are useful in counseling. We believe that behavior modification approaches are most appropriate for clients who have developed choice patterns involving words, actions, and thoughts that are quite strongly ingrained. As with other more active theoretical formulations, the position is taken in Choice Awareness that humanely-applied behavior modification approaches should follow reasonable opportunities for clients—even those who have strongly ingrained thought or behavior patterns—to air their concerns and evolve their own solutions.

> SELF-EXAMINATION—JOURNAL ENTRY: Take a few minutes, preferably at least five, and discuss the extent to which you use some of the strategies of behaviorism (e.g., self-management, thought-stopping, behavioral rehearsal) in coping with the difficulties you face from time to time. Further, discuss the extent to which your use of behavioral strategies is consistent with a pattern of effective thinking/working choices. Head your entry MY BEHAVIORAL STRATEGIES.

We encourage you to share these ideas with your clients, inviting their reactions and helping them see that focusing on their behaviors and thoughts and making effective thinking/working choices involving self-monitoring, cognitive restructuring, reframing, and so forth, may help them achieve some of their most important personal goals.

COUNSELING APPLICATION—JOURNAL ENTRY: Discuss the extent to which you believe it is important for you to use behavior modification techniques with your clients. Consider with at least one specific or hypothetical client how you might incorporate a behavior modification technique you have not previously used in your counseling. Head your entry BEHAV-IORAL STRATEGIES AND CLIENT THINKING/WORKING CHOICES.

Thinking/Working Choices: Planning Ahead

Choice Awareness theory suggests that planfulness is appropriate in the implementation of effective thinking/working choices. Clients who think or act in shallow, circular, or self-destructive ways can learn to make different patterns of choices. Some clients will gain if they merely decide to remain alert to opportunities to think and work at deeper levels. Others will need to be more intentional, arranging for opportunities to read expansively and to otherwise challenge their own thoughts and give their energies to tasks that will enhance the sense of meaning in their lives.

You can help your clients learn to cope more effectively in the moment with the frustrations and concerns they face. Perhaps more important, you can help them learn to anticipate events that are similar to those they have faced in the past, and to encounter those events with a broader repertoire of more effective choices, including thinking/working choices. You can help your clients to think through and rehearse how they might implement their choices in ways that better serve their goals. Planning for thinking/working choices is supported in Choice Awareness theory as an essential element in helping clients take more effective control in their lives.

Most people have two or three subjects—often work- or family-related—on which they have some expertise, and about which they may be able to discourse at considerable length. They allow themselves a few other topics on which they are comfortable chatting for brief periods of time; and there may be dozens more avenues of discussion on which they feel free to make brief comments. Many individuals can exhaust their stories and share their knowledge and opinions in a matter of days, weeks, or months; few are effective in sustaining deep relationships over a period of years. Add to that two realities: that the majority of people see themselves as responders, and that males consider light chatter to be a female preserve, and it is little wonder if people, males especially, run out of things to communicate about with those who are constantly in their lives. Boredom sets in. People are tempted to form new relationships through which they can renew the feeling of excitement that comes with sharing their stories and discussing what they know. A great many individuals need help in making their long-term interactions meaningful. To say it another way, a great many individuals need help in making more effective thinking/working choices as they communicate with others.

When we meet people who are good listeners, our early perception is that they are good conversationalists. The listening strategy works especially well during superficial interactions—at parties, for example. But more than skill in listening is needed to sustain relationships over time—especially when two responders find themselves together. For many people to become really good conversationalists who can sustain relationships over time, they need (1) skill in listening, (2) skill in drawing others out, and (3) skill in sharing.

Listening requires more than saying "uh huh" while reading a newspaper. It involves a variety of verbal and nonverbal skills such as those we explored in Chapters 3, 6, and 7 (Counselor Choices, and Caring Choices: Exploration and Application). We all need the sense from time to time that someone is listening to us attentively. We thrive on that sense—when it occurs. We need to listen to others with that same kind of attentiveness, and many counseling clients need to develop better skills of listening to others—beyond the point of finding the place where they can begin to talk.

Skill in drawing others out is an important aspect of listening. In our everyday communication we can reflect the feelings of others, ask good open-ended questions, and make invitational statements: "That sounds interesting, I'd like to hear more about it." We need to reflect on our knowledge of other people and the life events they face, and be ready to ask them about the new business venture, the sick relative, the busy sibling, the growing child, the mutual friend, or the adventures of their well-loved team. Initiate with a positive invitation, and the responder feels our permission to tell the story or flash the picture that might otherwise have remained unmentioned or unshown. We need to draw others out; and counseling clients can gain in the same way, instead of centering their conversation totally on self.

Skill in sharing may be even less well developed than the skills of listening and drawing others out. As we have suggested, people give themselves permission to dialogue in depth on a few topics and allow themselves limited freedom beyond those selected issues. Often they see others' eyes glaze over after the first few minutes of discussion, and if they are responsive they drop the matter under discussion. Alternatively, they make a few observations about the latest political maneuver, the latest bit of information about the exploration of space, or the weekend's sports results, and then drop the subject. Their store of thinking/working choices is thin.

What is the alternative? A Sunday supplement piece about Rose Kennedy that appeared some years ago offers a clue. Each day Mrs.

Kennedy selected an article from the morning paper and posted it in the pantry. Every member of the family was expected to read the article and have something to say about it at dinner. That simple act led to genuine, deep, challenging discussions, and members of the family made every effort to be present, in part because they wanted to participate in the dialogue. The message is clear: if we do not have enough to talk about to create absorbing involvement with those in our households or in our lives, we can do something about it. That something can be constructed in the way the Kennedy clan's dialogue was, or each person can be expected to bring up a topic for discussion on his or her own, or both expectations can occur.

Other alternatives abound, and they need not be restricted to the dinner table. We might read aloud from a brief news article, share a piece of poetry or a brief essay from an anthology or collection, use an object —a photograph or a souvenir—as a basis for dialogue. We need to share with others, deeply and regularly—and counseling clients need to permit themselves, even obligate themselves, to do the same if they want to enhance their communication with others.

Many of your clients would gain if you engaged them in a process of education toward more effective thinking/working choices. Some clients may find it difficult to change ingrained patterns of choices— of unendurable silences or brief-as-possible responses—and counseling as relearning is likely to be necessary, while for others the process might be that of learning. For many clients, expanding the range of thinking/ working choices and finding challenge through listening and sharing may mean that they achieve the level of spa. One client whose efforts had changed the flow of dialogue in her family said ecstatically, "I've got the excitement back in my life now."

Planning and spontaneity are at different points on a continuum, but most clients need to broaden the spectrum of choices available to them before they can be truly spontaneous. Once they have expanded their range of thinking/working choices, they are able to respond more effectively to events as they occur. Planfulness in thinking/working choices is supported in Choice Awareness theory as an essential component in enabling individuals to be more effective in living their lives.

CONSIDER THE FOLLOWING:

In prior chapters we discussed Julia's relationship with her roommate, Maria. Her Resident Assistant encouraged Julia to expand the range of her behavior to include all the CREST choices in her interactions. Julia thought deeply and worked assiduously on her relationship with Maria. Many of the gains the two experienced resulted from Julia's skills in sharing.

Here are three thinking/working choices Julia used to initiate effective dialogue with Maria.

J: Listen to this quote by Machiavelli—I always thought of him as more cynical: 'God is not willing to do everything, and thus take away our free will and that share of glory which belongs to us.'

J: How would you like it if we alternated each day in suggesting an article from the newspaper or a news magazine to talk about? This piece I found about a new book could get us started.

J: One of my profs keeps saying, 'No good deed ever goes unpunished.' What do you think of that?

Many of your clients would benefit if you asked this question: "Who in your world would benefit if you thought more deeply about ways you might interact better, if you implemented the resulting ideas through more effective words and actions, if you contributed interesting topics to your dialogue, or if you balanced your thinking/working more suitably with the other CREST options?" You contribute to your clients' relationships with others and to their feelings of self-esteem when you assist them to expand and rehearse their repertoire of thinking/working choices—always encouraging them to balance thinking/working with the other CREST choices.

Thinking/Working Choices

Choice Awareness theory suggests that if clients are to act responsibly, they need to have available to them a broad repertoire of thinking/working choices—and counselors need a broad repertoire of thinking/working choices as well. Ideas from Reality Therapy can be useful to counselors when they want to help clients to become more goal-directed and to take responsibility for achieving their goals. Ideas from Rational-Emotive Therapy can be useful when clients think irrationally about the world and about some of their own feelings and behaviors. Ideas from Transactional Analysis can be useful when clients could benefit from encouragement to think for themselves, to express their feelings, and to reduce their game-playing. Ideas from Behavior Therapy can be useful when clients need help in examining the ways in which they interact, in reframing their thoughts, and in changing patterns of action. A variety of approaches can be incorporated in counseling to lead clients to become more planful and effective in making thinking/working choices. The results should be that they see themselves as effective choice-makers, they acquire the skills they need to encounter the difficulties they face, and they grow in their feelings of well-being.

References

Bandler, R. & Grinder, J. (1982). *Reframing.* Moab, Utah: Real People Press.

Berne, E. (1961). *Transactional analysis in psychotherapy.* New York: Grove Press.

Berne, E. (1964). *Games people play.* New York: Grove Press.

Berne, E. (1972). *What do you say after you say hello?* New York: Grove Press.

Cormier, W. H. & Cormier, L. S. (1985). *Interviewing strategies for helpers.* (2nd ed.) Monterey, CA: Brooks/Cole.

Ellis, A. (1971). *Growth through reason*. Palo Alto, CA: Science and Behavior Books.

Ellis, A. & Grieger, R. (1977). *Handbook of rational-emotive therapy*. New York: Springer.

Ellis, A. & Harper, R. A. (1979). *A new guide to rational living*. Englewood Cliffs, NJ: Prentice-Hall.

Gilliland, B. E., James, R. K., Roberts, G. T., and Bowman, J. T. (1984). *Theories and strategies in counseling and psychotherapy*. Englewood Cliffs, NJ: Prentice-Hall.

Glasser, W. (1965). *Reality therapy*. New York: Harper & Row.

Harris, T. (1967). *I'm OK—You're OK*. New York: Harper & Row.

Ivey, A. E., with Simek-Downing, L. (1980). *Counseling and psychotherapy: Skills, theories, and practice* (2nd ed.). Englewood Cliffs, NJ: Prentice-Hall.

James, M. & Jongeward, D. (1971). *Born to win: Transactional analysis with Gestalt experiments*. Reading, MA: Addison-Wesley.

Lundin, R. W. (1977). Behaviorism: Operant reinforcement. In R. Carson (Ed.). *Current personality theories*. Itasca, IL: F. E. Peacock.

Meichenbaum, D. H. (1977). *Cognitive-behavior modification: An integrative approach*. New York: Plenum.

Skinner, B. F. (1948). *Walden two*. New York: Macmillan.

Thompson, C. L. & Rudolph, L. B. (1988). *Counseling children* (2nd ed.). Pacific Grove, CA: Brooks/Cole.

Wolpe, J. (1973). *The practice of behavior therapy*. Elmsford, NY: Pergamon Press.

Part III
Choice Awareness in the Counseling Process:

Changing a Life Script

Maintaining Desirable Body Weight

Enhancing Self-Concept

Child Counseling

Counseling Older Persons

A Group Counseling Process

The chapters that follow show how Choice Awareness theory may be applied to specific concerns. These discussions are brief because we have explored how this theory might be applied throughout this work. We invite you to examine these discussions with a view to considering how you might particularize Choice Awareness for the counseling clients and concerns you encounter. To some extent the individuals discussed and the group situations explored combine elements of more than one individual or group counseling process.

Chapter 16

Changing a Life Script

The Life Script of Wilma Adams, Wife of an Alcoholic

Wilma Adams presents a model of the life script issue raised in Transactional Analysis. Wilma sought counseling as the wife of an alcoholic who had grown up as the daughter of alcoholic parents. She felt dragged down, burdened, by the evidence she saw that she and her husband might be repeating the pattern of her parents. Troubled by this concern, and spurred on as a result of an evening class in human relations in which she enrolled, Wilma decided to take advantage of the help available to her through a university counseling service. Sol Warren was assigned to her as counselor.

Wilma poured out her feelings of anguish and concern and her somewhat intense recent feelings of attraction to the periodic, if temporary, oblivion of alcohol. She spoke of her parents' alcoholism, their apparent search for comfort, and their avoidance of problems through drinking. Neither parent exhibited the kind of drunken stupor commonly associated with alcoholism. As a result both her mother and father had resisted for years applying the alcoholic label to their own behaviors; and, until she was a teenager, Wilma had resisted allowing that label to enter her mind.

Wilma's family began to face the reality of alcoholism only when the economy suffered a downturn a few years earlier and Wilma's father was riffed from his job as an accountant in a medium-sized firm. Wilma vividly recalled sitting on the stairs, overhearing the dialogue that occurred when Mr. Larkin told his wife about being terminated—several days after the event actually happened and after he had lied repeatedly concerning his whereabouts. Wilma's mother plied her father with drinks and probed with incessant questions to fill in the major pieces of the puzzle.

No, Wilma overheard, not all people in Mr. Larkin's situation had been let go. Yes, some employees with less seniority had been kept on. Yes, Mr. Larkin had raised that issue rather gently, and had been put off with the rationalization that those who had been retained had skills that could not be dispensed with. Mrs. Larkin poured them each another drink and continued to probe. Eventually she learned that he had been told that one of the reasons he was not viewed as indispensable was that he had made serious errors from time to time that were taken as a sign of his unreliability. Wilma heard muffled sounds for many moments—tears, she thought. She felt a strong urge to run and comfort her father, but she remained where she was, and he provided further information.

"I couldn't think of anything more to say, so I said I'd just go it on my own. 'There's plenty for a good accountant to do,' I told him."

"Then what?" said Mrs. Larkin.

Wilma heard her father start to speak, then stop.

"C'mon, tell me. I know there's more," her mother's voice was gentle, persuading.

"You don't want to hear this," said her father.

"Let it all hang out. You know, I've never thought as much of Bob as you have, so nothing will surprise me."

After some time Wilma heard her father speak again, interrupted by pauses of several seconds each. "Bob put his arm around my shoulder. . . and said, 'Because we've been friends for years, I'm going to tell you something. . . . I argued for keeping you on but I was overruled. . . There is a concern in the company that you have a drinking problem that isn't under control. . . I don't like having to tell you this, but I agree.' Then he looked at me and added, 'It's unlikely that we're going to have a place for you even when the economy turns around, but whether or not we do, for your own sake, get that problem under control.'"

Wilma had been reminded of overhearing her parents' discussion when her course reading list led her to *What Do You Say After You Say*

Hello? a book on Transactional Analysis (Berne, 1972). "Several of Berne's ideas seemed to me to be particularly relevant," she told Sol Warren. She located a piece of paper in her purse and read from some notes she had taken. "The key question often is: 'What did you have to do to make your parents smile or chuckle' (p. 282). When I was little they laughed if I sipped on one of their drinks. And they laughed, too, when I told them about the parties we had—even in high school. The other thing Berne said was that for most alcoholics the parental prohibition is: 'Don't think! Drink!'"

"You know, Mr. Warren," Wilma continued. "What I heard from daddy that night still rings in my ears. And what did my mother say? She sounded like Scarlett O'Hara. I can't recall her exact words, but the message was, 'Let's worry about that tomorrow.'" Wilma sighed a long sigh. "Then of all things, I heard my father pour drinks and propose a toast to 'Tomorrow.'"

When Sol Warren probed a bit, Wilma shared her recall of her feelings way back then, as she sat on the stairs. "Appalled at first, and then strangely comforted, 'cause mom and dad both laughed."

Wilma's reading of Transactional Analysis led her to the conclusion that her father's parental prohibition was *thinking*, and she recalled how often her father had told her, "Now don't you worry your pretty little head about that, my dear." She decided that what made her grandparents and her mother laugh most at her father was when he became warmly conversational or intimate after a drink or two; and she recalled that more than one boy friend of hers had complimented *her* on how relaxed and comfortable she became after she had a couple of glasses of wine.

Wilma's report of her self-analysis continued as she told about her interactions with Patrick, her husband. She saw in the two of them emerging mirror images of her parents. "I can see that from time to time I act as rescuer, as persecutor, and as victim," she said. "Mostly, I guess, I'm a rescuer. I'm always pulling the fat out of the fire and making excuses for him, encouraging him—pleading and cajoling and setting up circumstances designed to minimize his drinking, or at least to soften its effects." From time to time, she reported, she also saw herself as persecutor, lashing out at Patrick, attacking him for his weaknesses and demanding that he straighten himself out. More and more often lately she had begun to think of herself as a victim, worn down by the responsibility of trying, often without hope, to improve circumstances.

"What frightens me most, though, is the recurring thought that I might just give up and join Patrick and my dad and mom in a pink glow of alcoholic behavior. I don't know who would take care of all of them—all of us—but I feel too burdened to go on in the same way much longer." She paused for a moment and sighed. "The thought, 'If you can't lick 'em, join 'em,' occurs to me more and more often. It's both appalling and attractive to me."

The Initial Interview

In the major portion of the first interview, Sol Warren's efforts were directed to the creation of a warm and comfortable environment. He encouraged Wilma to talk with him in any way that was helpful to her; and he concentrated on listening, deeply and fully, as a way of helping Wilma get her feelings out in the open. Sol used nonverbal messages of encouragement, minimum verbal responses, clarifying statements, and reflections of feeling as his major tools in the dialogue, and Wilma rewarded his efforts by sharing with him easily and deeply.

With fifteen minutes remaining in their hour, Sol took a more active role. "To sum up, I see that what you have been telling me in many ways is that you fear being drawn into the web of drinking that surrounds you, and you want help in choosing to combat that attraction."

"Yes, that's right," Wilma replied with a sigh. There was nothing new in the summary, but it comforted her because of its combination of gentleness and directness.

"So we might consider that our job—our contract—is finding ways to help you control your choices so you don't move in that direction." Wilma nodded.

"All right, then, let me say first that I believe we can probably plan on eight or ten sessions, then a follow-up from time to time—but we'll leave that open for now—and that I'd like us to spend most of the time directly working on helping you take better, fuller control of your choices," said Sol.

"That sounds good to me," Wilma responded. She was surprised to have the number of sessions projected at all, and particularly at such a modest number, but she sensed a rising confidence in her that Sol would help her find her way.

"First, Wilma, I'd like to have you make a commitment that you won't drink any alcohol between now and next week when we see each other."

Wilma looked puzzled.

"You've told me that you're worried you might give up and be drawn into a severe drinking problem yourself. The truth is, from what you've told me about your experiences, I believe you already have an alcoholism problem—one that you may be able to master if you take control now."

Wilma's face was a study in changing emotions. Finally she spoke. "I was thinking I might just limit myself—not quit cold turkey—have one glass of wine a day maximum, for example," she said. Her tone was convincing. She smiled, and her eyelids fluttered slightly.

"You have to make your own decision. I won't make it for you. I believe, though, that if *you* commit *yourself* to abstinence, it will give you confidence in yourself and your ability to control what you're most worried about," Sol replied.

Wilma was quiet for several seconds, then she nodded. "I see what you mean. I guess it would be good for me to show myself that I can do without alcohol altogether for a few days."

"For a few days," Sol repeated. "So that means. . . ," he said and paused.

"That I'll try not to drink anything, even wine, over the next seven days," Wilma sighed.

"You'll try, you said. And you sighed. I'm not sure what that means."

Once again Wilma was quiet. "OK, I think you're right. I'll take the pledge. Nothing alcoholic for the next week. I won't even sip on the cooking wine," Wilma said, then smiled.

"Talk about your smile. What it meant just then," said Sol.

"Just that it feels good to make a commitment. I know I can do what I've said I would, and I think it will help me to have a plan."

"So it seems that the plan doesn't feel like a burden. It's something you can do and feel good about," Sol stated.

Wilma nodded enthusiastically. "It'll be like a test. I know I'll be able to pass it."

"I can tell you feel good about that as a commitment."

"Yes. It's a small thing, but it feels good."

"And maybe it's not so small, since it relates to what you're most worried about."

Wilma smiled once again.

"There's something more I think you need to do," Sol's voice was soft and gentle, but there was no mistaking its intensity. "I think you need to become active with AA and strongly encourage Patrick to do the same." He raised his hand when she scowled and opened her mouth to speak. "I know you told me you've tried to persuade him to go. But from what you said you never offered to attend yourself. I suspect from Patrick's point of view you two are in the same ball park."

Wilma stared out the window for a while. Sol spoke. "I see this as a family problem, and I believe that as long as you think about it as just belonging to Patrick you won't make real progress."

Wilma nodded. "The other day. . . ," she began slowly and stopped. "The other day Patrick said to me that I drink about two-thirds and I weigh about two-thirds as much as he does, so if he's got a problem, I do too. That's an exaggeration, but. . . ." Her eyes were glassy, unseeing, fixed on something beyond the counseling office. "Anyway, the drinking is interfering with his work, and it isn't having any effect on mine. At least I think it isn't."

"So you're saying you think it isn't a big problem for you—yet. But I sense acceptance of my suggestion in what you're saying." Sol's voice was gentle.

"I'll go if it'll help Patrick—if he'll go."

"I want you to agree to more than that. Go because it will help *you*. Go because it will model for Patrick what he needs to do. Go even if Patrick won't—but insist strongly that you *want* him to, that you believe *he* needs to go—too."

After several seconds Wilma agreed and Sol introduced a new topic. "In the three or four minutes we have left today, and since you now have a plan to work on, I'd like to have us spend a little time bringing joy into your life."

Wilma's smile was immediate. "I'm not sure what you mean, but I could use some joy."

"Have you ever been to a spa?" Wilma shook her head. "Well, have you ever engaged in exercise and felt the pleasure of the warmth of your muscles and the nice tiredness that follows?"

"Oh yes," she replied. "I took an aerobics class for a while, and even now I use some videotapes I have to keep in shape. At first it was difficult, but for a long time now it's been a real pleasure—as long as I don't overdo it."

"Well, I'd like to introduce you to spa in counseling, Wilma. I'm not sure whether it will be hard or not for you at first, but I'm sure it will bring you good feelings that are similar to what you feel from aerobics. And if you agree we'll put some spa in each of our sessions together," Sol said.

"OK, I'll try most anything once, and things that feel good I usually keep on doing."

Sol reached into a drawer of the table beside him and brought out a plain white pad of paper and a blue felt pen. "All right. Let's begin to list things you can do and that you can take pleasure in. Most of us spend too much time focusing on what worries us and we lose sight of all the good things we have going for us. This list will have only things on it that you *can* do."

"Well, I can do aerobics." Wilma said tentatively. "Is that the kind of thing you mean?"

"Right," said Sol as he wrote the title, THINGS I CAN DO, and the word *aerobics* below it. "And to let you know that you can include the *simplest* of things, I'm going to add *breathe*. As a matter of fact I'd like to compliment you on that. I notice that you breathe deeply and fully, not quickly and shallowly as so many people do—it probably has something to do with your exercise pattern." Sol wrote *breathe* on the list.

"Well, if we're going for simple things, I can add several," said Wilma. "I can walk, talk, run, dance, eat, . . . drink—and maybe even drink too much at times."

"Wait, let me catch up," said Sol as he waved his free hand. He added those items to the list, including *drink too much*.

"And I can cook—some things—pretty well. I make a mean Spanish omelette and a superb chocolate mousse." Wilma rolled her eyes as she enumerated those items, and Sol wrote them down.

Over the next two minutes the list for Wilma was expanded to include: spend money, touch, make friends, compliment others, read, write, type, think, put on makeup, scratch, listen, sew on buttons, socialize, watch television, drive, play tennis, and use a computer.

Wilma's pleasure in the expanding list was evident. Sol picked up on that. "I want to add one simple, but important thing that reflects the way you have been *looking* over the time we've been talking about the things you can do," and he added *smile* to the list.

Wilma beamed. "Yes, and I can laugh, too, and gripe, and let myself be miserable. But I think it'd be a help for me to decide to smile more often."

"OK," said Sol, adding those items, "and with your permission I'm going to add both *decide* and *choose* to your list. Those words mean almost the same thing to me, but I use the word *choose* to cover all my choices, both major and minor, and I use the word *decide* mainly for major issues."

Wilma nodded. "Decide and choose," she said aloud, softly.

"Our time's up today. I think we've made some good progress. You have a plan that you think is attainable—to eliminate alcohol for the week, and to get yourself, and Patrick, if possible, to AA." Sol searched Wilma's face for any reactions, looked down at the pad on the table before him, and continued. "In keeping with the spa idea, I'd like to suggest that when you become upset or get down on yourself—or Patrick—that you recite in your head things you can do, or list on paper some more of the things that give you pleasure from time to time." At that point Sol tore off the sheet of paper before him and offered it to Wilma.

"Yes, I'll be glad to have this. Whenever I'm in a bad mood, I'll take it out and look at it as a reminder of the good things I've got going for me."

After clarifying the next appointment time, Wilma left smiling.

The Second Interview

Wilma arrived out of breath for her second counseling session. "I couldn't find a place to park close by, so I had to run to get here on time," she explained.

"So I *chose* to run so I could get here on time," Sol offered his revision of her statement gently, tentatively.

"Oh, yeah," Wilma replied. "I chose to run."

Wilma mentally tucked that thought away for later consideration, then launched into a report on her activities. Keeping her no-drinking pledge had been easy, she reported, and she had mused several times over her THINGS I CAN DO list at odd moments and added several items to it. Her own buoyant attitude had served her well during a gathering with Patrick, her parents, and some old friends of the family on the evening after her first appointment with Sol. Even when Patrick and her mother and father started to get high, she had been able to distance herself from that and to see it first and foremost as their problem, and she had resisted their entreaties to "have just one little drink."

"I don't know what's different. Maybe just that I'm beginning to feel more confident that I can lick this thing—but in several ways I seem to be doing better," Wilma commented.

The following evening, she reported, she had brooked the AA issue with Patrick, emphasizing that she planned to join a group, that she *wanted* him to go, but that she *intended* to begin to attend meetings of an AA group in any case. "His response was not as negative as I expected it to be. 'Go if you want to,' he said, but he wouldn't say he'd go," Wilma reported.

"I don't know if he will, but I've told him I'm going to my first meeting tomorrow night," she said, her voice filled with conviction and strength.

Sol had used minimum verbal responses, silence, head nods, and reflections of feeling to encourage Wilma to open the session in her own way. He summarized, "So things have been going rather well for you; you're not sure what will happen with Patrick concerning AA, but you're feeling more confident, and your movements seem to be saying, 'Let's get on with it.'"

Wilma chuckled and said, "Yes."

"Well, I'd like to tie two things together, something you said just a moment or two ago and something from your commentary about Transactional Analysis last week," Sol began.

"A few moments ago you said that you stepped back and saw your parents' and Patrick's getting high as their problem. I'd like to encourage you to see that in a little different way." Wilma nodded and Sol continued. "I'd like you to see that as *you* making the *choice* to let them be responsible for their own behavior—especially Patrick—to let him make his *own* choices." Wilma nodded again. "I see that as different from last week, when you seemed to think that you had to be a persecutor, a rescuer, or a victim."

Wilma scowled. "I don't see your point."

"Which role were you taking when you let Patrick be responsible for his own behavior?"

Wilma looked at the ceiling and thought for several moments. "I can't figure out which."

"That's because you weren't fulfilling any of those roles. And it points the way to the most constructive direction you can take." Sol paused. "Your facial expression changed just now. I think you see it."

"Yes, I believe I do. What I need to do is what I've long known I should. Not let myself get caught up in any of the roles," Wilma mused. "I've been telling myself that for years. . . but. . . ." A long silence followed.

"But you haven't known what role to take or what choices to make to avoid being a persecutor, a rescuer, or a victim," suggested Sol.

"That's right. I try for a moment, then somehow I get caught up in it like it's a spider's web, and I'm a fly, and I can't get away."

"Yes. So I believe our objective ought to be to help you see a wide range of other choices you can make so you don't get caught," said Sol.

"Sounds good to me."

"OK. Talk about what you did that was different in the way you performed with Patrick when he started getting high at your parents' house—your *non*-victim-rescuer-persecutor behavior."

Wilma paused for several moments. "Well," she began, slowly, "I remember just telling myself that Patrick is Patrick and I am I, and I have all these good things I can do, and maybe I can help him see all the good things he can do, but now is not the right time." She paused again, then continued. "I kept thinking, 'We came in my car so I don't have to worry about him insisting on driving if he's had too much to drink; and if he won't go with me when I need to leave, I'll just tell him I'm leaving and to call a cab if he drinks too much.' Somehow, for the first time in a long time, I let him do his thing and I didn't bug him. I got caught up in a good conversation with Mrs. Smitherman, who's been in an aerobics group too, and I had a really good time. It worked out OK."

Sol reached into the table drawer for the pad of paper and felt pen as he had done before, and was to do in other sessions. TO AVOID BEING A PERSECUTOR, RESCUER, OR VICTIM, he titled the page. "Some of the things you did that helped you avoid being a persecutor, rescuer, or victim were: you let Patrick be Patrick. . . ," and Sol wrote the last four of those words on the page.

"I reminded myself of all the good things I can do—so I wasn't thinking about my not being a good, protective wife." Wilma's lips were pursed as she pronounced the words *good* and *protective*.

Remind myself of things I can do, Sol wrote.

"I tried to think about the situation as optimistically as I could," said Wilma.

Be optimistic, noted Sol.

"And I got involved in a conversation of my own," Wilma commented with an air of finality.

Sol added, *Get involved*.

"There was at least one other important element in what you told me. You thought through a strategy. You planned. You decided if necessary that you'd leave on your own and let Patrick call a cab if he drank too much." Sol waited for Wilma's nod, then added, *Plan what to do.*

"I'm going to put this aside now, but we can add other items any time—and I'd encourage you to think about and write down other ideas between sessions, too," Sol commented as he moved the pad to his left. "It's a great beginning for deciding what kinds of choices you can make instead of letting yourself get caught up in the game you so often play with Patrick."

"And my parents," Wilma added.

"And your parents," Sol agreed.

"What I'd like to do now," Sol continued, "is to give you just a little bit of a handle on my philosophy—Choice Awareness."

Wilma looked expectantly at him and Sol cited some of the key bases for the choices she and other people make, during which Wilma interjected several questions and offered possible examples.

Sol defined the word choice as any behavior over which a person can exercise some degree of control, and pointed out to Wilma that her acceptance of that definition meant that she needed to see her words and actions, and to some extent even her thoughts and feelings, as choices. He asked her what she saw as the implications of that generalization.

"Why that means that practically everything I do is a choice," she said, then paused. "I'm probably hardly ever *really* a victim. Maybe I just *choose* to be one. I go along day by day with my blinders on, doing things the way I've always done them, feeling sorry for myself when things don't work out, convinced there's little I can do to affect the world. But at least in my own little world I can probably have a lot of effect."

Sol complimented Wilma for her comprehension and insight.

"Doing things the way we've always done them—following habit— is a problem for most of us. Habits can be useful as a kind of shorthand so we don't have to think through everything in every moment, but the problem is that most of us use habit as a substitute for thinking." Sol commented. "And the implications of that for you are. . . ," he began and paused.

"Well, that hits the nail right on the head for me," Wilma replied. "It seems to me I m a real creature of habit. I have a lot of difficulty taking new roads and making new choices."

For several minutes Wilma shared with Sol the nature of her habit patterns, and together they explored ways in which she might break some of her less effective habits. Sol helped Wilma see that she built specific, narrow, habit patterns in particular relationships—like that of being a rescuer with Patrick and her parents—then pointed out that she made very functional choices in many of her other relationships. He pointed out that she could use those more functional choices with the three people who were closest to her. Sol then asked Wilma about the goals she had with those three people.

"I think with Patrick I just want to have a nice, warm, mature relationship—like two grown-up people who love each other," Wilma said after several seconds, then she sighed. For some time she and Sol talked about what choices that meant she might make.

"I like to call all of those OK choices," said Sol, "as opposed to OD choices—choices that are overdone or an overdose or overdrawn." Sol went on to develop with Wilma the banking analogy and introduced her to the concept of the interpersonal account. He suggested that she conceptualize that she and Patrick each symbolically contributed to and withdrew from an imaginary joint account—that she should not expect always to make OK choices, but that she could strive to make OK choices that would overbalance the OD choices she inevitably made.

Wilma was intrigued with the idea. "That's neat," she said.

"A few minutes ago you said your goal was a mature relationship. I like that word mature," said Sol. Because of time limitations in the session he elected not to introduce the CREST choices at that point, but he covered the flip side of four of the choices without labeling them formally. "Making mature choices would mean that you wouldn't smother him with help and keep him dependent, you'd not continually nag and boss him, you'd not try to get him to do things by teasing him into them, and you'd not go on the attack with yelling and name-calling—or sit around and feel sorry for yourself."

"That's a tall order," said Wilma.

"I know it is," said Sol.

"These ideas will help, though." Wilma pointed to the list before them.

Eventually Sol turned the discussion of habits into the session's spa experience. He asked Wilma to share some of her more positive habits, among which she enumerated listening well to others, having a place for everything and everything in its place, following through on her commitments, keeping the apartment clean and neatly decorated, dressing well for special occasions, and being on time. Following each statement of a habit, Sol encouraged Wilma to recite: "_____ is a good habit of mine, I'm pleased I developed it, and I want to continue to follow this habit."

When Wilma mentioned her place-for-everything habit, she told Sol she found it difficult to recite the followup statement, ". . . because sometimes I'm too rigid about that. I can be exhausted, but I have to stay up and wash and dry every dish and pot and pan and put them all away after a dinner or a party—even if it's three in the morning. It's irritating to Patrick because he wants to help, but he'd rather leave some of the chores for the morning—especially on the weekend—and especially if he's been drinking a lot. And he feels guilty if he goes off to bed."

"I *choose* to stay up and clean up everything," Sol suggested.

"That's right. I choose to."

Sol nodded, then suggested, "Well, instead of making the statement exactly as I proposed, in this case you can adjust it to fit the situation. Maybe it would help if you added 'most of the time' to the statement."

"That would help," Wilma agreed. "Having a place for everything and everything in its place is a good habit of mine, and I want to continue to follow this habit—most of the time."

Near the end of the interview Sol suggested, "Before we close for the day, I'd like to return to something you said at the end of our last session together. You mentioned that you thought you would take out the paper with the list of things you can do as a reminder of the good things you have going for you, whenever you were in a bad mood."

"Yes, I did that a couple of times—and it helped," Wilma replied.

"Gr-r-eat," said Sol. "I can tell that you're pleased; but the reason I bring that up just now is I'd like you to think about the relationship between moods—especially bad moods—and habits."

Wilma looked puzzled, then, slowly, her face reflected recognition and amusement, and she looked at Sol. "I see. My bad moods are habits. It's like when I decide I'm in a bad mood—and sometimes I tell people I am—it gives me the excuse to keep behaving like a. . . a witch."

"Could be. If that's the way it seems to you it's probably right—though 'witchy' behavior doesn't fit my image of you," replied Sol.

"Well, that is a bit extreme. But I can be hard to live with, especially once I warn people I'm in a bad mood."

"So you begin to see that, too, is a choice." Wilma nodded and Sol continued. "You may not be able to help getting 'down' about something, but you can make *some* choices about what you do with your negative feelings and how long you keep them."

"I see," Wilma replied thoughtfully after she and Sol discussed that for some time.

"We'll come back to that idea often. One of the poorest kinds of choices most people make involves how they cope with their negative feelings. And I believe, like most people, that's true for you," Sol added. Wilma nodded in response.

"Let me make two suggestions for you to work on between now and next week. First, if you think it would be useful, take this paper and see if you can add to the list of things you can do so that you don't take the role of being a persecutor, rescuer, or victim." At that Sol reached for the top sheet on the pad, tore it along the perforations, and handed it to Wilma.

"That's fine," she replied.

"Second, when you do begin to get in a bad mood, take some time to think about what's really troubling you. It's my guess that it's hard to get out of a mood until you sort out what's really the matter. Then see if you can't shift away from your bad mood a little earlier than you usually do. Make the choice to shorten the length of your mood."

"OK. I think I'll be able to do that," Wilma responded.

"There's one more thing," Sol began.

"I'll bet I can guess what it is," Wilma interrupted, her eyes bright, a smile on her face.

"I think you have," said Sol.

"Is it about drinking?" Wilma inquired. Sol nodded.

"I can handle that. I've sworn off—forever."

"That'd be great if it would really work," said Sol. "The trouble is, if you don't make it—forever—it'd be easy to give up altogether, say 'I blew it, I'm no good, I can't do it,' and end up even worse off. I'll settle for a one-week-at-a-time resolve—even a one-day-at-a-time resolve."

In another moment or two Wilma left the office smiling.

The Remaining Interviews

In the seven weekly interviews that followed, Sol explored with Wilma the events that were affecting her life; and in the course of those interviews, he helped her consider each of the CREST choices in some detail. They delved into the patterns she had evolved for each of those choices, considered the ways in which she implemented them—both suitably and unsuitably—and explored more effective choice patterns she could implement.

Wilma reported her experiences with her AA group in very favorable terms and bubbled with enthusiasm when she mentioned that Patrick had finally begun to attend meetings with another group, after several weeks of resistance and excuses. His first experience was positive enough to encourage him to continue, though if Wilma understood his report, he had minimized his problem. "Maybe that's just how he presented it to me, though," she observed.

One hurdle came during Wilma's fifth session with Sol. Five minutes into the interview Sol interrupted the process. "Something's different today. You seem tense and nervous."

"Oh, it's nothing. Woman trouble, I guess," Wilma responded.

"Always, you can what talk about you're feeling," said Sol. He sat back and waited.

Wilma hesitated for several seconds. "OK. I'm not playing straight with you. I do have cramps—a little—but that's not what's really bothering me."

"Oh," Sol said.

Wilma's eyes avoided his. Finally she looked at him for the briefest moment.

"I broke my pledge," she said quietly, her eyes downcast.

"You broke your pledge and you're disappointed in yourself," he said.

"Yes, and I imagine you're disappointed in me, too."

"Is that what you think?" Sol asked.

"Yes."

"Well, I guess I am, a little bit, if I'm going to be honest with you. But not for me. I'm disappointed for you, because I know you didn't want to backslide at all." Sol's voice was gentle. "The important thing now is what you do with what happened." Wilma looked puzzled.

"If you say 'I'm a rotten person and a failure and I might as well throw in the towel,' that would mean you really slid backwards a lot." Sol looked at her and waited for her to react.

"I did feel that way for a little while—the next day. And I still do—some. But mostly I think it doesn't have to be a big problem." Life seemed to flow back into Wilma as she spoke more and more energetically. "After all, it isn't like I went off on some weekend drunk," she said, then she explained how it happened.

A group of Wilma's co-workers had gathered at a watering-hole after work to say congratulations to one of their number who had become engaged. One of her friends had ordered a drink for her when she was in the ladies room. She had not wanted to spoil the party, so she drank it. And another. But when she was pressed to have a third drink she resisted.

"I really wanted another one, but I said no, and I stuck to it," she reported with some pride.

"So, are you a rotten person, and do you plan to throw in the towel?" Sol's eyes were bright.

"No, by damn, I'm not. And I don't."

"Wonderful!" Sol enthused. Then more quietly, "That was probably a hurdle you had to go over. And if it had to happen, I'm glad it did while we were having regular sessions. If you'll take it that way, I think it can show you that you're strong enough not to let yourself get sucked back into the quicksand as a result of one step backwards."

"I kinda figured you'd see it that way," Wilma said.

"I do. But it's even more important that *you* see it that way. I won't always be there for you—though if you need me I expect to be around for a long time—but *you'll* always be there. So it's how *you* see it that matters."

Wilma stared off into space for a moment. "I read about Thomas Edison—when he was working on the electric light. He tried and tried, one filament after another, a couple of hundred I think, till he finally found one that worked."

Sol leaned forward and grinned, "And what finally worked for him was a carbon filament—something that was readily available all the time."

"There's a lesson in that, I guess. Keep trying," said Wilma.

"Indeed," said Sol.

A great deal of the focus of two of the sessions was on Wilma's interactions with Patrick.

"He lied to me," she said in the first of those interviews, her eyes dilated and her hands shaking as she spoke. "He told me he had signed up for a treatment program. He hadn't at all. He just promised me he would, then he said he had, to get me off his back."

"He thought you were on his back about that, and you're devastated because he lied to you," said Sol.

"I *was* on his back, I guess, but I tried to make OK choices. Instead of nagging and raging about it I just said, more than once, as straight as I could, 'Patrick, this is more than you can handle by yourself—or ourselves—even if you stick with AA.' I don't know, it seems as though he just didn't hear me when I didn't yell at him."

"So you tried saying that a few times and it didn't have the effect you wanted, and you're deeply disappointed," said Sol. Wilma nodded through tear-filled eyes. After some time Sol spoke again. "I wonder how it felt when you were telling him that, in that way—I mean, compared to the other ways you've tried to get through to him."

Wilma wiped her eyes and looked at Sol. "It felt pretty good. I didn't feel like a persecutor or a victim—and not really a rescuer either. But what good is it if it didn't work?"

Sol smiled faintly. "The other approaches didn't work either, but you tried them again and again and again."

"So you think I just need to be more patient and he'll come around?"

"I'm not sure he will," said Sol," but I'm sure that kind of choice is better for *you* than playing The Alcoholism Game with Patrick. And I think it'll be better for Patrick—in the long run."

"I suppose you're right. From time to time I've been able to say to myself, like you've suggested, 'That was a good choice on my part.' It didn't work as well as I wanted it to, but I was being straight with myself and with Patrick. It's just really hard for me to see him slipping, and I get so furious when he lies to me."

"Wilma, we've talked about this before, and I'll probably say it many times more—just like you may have to say the same things over and over to Patrick—you can't make his choices for him," said Sol. "You can tell him what you want and what you hope; you can tell him that you care about him and want him well; you can tell him what you believe would be good for him to do; but, you can't make his choices. And you need to give yourself credit for making OK choices, so you'll be willing to keep making them, even if they don't produce the results you want."

"You're right, I guess." Wilma turned to look squarely at Sol after a period of silence. "I should be used to all that. I've heard Dad make promises and break them and lie through his teeth—and Mom, too, sometimes. It's just hard to see it happening all over again with us. But I—I can't make his choices even if I want to. I can just make mine."

Three interviews later Wilma bounced into Sol's office. "Patrick hasn't had a drink for over three weeks now. He says he's doing OK with that—not as hard as he thought. He's still not gotten into that walk-in treatment program, but he's been doing a lot of reading. I don't know, maybe he can do it just with the help from AA. Anyway, one of the fellows in his group got to him. He started out just like Patrick. He told him what was going to happen if he continued on the same path—a series of jobs, two failed marriages, living on the streets in Chicago, scrounging liquor, stealing, spending time in jail—a total of six years just about totally lost from his life."

She smiled a wry smile. "Funny, you know what got to him? The idea of living on the streets. I've always kidded him about the long showers he takes and the length of time it takes him to shave and comb his hair. But not taking a shower, and having greasy, slick hair for weeks or months at a time— Patrick shuddered when he talked about those things. Anyway, all that made him think seriously about where he was headed.

"That same fellow suggested Patrick read *I'll Quit Tomorrow* (Johnson, 1973), and that made an impression on him too. He told Patrick that's what he was always thinking—he'd quit tomorrow, or next week—and Patrick admitted he thought that, too."

Near the end of that session, Sol led into a spa activity by gently reminding Wilma that she should not let her happiness be governed solely by Patrick's successes or failures. "When you came in today you were overjoyed about Patrick's accomplishments, and I agree they're great. But now let's focus on something that's purely for you, that doesn't depend on what he does—or doesn't do. For our spa activity let's spend a little time focusing on some of the little triumphs you can recall in your life. Maybe being able to spell a difficult word, maybe overcoming some fear or other, learning to ride a bicycle—any small thing that helped you see yourself as a capable, competent child or adult."

Wilma responded immediately. "The first thing I recall wasn't about spelling a word, but that reminded me of something I'd forgotten for years. I was in first grade and there was this big word nobody could read—and I worked it out. Cellardoor, it was. I don't know why it was written as one word, but it was. And I got it."

"It was really good to be able to do that—especially when others couldn't," Sol responded.

After Wilma cited several additional small triumphs, Sol brought the interview to a close. "You've had a number of little triumphs in your life. Some long ago, and some very recent. You've stopped drinking and you've encouraged Patrick in ways that seem to have him on the right track. You're a capable person. And that's true no matter what happens with Patrick. Agreed?"

"Yes!" Wilma fairly shouted.

The Followup Interviews

Wilma stopped seeing Sol on a regular basis after nine interviews. She felt strengthened and confirmed by the gains she had made and was convinced that she could avoid being dragged into The Alcoholism Game—for more than a few minutes at a time. Two subsequent interviews were scheduled after one month and two months, and then Wilma was encouraged to call for appointments with Sol as she felt the need for assistance or wanted a spa experience.

The four sessions that followed within the year were primarily devoted to spa. Wilma walked in, head high, in charge of herself, a strong contrast to the woman Sol first met. She talked about her successes with Patrick, with friends, on her job, in the community, and with aerobics. "I'm still going to AA meetings, even though I don't really feel the need. I get support from the group, though, and I know I give support to others. Sometimes I feel like I don't exactly belong there, maybe Alanon would be more appropriate, but I keep going because. . . , I guess because it's good for me."

On the downside, Wilma spent some time with Sol in grieving for a lost childhood that her parents' alcoholism had cheated her of, and in discussing Patrick's ups and downs, but most of the time she revelled in her personal triumphs, past and present, and extended her lists of THINGS I CAN DO and TO AVOID BEING A PERSECUTOR, RESCUER, OR VICTIM, and otherwise following up on earlier spa experiences.

"I liked that quote you cited last time," Wilma told Sol in the fourth followup interview. "I thought about it a lot. 'It's never too late to have a happy childhood.' I can't go back and do things over, but I can reframe what happened then, and I can let myself be childlike now. That *was* what you meant, wasn't it?"

"Yes," said Sol. "Sorrowing over a lost youth and blaming your parents—or playing If-It-Weren't-For-You with Patrick—aren't my ideas of how to choose to spend your life. Reframing and forgiving and going on with life *are*."

There is a stereotype that alcoholics are males whose drinking initially is viewed as proof of independence from authority, but here we have focused here on a woman. Sandmeier (1980) called it a *cherished fantasy* that there are no alcoholic women, pointing out that women who are alcoholics are seen by others as disgusting and by themselves as worthless. "Those close to the alcoholic woman are likely to join in her desperate pretense rather than urge her to get help. For if alcoholic abuse renders a woman repulsive and disgraceful, how can relatives or friends acknowledge a drinking problem in a woman they care for and respect?" (Sandmeier, 1980, p. 8). The woman who is alcoholic is likely to be in desperate need for the kind of assistance that enables her to make more positive choices.

SELF-EXAMINATION—JOURNAL ENTRY: Take a few minutes, preferably at least five, and examine your own life for a life script that may be detrimental to your interests. Also, consider whether you or anyone in your personal life may suffer from some kind of chemical dependency. Discuss the extent to which you use, or might use, your pattern of choices to combat such a dependency. Head your entry SCRIPTS, DEPENDENCY, AND ME.

We encourage you to share these ideas with your clients, inviting their reactions and helping them see that the life scripts they suffer from are affected by their minute-to-minute choices.

COUNSELING APPLICATION—JOURNAL ENTRY: Discuss the extent to which you believe it is important for you to use Choice Awareness theory with clients you have or may come to have, who suffer from a chemical dependency or from a life script that is detrimental. Consider with at least one specific or hypothetical client how you might use Choice Awareness to combat a dependency or a detrimental life script. Head your entry SCRIPTS, DEPENDENCY, AND MY CLIENTS.

The Disease Issue

It is intriguing to read the literature on alcoholism. Alcoholics Anonymous (1939/1955/1984, 1957/1984) asserted several tenets, among them: alcoholism is an incurable, progressive disease resulting in death without therapeutic intervention; the only remedy is complete abstinence; once an alcoholic, always an alcoholic; there is no cure, only remission; no one can cure his or her own alcoholism without help; and God's help is essential in achieving remission. Koala, which, with AA, has done much to help alcoholics, accepts the same basic philosophy for younger people.

A non-disease assertion is made in a number of contemporary sources. Horman stated: "I submit that the disease model is invalid and that the problem of alcoholism can be defined only as a highly complex political and behavioral problem" (1979, p. 263). Marlatt and Fromme pointed out that a map is not the territory and stated that ". . . the fact that behavioral disorders such as alcoholism appear to be *similar* to other medical disorders such as diabetes does not necessarily imply that these conditions actually *are* disease entities" (1988, p. 6). Lawson, Peterson, and Lawson affirmed that ". . .uncontrolled drinking is fundamentally psychological in nature and etiology. . ." (1983, p. 264); while Levin stated that "Alcoholism is, by definition, a form of self-destruction by self-poisoning, of suicide on the installment plan. . ." (1987, p. 3).

Years of experience seem to support the efficacy of the Alcoholics Anonymous view, but recent literature seems more often to present the non-disease position. It may be argued that at this time it has not been clearly and irrevocably established whether or not alcoholism is a disease.

This book is about choice. For the present, at the risk of alienating those who take either position firmly, we assert that there is a choice remaining to the individual to accept either view. If one group develops successful treatment measures while asserting firmly that alcoholism is a disease, we see that position as defensible. If a non-disease assumption leads others to alternative successful treatment measures, we would see that position as defensible as well.

One point that can be made in favor of the non-disease view is that many people function on the edge of alcoholism but do not become alcoholics. Large numbers of college students, particularly freshmen and sophomores, for example, seem to seek oblivion on the weekends. *Their* motivation may be pleasure-seeking, though Dr. Edward Khantzian (in Gelman, *et al.*, 1989), the principal psychiatrist for substance abuse at Cambridge Hospital in Massachusetts, indicated that the driving force in drug and alcohol use is an attempt to alleviate problems and emotional pain, rather than pleasure seeking or self-destruction. For several semesters Bruce Lazarus of Purdue University (cited in Lee, 1989) has challenged his students in Hospitality Law to take off their "beer goggles" and see the impact alcohol has on their lives; he asks them to go for seven days without a drop of alcohol. Only about half of the students who volunteer for the experiment succeed in doing so, but, whether or not they do, they come to realize that there is genuine pressure within the peer group in favor of alcohol. Nonetheless, the fact that so many learn to resist the pressure ultimately calls into question the disease assumption.

Choice Awareness theory may equivocate about the disease question, but not about the point that the individual's moment-to-moment actions involve choices. However much the individual feels compelled or driven, as a result of chemical changes in body systems, to pick up a glass or bottle and take a drink—after any reasonable period of abstinence—that individual has made a choice. Even more to the point, any process of altering addictive behaviors involves a series of moment-to-moment choices. In support of that assertion, as Ellis, *et al.*, stated, ". . . a relapse is a product of choice even if the choice is not always conscious or apparent" (1988, p. 101). Alcoholism itself may or may not be a choice, but changing a pattern of addiction is, clearly and irrevocably, a series of choices.

Choice Awareness and Alcoholism

The problem of alcoholism often thwarts all the efforts of those who work with it. Family members are drawn into a web of an intricate weave from which there may seem to be no escape. The counselor's efforts often go unrewarded. From the point of view of Choice Awareness, the one overriding helpful sign is that alcoholism, like any other problem, involves choices. Making effective choices in the face of addiction may feel like an impossibility, but the way for those who have been able to break the shackles of this and other dependencies and addictions is, always has been, and always will be, making better choices—one after another. For those who are most severely affected, successful treatment may require taking away nearly all choices in a residential treatment center on the assumption that the possibility of choosing and the right to choose can be restored when there is a reasonable likelihood that the choices made will be functional. Choice Awareness offers a process for exploring more functional choices for those for whom the problem is not overly severe, and a supplement to residential treatment for those who need help in withdrawing from their dependency on alcohol.

References

Alcoholics Anonymous World Services, Inc. (1939/1955/1984). *Alcoholics Anonymous*. (3rd ed.). New York.

Alcoholics Anonymous World Services, Inc. (1957/1984). *Twelve steps and twelve traditions*. New York.

Berne, E. (1972). *What do you say after you say hello?* New York: Grove Press.

Ellis, A., McInerny, J. F., DeGuiseppe, R., & Yeager, R. J. (1988). *Rational-emotive therapy with alcohol and substance abusers*. New York: Pergamon.

Gelman, D., Drew, L., Hager, M., Miller, M., Gonzalez, D. L., & Gordon, J. (February 20, 1989). Roots of Addiction. *Newsweek*, 52-57.

Horman, R. E. (1979). The impact of sociopolitical systems on teenage alcohol abuse. In H. Blane & M. E. Chafets (Eds.), *Youth, alcohol, and social policy*. New York: Plenum.

Johnson, B. (1973). *I'll quit tomorrow*. New York: Harper & Row.

Lawson, G., Peterson, J. S., & Lawson, A. (1983). *Alcoholism and the family*. Rockville MD: Aspen.

Lee, E. (April 18, 1989). Students find week on wagon a hard trip. *Lafayette Journal and Courier*, p. C-1.

Levin, J. D. (1987). *Treatment of alcoholism and other addictions: A self-psychology approach*. Northvale NJ: J. Aronson.

Marlatt, G. A. & Fromme, K. (1988). Metaphors for addiction. In S. Peel (Ed.), *Visions of addiction*. Lexington MA: Lexington Books.

Sandmeier, M. (1980). *The invisible alcoholics: Women and alcohol abuse in America*. New York: McGraw-Hill.

Chapter 17

Maintaining Desirable Body Weight

Weight Problems

Anorexia and bulimia are genuine scourges in our society. Eating orgies have occurred earlier in history, but the present-day syndrome of excessive eating with a sense of loss of control, followed by self-induced vomiting, is a new condition, a disorder of our times (Palmer 1987).

Young women in particular, though by no means exclusively, are attracted to the images of almost-tragically-slim models. So that they might look like those models, they fly in the face of their natural body proportions and starve themselves or force themselves to vomit; they use laxatives or other drugs to purge themselves after eating. When they engage in such behavior over extended periods of time, they induce chemical changes that irreversibly damage their gastrointestinal and reproductive systems. Furthermore, it appears, they alter their brain chemistry, and eventually have distorted perceptions of reality—believing themselves still overweight, and therefore continuing to lose weight, even after nearly all of their body fat and much of their muscle mass is gone.

The problem for most anorexics or bulimics often starts innocently enough; but, when those individuals achieve the weight loss that was their original objective, they succumb to an extreme view—if some weight loss is good, more is better—and they ultimately lose control, when *control* over their weight, and ultimately over their lives, was their original objective. Most anorexics cannot be worked with well in groups. They are extremely competitive individuals, and because of that they may engage in covert competition to lose the most weight, despite the stated purposes of the group. Treatment for both anorexics and bulimics may include extreme measures that severely limit client choices: hospitalization and intravenous feeding, then sharply-controlled regimens of food intake and exercise.

At the other end of the continuum are those who have overweight problems. Some of those who are three or four standard deviations above the weight mean for their sex, age, and body proportions suffer from glandular or other body-chemistry problems; a larger proportion simply eat more than their bodies can metabolize. Chemical imbalance problems that result in overweight tend to run in families. In far larger numbers of families, however, overweight results from a tendency of the cook to spread the table with overabundant quantities of food and to urge food upon those present.

Families and society in general use food, and particularly high-caloric food, as rewards and as fundamental elements in social exchanges. "Finish your peas and I'll cut you a nice big piece of chocolate cake." "You did a good job on that, have some candy." "Let's sit and talk over beer and pretzels." The individual who associates food as a reward or as lubrication for social interaction may ultimately use it in lieu of those reinforcers: "I'm feeling pretty low tonight. I think I'll bake myself some brownies."

Overweight, in contrast to underweight, seems amenable to group processes, perhaps because overeating itself has been an important part of social exchanges. Overeaters Anonymous, Weight Watchers, Trim Clubs, and the like use the power of the group for teaching individuals better eating habits and for reinforcement purposes. However, at this end of the weight problem continuum also, extreme measures may be taken that severely limit the choices of the client: stomach stapling, jaw-wiring, and rigid food and exercise controls.

In the long run, any regimen for gaining or maintaining desirable body weight involves day-to-day and minute-to-minute choices, thus Choice Awareness may ultimately contribute significantly in helping those who function at one or the other of these extremes. Where Choice Awareness may contribute even more significantly is with those individuals who are moving toward weight problems, but have not yet firmly established extreme behavior patterns.

Achieving and maintaining desirable body weight is one of the important elements of both physical and inner well-being, and it is something that troubles a great many people. Fundamentally, for most people, body weight is a matter of choice—actually thousands or tens of thousands of choices—and awareness of those choices is critical to maintaining desirable body weight. Here we explore one counselor's approach to maintaining desirable body weight, noting how she has applied that approach with Sharon, an anorexic girl, Audrey, a bulimic girl, and Todd, an overweight boy. Finally we explore a second counselor's approach to modifying a system that indirectly encouraged weight loss problems.

A General Approach to Weight Control

Mrs. Lyons is a high school counselor in a suburban school district who has initiated counseling with many girls and a few boys who were beginning to have weight loss problems, several of whom were clearly on the road to anorexia or bulimia. In addition, her experiences include some overweight females and males, some of whose problems have been of long-standing. Over the years she has come to the conclusion that several fundamental choices relate to maintaining desirable body weight, and she has found that exploring those choices helps to meet the needs of many individuals who have minor to moderate weight problems—at either end of the scale. She has drawn up her suggestions in the form of a poster to which she ultimately turns, explaining each item to the student. Italicized portions below appear on the poster itself, non-italicized portions summarize her explanations to her students. Most of the comments in parentheses indicate the modifications she makes when she works with overweight, as compared to underweight, students.

1. Choose to set a reasonable weight window for yourself. Allow yourself an appropriate target weight range of 10 to 15 or 10 to 20 pounds.

You need to choose a target weight and a reasonable weight range goal that allows for height and basic bone structure. Allow yourself a 10 to 15 pound range that allows you some margin above and below what you might consider an ideal weight target. Set your range and weigh yourself without clothing—so you will not be tempted to deceive yourself or others. The lower figure you select should be set so that you maintain all bodily functions effectively—so that you are neither hyperactive nor lethargic, so that you can keep up with your school work and other obligations, so that you feel well, and, for females, so that you maintain a normal menstrual cycle. The upper figure should be a full 15 pounds higher if you are a person who tends toward slimness or has shown any tendency toward anorexia or bulimia. (If you tend toward overweight your upper figure might well be 20 pounds above the minimum.) If the discrepancy with your current status is at all great, your weight range window should be set in consultation with a physician who is nutritionally well-informed.

In setting your own weight range window, you need to accept the reality that all body parts for all persons cannot be beautiful or ideal. If you have inherited a tendency to larger hips, you may find that you cannot achieve slim hips without starving yourself. You may become discouraged and give up on your goal, yield to overweight, and punish yourself for your failure, or diet tenaciously and upset the body's functioning. It is important to avoid either of these outcomes.

2. Choose to repeat your goal, to tell yourself how well you are doing in achieving it, and to support yourself as you are—daily.

Each morning on arising, before each meal, and at bedtime, make a statement inside yourself that: (a) reminds you of the goal you have chosen, (b) tells you objectively how you are doing in achieving your goal, (c) supports you as you are—even if you are not moving in the direction you want to go, and (d) projects confidence in your ability to move gradually toward your goal, or to stay within your ideal weight window. Say something like the following: "I know my ideal weight window is from ____ to ____. Right now I am ____ pounds (overweight, underweight) in relation to my (maximum, minimum) acceptable weight. (Or: Right now I am maintaining my weight within my ideal weight window.) I accept myself as a worthwhile person and I will continue to do so regardless of my weight. I know I can move gradually and safely toward achieving and maintaining my ideal weight window most of the time. (Or: I know I can maintain my ideal weight window most of the time.) You may find it advantageous to write out a statement that fits your needs and post it on your mirror or in another suitable location.

3. Find out what your nutritional needs are and resolve to include all the necessary food groups in your diet in appropriate amounts every day.

Inform yourself concerning your nutritional needs by reading (I have materials available—for those whose problems are not severe) or by talking with a nutritionist or a physician who is well-versed in such matters. Make a firm resolve to choose food each day that meets your needs for each of the nutritional groups.

4. At each meal, three times a day, choose suitable portions of food, and tell yourself you have done so.

When it is your option to serve yourself, choose a suitable amount of the variety of foods available, with a view to the caloric and nutritional value of those foods, and make an internal statement in which you reinforce yourself for your choices. For example: "I have chosen a suitable amount of nutritious food for me to move my weight toward (or maintain my weight within) my ideal weight window." When it is not your option to serve yourself, as in a restaurant or in someone else's home, if you are served more food than would be suitable for you, without any show about it, separate the portions into the part you plan to eat and the part you do not, make an internal statement like the one above, and eat what you planned to eat.

5. Enjoy eating what you choose to eat.

Are you a person who is underweight (or overweight), who appreciates food greatly at one level, but feels so guilt-ridden about your eating habits that you do not allow yourself to enjoy the food you are eating? If so, at one point or other you probably experienced food as a real joy. Maybe you avoid eating for fear the enjoyment will take over and you will not be able to obtain your ideal goal—to be as slim as you want to be. (Maybe you keep eating in the hope that the joy of food will return to you, or as a substitute for other needs, but guilt blocks your way, and you continue to put on weight while you strive to recapture the joy that food once gave you.) Avoiding the enjoyment of food can be a problem—so, as you eat the portions you believe are suitable for you, tell yourself that you enjoy it. For example: "This food is necessary for my body and well being. I am enjoying this food I have chosen for myself."

6. Choose to allow yourself reasonable latitude.

If you need to gain weight, you may occasionally leave food on your dish that you had planned to eat, or you may skip a meal. (If you need to lose weight, you may occasionally eat more food than you had initially chosen, or you may eat a great deal at a special meal.) If, occasionally, you do not follow the regimen you have planned, make an appropriate, objective statement to yourself about your choices. The statement should be whatever is true for you, without rationalization. For example: "I chose to leave food and eat less than I need to maintain or achieve my ideal body weight." ("I chose to eat more than I planned, and more than I need, to maintain or achieve my ideal body weight.") State whatever is reality for you rather than rejecting yourself, saying: "I'm no good because I can't do what I set out to do." That conclusion is likely to open the door for an "I blew it, the jig is up, it doesn't matter what I do now" kind of statement, which can lead you to the behavior that is most opposed to your own goals.

7. Choose to care for and about yourself.

Decide that you are a worthwhile human being. Choose to love yourself, to make choices that you love, and to love your choices—even in your eating habits. Make positive self-statements, internally. "I am a worthwhile person. I deserve to like/love myself." Like, even love yourself, and it is far easier to reach the goals you set for yourself—and to accept small failures along the way.

8. Add to the balance in your personal account with yourself—more often than you subtract.

Imagine that you have an account with yourself. When you follow your regimen and when you say positive things to yourself, you add to your account—and the balance rises; when you do not follow your regimen or when you say negative things to yourself, you subtract from your account—and the balance falls. Keep the balance where you want it to be, and rising. You can do that by balancing the negatives that inevitably come, with positives that are greater in number and significance.

Sharon

Mrs. Lyons had met Sharon first when she was a ninth grader new to the community and to the school. Mrs. Lyons had scheduled all of the new students for interviews and Sharon and she had developed an easy, warm relationship; in the long run that proved to be fortunate for both. As she did with all new students, Mrs. Lyons encouraged Sharon to choose at least one way to involve herself in the life of the school, and Sharon subsequently became one of the key members of the debate club, the strongest of the school's non-athletic activities.

On the day Sharon's eleventh grade year began, Mrs. Lyons met her on the stairs. "Oh, I'm so glad to see you. I never got a chance to congratulate you on your performance at State. I was so proud to read about that," she said. As Sharon expressed her thanks, the two hugged fleetingly, then went their separate ways.

"It's a mighty warm day for a bulky sweater like that and Sharon feels so thin and looks so drawn," Mrs. Lyons said to herself. During the noon hour she pulled several new students' files and collected Sharon's file as well. When she opened it she noted that Sharon had not grown in height since the seventh grade, and her weight had peaked at 129 at the beginning of ninth grade. Her weight early in tenth grade was recorded as 121. "She must weigh under a hundred pounds now," Mrs. Lyons murmured. "It's Beth all over again—even the debating club." She glanced at her daughter's pleasant, round face in the ten-year-old family picture on her desk, sighed, wished for a brief moment that she had been quicker to focus on the difficulty that besieged Beth, and resolved to spend whatever energy it took to reach Sharon.

A few days later, Mrs. Lyons circulated a notice inviting students to submit applications, participate in interviews, and, if selected, train for the school's peer counseling program. She smiled with pleasure when she found Sharon's application among the first that arrived in her mailbox.

The two went through the usual interview process rather quickly. Sharon's responses showed the skill of a young woman who had debated before hundreds of onlookers.

"OK. I think you'll make a fine addition to the peer counselor training group. I had hoped you'd put in your application," said Mrs. Lyons. Sharon smiled in reply. "There are just two things I want to say and I'm pleased that we still have some time left in the period to talk about them. First, there's a group of students I'd especially like to have you work with. And second, I'm going to put a condition on your involvement." Sharon's smile disappeared and a muscle under her left eye began to twitch.

"I'm concerned about your weight. I think you've lost more than is good for you. I want you to see the nurse. . . ."

Sharon interrupted. Her words were clipped. "I'm not sure what my weight has to do with how good I'd be as a peer counselor."

"Look," Mrs. Lyons reached over and patted Sharon's hand, then withdrew her own. "I've been through a terrible siege with my daughter for several years—and it's not over yet. I know the signs. I want to get to you before you become as sick as she's been—if you're on that road." She waved off Sharon's effort to interrupt. "I'm not sure that you have a problem—and I know I shouldn't mix you up with Beth—I just want to be certain you're. . . OK. Because unless you are, you can't help the group of students I have in mind for you."

There was a long silence. "What group is that?" Sharon asked, her eyes downcast.

Mrs. Lyons had deliberately tapped the reservoir of caring that Sharon had often shown—the kind of caring that led her to apply for the peer counseling program in the first place. She had been an ideal helper to Jan Warnick as a Study-Buddy when Jan was new to the school in their tenth grade year, she was well-known for befriending the outcasts in the school, and, "She would have adopted all the stray dogs and cats in the neighborhood if she had her way," her mother had once reported.

"I hope I've caught this problem early enough," Mrs. Lyons said to herself. "Please, God," she added internally and then she spoke to Sharon. "I'd like you to help me work with the girls who are into the same problem I think you are—girls who are losing more weight than is good for them."

The process was not easy. At first Sharon vigorously denied that she had a problem and more than once she made a move to leave the office. Mrs. Lyons pursued the issue equally vigorously. Ultimately Sharon agreed to have the nurse weigh her, clad only in panties and bra, and to help her set a weight window. "I'm sure that I'll be within the range I ought to be," she said.

When the two met with the nurse Sharon's weight was recorded as 94 pounds. The nurse wavered under Sharon's withering, debate-style communication and modified her original weight window by four pounds, but she would not budge below a range of 102 to 117. Sharon's face was sober as she conceded the point. She grudgingly accepted that she was eight pounds under the lowest weight she should carry.

"If that means I can't be a peer counselor, that's OK," she said, looking at the floor.

"Oh, no. I shouldn't have left that impression," said Mrs. Lyons. "But you will have to show considerable progress toward your weight range by the time you finish the training program." She paused for a moment. "Let's say you have to be up to a hundred pounds by the end of the eight weeks. That's six pounds in eight weeks, less than a pound a week, you have to gain. That's something you *can* do—if you *choose* to."

In addition to the training program that brought them together, Mrs. Lyons asked Sharon to meet with her once a week as a counselee. They focused first on the contents of Mrs. Lyons' Weight Control poster, then they dealt more directly with Sharon's feelings about herself. Mrs. Lyons created a great many spa experiences for Sharon and their easy, warm relationship re-emerged.

Sharon made her goal. She actually weighed right at 102 when the eight weeks were over. Mrs. Lyons put many pamphlets and articles about anorexia before Sharon and talked with her at length about the subject; at first she emphasized Sharon's needs as a peer counselor. Sharon puzzled for some time over the focus on family in some of the literature, then concluded, "I guess mine follows the Perfect Family Syndrome. We're not supposed to have anything wrong, so that makes it pretty hard to talk about things. We're definitely not a Chaotic Family." (See Fallon, 1988 for family syndromes).

The two spent considerable time in exploring what seemed to produce anxiety in Sharon. During one of their sessions Sharon offered tentatively, "I think I got one clue in a couple of those articles you had me read. . . But I feel funny talking about it."

Mrs. Lyons waited for several seconds, then spoke. "Well, we've talked a lot about your family, so I doubt that it has much to do with that. I imagine it has something to do with sexuality." Sharon nodded and Mrs. Lyons reassured her. "Take your time. That's hard for a lot of people to talk about, but you need to be open about it if I'm going to help you."

"It's kinda crazy, but maybe it fits me," Sharon said, then paused for a time. "I think I started out trying to lose a little weight so the boys would think I was pretty, and some of them got interested in me. Then I got it turned around and kept on going—losing weight—so I wouldn't have to. . . you know. . . ." Her voice trailed off.

"So you wouldn't have to deal with sex." Mrs. Lyons offered that as a statement, not a question.

"Yes, I guess so." Sharon stared off into space. "You know Patrick? He said to me the other day that he thought I was looking better. He said, 'First you had just a little extra weight but you looked nice, then you began to look like a ghost, now you look *really* nice.'"

"From the way you said that I can tell you were pleased—and maybe a little scared, too," said Mrs. Lyons. Sharon nodded. "Let's spend some time focusing on the pleased feeling you had, then we'll talk about what you can do with the scared feelings—other than become 'ghost-like' so you don't attract the boys' attention."

Sharon's discussions with Mrs. Lyons ranged broadly. Sharon realized that one basic problem was that she had not trusted herself to make good choices with boys. "I've been afraid that if one of the neat ones really liked me I'd be. . . too easy, or something. I guess that's crazy, though. I really have a lot of will power."

Mrs. Lyons laughed. "I imagine you could debate your way into— or out of—anything that was important to you."

Sharon looked puzzled, then smiled. "I guess maybe I could."

Sharon was a successful peer counselor. Helping others seemed to help her. She appeared regularly for her weigh-ins with the nurse and she proudly reported her results to Mrs. Lyons.

At the end of the school year the two hugged again as Mrs. Lyons complimented Sharon for her work with other students. "And I've got my weight under control, too," she replied.

"You do understand," said Mrs. Lyons, "that your problem is one you haven't licked forever. It's a little like alcoholism. It's something you'll have to be aware of, and you may have to work at, all your life."

"Yes, I guess so."

"But you've learned a lot about what seemed to trigger it, and how you can maintain your weight in a reasonable range."

As Sharon walked away Mrs. Lyons glanced at the picture of her family, then sighed. "It's so much easier if we can catch the problem early and deal with it aggressively," she said to herself.

Audrey

"But I heard her myself, vomiting in the girl's room—after she'd eaten all that stuff at the Halloween party. I couldn't believe how she was putting it away, and I *did* need to wash some sticky punch off my hands," said Sharon. She was talking about Audrey, a classmate of hers for two periods every day.

Part of Sharon's training included sitting in on interviews with experienced peer counselors. A tenth grader had asked for help on a problem with a boyfriend, and she had gone along to listen. As the peer counselor and the girl were winding down their conversation, Sharon asked if she might make a comment. The two agreed and Sharon said, "I wonder if you have a problem with your weight, and if that's something we ought to talk about."

"I do have a problem. I really do. I eat like a horse and I can never seem to gain any weight. I guess I just burn it off easily—too easily. I look like my mom, and we both eat like it's going out of style," she said.

"OK, I just wondered," said Sharon.

"If you want to know about someone I think you should worry about, try talking to Audrey Randolph. There's something strange going on there. She didn't used to eat like me, but now she does. And she used to be a little on the chubby side, but now she looks skinnier than I do," she said.

The party at which Audrey had vomited occurred just two days after Sharon had heard that comment. "You better see her. I'd bet my bottom dollar she's bulimic," Sharon said to Mrs. Lyons.

When Audrey arrived at Mrs. Lyons' office, she seemed open enough. "You wanted to see me?" Mrs. Lyons' reputation among the students was quite positive, so few students immediately assumed they were in difficulty when they received a note like the one she had sent to Audrey: "I have the time open during your fourth period study hall. I'd appreciate it if you'd stop by my office to talk."

Mrs. Lyons noticed Audrey's gaunt, pale face and the dark circles under her eyes and observed that she had pulled her bulky sweatshirt down over her left hand. For a moment she was tempted to skirt the issue, to talk about the football game on the previous Friday night, or to ask Audrey how her classes were going, but she decided to get right to the point.

"You were in one of my guidance classes in ninth grade and so you know I deal pretty straight with students." Audrey snickered and then fell silent. "I'm concerned that you have a weight loss problem—that you're bingeing and purging."

"I don't know what you mean," said Audrey, her eyes half-closed, her teeth clamped together.

"I mean that you eat a lot and then force yourself to vomit," she said.

Audrey smiled sweetly and spoke rather breezily. "Oh, you must have heard about what happened after the Halloween party the other day. I'm so stupid about all that kind of thing—popcorn and cake and candy. When I'm around it I just can't seem to stop eating. And then all of a sudden I had this big pain in my stomach and I rushed to the rest room and had 'a big burp'—that's what I used to call it when I was a little girl." She waved her hand to dismiss the issue. "So is there anything else?" she said and stood in front of her chair.

Mrs. Lyons made a short sweeping motion with her hand inviting Audrey to seat herself again. Audrey pretended not to notice. "So you're saying that you didn't force yourself to vomit. It just happened. That could be. How often does that happen?"

"Oh, it hasn't happened for years," Audrey said and blinked her eyes and opened them wide.

"I'm afraid I'm not convinced. Please sit down," Mrs. Lyons said gently. As Audrey seated herself, Mrs. Lyons came out from behind the desk and sat on its front edge. She held out both her hands silently.

Audrey reached her right hand out, looked up at Mrs. Lyons, worked her left hand out of her sleeve, and reached out palm up.

Mrs. Lyons' voice was hardly more than a whisper. "Let's stop playing games. I want to see the back of your left hand."

The breezy voice again. "Oh, this? You won't believe how that happened. I was cutting cheese the other day, fortunately the knife wasn't very sharp. . . ."

"I wasn't born yesterday," Mrs. Lyons said gently. "Those are teeth marks. You are bulimic. It's time to stop pretending."

Audrey's breezy style disappeared at that point. She stared at the floor a great deal and for a long time she responded, after protracted silences, in the briefest way that she could. To her credit she did reply, and if briefly, then openly, as Mrs. Lyons checked with her concerning the patterns of behavior bulimics tend to follow.

Audrey's bulimia had evolved over the previous seven months. "I just had to be able to wear one of those brief bathing suits and look good in it. When I tried it on in early April, I looked like some painting of one of those middle ages nudes with a little piece of gauzy cloth. I couldn't stand it." She admitted to gorging and vomiting as often as five times in a day. She had tried a variety of approaches, laxatives, Ipecac, other over-the-counter drugs, but sticking her fingers down her throat was the most reliable technique.

"How have you been getting away with all this at home?" asked Mrs. Lyons.

Audrey's first approach took her back into her breezy, chatty, self-assured way of responding for a few moments. "Mother's so careless about food. Besides she lets me do some of the buying and she never notices how much I spend." Mrs. Lyons thought some of Audrey's responses did not ring true so she pressed her gently, but firmly, and continually. At one point she invited Audrey to telephone her mother and ask her in to discuss the matter on the spot. That turned the conversation around. In the several minutes following, Audrey admitted to taking money out of her mother's purse, lying to her mother about her eating habits and purchases, hiding food for later consumption, and shoplifting food items and slipping them into her pockets or under her bulky sweater.

"Sometimes I think, 'Why should I bother paying for all that stuff when I'm just going to get rid of it.'"

Mrs. Lyons stifled a sigh. It was such a familiar story. She shifted directions. "I assume you make choices—at least some of the time—to avoid vomiting. I'd like to know about those." Audrey looked blank. Mrs. Lyons continued. "Sometimes you *do* hold down your food, I'm sure." Audrey nodded. "What's different about those times?"

Audrey talked about staying with people for an hour and a half or so after eating. "That helps—sometimes. And sometimes I take a walk and I tell myself I'm not going to upchuck—especially if I haven't eaten a *ton* of stuff." She fell silent.

"OK, I hear three choices you make in that. Sometimes you choose to stay with people and that helps; or you choose to take a walk and tell yourself that you're not going to purge yourself; or you choose to eat less and then you can keep your food down." Mrs. Lyons tapped her right index finger in the palm of her left hand as she ticked off each of the three choices.

"And one time, just the other day, a while after dinner, I took a long slow bath, with bubble bath, you know. And when I got out of it I didn't have the urge any more," Audrey said.

"So that's four techniques you can use—when you choose to," said Mrs. Lyons.

The situation was a textbook one. Bingeing, purging, stealing, lying, hiding food. But Audrey had some strategies for combating her urges—and the main thing on her side was a combination of her age and the short duration of the habit. Under eight months.

One of the most difficult aspects of that first interview came when Mrs. Lyons brought the topic around to involving Audrey's parents, at least her mother, in the matter. "They've *got* to know. You need their support and assistance if you're ever going to lick this thing—you have no idea how difficult it can be." After resisting for many minutes Audrey agreed to explore the issue with her mother, but only if Mrs. Lyons would be there to act as a buffer between the two.

On the following Monday Mrs. Randolph breezed in with the same light-hearted air Mrs. Lyons had observed many times in Audrey. "Now what's all this about? My little girl been ditching class a time or two? I know her grades are in good shape. Oh, Lord, I could tell you stories from when I was in high school—but I wouldn't dare in front of Audrey. Might give her ideas."

"No, her attendance has been fine, and her grades are holding up nicely," Mrs. Lyons replied, then she turned to Audrey. "I'd like you tell your mother what this is all about."

Audrey hesitated and her mother rushed in with an observation that she had never known her daughter not to have something to say. Then she began to launch off in a new direction: "Why, when I was her age. . . ," but Audrey interrupted her.

"Mother," she began and waited for her mother to stop and look at her. Then she continued in the words she had rehearsed with Mrs. Lyons. "Mother, I need you to listen, and I need your help."

"Well, dear, don't look so grim. You know I'm always there for you, as I say—except on Tuesdays when the bridge club meets." Her laugh was hollow.

"I'm bulimic. I've been eating huge amounts sometimes and then I force myself to, you know, upchuck," she said.

For many minutes Mrs. Randolph tried to pass the issue off as a minor problem, but with periodic interruptions and invitations by

Mrs. Lyons, Audrey got the whole story out—the bingeing, purging, hiding food, taking money, and shoplifting. Mrs. Randolph's breeziness gradually ebbed and real concern for her daughter showed on her face.

"This is a time when your daughter needs you to understand her and to help her," said Mrs. Lyons. "She's lost over thirty pounds, and even though you may be proud that she's lost the chubbiness she had, she's built some patterns that for some girls and women are irreversible."

Mrs. Randolph's voice had an edge to it. "What do you mean?"

Audrey waved off Mrs. Lyons' attempt to respond. "Mom, Mrs. Lyons tells me that lying is a pattern with us bulimics, and I've already done a lot of that. But here, I'm being honest with you. I thought it was great that I stopped having my period, but maybe that means that I'm messing things up inside myself and I won't be able to straighten them out—by myself, anyway." She burst into tears.

After many moments, when Audrey was able to calm herself, she turned first to her counselor then to her mother. "I haven't even told *you* this, but three times in the last two days I didn't have to *make* myself vomit. It just came up. You said that might happen. Mom, just listen to both of us."

"I think you need specifics, Mrs. Randolph. Let me try to give you some," Mrs. Lyons said. At that point she called Audrey's mother's attention to her poster, and the three talked about it for some time. "I think where you can help most is to be there for Audrey every day. Talk with her about her eating choices that day. Reinforce the fact that *she's* pleased when things are going all right. Give her your support. Let her know that you're distressed when she breaks her resolve—but help her understand that you love her no matter what she does. Help me keep convincing her that she makes eating choices one after another—and that she can remain in control."

Over the next several months Mrs. Lyons saw Audrey frequently. She had her ups and downs. In some ways that first air-clearing discussion and the follow-up interview with Mrs. Randolph were the high points of the counseling process. The problem kept rearing its head as soon as Audrey began to gain a little weight. Finally, after Audrey had heard the same points from a physician who had treated many bulimics, a nutritionist who worked in the same clinic, and a bulimic who had struggled with the problem for years, the point penetrated— and seemed to stay.

Audrey put it this way. "I guess I've got a life-long fight ahead of me. But I can see that the key to winning it isn't some big thing, it's all the little choices—of eating, and of feeling good about myself—that make the difference."

In a note to her own mother, Mrs. Lyons wrote, "Sometimes I feel like I'm trying to bail out a half-sunken boat with a teaspoon. I think I've got Sharon on the right track, and some of the time I'm convinced that Audrey's going to make it—mainly because we've gotten to her before the problem was a habit of years—but when I'm convinced that I've succeeded with a couple of students, four more show up at the door, or I think about Beth's never-ending struggle.

"Whoever coined the phrase originally, 'You can never be too rich or too thin,' had no idea what he or she was unleashing into this world—and the same for whoever decided that models on the cover of magazines ought to look like they hadn't had a decent meal in their lives.

"It's an uphill fight, but I'll keep at it because I know if I don't, a lot of these girls, and a few boys, will face far worse problems the older they get. And maybe some day the media will decide that looking natural—*whatever* that may be—is better than looking undernourished."

Todd

"Pudge, they call me—all the time. I don't let 'em know it gets under my skin, but it does," Todd told Mrs. Lyons. The precipitating event that had brought him to counseling was that he had wanted the lead in the high school play, but he had been cast as the father of the heroine.

"I can act rings around the guy they picked. The part doesn't call for someone who's slim or good-looking. But even the teachers can't see me as a leading man." He looked down at the floor for several seconds. "I heard one of the kids in the back say, 'And he-e-e-re's Orson Welles,' as I stood up for the reading. I think that cinched it. Can you help me, Mrs. Lyons?"

Todd, a high school junior, recited his history of overweight. Food had been used as a reward at home. His mother followed what she called Grandma's Law—no dessert until you finish your vegetables—and she treated Todd to larger pieces of cake and pie than others in the family received when he had gotten a good grade or done well in a recitation at church or in a part in a school play. "And sometimes when I felt bad about something, she'd take me out for a sundae or a pizza. When I got a little older and had some spending money, I'd go buy some donuts or something when everything was great—or when things were going sour. It'd perk me up again—like it did when mom treated me."

Todd summarized. "Truth is, I guess I've always been a little. . . pudgy—I hate that word—as long as I can remember. For a little while when I grew five inches in the year after my fourteenth birthday, I looked pretty good, but then I let things get out of hand again."

Mrs. Lyons listened to Todd's recitation, reflected his feelings, and asked questions now and again. She probed at length about his relationships with boys and girls his age, and at one point she offered a speculation: "Could it be that you felt threatened when the girls began to hint that you were attractive, and you couldn't stand the pressure, so you let your weight go up again?"

Todd dismissed the idea out of hand, but returned to it a few minutes later. "What you said about girls a bit ago—maybe that's right. I never thought about it that way, but. . . that could be."

"So if you choose to lose some weight now, what do you think will happen?" she asked.

"D'you mean, will I get scared if the girls pay attention to me, and will I balloon up again?" Mrs. Lyons nodded. "Naw. I don't think so. I feel a lot different about girls now. In fact, I'd like it if they did pay me some attention. Besides, now I'd have a better idea of what was happening, and that'd make a difference."

Todd was a pleasure to work with. He had no interest in thinning down to an unrealistic level. He undertook an exercise regimen and did not overdo it. He sought the aid of his mother who modified her cooking patterns to some degree for the benefit of the entire family. He seized upon the idea that each mouthful of food he ate involved a choice, and he readily accepted the notion that eating modest servings of a variety of foods was in his interest. He responded wholeheartedly to the spa opportunities Mrs. Lyons offered, and he used them to build up his self-concept.

A moment of triumph came on the evening the play opened. "I just loved your performance," said a female stagehand whom Todd thought was most attractive. "Greg's nice enough, but you'd have done a much better job in that part." That night he looked in the mirror and weighed himself. "You've come *down* a long way, baby," he told himself, then he recited his goal statement proudly. "My ideal weight window is from 155 to 175 pounds. Right now I'm 18 pounds heavier than my top weight. I accept myself as a good guy and I'm going to keep thinking that, no matter what I weigh. I know I can get to my ideal weight window and stay there—and I'm well on the road."

He smiled and added, "By next year I'll be a real candidate for the leading man role in the school play—and my weight won't be a problem."

Mrs. Lyons had built a reputation for dealing effectively with weight problems and Todd was the third overweight student who had asked for help shortly after the beginning of the new calendar year. Initially Mrs. Lyons saw the two girls and Todd individually; eventually she formed a group, and four other students, two boys and three girls, joined in. The group process proved to be highly effective for Todd, who had the least weight to lose because of the progress he had already made.

"I used to feel so alone, even though I could see that other people had weight problems," Todd observed to the other group members during their third meeting. "I guess I thought everyone else who was fat felt OK about it. I know better now."

Lucy, the heaviest member of the group, looked thoughtful, then responded. "I always spent the time thinking about myself and my problems. In these last couple of weeks, I've really looked around at the other kids. I think almost all of 'em have problems. If it isn't over-weight, it's underweight, if it isn't too few friends, it's too many friends—and too many temptations; if it isn't poor coordination, it's too much pressure to be a super-star on a team—or one of the cheerleaders."

Todd nodded several times as he thought about his closest com-panions and others he admired. "That reminds me of a poem I memorized for English class a month or so ago," he said. He identified the poem to Mrs. Lyons and she encouraged him to recite what he could recall of it. To sum it up, "Richard Cory," by Edwin Arlington Robinson, tells of a man who was handsome and well-dressed, who "fluttered pulses," who was "always human when he talked," who was "richer than a king," and who made others "wish that we were in his place." Todd's rich voice unfurled the last verse:

And on we worked, and waited for the light,

And went without the meat, and cursed the bread;

And Richard Cory, one calm summer night,

Went home and put a bullet through his head.

There was a long silence. Lucy finally spoke. "So even the people I can't figure out a problem for may have one."

"And none of us has an option to be anyone but who we are," said Mrs. Lyons. "All we can do is make all the little choices we face every day the best way we can—at least most of them."

Modifying a System

All over this country, in fact all over this world, there are systems that contribute to problems involving weight. Athletes in such sports as wrestling and football may be encouraged or required to maintain their weight within particular ranges, while others in such sports as volleyball and gymnastics may be encouraged or required to keep their weight below specified limits. The weight requirements that are im-posed on athletes in some instances ideally fit the needs of those individuals. In many other instances those requirements create genu-ine difficulties during the athletic career, and difficulties often increase when the athletic career is over. Weight-related problems are not restricted to athletes, however. Twirlers, cheerleaders, and flag-bearers are commonly required to meet weight requirements, as are members of music or dance groups or others with high public visibility.

In this section we examine briefly the impact of weight require-ments on students in a college marching band. The process may offer guidance to the professional counselor who becomes aware that systemic difficulties may be contributing to problems of individuals in maintaining desirable body weight. Student affairs personnel in the college became aware of the problem and worked with the leadership of the band to the advantage of the students.

In one of the earliest events that tied the weight control issue to band students, a member of the student affairs staff was asked by leaders of a residence unit to help with their concerns about a bulimic student we call Mara. A number of times food marked with the names of students had been taken, but the precipitating event occurred when Mara consumed dozens of donuts that had been purchased for the whole unit. At the insistence of others in the unit, Mara referred herself for assistance, and it soon became apparent that her concern for controlling her weight came in part because she was a member of a group of women who dance and lead cheers at athletic events. Mara supported the right of band personnel to impose weight requirements, but it was clear that her tendency toward bulimia was aggravated in part because she was required to weigh-in periodically, and her status in the group depended on her maintaining her weight within preset guidelines.

Other events also raised concern. The same staff member was asked to work with chapter relations for a social sorority. In more than one meeting the topic turned to band and auxiliary band members, weight requirements, weigh-ins, and the relationship of grades in band to weight standards. One student who was not selected as a flag bearer was told what the weight requirements would be if she were to apply again the following year. She worked assiduously, made the standard, still was not selected, and left the college. In addition, in their contacts with hall directors, other student affairs personnel heard similar concerns expressed for residents.

Two events made the time for action seem appropriate: in its annual report, the college health advisory board cited weight control problems as one of its primary concerns, and a member of the student affairs staff was asked to help select key twirlers. Student affairs office personnel used those events as opportunities to offer their expertise concerning weight control issues. From the beginning, band staff members were open and positive, and their attitudes were character-ized as reflecting "excellent cooperation."

In the meeting that resulted, those present from the staff of the bands focused primarily on practical matters—how to maintain rea-sonable standards without harming students. They freely discussed the inconsistency of weigh-ins for female students in some groups, while there were no such requirements for males. They took a healthy view of participants as students first, rather than as performers. They discussed alternative criteria to weigh-ins, and they expressed willing-ness to consider using parts of some band sessions for educational programming—as a result nutritionists and others were invited to speak to students and to discuss their questions and concerns related to weight control issues. The objectives of the program were to help students understand that they have choices in their eating habits and to encourage them to make choices that are personally reasonable and effective.

The conclusion that can be drawn from this effort is that where systems may contribute to the problems of individuals, people of good will can come together to work them out. Among the individuals who are most likely to perceive the dimensions of the problem are those who serve in various counseling capacities. When those individuals become aware of student or personnel concerns, they need to enlist the cooperation of others in resolving such matters.

Whether the onset of a problem results from systemic conditions or not, three family types appear to be at risk for producing bulimics; it may be assumed that similar types of families produce anorexics. *Overprotective families* use age-inappropriate rules and overprotect family members; food becomes a way of expressing nurturance and connection, and bulimia serves as a way for the young person to separate, to create boundaries, or to solicit protection and nurturance. *Chaotic families* are overtly distressed and have numerous problems; individuals feel victimized and powerless and resort to routine, compulsive behaviors, particularly around food; and bulimia may serve as a predictable recourse in an unpredictable world. *Perfect families* present a veneer of coping "perfectly" with stresses within and beyond the family; achievement and appearance (especially physical appearance) are valued more than connectedness; bulimia is a way to belong and to rebel simultaneously (Fallon, 1988).

Counselors should not take responsibility for "fixing" a bulimarexic, since failure leads to feelings of incompetence for both persons, and success leads to dependency. Bulimarexics must initiate the process of change and commit themselves to positive actions on their own behalf (Boskind-White & White, 1983). Bulimia and anorexia are not solely eating disorders; they are problems ". . . related to an underdeveloped sense of mastery, control, and power; treatment must take place at this level" (Hawkins, *et al.*, 1984, p. 223). Counseling is not likely to be beneficial if it repeats the pattern of a lifetime: individuals being told what they feel and how to think, with the implication being that they are incapable of helping themselves. Instead, clients must be helped to develop awareness of their capabilities and potentials so that they may become more competent and effective in handling their own problems of living (Bruch, 1983). In short, they must learn to make more effective choices.

SELF-EXAMINATION—JOURNAL ENTRY: Take a few minutes, preferably at least five and examine your personal attitudes and choice patterns concerning weight maintenance. Consider whether you have, or have had, genuine difficulties in this area, and to what extent you are understanding of others who have such difficulties. Discuss the extent to which you use, or might use, your patterns of choices to prevent or resolve such difficulties. Head your entry WEIGHT MAINTENANCE AND ME.

We encourage you to share these ideas with your clients, inviting their reactions and helping them see that maintaining desirable body weight depends on a great many everyday choices.

COUNSELING APPLICATION—JOURNAL ENTRY: Discuss the extent to which you believe it is important for you to use Choice Awareness theory with any of the clients you have, or may come to have, who suffer from weight control problems. Consider how you might use Choice Awareness to combat a weight control problem with a specific or hypothetical client or system. Head your entry WEIGHT MAINTENANCE AND MY CLIENTS.

Maintaining Desirable Body Weight

For many individuals weight control problems are a lifelong matter. Some swing upward into overweight, then use extreme measures to overcome their difficulties, and become anorexic or bulimic. In some instances it appears that chemical imbalances distort the perceptions of those involved and the difficulties become so great that extreme measures may be necessary, including hospitalization and force-feeding. Even then, in the most severe instances, death may result.

Although examples can be cited in which problems of long duration have been brought under control successfully, the best hope for combating the scourge of weight control problems is often early assistance. Thus the examples cited in this chapter have focused on young persons whose difficulties were of comparatively short duration.

Ultimately, for moderate or extreme manifestations of weight-related problems to come under control, individuals who face those problems must learn to make effective choices, moment to moment, regarding at least two matters: their intake of food and their feelings about themselves. Those who counsel individuals with weight control problems would do well to help clients become aware of the choices they have available to them, and assist them to take more effective control over their food intake and over their self-perceptions.

Our cultural norms value physical perfection and thinness and cast women in the role of sex-objects. Changing those norms may appear to be an overwhelming challenge, but just as mountains are worn away over time by wind and rain, challenges to those norms can be expected to wear away those norms, eventually. Meanwhile, the work of the counselor must include that of helping all people, and young women in particular, to accept themselves as they are, and to make only those changes in themselves that are both reasonable and healthy for them.

References

Boskind-White, M. & White, W.C. (1983). *Bulimarexia: The binge/purge cycle*. New York: W. W. Norton.

Bruch, H. (1983). Psychotherapy in anorexia nervosa and developmental obesity. In R. K. Goodstein (Ed.). *Eating and weight disorders: Advances in treatment and research*. New York: Springer. Pp. 134-146.

Fallon, P. (1988). A feminist/systems approach to the treatment of bulimia. Unpublished paper. International Conference on Eating Disorders.

Hawkins, R. C., Tremouw, W. J. & Clement, P.F. (1984). *The binge-purge syndrome: Diagnosis, treatment, and research*. New York: Springer.

Chapter 18

Enhancing Self-Concept

A Damaged Self-Concept

Many individuals can benefit from Choice Awareness counseling that helps them (1) explore both their general self-concept and the specific components of their self-concept, (2) understand how their negative views of themselves affect them, and (3) make choices that allow them to see themselves both realistically and positively. Warren Rasmussen, a thirty-year-old bookkeeper for a manufacturing concern, was an ideal candidate for self-concept counseling.

It was one of Warren's least-liked tasks to carry the firm's deposits the four blocks to the bank once every two weeks. One hot July day, immediately upon entering the bank, he heard a loud, but muffled voice yell, "Down on the floor!" Instantly he flung himself down.

A robbery was in progress; the police arrived on the scene; bullets flew; two of the gunmen and one policeman were killed; and the third robber and three bank customers were wounded, one customer quite seriously. Warren was carted away in an ambulance, treated for a scalp injury, and then his statement was taken. Before he was released he was strongly urged to take advantage of the post-traumatic stress counseling by one of a team of counselors the bank called upon for assistance. Whatever Warren was strongly urged to do, he did; as a consequence, he made an appointment with Dr. Dorothy Thomas, who had recently retired from her university counseling position and was pressed into service to help those who were in the bank during the attempted robbery.

Warren's learned reticence, added to a sense of embarrassment, in part because he could contribute nothing that would shed light on what had happened—though he was asked repeatedly by the police, family members, and his fellow employees to provide details—resulted in a hesitant and garbled first twenty minutes with Dr. Thomas.

The First Interview

"Something is bothering you about all this. I don't think you're hiding anything that the police need to know, but I do think you need to talk about what's troubling you," she said after a time.

"It's just stupid. . . and. . . and embarrassing. I want to tell you what you want to know, but," he paused and gulped, "I don't really know anything."

"Look," said Dr. Thomas, "the police report makes it clear that you were unconscious and couldn't tell them anything; their guess is you hit your head on the table they found you near. What's embarrassing for you in that?"

"Can't you see?" Warren responded, glancing up from the floor, a pained look on his face.

"No, but I'd really like for you to help me see," she said gently.

He rolled his eyes to the ceiling and took a quick, shallow breath. "I think I fainted," he said.

"Oh, so that's it," she said.

"Yes, you see," he said, and followed with a sudden rush of words, "I'm taking all this time from you under false pretenses. I know as little about all this as the people who got it from the newspaper. I'm such a coward. I didn't even *see* anything. I just heard someone yell to me to get down and I guess I fainted and the next thing I knew I was in the hospital. I didn't hear any of the shooting. I didn't even get to see any of the blood. It was all over so fast I don't think I have any of that post-traumatic stress disorder, as they keep calling it. Someone from the bank even took the bag out of my hand and made the deposit for me—and everything was there."

Once the flood gates were open Warren talked openly and freely. At one point Dr. Thomas drew a collection of papers out of her leather folder and located a page. "This is from the statement by one of the other bank customers I talked to. It's a transcript of the police report, but I can't see that it'd violate a confidence for me to read the part that relates to you. 'So these guys are grabbing the money and the door opens and this guy comes in and they yell to him to hit the floor and he throws himself down so fast that he cracks his head on this big marble table where you make out your deposit. . . .'"

"That doesn't sound like you fainted. It sounds like you just went down fast and hit your head—if that's any comfort to you," she observed.

"It's a great comfort," he replied, and over the next several minutes he visibly relaxed.

Near the end of their scheduled hour, Dr. Thomas said, "I'm pretty well satisfied that you don't have any trauma resulting from the bank disaster—though sometimes the reaction sets in later as it did with some of the people who served in Vietnam. The bank has contracted with me to see you as often as you want over the next two months, and I think it'd be a good idea for us to get together several times."

Warren nodded politely. If those were the rules, those were the rules. He knew about rules. "Besides," he said to himself, "it's comforting to talk to someone, and she's not judging me harshly. And I've always been able to talk to older women all right."

"I think there's something we *could* work on during our time together if it'd be OK with you—and we can go into gear on the bank matter if something about that begins to bother you." She watched him while he traced the crease in his trousers with his index finger and thumb. "If you'd let me, I'd like to work with you on your feelings about yourself." Her voice was gentle, soothing.

He stared at the floor for several seconds and then looked up at her. "That'd be OK with me," he said. His eyes were suddenly, unaccountably, irritated, and he reached up to press his knuckles lightly against them. Dr. Thomas patted his arm. He found tears coursing down his cheeks, his shoulders heaved once slightly, then vigorously, and soon he was sobbing uncontrollably.

"It's OK. It's OK. Let go. Let it out. It's been in there a long time. It's OK," she said.

Warren's story was a familiar one to Dr. Thomas. He spoke at length about his cold, demanding parents, and the cold, demanding grandparents who had raised them. Nothing he ever did was good enough. They never spanked him or beat him. But they seldom smiled at him either. They sent strong speak-when-you-are-spoken-to messages and preached hell-fire-and-damnation at him whenever he slipped, or whenever they heard about him "taking up" with anyone about whom they knew anything questionable. And they knew something questionable about nearly everyone.

"So you see, if my feelings about myself aren't in very good shape, at least there are reasons for it," he said, and he sighed, sat back in his chair, and rubbed his eyes and wiped his nose with his handkerchief.

"I never doubted that," said Dr. Thomas, adding after a moment, "and I think taking some time to work on your feelings about yourself might be highly worthwhile."

When Warren agreed, Dr. Thomas said, "Let me clarify what I see as our purpose, then. I think we can spend our time together first exploring ways in which you feel good and not so good about yourself, and second considering what you may be able to do so that your feelings about yourself are more positive. At the same time, we'll see if other things emerge that we'll want to work on—especially if they're related to the holdup."

"Sounds OK to me," said Warren in a lifeless voice.

At that point Dr. Thomas reached into her desk and pulled out a pad of paper and a felt pen. Across the top of the first page she printed, HOW I SEE MYSELF AS A PERSON. Below that she labeled three columns: THINGS I CAN DO, MY SKILLS AND ABILITIES, and THINGS I WANT TO CHANGE.

"Let's start here," she said, pointing to the first column. "A lot of people who don't feel good about themselves overlook the everyday things they can do—and feel good about. Let's see if we can build a list of several things that fit that category." Warren looked hesitant, so she added, "I'll help too, and we can start with the simplest possible things. Let me write down three." And she wrote the words *breathe*, *walk*, and *read*.

"Oh, I get it. Really basic things," he said.

Over the next several minutes, with minimal prompting from Dr. Thomas, and with Warren smiling occasionally, the two listed twenty-three entries in the column, with the only complex one being *play chess*.

"That's one you have on me," said Dr. Thomas, when Warren mentioned that skill as item number nine. He nodded at her comment.

"OK, now, let's tackle this second column and list some more personalized skills and abilities—maybe try for five or six. If it were mine I could write, 'I can sing well enough to be in the church choir. I'm better than fair in math. I make friends slowly, but once I make friends it sticks. And I understand people pretty well,'" suggested Dr. Thomas, and she waited for Warren to speak.

"Five or six? I don't know if I have that many, but two things you said work for me. I can sing OK, and I remember lots of words to songs. And when I make a friend I'm a pretty good friend—loyal, you know— I don't have enough friends so I can afford to turn one off," said Warren.

"I hear *three* things in what you said." Dr. Thomas wrote, *I can sing, I remember the words to songs,* and I'm *loyal to my friends.* "For the time being let's stay away from the criticism—not having enough friends. What else is positive?"

Warren paused for several seconds. He looked at Dr. Thomas for inspiration but she waited for him. "I know my own mind pretty well," he said.

"Hey, that's neat," said Dr. Thomas as she entered those words on the list. "Tell me more about that."

"Well, I don't always say very much, but I have convictions—I know what's right and wrong, and I do what's right, most of the time anyway," he said.

"That's the strongest voice I've heard you use so far. I really believe that. And it sounds like it's not just a matter of doing what you were told to do as a child," she said.

"No, I guess not. Actually, to put a label on it, I'm much more liberal than my folks—not just because they always tell me what to do. I really believe—what I believe."

"OK, that's great. And maybe we can get you to believe some new, positive things about yourself in here," she said. "I'm going to add two things you said to the list." Dr. Thomas wrote, *I know what's right and wrong*, and *I do what's right*. After a brief pause she added, "Also, you're the kind of person who is good at remembering detail—judging by what you told me about your interactions with your parents and grandparents and friends—and you express yourself clearly, too," and she made two additional entries on the list.

Warren half smiled. "This is kinda fun for you, isn't it." said Dr. Thomas.

"Yeah." He smiled more fully.

"It's meant to be. I think an important part of counseling ought to be rather like going to a spa. It ought to help you feel really good about yourself. We have to have the other part, too, but some of the time we ought to get you to feel really good about who you are."

"OK. But what about that third column, THINGS I WANT TO CHANGE?" said Warren. "That's the one that worries me. I've been putting it off, I think. I might be ready for it now."

"All right, if you're ready—but let's go for just a couple of things to list here," she said, "and let's begin with the thing we already agreed on. You want to feel better about yourself."

As Dr. Thomas entered that below the heading, Warren commented, "And I guess I'd like to make more friends, you know—so I'd have more people to be loyal to," then he chuckled.

"I'm sure you can find other things you want to change, but these are enough to work on from my point of view," she said.

"But there are so many things. . . ," Warren's voice trailed off as Dr. Thomas raised her hand.

"It's easy to go off in too many directions and make no progress at all, and I don't want that to happen."

"You're the boss," he replied.

"I think I'll leave that alone just now since our time's about up, but we'll come back to it another day." Warren nodded in response. "Before we quit, though, I want to tell you that I really like your openness with me and I see some directions we can take in the future," she said.

"This page we've started—the Things I Can Do and the Skills and Abilities columns—I'd like to ask you to add to these in the next few days. Put down anything that comes to mind, and they don't have to be things you can do perfectly or skills you're an expert in," she said.

"I think I can do that," he replied.

"OK. And I'll ask you to do one other thing with the list. Spend some time every day thinking about and enjoying each item. Revel in these things you've listed and those you add." Warren frowned, so she explained further. "Take the first thing *you* listed: *talk*. As you read that, think about it, think what a wonderful skill it is, appreciate it, and appreciate yourself because you can do it—and very well, I might add."

Warren blushed. "There are lots of things I'm tongue-tied about. But with someone like you, a counselor, I can talk about myself a little. That's nothing special."

"I guess if you want to, you can choose to believe it's nothing special—but I think it's wonderful. Speech is a miracle to me. No creatures except human beings can do it—at least in no way that compares to the level you can." Dr. Thomas paused a moment. "I guess what I'm telling you is to smell the roses. Decide that the things you can do are wonderful. They really are, you know."

"I think I see what you mean. It just seems so ordinary. But when you really look at it. . . ," his voice trailed away.

"When you really look at it, it's an amazing skill. And so are all the other things you have on that list. Think what it'd be like, what it would mean, if you couldn't do those things—walk, and smile, and tie your shoes, and the most basic one of all—breathe."

"I get you. I really do." He paused. "Smell the roses, you say. I guess I *do* have a rose or two of my own to smell."

Dr. Thomas had a few moments to reflect on the interview after she scheduled the next meeting with Warren and before her next client arrived. "We really got to spa," she said to herself and smiled. "I think the 'assignment'—the directed activity—will do him a world of good because it's so achievable." She smiled again when she compared Warren's bearing during the time he was sharing his sterile childhood to the way he looked at the end of the interview. "I'll wager no one ever complimented him for his openness—the way I was able to before he left. That'll help, too," she told herself.

The Second Interview

In the second interview Dr. Thomas invited Warren to begin wherever he wished. He immediately shared his extended lists of things he could do and his skills and abilities, summing up, "It made me feel pretty good to think about those things."

"I'm glad they felt good to you." After a pause she added, "But I'd like to point out that you *chose* to let them feel good to you. They didn't really *make* you feel good. You could have discounted all those things, for example, and decided they aren't really important—even though they are."

"I guess you're right." He looked thoughtful and Dr. Thomas waited for him to continue. "A time or two someone tried to tell me I have a lot going for me—like a high school teacher I had years ago—but I didn't really listen. I guess I didn't *choose* to listen."

Dr. Thomas smiled. "You're really getting the point. And maybe it's time for me to bring up something you said last time, that I said I'd come back to." Warren scowled and she waved her hand. "It was no big deal," she said. "Lot's of people say it without thinking—'You're the boss' was what you said."

"Oh, that." Warren's voice and smile dismissed it as minor.

"I just want you to know that it's your life and you're really the boss. I can help you think through things, but like with the lists on that paper, you're the one who decides whether or not you'll let those things in. And you're the one who has to make changes if any are going to be made."

He sighed. "I guess so."

"You don't need to be discouraged. A few little changes and I think you'll have a new outlook on life," she reassured him. "Already I see some important gains. I noticed how upbeat and shoulders-back you were when you left the other day, and when you were sharing the additions you'd made to your list today. Those are neat changes—and you're already making them."

Warren nodded. "So that's what this is all about," he mused.

"Right. It's about you making better choices—mainly in how you feel about yourself. And the little choices add up," she replied. "I jotted down something Ellen Goodman wrote in her column in June of 1988, and I keep it on a card here in front of me," she said, and pointed. "'How do you make a life?' she wrote. 'Put one foot in front of the other. Make some choices. Take some chances.'"

"That's neat," Warren mused.

"Instead of believing that something *made* you feel good or bad, which suggests you have no choice, you can say, I *chose* to feel good or bad about that. You see how that puts you in control?"

Warren nodded. "Then I guess I shouldn't let things make me. . . I mean, I shouldn't feel bad about things?"

"No, I wouldn't say that," she replied. "It's OK to feel bad—to let something get under your skin and have negative feelings. But it's important to know that you have a choice about whether you let yourself go with that feeling or not—and you have a choice about how long you let yourself stay with it too."

"Hmm." Warren rubbed his chin.

"Take an example of a situation you mentioned last time that involves your parents. They heard you were palling-around with Jimmy from work and they say they disapprove of you spending time with him." Warren nodded. "OK. First you have a lot of feelings; you love your folks; you like Jimmy; you feel resentful that your folks are still interfering in your life; you believe in Jimmy; and maybe you're just a bit amused—'they'll never change,' you think to yourself. Is all that possible?"

"Yeah. I guess so. All but being amused. I never think that way—but I guess I could," he replied.

"All right. So you have some of those feelings—and more. And you have a choice about which feeling you'll pay attention to first, what you'll do with it, and how long you'll stay with it." Warren nodded again and Dr. Thomas continued. "Let's say you choose to pay attention to your hurt feeling. There are several things you could do with it. For example, you could go off and sulk. Or you might say, 'Come on, Dad and Mom, it hurts when you don't give me credit for good judgment. I *know* Jimmy and I think he's just fine. Besides, he's even said I'm a good influence on him.' As I recall that's something you mentioned when you were talking about Jimmy last time."

"It was. And, boy, I'd *like* to say that to them. But I'm not sure I ever could," he replied.

"Well, you don't ever have to. I just want you to know that it would be possible. And maybe one of these days we could role play a little and find *some* way for you to say something similar that would feel OK to you," she said.

Warren nodded. "Well, maybe it'd be worth a try, but. . . ." His voice trailed away.

"The other point I want to make is even if you let the hurt come through from your parents, you have a choice about how long you'll let it stay with you," said Dr. Thomas.

"I think you may be right there," said Warren after a thoughtful pause. "Sometimes I just go for a walk and that helps. Or I go work out at the gym. The other day I did that and it felt pretty good. I even started humming after a while."

A few moments later Dr. Thomas changed the focus of the interview by suggesting that Warren share with her one or two of the labels he put on himself. It took him some time to figure out what she meant and to sort out labels that fit him.

"Shy," he suggested, "especially around women, my age—but I've always been that way."

"That's exactly the point," she replied.

Over the next two or three minutes as a result of Dr. Thomas' probing, the two built a list of ways Warren showed his shyness, and she made note of them with her ever-present felt pen and paper. *I don't look at people directly. I wait until others smile first. I don't say "hello" first.*

At work I don't speak up for myself. Then for several minutes she explored with Warren the yardsticks by which he could measure success—how he might be able to tell if he were not being quite so shy. His own yardsticks were very demanding.

"If you set a goal of making eye contact with a woman *all* the time, instead of the five to ten per cent of the time you estimate you do, you'd be bound to fail. And if you continue to use your minister, who's so good at talking to people one-to-one, and looking directly at them, as your model, you might never be able to reach his level. It'd be more realistic to make your goal increasing your eye contact with women to ten to twenty per cent of the time, and with your friends you might go for forty to fifty per cent of the time," she said. Through Dr. Thomas' gentle probing, the two explored each of the ways Warren cited that he showed his shyness—ways he "chose to live up to his label," as she put it.

Another avenue the two explored for several minutes was that of gains and losses for Warren from his shyness. Dr. Thomas summed up that discussion: "So, being shy keeps the pressure off to some degree, since nobody expects too much of you. But then you don't get noticed when you want to be—by women, or when opportunities come along for advancement at work."

Before Dr. Thomas shifted the focus to a spa activity and closure, she invited Warren to choose one action he might take before they got together for their next appointment; "Make it something simple and easy to achieve, something you can do at least once, that goes against your label of shyness," she suggested, and she was pleased with the action he resolved to take.

"I guess I could try to speak first at least once this week to Judy—at work. I told you she always says something to me whenever I pass by her desk, and I always say something back to her. But I think I could say something first—once or twice." Warren's neck and ears were tinged with pink as he said that.

"That's great. I'm sure you can do that," she replied.

The Next Four Interviews

"That wasn't so hard—talking to Judy first. I did it a couple of times. And I made sure to look at her when I talked," Warren began, after Dr. Thomas invited him to start wherever he wished.

"Wonderful. And I can see how pleased you are that you were able to do that," she replied.

In that interview and the one following, Dr. Thomas explored with Warren extensively concerning the choices he might make that would counter his shyness label. At one point she waved toward the Ellen Goodman quote and paraphrased it: "How do you make an 'un-shy' life? Put one foot in front of the other. Take some chances. Make some 'un-shy' choices."

Gently, one at a time, over those interviews, Dr. Thomas introduced the five CREST choices. At first she accented self-caring and self-ruling. "Keep it reasonable. Don't expect so much of yourself all the time," she said on the latter point. Next she stressed self-enjoying. "That's what spa activities, like the list of THINGS I CAN DO, accomplish for you. They help you appreciate and enjoy yourself." She directed Warren's attention to ways in which he made all five choices with others, starting first with his choices with friends and co-workers, then turning to the choices he made with his parents.

After some detailed exploration concerning Warren's relationship to his parents, she summarized, "I think it's because you've built up so much resentment with your parents that even though you love them, you hardly ever make caring choices with them. And making enjoying choices with them seems to be out of the question—at least it has been so far. You're mostly modeling what they do or responding to the kinds of choices they make. They're into ruling and sorrowing and thinking/working choices. And you don't feel like you can make ruling choices, so you get into mostly sorrowing and thinking/working choices *inside* yourself."

Warren conceded the point and sighed. "That's what's so discouraging. It's like I'm stuck on dead center and I don't see that making different choices will help me all that much—with them."

"Well, let's try to figure out some little ways you might be able to turn that pattern around; let's find some choices you can make that you'll like and that ought to be good for the relationship."

The two discussed and role played at length. Subsequently, Warren tried out several suggestions in his interactions with his parents. He reported a few successes and some failures; but even with the failures, he eventually came to see that he could feel good about the attempts he had made.

"When Mom had a tension headache I suggested she sit down and I'd make her some tea and do the supper dishes. Those—what were they?—caring choices worked pretty well," he recalled.

Reporting on another event he said, "I spent a long time untangling Dad's fishing line, then I asked him to come out on the porch. He said "thanks" and smiled a little—as much as he ever does—and I made a perfect cast to show him it worked, even though I just missed a bird feeder. That was an enjoying choice, I guess—even while I was working on it."

A few moments later Warren reported to Dr. Thomas how discouraged he felt when he tried to reach out to a new female employee in his department at work. "She's pretty and she's nice. I heard she was divorced and I think she's almost my age," he said. "She came by when I was at the drinking fountain. Well, actually I knew she had to go by there to get back to her desk, so I went to get a drink. I tried to say something to her and I couldn't even get one real word out. I just made some kind of stupid sound and then I went back and sat down." He stared at the floor.

"I can tell you're pretty discouraged about that," she said.

"Yeah. I thought I was making progress," he sighed.

Dr. Thomas waited several seconds, then spoke quietly. "You were, even then." Warren looked up at her and frowned. "Think about it," she continued. "A few weeks ago I'll bet you wouldn't even have thought about going up to the water fountain while she was anywhere around. No, let me change that—you might have *thought* about it, but you certainly wouldn't have *gone* up there, and you wouldn't have let anyone see you even *try* to speak to her."

"I guess you're right."

Dr. Thomas used that discussion as a launching platform for presenting a new idea to Warren. She helped him see that his feelings about himself, the feelings that made up his self-concept, were both global and specific. "You've got this general feeling that's not very positive about yourself—but we seem to be nudging that up and up and up. In addition you have feelings about yourself in several specific areas, like you rate yourself quite low in your ability to get along with women your own age."

"That's for sure," he said.

"But you have a different feeling about yourself when it comes to men who are your own age."

"Yeah, but that's different," he added and leaned forward.

"That's exactly the point," she said. "We all have a lot of specific areas that we either feel good or bad or neutral about inside ourselves. Sometimes I think the biggest difference between people who have a positive self-concept and those who don't is that those who feel good about themselves focus on the things they have going for them, and those who don't feel so good about themselves spend a lot of their time focusing on what doesn't work well for them."

Warren stared at the floor and nodded several times. "I see what you mean, I think."

"From what you've told me, I think you feel pretty good about yourself as a bookkeeper, while your lowest feelings about yourself come when you think about your interactions with women your age," Dr. Thomas said, and Warren nodded in agreement. At that point she drew from her desk her felt pen and paper, headed the page SELF-CONCEPT, topped three columns with a plus, a check mark, and a minus, and listed the word *bookkeeper* in the first column and *interactions with women* in the third." From that beginning the two explored a number of dimensions of Warren's self-concept. Two other items in addition to *bookkeeper* in the plus column were *singer* and *friend*. In the minus column one item Warren added was *shy*—"Even though I'm making a little progress." When the two were working on the neutral column Warren laughed and suggested *bravery under fire*—"I guess I can't really be faulted for what happened in the bank," he said, "— and *son*. Some of the time anyway I think I do an OK job there, even if my parents wouldn't always agree."

"It's great that you can see both of those things the way you do now. Lot's of people find it difficult to show approval to their children, and some younger people have to read into their parents' reactions even *neutral* messages. That and your feelings about what happened in the bank are two ways I can see that you're making progress," she said.

Warren and Dr. Thomas spent a considerable amount of time in the fifth interview exploring and then role-playing how Warren might brook the issue of Jimmy with his parents—as a way of letting them know that he planned to be his own person and make his own decisions in his relationships. It was not easy for Warren to come up with ways he was comfortable in expressing his feelings, even in role play, but when Dr. Thomas asked him if he would like to leave that issue for another time, he said he wanted to go ahead with it. "I need to make more OK ruling choices with my parents—and for myself," he said finally.

"I'm not sure how well that idea worked," he reported the next time the two met. "It was like a deep freeze. For a long time they didn't say anything. Even then they wouldn't look at me. And they hardly talked about anything after that."

"So they chose to be silent," Dr. Thomas said matter-of-factly. "And you?"

"I figured I'd try to ignore it. So I read the newspaper and I rattled on about a couple of things I saw in it. Then I took a walk." He sighed.

"Well, wasn't that a lot better than what you feared?" she asked.

"Yeah, I guess so." He half-smiled.

"Hey, you can call that a failure if you want. To me, it looks like you were a great success. Surely you weren't expecting them to hug you and tell you how brave you were to speak up for yourself like that," she said.

Warren laughed. "I guess it *was* about the best I could have expected," he said after a moment.

When time came for the following interview, Warren strode in, beaming. "I did it," he said. "We've been talking about putting on a door and a stairway from my room down the side of the house for years—at least *I* have. But they never got around to it. I said that they either call on Monday and get the work scheduled or I'd move in with Jimmy until I could find an apartment of my own."

"That's terrific. And the way you're standing and your smile tell me that it worked out for you and you're thrilled that you made the choices you did."

"You're right. And as it turned out the guy they called can work it in within the next couple of weeks. There's going to be a delay on a big job he has ahead of him and he can squeeze it in."

"Can you feel the change in yourself from when we first started to talk?" Warren nodded. "Your living arrangement is something I was going to get around to talking about with you, but you figured out what you wanted on your own and did what you decided needed to be done. I hope you're pleased with how far you've come in just a few weeks," she said.

"And I owe it all to y. . . ." He stopped before he completed the word *you*. "I owe a lot of it to you. But I had to make the choices," he said.

"Wonderful!" she replied.

Warren and Dr. Thomas spent many minutes in those interviews on other labels he put on himself and they explored choices Warren might make to counter each label. Periodically Dr. Warren tied those labels and choices back to the two things Warren wanted to change: his feelings about himself and the desire he had to make more friends.

"It's funny—well, not really funny—but I can see when I stop thinking that I have to wait for the other person to make the first move, it's easier for me to make friends, and I feel better about myself too. One thing leads to another. It's still not easy for me, but it's working—some," he said.

Dr. Thomas laughed. "That reminds me of something. I probably shouldn't have done it myself, but the other day when it was raining so hard I noticed one of the downspouts wasn't flowing. I called to see if the neighbor boy could go up and pull the leaves out of the gutter, but he wasn't home. I didn't want to go up on the roof in the rain, so I put up a ladder from below and reached under the gutter screen and pulled out a small handful of leaves. Well, the downspout started trickling, and pretty soon a clump of leaves came out and then the water began to gush out freely. I made one little change and the rest took care of itself."

"Neat-o," he said. "I see what you mean. I guess maybe I've been like a stuck downspout."

The two considered and rehearsed ways Warren might let his superiors at work know that he was feeling more confident and that when another promotion chance came along he would like to be considered. "Nothing's coming up right away," he said after he had taken action, "but I think they'll give me a chance when it does. And if I hadn't talked to them like I did I'm sure they wouldn't have given me the first thought."

Dr. Thomas used that as an opportunity to encourage Warren to be persistent and consistent. "With your bosses you need to be sure not to fade into the background. That way you let them know, maybe even on a daily basis, that you're around, that you're competent, and that you're ready." He nodded. "And it's the same with your parents. You've made a good start by getting them to make an outside entrance for you. You need to keep thinking about the ways you want things and consistently make positive and assertive choices that help keep your relationships with the two of them on the upswing. Both at home and at work the same things will come up again and again. You need to think ahead and rehearse how you want to deal with them—like we've done here."

Warren began his final interview with Dr. Thomas by reporting enthusiastically, "You know what you said about going after what I wanted consistently? Well, I decided I wanted to have Sunday dinner with Jimmy—that's a meal that's always special at our house. I said to Mom, 'I'd like to ask Jimmy to come to dinner next Sunday. I know you think you won't like him, even though you've never met him, so I don't want to push him on you. If you don't want him to come here I'll ask him to go out for dinner with me instead. It's OK with me either way.'"

"So you put her in the position where she had to make a choice, and either way you'd get what you wanted," she said. "Great."

"Right," he replied. "And it worked like I hoped it would. She said I could invite him home. We don't have anybody in for a meal very often, but Mom's always polite when people come to the house, so I know I don't have to worry. And Jimmy's a big talker and she'll like him, I'm sure. That stuff she heard about that he got into was years ago. They'll get along fine. I think."

Two weeks before their last interview Dr. Thomas shared her emerging plans to make a lengthy western driving trip with a friend. Late in their last session she said, "I'll call and let you know when I'm back. Keep notes and we'll get together and you can regale me with all the little gains you've made and the things you feel good about that you've done. You've made some real strides in feeling better about yourself and you can see that friendships are working better for you too."

Warren was quiet.

"Say what you're thinking—and feeling," she said gently.

After several seconds he said, "I wish you weren't going just now."

"I'll miss you, too," she replied, and he half smiled. "You'll be fine. You might backslide a little—it does help to have someone to talk to, someone in your corner—but you're doing so well that I'm sure you can go it alone. And if not, maybe Jimmy can give you a little of the backup you need."

The last spa experience for Warren came at the close of the final interview when Dr. Thomas said, "Let's build a list of all the little and big ways you've progressed since you walked in here feeling sure that you'd fainted in the bank."

He chuckled and began to tick off a number of large and small triumphs. The last thing he suggested for the list was, "I believe in myself a lot more than I did then." Dr. Thomas wrote, *I believe in myself,* tore off the sheet, handed it to Warren, and shook his hand.

"You always had reason to believe in yourself. You just didn't know it," she said.

SELF-EXAMINATION—JOURNAL ENTRY: Take a few minutes, preferably at least five, and examine your own self-concept. Discuss the extent to which you make choices that support a positive self-concept. Head your entry SELF-CONCEPT AND ME.

We encourage you to share these ideas with your clients, inviting their reactions and helping them see that their self-concepts are affected by their minute-to-minute choices.

COUNSELING APPLICATION—JOURNAL ENTRY: Discuss the extent to which you believe it is important for you to use Choice Awareness theory in enhancing the self-concepts of your clients. Consider with at least one specific or hypothetical client how you might use Choice Awareness and spa to build a positive self-concept. Head your entry SELF-CONCEPT AND MY CLIENTS.

Self-Concept

Effective Choice Awareness counseling helps clients examine their self-concepts and the choices that affect their self-feelings. When it is appropriate, the counselor gives attention directly to the matter of building more positive client self-concepts. The process generally begins with an exploration of how the individual sees him/herself as a person and an examination of the labels that affect the individual's self-feelings. The next effort involves exploring the possible choices that might counter negative labels. Third, the attention of the client is directed to selecting, rehearsing, and trying-out alternative choices. Finally, the individual is helped to explore the effects of new choices on the self-concept, recycling through the process if necessary. Views of self, like so many other matters, are seen here as choices; making different choices often enables clients to change their views of themselves.

Chapter 19

Child Counseling

Four Children

Children are neither little people with whom *any* adult counseling process may be modified slightly and used successfully, nor unique creatures with whom a series of unique counseling procedures must be used. As with adults, children vary greatly in their needs for counseling; they vary even more than adults in their capabilities for responding to counseling, as a result the processes involved may need significant modifications with some children and little modification with others.

In this chapter we describe two children who were referred for counseling and two who sought counseling on their own. Some children are ready to deal directly and openly with the issues that face them, and they are perfectly capable of entering fully into the problem-solving process. Though parent-referred, Jennifer turned out to be one of those children. Steve was a great contrast to Jennifer. It is unlikely that he would have sought counseling on his own, he was somewhat resistant to the process, and he responded to the verbal challenge of counseling in a limited way, but he gained greatly from the process. Denise, like Jennifer, was highly verbal. The counseling process with her made it clear that there are children who can enter fully into a behavior modification process. Rich illustrated the benefits of play media in counseling, even for a rather mature elementary school student.

Jennifer

When ten-year-old Jennifer walked into the reception area with her mother, her eyes downcast, unsmiling, my first impulse was to switch clients so she would not have the practicum counselor to whom she had been assigned. R. J. Lee had one major string to his bow: questions, questions, and more questions.

The encounter between Jennifer and Mr. Lee occurred early in my career as a supervisor and at that time I did not feel as free as I do now to state strong expectations to the counselor. I had encouraged him to broaden his skill base, but through five previous interviews he had ventured away from questions only when it was virtually unavoidable. I determined that there was no reasonable way to switch clients, so I decided to observe the interaction closely behind the one-way glass. Jennifer taught Mr. Lee a great deal, and I learned a lot, too.

Mr. Lee started awkwardly with a long speech interspersed with questions to which he did not wait for answers. The essence of the speech was: "This is what counseling is about; I'm here to help you; I know your mother was the one who wanted you to come here, but you can talk about whatever you wish, it's your choice. Have you ever seen a counselor before? What do you think a counselor does? How do you think I could help you? I'll try to help you with whatever you want me to." Throughout the speech Jennifer stared at a spot near the floor so intently that I stood up and looked so I could see what was capturing her attention. The only thing I could see was the electrical outlet into which Mr. Lee had plugged his tape recorder.

Jennifer turned her head briefly in Mr. Lee's direction without making eye contact, said no to the question about prior counseling, and returned to monitoring the electrical outlet. Mr. Lee leaned forward and asked, "Is there something in particular you want to talk about?" He had opened his mouth to override that question with another, but stopped because Jennifer nodded her head.

"And what is that?" said Mr. Lee.

"Homework," she said immediately, her word barely audible.

"What about homework?" Again, Mr. Lee's nonverbal behavior said he planned to ask a second question, but Jennifer was not looking at him.

At that point Jennifer launched into a three- to four-minute flood of words, her eyes fixed on the outlet, oblivious to Mr. Lee's dozen signals that he wanted to insert questions. Her concern was that she had not had homework until this year in fourth grade. She used to be able to read or sleep with the television on the other side of the wall, but now when she tried to do her homework in her room, it took a long time because she would begin listening to the television and forget what she read or what the question was she needed to answer. When she did finally get her work done, she would be worried about whether it was right, she would lie there unable to get to sleep for a long time, distracted by the television, then she would go to school the next day and yawn a lot and not get all her work done and have more homework as a result.

Mr. Lee's signals that he wanted to interrupt slowed a bit when he saw that he was not able to get a word in edgeways. As a result he was not quite quick enough to insert a question when Jennifer half-turned toward him for the briefest instant. "And another thing," she said, and started on a second problem. She complained that her younger brother took her things and broke them, and that seemed to be OK with her parents, but she got scolded if she so much as looked at her older sister's things.

That pattern was repeated until by actual count she had cited fourteen problems either briefly or at some length. "And another thing," was her transitional statement before each new topic, which ranged from her aunt's illness, to the bracelet she lost, to her kitten who had been killed, to seeing starving children on television. Mr. Lee interrupted twice to ask questions to clarify something Jennifer said, but otherwise was silent. Initially his nonverbal behavior showed he wanted to interrupt constantly, but eventually he sat back in his chair and let her words wash over him.

In our supervisory session following the interview, Mr. Lee and I concluded that Jennifer had been wanting someone to hear all her complaints for a long time, that she had them cataloged in her mind, and that she saw counseling as a place where she could unburden herself of them. At one point in our session Mr. Lee observed sheepishly, "I guess some kids have a lot to talk about. Maybe I don't have to ask questions all the time." I complimented him on his insight.

After the two exchanged greetings at the beginning of the second session, Jennifer's first words were, "I did what you told me to." I could hardly believe my ears. I concluded that Mr. Lee had buttonholed Jennifer after they left the counseling room following the first interview and had offered her a solution to one or more of her problems. That turned out not to be the case, however.

Jennifer told of spelling out her problem about homework to her mother, asking if she could exchange rooms with her younger brother so she would not be right next to the television, arguing that her room was better than her brother's so he would like it—and besides he could sleep through anything. The change was made, and Jennifer had already found that she was able to complete her homework more quickly, get more sleep, and accomplish more in school.

Throughout Jennifer's recitation, Mr. Lee sat still and did not signal his desire to interrupt. When it was evident that she had finished her story, he leaned forward, touched her gently on the arm, and said, "Jennifer, I want you to know that you figured all that out for yourself, and you did a great job. I didn't suggest it, it was your own idea. You made all those choices." Mr. Lee said later that he had me in the back of his mind when he gave Jennifer the credit for solving that problem, but mostly he wanted Jennifer to feel good about her creative action.

Jennifer's eye contact improved somewhat after Mr. Lee gave her strong support for her initiative, and the counseling process gradually became more of a dialogue and a mutual sharing of ideas. Mr. Lee still relied heavily on questions, but not to the exclusion of other responses. He showed admirable patience in waiting for Jennifer to come up with her own solutions when she again complained that her brother borrowed her things, and in helping her realize that there was no solution, just a need to continue the grieving process, when she once again talked about the kitten who had been run over. In some instances, Jennifer was ready to take action on her own behalf with no more encouragement than the opportunity to state the problem. At other times all she needed was to be helped to expand the range of choices she might make, and she was ready to solve the problem herself.

Jennifer took advantage of counseling in the way an experienced counselor might have wanted her to—she used it to find her own routes to more effective patterns of choices. In a real sense she was like those students who show great initiative in learning; with such children, teachers need to provide some kind of structure, then get out of their way. Some children in counseling, too, need minimum assistance to grow on their own, to learn to make more effective choices.

Mr. Lee's experience with Jennifer helped him make three important generalizations concerning counseling with children: (1) Some children will voluntarily provide the information the counselor needs—if he or she listens patiently. (2) A topic need not always be dealt with in depth the first time a child brings it up; if it is important it will resurface—it is not necessarily an opportunity that is lost forever. (3) Some children can deal directly, openly, and effectively with the issues that face them; those children may require little more than the chance to think through and talk about what they need to do.

Steve

Steve was a teacher referral. Mr. Long, his teacher, stopped the school counselor, Mrs. Gorman, in the corridor one morning while his third graders were in the gym. "I don't know how to tell you this. I know we're supposed to report any instances of possible child abuse, and I suppose it could be that Steve is a victim, but I know his parents and I can't believe that's the case."

Mrs. Gorman invited Mr. Long into the counseling office, listened for several minutes, and decided the situation was indeed marginal. Mr. Long had noticed Steve sitting to one side and had asked about it. Through nods and one word responses, he learned that Steve's mother had swatted him on the rear with a ruler. "That sounds close to what parents are allowed to take as their prerogative. I'll stop by the assistant principal's office and mention it to her. My guess is we'll just want to stay alert to any future problems. If you stop by my office during the noon hour I'll let you know what kind of reaction I get," Mrs. Gorman said.

When the two met at noon, Mrs. Gorman reported that her discussion with the assistant principal confirmed her judgment. "But we both think it'd be a good idea for me to talk to Steve."

"Fine, fine. How about if I just send him down or you come get him this afternoon? Two-thirty would be the best time for me, but you can take him any time," said Mr. Long.

Mrs. Gorman paused for several seconds. "Remember in our first faculty meeting when I talked about my ideas concerning teacher referral? It may be difficult to get Steve to refer himself, but it would be a lot better if we can get that to happen."

For a time the two discussed strategy. Eventually Mr. Long summarized his thoughts in this way: "OK, I'll tell him that I think it'd really be a good idea if he put a note in your mailbox and got to talk with you. I'll say I plan to talk with you too and see if you can help us both, because I've been on his case a lot lately about getting his work done. And I'll add something to the effect that it sounds like things aren't going too well at home either, and maybe he can talk about that, too."

"Great, that's the kind of thing I had in mind."

Steve's scrawled note appeared in Mrs. Gorham's mailbox three days later, and the next day he came to her office for the first time. The process was slow, almost painful, for Mrs. Gorman. Steve's responses were invariably phrased in as few words as possible, and, try as she might, Mrs. Gorman found herself asking more questions and making more suggestions than she wanted to, and she endured long pauses both before and after her comments. "I'll try to develop his trust by focusing on the school problems first," she had told Mr. Long, and she was true to her word.

Finally she broached the subject that had brought the two together. "Mr. Long mentioned that there was some kind of problem at home a few days ago—something about a ruler."

"Yeah. Mom whacked me. It broke."

"I imagine that hurt, and hurt your feelings, too," said Mrs. Gorman.

"Yeah." A long silence. "Mom's always yelling at me and twisting my ear. Stuff like that."

Later that day Mrs. Gorman told Mr. Long about her interview with Steve and mentioned that he had just volunteered two real sentences up to that point. Mr. Long put the matter in perspective. "That's two more sentences than I've ever heard out of that boy—and he's been in my room for over two months now."

To Steve, at the time, she had said, "So your mom does things like that a lot of times."

"Yeah. Sometimes."

When Mrs. Gorman noticed that she had only six or seven minutes left with Steve, she wanted to get him to spa level, but before she did that she followed a thought she had in the back of her mind for several minutes. "I need to let you get back to class pretty soon and I want us to do an activity together before that, but I have something to suggest first. I imagine your parents have an alarm clock in their room, but I wonder if there's an extra one in your house you could use."

"Dad keeps one in his suitcase, I think."

"Would you be willing to borrow it, set it at the time you have to get up, and make the choice to get up on your own—without your mom yelling at you?" Mrs. Gorman asked.

"Yeah, but why?" asked Steve in return.

"I have an idea that if you'd do that on your own, it'd get you off to a better start with your mom and you'd have a better day." Steve shrugged his shoulders and agreed to take the action suggested. Before Mrs. Gorman switched to the spa activity, building a list with Steve of THINGS I CAN DO, she added one further suggestion. "How about stopping by my office as you come into the building tomorrow and let me know how it goes?" Steve nodded agreement, Mrs. Gorman introduced the activity, and a few minutes later he left the office, smiling.

The next day Steve ran up to Mrs. Gorman. "Mom didn't scream at me or pull my ear or whack me this morning. She hugged me—said she was proud of me!"

"I can tell you're really pleased about that."

"Gosh, yes. She said if I get myself out of bed the rest of the week on my own, we'll get to do something special this weekend, maybe go to a Purdue football game, or something."

"So if you choose to get up on your own, things are different for you—in lots of ways."

"Yeah. Well, I gotta go now," said Steve as he headed down the hall.

"I'm glad it worked out for you," Mrs. Gorman called after him.

Although Mrs. Gorman spent five twenty-to-thirty minute sessions with Steve, he never entered into the counseling process in a highly verbal way; but from time to time he burst forth excitedly, telling Mrs. Gorman of his progress in one venture or another. It was clear that although he initially thought of himself as a victim, powerless to change his mother's reactions to him, he learned that he had a great deal of effect on the relationship between them. Mrs. Gorman helped him see that he could anticipate the reactions his choices would receive and that he could initiate with positive choices—not merely follow his habit patterns and wait for his mother's inevitable, negative reactions.

After her last interview with Steve, as Mrs. Gorman began to draw together her notes so that she might write a brief report, she reflected on the counseling process. She was confirmed in her conviction that it was desirable, whenever possible, for children whose teachers wanted them to participate in counseling, to be approached by them, rather than be sent to the counselor with little more than a vague statement, or none at all. Steve readily agreed that his teacher should be kept informed about the progress they were making, and Mrs. Gorman was able to help Mr. Long think of ways of handling minor difficulties he was having with Steve and three other children in his class.

Mrs. Gorman recalled her inclination as a beginning counselor to be impatient with low verbal children and was pleased that she had accepted Steve's hesitant, abbreviated speech and long silences. "By his yardstick he was chatting up a storm," she thought to herself. "I have no right to expect more. It is not my yardstick that ought to be the measure of success in counseling—it is the child's."

A number of other factors may be viewed as strengths of the counseling process between Mrs. Gorman and Steve. Because Steve participated in counseling at a low verbal level, Mrs. Gorman slowed her usual verbal pattern to match his. She reflected, waited, used minimum verbal responses, and otherwise helped him see that she wanted the counseling process to take the direction he needed to have it go. When Steve commented that his mother *always* yelled at him and twisted his ear and the like, Mrs. Gorman accepted his statement without either minimizing it or challenging it: "So your mom does things like that a lot of times," to which he simply nodded, when he might otherwise have either cataloged other abuses, or avoided further mention of the subject. When Steve reported that his mother hugged him and said she was proud of him for getting up on his own, Mrs. Gorman reflected *his own* pleasure. "I can tell you're really pleased about that," she said. She wanted him to learn that he could take pleasure in what happened when he acted responsibly. Finally, Mrs. Gorman used language to help Steve see that he was not just a victim in his world, but that he made choices continually that affected those around him, and ultimately himself.

Denise

Denise was a highly-verbal fifth grader who referred herself to Mr. Penrod and within moments put the problem before him. "I cry all the time. I'm such a baby. I hate it, but I just can't help it. And I cry over such dumb things." As if to prove her point, she cried about crying.

Mr. Penrod showed caring and concern primarily through listening and reflecting feelings as Denise detailed some of the events that occurred in the previous weeks about which she had cried; some were indeed trivial, while others seemed to be very legitimate. Initially she seemed not to be able to differentiate between major concerns and those to which she might choose to respond without crying. By using two extreme examples, her aunt's serious illness and her misspelling one word on a long spelling test, Mr. Penrod helped Denise begin to sort the events about which she cried into OK and OD choices.

Next, Mr. Penrod introduced Denise to the bank account analogy. He helped her see that she could think of herself as having imaginary accounts with her parents, her sister, and two of her friends. Once she seemed to have those ideas in hand, he said, "Now imagine you have an account with yourself, too. If you cry when there are things that are all right to cry about, those are OK choices. You should respect yourself for acting in a very human way, and you can think of those choices as adding to your account with yourself—or at least not subtracting from it. On the other hand, when you cry about trivial matters, that's not a disaster, but it subtracts from your own good feelings about yourself, so those are OD choices."

A few moments later Mr. Penrod shifted the focus to a spa experience, THINGS I SMILE ABOUT. He pointed out that each item they thought of could add to Denise's account with herself.

Mr. Penrod asked Denise to make a note every time she cried, to indicate what happened that resulted in her crying, and to decide whether or not it seemed to be an OK or an OD instance of crying. "And see if there are any times when you felt like crying, but didn't," he suggested, before closing the interview.

Denise came to counseling a week later armed with a crude chart she had made. "I thought I cried all the time, but this week, anyway, I only cried six times," she said as she spread the chart in front of Mr. Penrod.

"That smile tells me you're really pleased that it was only six times," he said.

"And three of them were OK," she said, and she explained her chart.

When I Felt Like Crying

	I cried		I didn't cry	
	It was OK	It was OD	It was OK	It was OD
Broke my award bracelet	√			
Saw a dog almost hit by a car			√	
Talked to my aunt on phone	√			
Didn't do my math right		√		
Saw a sad movie	√			
Freda couldn't come over			√	
Heard a funny noise outside		√		
Couldn't get my story right		√		

"I cried about my award bracelet. Maybe it was stupid, but I didn't know if it could be fixed and I won it for a story I wrote. It was important to me, so I decided it was OK," Denise looked to Mr. Penrod for approval.

"Hey, it's your life—your choice—if it was OK for you, that's all right by me," he smiled.

"And when I talked to my aunt on the phone—she's still pretty sick, but doing better—and when I saw a sad movie, I thought those were OK times to cry."

Mr. Penrod nodded. "You said those two things like you're becoming more sure of yourself—like you don't need me to tell you whether or not those were OK times for you to cry."

"Yeah," Denise said with conviction, and she pointed at her chart again. "But when I cried 'cause I couldn't get my math right and I had trouble writing my story, I thought that was kinda dumb afterwards. And it's OK to be scared about a noise, but I wouldn't even peek out the window. When I finally did, it was just a dog that knocked over our garbage can."

"And you thought those were times you could learn in the future not to cry," Mr. Penrod said.

Denise nodded and continued. "Here I listed two times when I didn't cry and it was OK. My heart was in my mouth when I saw a dog run right in front of a car—I don't know how he made it across the street without getting hit. And when Freda couldn't come over I felt like crying, but I told myself I didn't have to—and I didn't."

"So there were two times when you might have cried, but you didn't. And you're pleased."

Denise smiled, then pointed to the final column. "I didn't have anything over here."

Mr. Penrod commented, "So there weren't any times when you didn't cry and it would have been OK if you had."

"I don't think that *ever* happens," Denise said, and she chuckled.

Mr. Penrod saw Denise three times in three weeks, then three times in the final four months of the school year, with the primary focus on spa in the latter interviews. When he mentioned his contact with Denise to another counselor, Mr. Penrod said, "Denise reminded me that accurate counting is really important. She was genuinely surprised to find out that she'd only cried six times in a week, since she was convinced that she cried constantly. Just the fact that she counted helped her realize that the problem wasn't insurmountable.

"And it's the same with teachers. I notice that if they keep accurate counts, how many times Johnny is out of his seat without permission, and the like, and then they try some kind of approach that helps him get attention for cooperating, they see gains. But if they don't keep a count, and Johnny's out-of-seat behavior reduces from, say, 22 times in a morning to 18, and then to 16, they aren't likely to notice any difference. The teacher who counts is encouraged and keeps up the effort, and the changes keep coming; the one who doesn't count gives up and goes back to the old ways and the child's behavior doesn't improve at all."

Many of the problems children face involve countable behaviors, or choices. For example, they are out of their seats without permission so many times an hour, they interrupt so often, or they could make so many more OK enjoying choices each day with a younger sibling. When countable behaviors might be expected to be increased or decreased, many children can beneficially become involved as direct agents of change in their own lives. In Choice Awareness theory the view is taken that behavior modification approaches are most effective when they help children engage in more positive behaviors, when children are helped to see their behaviors as choices, and when they experience gains as a result of making more positive choices.

Rich

Child counseling has often incorporated the use of play therapy, also referred to as play process, or counseling with play media. The more traditional term, play therapy, has been used to describe two quite different processes: one is Freudian, analytical, and structured, while the other is Rogerian, person-centered, unstructured. The term play media, the designation preferred here, denotes a person-centered process used by many school counselors, akin to the Rogerian model, but providing limits, structures, and expectations that are consistent with the realities of the school setting.

Miss Procopio, an elementary school counselor, arranged her office so that a single four foot shelf of a bookcase, containing a variety of play media, was within easy reach of children who took their place in a low, overstuffed chair a few feet away from her desk. When younger, less-verbal children were having difficulty sharing their concerns, Miss Procopio called their attention to the paper, felt pens, clay, pipe cleaners, hand puppets, and other media. "Many boys and girls like to do something with their hands while we talk," she often said. Frequently younger children, and occasionally older children, reached for items on the shelf without encouragement, or they sought her approval non-verbally by looking toward the media and glancing back at her.

After Rich made a sweeping visual inspection of the room, he fixed his eyes on something on the shelf. "If you see anything you want to use, please go ahead," Miss Procopio told him.

"They're not just for little kids?" he inquired.

"Lots of people of all ages like to do things with their hands while they talk," she replied.

Rich, a very bright sixth grader Miss Procopio had talked to briefly once before, tore a piece of buffy-colored paper from a pad, unwrapped a chunk of clay, and began to work it with his hands, fastidiously, over the paper. "My uncle is always fiddling with his pipe. I guess it's kinda like that," he offered.

"Exactly," replied Miss Procopio, smiling broadly.

Rich, a boy with a scientific bent, had a lot on his mind. An international issue of the moment had him worried about the H-bomb; he was concerned about pollution and the loss of the ozone layer above the earth; he wondered whether SDI made any sense or whether it might provoke the Russians to "do something" some day; he mentioned the problem of AIDS; and he talked about the homeless in America. "Some day I want to work on one of those problems. I can't decide which right now. But I guess I've got plenty of time."

Miss Procopio reflected his feelings and encouraged him in expressing his concerns. "There are lots of things on your mind today, Rich." He nodded and she continued. "You know, I think maybe you're the kind of person who might really help solve one of those problems some day."

He smiled.

Throughout his discussion Rich's fingers were busy with the clay. For some time the movement seemed to be random—he worked the mass, stretched it out, pulled off pieces, then mashed them back into the whole and started over again. When his conversation was animated and rapid, his hand movements matched his verbal speed. When he became more thoughtful or when he paused to search for a word, his fingers hovered over the clay or manipulated it gently, slowly. At one point he began arranging an elongated oval on the paper before him; he pulled the two ends into points; and he worked the clay into what appeared to be walls on either side.

Rich finished what he was saying, looked at his creation, scanned the bookshelf briefly, and reached for a package of pipe cleaners. Miss Procopio searched for a response, "You've figured out what you want to do," she thought, but decided she wanted her response to include mention of the clay structure as well. Before she got her thoughts together Rich began to verbalize his concern about the homeless. "A lot of them are children, you know," he said.

"That concerns you a lot," Miss Procopio reflected, and he nodded.

As Rich talked about how he believed people became homeless and what he thought that kind of life would be like, he formed pipe cleaner pieces into one figure, then another, somewhat smaller. He carefully manipulated the two figures into what appeared to be sitting positions and arranged them, facing one another, at either end of the clay structure.

He paused for a moment, half-smiled, and recognition lit his eyes. His first words brought the same light of recognition to Miss Procopio's eyes.

"I wish my dad would take me fishing," he said, simply.

"That's something you'd like the two of you to do together," she replied. Internally she was both delighted and amused—delighted that the figures and the structure now meant something—amused because it showed that Rich had been thinking on two levels at the same time. Apparently while he had been talking about global and national concerns, somewhere in another part of his mind he was working on a concern about his relationship with his father.

"So there you are in a boat together—the way you'd like it to be," Miss Procopio offered.

"Yeah," he sighed. "That's the way I'd like it to be."

"It'd feel a lot better if it really happened," she said after a wait of several seconds. Rich nodded. He took out a cleanly folded handkerchief and began to rub the clay off his hands. "Would you like a tissue?" Miss Procopio moved the box on the top of her desk toward him. He pocketed his handkerchief, thanked her, pulled two tissues, and rubbed his hands vigorously.

"Yeah," he said, "Dad won't ever take me with him." He detailed an event that had occurred three years earlier when his father took him out in a canoe; it had drizzled, he had gotten cold and asked to go home, and his father had said, "I'll never take you fishing again." True to his word, he had not offered the opportunity, and Rich really wanted to have that kind of special time with his father.

"He calls up Uncle Terry—he's the one who smokes a pipe—ugh!—and gets him to go. But I can tell he has to talk fast 'cause Uncle Terry doesn't like fishing all that much."

"You're frustrated because your dad has to talk your uncle into going fishing and you'd *like* to go with him," said Miss Procopio.

"I've asked him. . . sometimes, but he always talks about my wanting to come home—'after less than an hour,' he always says."

The two talked for a few minutes more. "Maybe if you had a talk with him—man to man, sort of—and you told him how you see it, said you're sure you could handle it now, mentioned that it bothers you that he has to talk your uncle into going when you'd like to go, maybe that would help."

Rich role played and made various changes in what he would like to say, then Miss Procopio moved the session to spa level by asking him to make some statements about his strengths. She jotted those down and gave the paper to him, and the interview closed very positively.

The next interview began on an even higher note. "You won't believe it. I talked to my dad the way we tried it out last week. He said if I was sure, he'd be glad to have me go with him. And we went and had a great time. We didn't catch anything, but the weather was great and we had good talks," Rich said and he grinned from ear to ear.

"I can tell you're really excited about that. And I'm pleased for you that it worked out so well."

"Me, too," he replied.

"I wonder what was different this time—that he said yes. If you could figure that out, it might help in the future," said Miss Procopio.

Rich shuffled his feet, twisted his hands together, and looked down at the floor.

"You seem a little uncomfortable," she said.

"I guess I didn't ask him a lot." He paused. "Maybe I didn't *really* ask him at all." Another pause. "I think I hinted about it sometimes. And I know I *thought* about asking him a lot," he said.

"Hey," she patted his shoulder gently. "That's OK. Lots of people think and think about things without doing anything about them. After a while they can even imagine they've done something that didn't work out—they've pictured it in their minds so often."

Rich looked at Miss Procopio for the first time in several seconds, and he smiled wanly. "I guess that's what I did," he said.

"The important thing is that you learned something. When you actually made the choice, and probably in the nice mature way you rehearsed, it worked out."

"I guess if I don't just do it in my mind, and I don't just hint about it, it works better," he said.

"Exactly. It won't work every time, but it's better than just thinking and thinking about it or making one sorrowing choice after another," said Miss Procopio.

"Yeah." Rich looked puzzled for a moment. "What was that kind of choice I made when I asked my dad about going fishing? A leadership choice? What are those called?"

"My goodness, you remember that from last year?" Rich nodded and smiled. "Choices that show leadership—they're what we call ruling choices," said Miss Procopio, pleased that her classroom guidance activities had carryover that endured for more than ten months with Rich.

"Dad said, 'Ask me again, sometime. I'm going to be really busy for a couple of months until the holidays, and I may forget to take time off. You ask me and I'll break away as soon as I can.' So that means I get to make another ruling choice pretty soon," Rich said, and smiled once more.

For the remainder of the school year, on the average of a little less than once every other month, Miss Procopio found a note in her mailbox from Rich and talked with him for forty minutes or more. In her report concerning her work with Rich she noted: "Rich thinks deeply about a great many issues. Once it occurred to me that continuing my work with him might not be the best use of my time, then I thought about the great potential he has, and the quick gains he made in his relationship with his father, and I changed my opinion. We always ended on a spa note for him—that has been good—and the whole process has been spa-like for me. When I think about my work with Rich and a few of the other exceptionally bright children in this school, I become convinced that spending time with them—helping them unleash their potential by releasing them from some of the burdens they face—is a really important part of my contribution to this school and even to the community at large."

Miss Procopio's work with Rich validated the listening process and illustrated the benefits of play media in counseling, even for a very mature elementary school student. Much of the time the use of media took a back seat, becoming something Rich worked with "while they talked"; but when it seemed appropriate, Miss Procopio reflected Rich's actions and the feelings he seemed to be projecting as if they were words: "When you have a lot to say, your fingers fairly fly; but when you're thinking deeply your fingers slow down, 'til they almost stop." "When you talk about what people are doing to the ozone layer, you squeeze on that clay like you're really annoyed." "You moved the two figures closer together in the boat—the way you want them to be."

Miss Procopio made a strong effort to keep her observations as close to "the givens" of the situation as possible. In so doing she avoided making leaps of logic into unsupported interpretations, working instead in small increments toward the idea she had in mind. As a result, instead of having to test an hypothesis through interpretation, she frequently found that Rich either confirmed her conceptualization or helped her make a shift of logic before she was moved to bring it up.

Play media with children of various ages allows the counselor to enter the world of the child; it takes away the pressure on them and on the counselor to "fill the unforgiving minute" to which Kipling refers in his poem, "If"; and it provides opportunities for children to express themselves and to channel their energies in constructive ways. Miss Procopio selected a few unstructured, yet familiar, materials which the children who came to her office could use in a variety of ways that suited their needs; her work with Rich validated her selections.

COUNSELING APPLICATION—JOURNAL ENTRY: Discuss the extent to which you believe it is important for counselors to use Choice Awareness theory with children. Consider with at least one specific or hypothetical child how you might use Choice Awareness in the counseling process. Head your entry CHOICE AWARENESS AND THE CHILD.

Choice Awareness and Children

Choice Awareness theory suggests that effective child counseling may incorporate nearly all of the dimensions of adult counseling—*plus*. Contrary to what may be popular belief about the helplessness of children, many young people, given little more assistance than listening, are perfectly capable of coming to their own conclusions and taking action on their own behalf. Other children can benefit from approaches that have more impact. While some may need a great deal of direction and support, the majority may benefit from a limited number of such impact-oriented responses as alternative exploration. They need to be helped to enlarge the range of choices they have so that they can function better in the environments in which they find themselves. As with adults, children frequently have distorted perceptions that can be modified; a counseling process that assists them in making these modification can lead them to make more functional choices.

Children are more clearly action-oriented than adults, and more children than adults have difficulty expressing themselves and working through their problems verbally. That is where the *plus* comes in—the *plus* is play media. Many children can benefit from the use of play media in counseling. Through the use of play media they can more fully express themselves, and as a result of the combination of verbal and non-verbal expression, they are able to work through their concerns and build more effective patterns of choices.

Chapter 20

Counseling
Older Persons

Older Persons

Groups of people defy generalization. Few groups of people defy generalization as much as do older persons. The stereotypical picture of the older person as female, poor, in ill health, and living in a dependent status in the home of a son or daughter or in an institution, describes a small percentage of the aged. Many more older persons are vibrant, energetic, independent, and on sound financial footing—and some of them are male. Some readily accept counseling, many do not—preferring to work out their own concerns as they have throughout their lives. As a result of this variability, older persons differ greatly in their needs and in their willingness and ability to respond to counseling.

In this chapter we describe a woman who sought counseling on her own, a man who came to counseling indirectly, and a group process that helped a number of females. Some older persons are perfectly capable of defining their problems and entering fully into the process of solving them; Essie Monroe was one of those people. C. J. Lowenstein

---

Richard C. Nelson

"happened" into counseling; as we shall see, he was not entirely comfortable with the process, but he gained in at least one significant way. The women who participated in the Choice Awareness group described here fit several of the stereotypes held about older people, but they represent only a small portion of the aging population.

Essie Monroe

Essie was one of the first people to sign up for an appointment after the sign appeared in the Senior Center. TALK TIME, it said, then in smaller letters: COME AND TALK ABOUT YOUR IDEAS, TELL YOUR STORY, DISCUSS THE DECISIONS YOU HAVE TO MAKE, OR SHARE YOUR BURDENS OR JOYS. Further information on the sign indicated that people who were taking a university course in gerontology would be coming to the center for one-to-one interviews, which might be one-time experiences or might evolve into a series of meetings. So that those involved could get some help with their skills in communicating with senior citizens, all interviews would be recorded, but the contents of the interviews would be treated confidentially.

Essie's friend, Libby Hackett, was suspicious, and what Libby thought often influenced several women who came to the center regularly. "It's just another way to say, 'See a shrink,'" she announced. "I'll solve my own problems my own way, thank you."

Essie spoke up after a moment's hesitation. "Hmmph. As much as all of us like to talk, I'd think we'd welcome a chance to do it. And we don't have to say anything we don't want to. Anyway, there's a big decision I have to make and I think I'll just see if I can't get some help with it." With that she went to the reception desk and told the volunteer on duty that she would be interested in talking with one of the people from the class, indicated that she thought she might want to talk to someone more than once, and agreed to have her name placed on the schedule of one of the men in the group, a Mr. Aaron Fleming. She wondered what it would be like to talk with a young man about the momentous decision she faced. "At least I *assume* he'll be young," she thought to herself.

When she again took her seat beside Libby, her friend eyed her somewhat suspiciously. "You're not thinking of leaving us to go stay with your niece and help her with that brood of obstreperous children, are you?"

"Well," she said, and paused. "I have to admit something like that might come into the conversation."

"You know how I feel about that," said Libby. "Even though, as you know, I don't like to interfere in anyone else's business." Essie smiled faintly and patted Libby on the arm and Libby continued. "I do think you need to keep your independence unless you *have* to give it up." Essie thanked Libby for her kind advice but gave her no further satisfaction.

A week later Essie met Aaron Fleming for the first time. Thirty, she guessed, and not tall and slim as she had imagined; rotund would be the word—and genial—with a mop of red-auburn hair. She appreciated Aaron's intense green eyes and his directness as they passed pleasantries for many minutes and as she recounted her history: her family, her marriage, her children, and her work life.

"No," said Aaron, in response to Essie's inquiry, "I don't think I'm related to that Rhonda Fleming. I've had a couple of people ask me about that and say my hair reminded them of her. Maybe we're related, but I doubt it."

A few moments later Aaron cleared his throat. "I noticed on the card that you had something you thought you'd want to talk about, maybe more than once. I've enjoyed hearing your story. I do want you to know, though, that I'm a professional counselor. I've worked mostly with young people so far, but I don't want to be limited to that group. If there's something, some concern, you want to talk about, I'll try to help you in any way I can."

There was a long pause that was awkward for Essie, but when she glanced at Aaron he seemed quite comfortable. Finally Essie said, "I've got to make a big decision. I haven't talked about it with anyone yet—around here, anyway."

Aaron relaxed into his chair and maintained eye contact with Essie. "Tell me about it," he said in a quiet voice.

"My cousin died about three years ago. Rebecca. A wonderful woman, and a good friend."

"That must have been really sad for you," said Aaron. Essie found his voice soothing.

"It was. But I guess we've all gotten over it pretty well."

"Uh huh," said Aaron. "We've gotten over it," he added after a pause.

Essie looked out the window for many moments. "Her husband, Jack, is now a widower, of course. He's said he'd like to come to town for a couple of weeks. He wrote me and I put him off, then he called me on the phone ten days or so ago. I think. . . I'm sure, he wants me to marry him."

"I can see what you mean about this being a big decision," Aaron said quietly after a pause.

"It really is." Essie smoothed her skirt with the palm of her hand. "I probably should have asked to see a woman," she added hastily.

"So this is a little awkward for you," he said.

"A little bit."

"I'm not sure what to say to let you know you can talk about anything with me," he said.

"I've made most of my decisions all by myself for years," she said, after a moment.

"We all can use a little help from time to time," he replied. The room was quiet, hushed.

"Well, maybe I won't shock you too much," she said, then broke into a smile. "You said whatever I told you would be confidential?" Aaron nodded.

"Well, I'll just come out with it. I want him to come, and I don't want him to stay at a hotel." Essie looked intently in Aaron's eyes for a moment, evidently checking for signs of disapproval.

"You want him to come, and you want him to stay with you," he said. She nodded and looked down at the floor. "It's not my job to judge," he said. "You're the one who has to decide what's right for you. My job is to listen—to help you come to your own decision."

Essie spoke at length in a rush of words and Aaron nodded and punctuated her sentences with one and two word responses. ". . . I've learned to be very independent since Tom died. . . . I'm not sure I want to end up nursing and burying another husband. . . ." She hesitated a long time, then said, "All that bedroom stuff and nonsense wasn't anything special in my thirty-eight years with Tom. . . maybe it would be with Jack. . . . In some ways I think the best thing would be for me to just enjoy whatever time he'll spend with me—with no commitment. . . . But he's the kind of man any woman would want, even if she were half my age. . . and he just might be the most wonderful kind of companion I could imagine. He's always been such a fine person to talk with and be with. . . . And he's almost exactly my age. . . ."

"I can see you have a mixture of feelings about all this," Aaron said. Essie nodded and Aaron reassured her. "Mixed feelings seem really normal to me in a situation like this. You've got a lot to weigh here. It's a really big choice—really a whole great complex of choices."

Essie frowned for a moment, then looked at Aaron. "I get what you mean." She paused. "And maybe I don't have to make the decision all at once. After all, he hasn't asked me, he's just hinted that he wants to marry me."

Essie resolved the issue by deciding to see if she could have Jack stay in the apartment of a friend in the same building who planned to leave soon for a holiday in Mexico. "I was going to take care of her cats, anyway, but he can do that—he even likes cats." She nodded her head. "And I can take it one step at a time."

Later that afternoon as Aaron Fleming was reflecting on his experience with Essie he thumbed through the first few pages of the source for his course, *Infusing Gerontological Counseling into Counseling Preparation: Curriculum Guide,* by Myers (1988). The Preface by C. Gilbert Wrenn caught his attention as it had when first read it. The population of people over age 65 in the United States has surpassed the population of Canada; it is projected that there will be 35,000,000 people over age 65 in the year 2000, Wrenn noted. Forty new nursing homes *per month* will be needed for the next twelve years. On the other hand, "older people will be more traveled, better read, more socially aware and live longer than any previous generation" (Wrenn, in Myers, 1988, p. 9).

Wrenn continued with a number of suggestions for counselors: Many older people are sensitive about hearing; rather than speaking more loudly, the counselor should move closer and articulate carefully and a bit more slowly. [Aaron smiled as he read that. Essie's hearing was sharp, she missed nothing; but one of his classmates that same afternoon had run into a woman whose hearing was a significant problem.] Opening comments are important; everyday, invitational approaches work well with older people. [Aaron recalled that one of his first inquiries was whether or not Essie had worked outside the home. That had led to a long litany of part-time and full time jobs. Essie had quite a checkered work history; among other things she had folded towels in a laundry as a teenager, spent some time as "a live-in nanny" when she was "hardly dry behind the ears," detassled corn, clerked in a store, and had what she called "a real career" for over fifteen years meeting customers and doing the books in a drycleaning establishment.] Instead of offering "counseling," which suggests that the older person "needs" the counselor, make counseling a two-way street by seeking to learn from the older person as well. [Aaron had taken that to heart. He thought it was more than a coincidence that Essie began to share information about her relationship decision shortly after the two had wandered off into a side avenue and he had invited her to comment on a problem he was having with his cantankerous four-year-old.] Many older people have a sense of guilt that relates to their children, who have experienced a more fast-paced, challenging, tension-laden world than they themselves did; the parent may wonder what he or she did that was wrong or what he or she might have done differently that would have helped. Counseling that is focused on helping older people feel less responsible for what has gone wrong may reduce any burden of guilt. [The allusion Essie made to her conflict with her oldest daughter came to Aaron's mind. "You'd like her to come around and let things be the way they were before she was married, but it's pretty clear that she's got her own agenda and she's making different choices," he had said. Essie had sighed and gone right on to another subject.] Finally, Wrenn commented that he believed that older people need to "keep young" by opening themselves to the joys of travel, by allowing themselves to take in new ideas, and through the development of new skills. [Aaron mused over one point of ambivalence he had reflected back to Essie: "The way I see it you're not quite sure whether you want to put this relationship on a new basis, but you're afraid you'll sort of 'dry up' if you don't reach out and make effective choices when opportunities come along." She told him he'd "hit the nail on the head."]

When Aaron listened with his professor to his interview tape, he made the point that Essie proved to him that some older persons are perfectly capable of defining their problems and entering fully into the process of solving them. "And," he said, "perhaps even more than people of other age levels, they appreciate being listened to."

His professor beamed. "That's a considerable gain for one hour. And it's not just something you've memorized from a page in a book; it's something you *know* because you've experienced it."

Aaron Fleming's experiences with Essie Monroe were cut short after he saw her three more times over a five-week period. Essie was closing her apartment and taking off on a cruise with Jack, her new husband. Aaron recalled that she had looked down at her index fingers and rubbed them against one another when she first told him about her decision. "I guess playing hard-to-get worked for me this time as well as it did years ago."

"I think you're pleased, too, because you didn't have to compromise your values," Aaron replied.

"One thing, though, we've both agreed on. We're going to sign a prenuptial agreement and work out the money and property and things like that before we get married."

"I think that's very wise. But then, I was sure you'd make good choices for yourself."

Essie looked down at the floor and rubbed her fingers together again.

"I think there's something more you want to—maybe need to—say," said Aaron.

"Maybe I'm making *one* compromise in my values. I've always been against divorce," she began and paused. "I think people ought to stick with the contracts they make—especially when there are children involved. But I've told Jack it was going to *have* to work out. I wasn't going to sit around and watch some old unshaven man drink beer in his undershirt and stay home and watch the boob tube all the time. I've done my time with that arrangement. It'd be one thing if he was sick or something—but if not, I'll just fly off to Reno and shed 'the old poop.'" She laughed, then looked serious for a moment. "Jack said that was fine with him, but what was sauce for the gander would have to be sauce for the goose."

"You hadn't thought about it going the other way," Aaron reflected. Then, before Essie could reply, he burst out laughing, and continued until his eyes were streaming with tears. Finally he could speak. "I'm sorry. I was just picturing what Jack said literally—you, without a shave, drinking beer and sitting around in a man's undershirt." At that Essie began to laugh too.

The two had another laugh when Essie told of Libby Hackett's incredulous reaction when she finally learned what the big decision was about. "She just stared at me for the longest time and then said, 'You have to be kidding!'"

Essie was a wonderful experience for Aaron and indeed for the entire gerontology class. It changed many perspectives when, as circumspectly as possible, Aaron was able to share with those involved his admiration for this bright, articulate woman who at age seventy-four was willing to take on a new life, who knew her mind as far as marital expectations were concerned, and who was able to draw her own conclusions, with minimal assistance, on a major change of life style. Essie made the case that *some* older people, at least, require virtually no special adaptation of the counseling process.

C. J. Lowenstein

Clifton Jeremy Lowenstein, or C. J. as he preferred to be called, had moved with his wife into a small home on the grounds of the Presbyterian retirement village five years before his contact with Judy Gravenham. Almost a year to the day after he moved in with his wife, she had a severe stroke and died subsequently. Several times over the four years that followed C. J. had been encouraged to accept counseling services, but he had always declined.

C. J. was basically a rather quiet man, but when he spoke, his words had the air of pronouncements. It was easy to imagine him in the role of a bank officer, which had been his career for well over forty years, keeping to himself, and giving orders when he had to, in crisp, brief sentences. Two concerns about C. J. were that he had never given any evidence of having dealt with his grief over the death of his wife, and that he seemed to be communicating less and less with others.

In a relatively minor traffic accident that was clearly not his fault, C. J. had hit his head on the steering wheel and sustained a number of bruises; as a consequence he had been taken to the health center of the home for observation. He had resisted that placement at first, but the concern that pneumonia might set in made sense to him, so he capitulated. It was during his stay in the health center that Judy Gravenham, an ordained minister, had stopped by to see him for several days in a row. She chatted on with him about her life and asked him many questions about his own.

During Judy's fourth visit, C. J.'s phone rang. The call was for Judy. She spoke five or six times, then explained that her husband, Mark, was down at the desk needing to borrow her car keys. As she left the room C. J. mustered his commanding air and called to her, "If your young man has time, I'd like to meet him."

Mark was in a hurry, but he responded positively to Judy's urging. "I'm not sure what he has in mind, but it's one of the few signs of outreach we've seen out of him," she told him.

As he returned the keys forty minutes later, Mark stopped in C. J.'s room. "I'm Mark Gravenham," he announced. "My wife said you wanted to meet me."

C. J. looked him up and down and extended his hand. "Your wife seems like a fine person."

Mark blushed slightly at the bluntness of the statement, and said as he shook C. J.'s hand, "I think a lot of her, too." C. J. asked several direct questions—what Mark's work was, why the two had no children, what kinds of things they did together—then C. J. said he thought he had better rest and Mark knew he had been dismissed.

The following Monday Judy visited C. J. in his home. After the two had laughed over a bit of gossip in the home, Judy broached the issue she had in mind. "What was that third degree you gave Mark about? From what I heard it sounded suspiciously like you were trying to figure out whether or not he deserved me."

C. J. cleared his throat and began twice. "Well. . . Well, no, it's not that exactly. More like, did you deserve him?"

Judy scowled and C. J. explained. "My wife was scarcely in her grave when all these women began to fawn all over me. I wanted to make sure you weren't, you know, doing the same thing."

"Oh, so you thought I might have ulterior motives," she said and chuckled.

"Let's say I thought it was *possible*. But I didn't think it was likely."

What followed over the next several weeks hardly deserved the label of counseling, but it had clear elements of that process. Judy tried to encourage C. J. to deal with his grief over the death of his wife. She was convinced he had never effectively done so, but whenever she turned the discussion in that direction, he allowed it a brief play, then parried it neatly by bringing up a different subject. Several of Judy's direct statements touched on her belief about his reactions, e.g., "You just can't handle letting your grief out, but I think it'd be good for you." "I think you avoid talking about that because you're afraid of tears." C. J. did not argue against those assertions, but he stopped short of responding to them in any depth.

Another avenue was more productive—discussion of C. J.'s use of his leisure time. "Somewhere along the way I heard that women are better equipped for retirement because they pick up activities in grade school that they can use all their lives, while boys concentrate on team sports. Some of the skills that work best for retired people are those they learned early in life," Judy said the first time she brought up the topic. C. J.'s initial reaction was that of laughter and protest, but the two discussed the matter on and off over several days.

"I didn't have time for team sports; I started working so early," C. J. said at one point, then gazed off for several seconds. "I did enjoy fishing way back then. I couldn't ever afford anything but a little drop line, a hook, a cork stopper, and a stick I cut myself, but it was something I could do either by myself or with someone else—when I had the time."

The next time they met, Judy invited C. J. to complete an activity called TWENTY THINGS I LOVE TO DO BEST, while she recorded what he said. He wondered aloud whether he could think of that many, and for a time she regretted that she had asked for twenty possibilities rather than ten. Then, with a burst of energy, once he reassured himself that he could list some things he had not done for a long time, C. J. completed his list. For many minutes they pored over the items and C. J. found several activities that he could do—some of them only if he had someone to do them with. That was the catch, in his view. Key ideas were: fish, read, go to baseball games, go to football games, walk, drive, go to *good* meetings—like when people talked about their travels, and travel on his own.

Judy brooked the issue she had in mind from the beginning of the TWENTY THINGS. . . activity. In her view C. J. needed to get outside himself. He had never been a volunteer—in point of fact she had heard him laugh at "do-gooders" who did such things—but he proved himself open to the idea of forming a small travel group within the retirement home. He could, he said, drive people on day trips to state parks and events in the area. Then he surprised Judy somewhat by readily agreeing to look into opportunities through the local Reading Academy to assist someone to learn to read.

Over time the Reading Academy connection proved to be highly beneficial both for Brad, the fifty-seven-year-old man C. J. was assigned to help, and for C. J. himself. Brad was bright enough that after a slow start he picked up the skills of reading reasonably quickly. One of the reasons Brad had sought assistance was that his wife, who had covered for his lack of skills in reading for years, once their children had left the nest, had divorced him and become involved with a younger man. Brad was an avid angler, and it was not long before he and C. J. were taking off early in the morning for Brad's favorite fishing holes.

The process of communicating with C. J. fit a great many of Judy's understandings about counseling older persons. Reminiscences are often seen as the key to building rapport and trust with older people—this was certainly the case with C. J. Although assumptions are sometimes made to the contrary, counseling older persons can be very worthwhile; "the older person may indeed have plenty of time to learn new ways of coping, to make significant contributions, and to grow" (Landreth & Berg, 1980, p. ix). Judy found that the basic skills of communication, those that are characteristic of effective counseling, were essential in working with C. J., but that the process needed to be de-formalized and trust had to emerge gradually, in some measure due to the counselor-client age discrepancy, and different cultural expectations. C. J. gave clear evidence of a need for independence and an unwillingness to admit his need for assistance—or to accept the label "counseling" for the process —the unwillingness that in other clients might appear as hesitation to "air one's dirty laundry in public." Finally, Judy credited her experience with older people for fending off what might have been a problem; C. J.'s hearing aid worked well enough when he had it in—and on—but Judy prided herself on her careful, moderated articulation when she talked with patients and residents, so that was never a problem between the two of them.

A Choice Awareness Group Experience

C. Gilbert Wrenn suggested in the preface to *Infusing Gerontological Counseling into Counseling Preparation Programs* (Wrenn, in Myers, 1988, p. 13), "Speaking of 'counselors' and 'counseling'—don't!" Wrenn commented that older people have a sense of pride and are often vigorously independent, so unless they ask for it we should not offer them counseling *per se*. We should engage them instead in a process through which they can give as well as take.

The Choice Awareness group (Nelson, 1989) we describe here at some length allowed those involved the opportunity for give and take and for sharing experiences. An activities assistant in a retirement and nursing home, and a co-leader, both of whom were enrolled in a Choice Awareness seminar, offered residents the opportunity to participate in a group focused on choices. The topic itself was not a strong draw for the residents; they came because they wanted to help the activities assistant, to get a break in the routine, or to enjoy the refreshments that were provided.

In her journal the activities assistant described the residents of the home: from rural communities in central Indiana, religious fundamentalists, accustomed to exact and simple directions, fearful of anything new, and needing concrete results and frequent praise. She prepared them for the experience by talking with them informally and encouraging them to attend, since, as she noted, they seldom gathered on their own in groups of more than three. She anticipated that the leaders would need to speak clearly and loudly, break down directions in simple steps, and repeat them frequently.

Each of the meetings developed a particular Choice Awareness concept that derived from the definition of the word *choice* as *any behavior over which the individual can exercise any reasonable degree of control*. Many of the activities that were included in the meetings are described and discussed here because they demonstrate how such a group might be organized.

Meeting 1: *We make many choices*. Throughout our days we make one choice after another—through our words, actions, thoughts, and feelings.

Starting with the co-leaders, the twenty-two women present introduced themselves; the few male residents did not elect to participate. The leaders made the point that we tend to act on habits, and the question, "What are some choices you *can't* make?" led to the statement of a number of complaints, and involvement of group members clearly increased. Residents wrote down how many choices they believed they had made by mid-afternoon that day, which was the time of the meeting; the numbers ranged from 3 to 10. A segment of the whitewashing scene in *Tom Sawyer* was read aloud and residents were asked to count the number of choices they heard Ben and Tom make;

over 20 choices were found and the group members became more verbal. A skit was presented in which an older employee played the part of a nurse aide, and the activities assistant pretended to be a resident who was getting ready for bed, but who had to have everything done in a certain way. Following the skit, group members members told of the choices they had observed. Residents concluded that they had made far more choices that day than they had thought earlier.

It was clear to the leaders that the residents grasped the concept that nearly everything they do can be considered a choice. The journal entry of one of the co-leaders noted that we all make choices about what we say and how we act and feel, but that many of our choices are based on habit. "We can choose to change or keep habits. I think we communicated this idea to. . . a majority of the group."

Meeting 2: *We have many choices.* We may think of our choices as either-or, yes-no matters, but they are more complex than that suggests. We can make each of our choices in many ways. *How* we make each choice is as important as which choice we make.

Residents were asked to react to several hypothetical situations, e.g., someone sitting alone in the day room looking sad, someone needing a nurse aide. Those present mentioned their usual ways of responding, emphasizing that their choice depended on the other person. Next, each in turn was asked to pose a question or make a statement to another person in the group, that individual was asked to respond, and others identified the messages and feelings in the response. One resident asked another how she liked the band that had performed a few days earlier: "I liked what they played, but the drummer was too loud," was her response. Three of her messages were identified as "a good band," "good old music," and "annoyed." Residents were paired and each pair wrote down as many feelings as they could think of; the responses reflected mainly negative feelings. A volunteer passed out slips of paper with feeling words written on them and individuals were asked to act out the feelings so others could guess what they were. The activity went poorly; the leaders concluded that the activity put individuals on the spot too much, and that it would have been better for the leaders to have demonstrated first, and then to have had small groups, rather than individuals, plan and act out the feeling words. Finally, three groups were formed, with a co-leader or volunteer assigned to each, and each was given a situation they might encounter in the home, e.g., a family member who did not arrive at the agreed-on time to take them out, and they were asked to figure out as many choices as possible someone might make in such a situation. Active discussion followed.

Many of the residents were waiting in small clusters for the second meeting to begin. Group members were clearly beginning to understand that they could respond to the same situation in a variety of ways and that there were no right or wrong responses expected of them. Small group activities were clearly more effective than those that focused on individuals or on the total group. The sharing of food created a social situation and capped both meetings in a pleasant way.

Meeting 3: *We have five kinds of choices.* In the first meeting the idea of OK and OD choices was mentioned. That concept was expanded and the five CREST choices, Caring, Ruling, Enjoying, Sorrowing, and Thinking/Working were briefly introduced.

Residents were asked to give examples of OK and OD choices; they were able to suggest some choices that might be OK at one time, OD at another. A resident was asked to play the part of a person who made a lot of noise at night; an aide responded by getting angry, then one of the leaders calmly requested her to be quiet. Those present could see that when they were talked to in an OD way they more often made OD choices in return, and vice versa. The leaders introduced the five CREST choices by writing them on the chalkboard and asking group members to give examples of choices that would fall in each category. Residents were overwhelmed by the task, but they were reassured that time would be taken to talk about each of the five choices, and the next activity began to dispel their confusion. One of the leaders drew a pie chart in which she showed the balance among the five choices in her life. When residents were asked to make their own charts, many needed help, but all seemed to know what they wanted the chart to show. Most of the residents believed they made almost no ruling choices, few enjoying choices, many sorrowing and caring choices, and a great many thinking/working choices—with the emphasis on thinking.

The leaders noted that the well-oriented residents returned because they were interested; others came because staff members or their friends were present. The leaders speculated that OK and OD choices might have been handled better in a separate, earlier meeting, and that CREST choices should have been explored individually first, then combined later. Informal conversation and refreshments at the end of the meeting helped to lighten what had become a rather heavy atmosphere.

Meeting 4: *We make caring choices.* Caring choices are those actions and statements through which people meet their own needs and those of others.

One of the co-leaders briefly reviewed the CREST choices and noted that the day's meeting would emphasize caring. She told of caring choices she observed as the group was gathering, e.g., one of the members holding the door for another, then invited members to mention helpful things they had done for, or said to, others, and what caring choices they made for themselves. They were then asked to tell of a caring choice they received from another person. Responses emphasized physical caring, but one person mentioned a compliment that had helped her to feel better. A leader displayed a collage she had made using magazine clippings that showed caring pictures and words or phrases. It was nearing Easter, so she invited residents to clip pictures and words to make individual collages that might be hung for that holiday. She distributed magazines and scissors and handed out sheets of wallpaper samples for use as folders, and later for mounting the clippings. Discussion was active as people found items to clip, e.g., a woman having her hair done was selected as an example of caring for oneself. A time was set for the group members to arrange and glue the pictures.

Residents clearly enjoyed the collage activity; it helped them think about the many forms caring might take. During refreshment time a leader invited each resident to pretend the person sitting next to her was frustrated or disappointed about something, and make a caring choice. Choices were relevant and personal, not merely cliches.

Meeting 5: *We make ruling choices.* Ruling choices include actions and statements that show leadership.

Residents were convinced that they were ruled by others in almost every area of their lives, and the leaders wanted to change that perception. They had heard many complaints about food choices and diet rules, so they discussed residents' concerns with the kitchen supervisor prior to the meeting. The supervisor agreed to meet with the group and explain how decisions were made about what to serve, and how it felt to make necessary, but unpopular, rules.

The leaders defined ruling choices as leadership of any kind, and demonstrated OK and OD ruling choices. Residents shared their feelings about being led, and they discussed the relationship of self-ruling to conscience. They began to understand that they often made small ruling choices in their lives. They named "rulers" they had in the past and in the present; present rulers were the government, the administrators in the home, their consciences, and God. The kitchen supervisor explained rules and the reasons behind them. Residents responded positively; it was clear that they liked having the rules explained to them. They understood the supervisor's frustration about trying to make choices that would be acceptable for everyone. During the refreshment period group members were talkative and willing to express their opinions freely. They made it clear that they appreciated having the kitchen supervisor talk with them *and* that they accepted the necessity of having rules in the home.

The leaders noted that the residents were socializing more and getting to know one another better; they liked participating in a circle and hearing others talk. The concept of God's will came through strongly; it was clear that they believed His will should be accepted. They developed a clear sense that in making self- and other-ruling choices they were able to gain a sense of self-respect.

Meeting 6: *We make enjoying choices.* Enjoying choices are actions and statements that express positive feelings.

Group members were invited to offer examples of what they saw as enjoying choices they received or gave. Their responses included eating, reading, seeing family members, talking with friends, and giving or receiving compliments. In small groups, members responded to prepared questions or sentence completions, e.g., What I enjoy now that I could not as a child. I most enjoy eating ____. Residents formed a circle and gave the person ahead of them a back rub, then the favor was returned; clearly that was an enjoying choice for each person. Residents were asked to come to the meeting prepared to write down an enjoying choice for someone in the group. Early in the meeting they wrote their enjoying wishes on slips of paper and a volunteer tucked them into cookies that were similar to fortune cookies. Late in the meeting each member selected a cookie and read it to the group. Because of the homogeneity of the group, the wishes seemed personalized; they centered around health concerns and visits from family and friends. Some of the wishes were rather philosophical; one was, "I hope you never have to cry." Residents enjoyed the warm thoughts involved and they liked discovering who wrote the wish they received.

Group members were delighted to see their caring collages on display in the dining room. They clearly understood the concept of enjoying choices as comprising both events and the little things they can do for themselves and for one another. The comfort level in the group suggested to the leaders that the members had come to feel quite secure. They knew they would not be pushed into anything or ridiculed or threatened by an activity in which they would fail or that would point out the aging process to them in a painful way.

Meeting 7: *We make sorrowing and thinking/working choices.* Sorrowing choices are primarily actions and statements that express negative feelings. Thinking/working choices are primarily actions and statements that are cognitive or action-oriented.

As a result of the death of a well-loved resident, a craft meeting was substituted for a one session, and two concepts were combined during this meeting. Pairs were formed and individuals took turns responding to questions and statements involving sorrowing choices: What was a recent situation that led to sad or bad feelings for you. How did you express your feelings? What do you do about your worried feelings? What helps you feel better? One resident was paired with a co-leader and shared at a very deep level; she often felt worthless and not valued by the other residents, she said, but she did not let herself cry. The leader told her that it sometimes helped her to cry. The head nurse had asked if the group members might fill out a depression scale. All of those who completed the scale showed high states of depression, and two members even felt that there were others in the home who would like to see them dead. All admitted to a sense of feeling low and useless. Pairs discussed a number of questions related to thinking/working choices: What are the things you think about (not sorrow about) most? Do you make your own decisions? How do you do that? Who makes the decisions that affect you, if you do not? What work did you do most of your life? What did you like to do?

The leaders saw the meeting as very worthwhile. Residents looked at how they expressed their negative feelings and they considered alternatives they might use instead of their habitual behaviors. One of the leaders noted in her journal that the sense of powerlessness the residents felt could not be overcome in any total way by realizing that they were free to choose their clothes, watch television or not, or reach out to another resident. It saddened her to realize that these women, who had been self-sufficient all their lives, now depended on others to a great extent for their sense of well-being.

Meeting 8: *Habits and choices.* This meeting focused on recapitulation of CREST choices and allowed time for comparing and contrasting choices and habits.

In advance of the meeting residents were told that they might bring a poem that would illustrate one of the CREST choices. Also prior to the meeting the home administrator offered the opportunity for group members to make up the menu for an evening meal—within state guidelines.

Residents read poetry selections. Most were poems about relationships—the types of persons they would choose as friends, what a good friend meant. The activity was clearly a winner. Leaders gave residents slips of paper and asked them to write down a habit they could work on and change the following week; papers were collected and held for the next meeting. Some chose not to write anything. Leaders concluded that the members' self-concepts were fragile and this activity reminded them of that. It might have better if individuals had been asked to identify one positive choice they might make in the following week. Leaders told residents that they might make up the menu for a dinner meal, and they entered enthusiastically into the process of making suggestions and narrowing down the choices until the decisions were made.

Attendance for the meeting was down, but interaction was very good. Residents lingered to talk after the meeting. The menu idea was clearly appealing. Residents felt empowered because the administrator responded to their needs to make choices and had found a way to let them do so.

Meeting 9: *Choices and consequences.* We influence, but we do not control, consequences.

Group members who had worked on changing a habit were asked to talk about what had happened; individuals had changed such habits as nail-biting and choosing poor attitudes. One member said she talked too much and felt worthless; other residents reassured her and gave her positive feedback. Leaders introduced the concept of choices and consequences, indicating that we tend to get what we give. The group was quiet, but with the next activity the members became more involved. Small groups were formed and members were asked to complete sentences and share responses to such items as: If I cried in public, others would _____. If I want my dinner in my room I can _____. If I want someone to like me, I can _____. What would happen if I said "I love you" to a close member of my family? What would happen if I said "I'm tired today"? Group members played THE NAME GAME. Each person named all people ahead of her in the circle, herself, and the next person in the circle; this tested the memories of the residents in a positive way and helped them interact with others. Those present were proud when they could name most of the people in the room.

Attendance was the largest to date, probably because, as a result of the menu planning, the group was perceived as having some influence. Members had clearly broadened their friendship base. In her journal one of the leaders expressed surprise that members did not know all of the other residents' names. Involvement within the group had masked that lack of knowledge. Most likely many of the residents had arrived at the home resistant to being there and did not reach out to make friends. Later they were embarrassed to admit they did not know the names of others whom they had seen for weeks or months. The group afforded them a safe setting to get to know others and to make better choices.

Meeting 10: *Choices and feelings.* Feelings both influence choices and result from choices.

Leaders led off by mentioning events from their own lives in which positive and negative consequences had resulted when they acted on their feelings, then they asked residents to share similar experiences. The points were made that our feelings influence our choices, and that how we feel can be the result of choices we have made. Next, residents were invited to mention the feeling they experienced most. A new resident shared her feelings of loneliness and not belonging; a long-term resident said that she showed happiness to others but she often felt sad. Members were in touch with their feelings and were comfortable enough to share them. Three groups were formed, each group was given a description of a situation; and all were asked to name all the feelings they could think of that they might have had in the situation. The situation was made competitive; a leader or volunteer worked with each group, assisting and adding humor as needed; and the winners named nine feelings. The meal the group planned had occurred in the previous week, so during refreshments the residents were asked to react to the consequences of their choices. Responses were very positive, and members were told that in the future they would be allowed to choose the menu for one meal each month.

Group members shared their ideas and feelings freely in the group. Leaders concluded that their own sharing of choices that had negative and positive consequences helped the residents share freely. The competitive element worked because there were several people in each group, and because competition was introduced after trust in the group had developed. Had it been introduced earlier it might have had negative effects.

Meeting 11: *Choosing to feel good about self.* We all make choices in how we feel about ourselves. Negative self-feelings can be modified if individuals make more effective choices.

Small groups were formed; the concept of feeling good about self as a choice was explained; and residents were asked to give examples of OK and OD feelings they might have about themselves. The leaders brought up a problem they had observed in the home: critical remarks some residents made about others had hurt their feelings. The co-leaders role-played a scene in which one talked to the other about a third person in a negative way. Residents recognized the problem and connected it to behaviors they had observed in the home. Group members made suggestions for the individual who was criticized: go to the person and request that the criticism stop, confront her and demand an apology, or share the hurt with a friend. Residents participated enthusiastically in developing the menu for the month's special dinner. During the refreshment period the residents and the co-leader who was not part of the staff said their goodbyes.

The departing co-leader noted that she experienced sadness at leaving the women to whom she had become attached. She wrote in her journal that she admired the residents, each of whom attended the group meetings as if she was going to a party. She wrote approvingly of the sense of dignity of the women. Yet their lives offered little except the satisfaction of survival needs, she observed, since they lacked a sense of purpose and direction.

Despite the contrary assumptions that abound, relatively few older persons find themselves in institutional settings such as the combined retirement/nursing home in which this group was situated. These women, however, fit some of the stereotypes that exist. Many of them felt lonely and unwanted by their families and by others. They knew they were in the home to live out their lives with little to occupy their time. The Choice Awareness group process helped them see that although their choices were limited, within limits they had much freedom and many opportunities for involvement with life.

One of the leaders noted in her journal that she had made what was clearly an erroneous assumption: that people who were in daily contact would interact actively with one another. "As a result of socializing they feel less lonely," she wrote. The other leader noted that the Choice Awareness group experience had helped those involved develop "new, concrete choice possibilities for their present living situation." The leaders agreed that the group members gained in three ways: their loneliness was dispelled for a time, they became aware of the ever-present opportunities they had to choose, and they grew in skills in making new choices within the home.

COUNSELING APPLICATION—JOURNAL ENTRY: Discuss the extent to which you believe it is important for counselors to use Choice Awareness theory in their work with older persons. Consider with at least one specific or hypothetical older person how you might modify the counseling process to incorporate Choice Awareness. Head your entry CHOICE AWARENESS AND THE OLDER PERSON.

Choice Awareness and Older Persons

Choice Awareness theory suggests that effective counseling with some older persons requires little change in the process, while with other older persons minor or major adjustments need to be made. Beyond those that are obvious—relating to issues of vision, hearing, and physical comfort, for example—adjustments of a more subtle nature are often needed. Older persons who grew up before counseling had a broad level of acceptance may be unwilling to seek counseling *per se* from those whom they see as younger and therefore less well-informed; however, they may be drawn into the process through activities on their own turf, and they may benefit in particular from direct problem-solving processes. As in the group process discussed here, older persons may be willing to work on their concerns within group contexts that afford them opportunities to share, to socialize, and to learn to make more effective choices.

References

Landreth, G.L. & Berg, R.C. (1980), *Counseling the elderly: For professional counselors who work with the aged.* Springfield , IL: C. C. Thomas.

Myers, J.E. (1988). *Infusing gerontological counseling into counseling preparation: Curriculum guide.* Alexandria, VA: American Association for Counseling and Development.

Nelson, R.C. (1989). Choice Awareness: A group experience in a residential setting. *Journal for Specialists in Group Work, 14,* 158-169.

Chapter 21

A Group
Counseling Process

The Group

Mrs. Ramsey thought a great deal about the challenge she was facing. "No," she said to herself, "I can't think of anything I've ever done that was tougher." In a few moments, if they kept to their commitments, eight boys, the leaders of two emerging junior high school gangs, would walk into her office. "It needs to be done," she reassured herself. She had not expected to face the issue of rival gangs in a Midwest city of under fifty thousand people, and she certainly never expected that working out their problems would be up to her.

The vice principal had tried to be reassuring. "It isn't really up to you—it's up to them. Either they smooth things out or the next time a problem arises they'll be expelled—all of them."

"That might be fine if I didn't feel so strongly that those boys have something to learn and something to give. I can't let them go without a good fight. It'll be worse if they end up on the street. It'll be worse if they end up on the street," she said to herself as she tapped her fingers on her desk. "At least they aren't into the kind of drug war that's hitting so many cities—not yet anyway. And we know that a few of the parents will back us up." She picked up the card on her desk and half-smiled, reread the four lines for what seemed like the hundredth time: *Handshakes, Introductions, Admirations, Issues;* then, for reassurance, she glanced at the wall and scanned the hand-lettered poster she had adapted from *Choice Awareness: An Innovative Guidance Process* (Nelson & Bloom, 1975, p. 44). Among the listings were the CREST choices and their OD equivalent: caring —smothering, ruling—dominating, enjoying—teasing, sorrowing—being mean/miserable, thinking/working—overthinking/overworking; and habit, decision, OK/OD, initiation, response, goal, consequences, and responsibility. "Good reminders all," she told herself.

The Cools arrived first: four Blacks, three of them eighth graders, one seventh grader. Barry, the tallest, and clearly the leader, led the pack, snapping his fingers, slouching, and moving rhythmically, living up to his idea of the gang's name in every way. "Hey there, Mrs. Ramsey," he said, emphasizing the two syllables equally.

"Nice office you got here," said Suds, whose real name was Walter Walters. They eased into the four seats nearest the door. *The Rods*—the name officially related to cars, but laughter and sexual innuendo were often tied to the name—would have a longer walk into the room.

Mrs. Ramsey greeted all four by name. "Barry, Walter," Suds grimaced, then laughed good-naturedly, "Washington, and Len. Thank you for coming."

"A pleasure," said Len, mockery sounding in his voice. "Well, *we're* here, let's get on with it." The other boys laughed, and Barry clapped him on the shoulder.

At a sound in the hall all stiffened and the laughter stopped.

The door that had been left ajar swung open and The Rods stepped inside. Steely eyes set in white faces met steely eyes set in black faces all around the room. The hush was dramatic. "Mrs. Ramsey, if you'd just push your chair up a bit, maybe we can slide behind you," Terry spoke first. His strategy meant that his group would not have to pass behind The Cools and along the end wall to get to their seats. Mrs. Ramsey stood and let The Rods pass; a moment later the boys were arranged in two facing groups. Terry opposite Barry—the two leaders were face to face to the right and left of Mrs. Ramsey; Jack opposite Len—the humorists across from each other; Steve opposite Walter; and Spike opposite Washington—hostility eye to eye with hostility. Leers crossed the table; biting comments were passed down the line, softly spoken, but audible. "They did show up. You owe me," Jack said to Steve.

Mrs. Ramsey remained standing. She leaned forward, fingers spread, palms on the table, and spoke in a voice that sounded strange to her, but firm. "You all know why we're here. From my point of view I'm hoping we can do something about the rivalry between your two groups so you don't all get expelled and get into worse trouble outside of school." Before she resumed speaking two murmurs reached her. "Nobody'll care at my house." "I'll get killed, but. . . what the heck."

"I'm not going to lecture you or try to figure out who's at fault for the problem." She let that sink in. Smiles were exchanged within the groups along both sides of the table. "I have a simple idea. I want you boys to get to know one another better." She remembered that she had planned to avoid the term *boys*, so she hastily corrected herself. "I want you young men to get to know one another better."

"Are you kidding?" Terry snapped. "I know all I want to know right now."

Support came from both sides of the table. "Trash don't need knowin'," said Washington. Spike slammed his hands on the table, pushed himself to a standing position, and glared.

"Sit down, please, Spike." Mrs. Ramsey fixed her eyes on him firmly and said nothing for several seconds.

"You hear him say we wuz trash?" Spike hissed through clenched teeth—but he sat down.

"Look, as far as I'm concerned I'm not sure this get-together has a very good chance of changing things. If you want to leave right now, it's your choice—but I expect you'll clash in the hall right away and be out of school before the day's over." Mrs. Ramsey caught the eye of each boy, then she sat down. She continued in a softer voice that she tried to make as pleasant as possible. "Now, if you want to give yourselves a chance to work things out, I have some ideas."

"Trash," Spike grumbled softly to himself.

Terry leaned forward. "Hey, Spike, cool it. Oops." The use of the name of the rival gang brought nervous movement, then Barry guffawed and everyone but Spike laughed. He finally caught the joke and snickered.

"I'm not sure you've all got courage enough to do what I'm going to ask you to do," Mrs. Ramsey said after several moments, "but let me see if this'll work." All eyes turned to her, and several of the boys straightened their shoulders.

"Guts is what we got pu-len-ty of," Barry said, making a three-syllable word out of *plenty*, and he nodded to his fellow Cools. They returned his nod and smiled broad smiles.

"They don't know anything about g—," Terry's rejoinder was overridden by Mrs. Ramsey.

"Let's see if all that's just talk." She paused for several seconds. "Here's what I want you to do. Reach across the table and shake the hand of the fellow across from you."

After the briefest moment two or three hands were thrust partly forward. "Yuk," said two voices at the same time, one from either side of the table, and the hands were swiftly withdrawn.

"Cooties," said Jack, who'd reached the furthest—without touching. He whipped his hand back and wiped it on his shirt.

Mrs. Ramsey spoke quietly. "I'm waiting to see if all this talk of guts is just so much hot air. I'm not asking you to promise anything with your handshake. I know it's not going to all be over like *that*." She snapped her fingers. "Anyway, it's your choice."

Grudgingly, slowly, Barry pursed his mouth in imitation of a tough-guy smile and thrust his hand forward. His unspoken message was clear, "I've got guts enough to do that—first." Terry's hand met his over the middle of the table. Other hands met. Then Terry stood up and reached toward Len. It appeared to Mrs. Ramsey that he did not want to be outdone by Barry's first move. In a few seconds each of the boys had shaken the four hands across the table. Hands were slid down the sides of jeans as if to wipe off perspiration—or pollution.

"That's neat. I only asked you to shake the hand of the person across from you—and you *chose* to include everybody on the other side of the table."

"So —, that don't prove nothin'," Spike's voice was a challenge.

"You're right. By itself that doesn't prove anything, except maybe that there's a little hope we might be able to work things out." Mrs. Ramsey leaned forward and spoke in a husky voice just above a whisper. "Let's build on that."

"I'd like to ask you to take two minutes to get to know the person across from you, then I'm going to ask you to tell your group something about the other guy. When it's your turn, tell the person across from you about yourself—your favorite foods, what gets you all steamed up, what your family is like, what's something you have that's really special to you—things like that." And the other person ask some questions so you'll know more to tell the group. After we start I'll let you know when two minutes is up and then the other person gets a turn to talk and to be asked questions."

It took a couple of minutes before the pairs began to exchange information. A number of questions put off the inevitable. The pairs started slowly, with each person waiting for the other to begin, then voices hummed. Mrs. Ramsey noted with satisfaction that in two of the pairs The Cools spoke up first; in the other two it was The Rods; Terry and Barry moved close to her at the end of the table so that they could hear one another better, and she slid her chair back. Spike held his place and Washington moved to the one empty chair at the other end of the table. Voices waned after less than two minutes, then waxed again after Mrs. Ramsey called time and the second person began to speak.

When Mrs. Ramsey said, "OK, finish what you're saying, and then we . . . , " the boys stopped talking immediately. "Which one of you will get us started?" she asked, looking intently at Terry and then Barry. Jack waved his hand to gain attention. The smirk on his face concerned Mrs. Ramsey. "I'll get to you next, but I think I'd like to hear from Barry or Terry first." Barry gestured to Terry to go ahead.

Terry cleared his throat, smiled, then frowned thoughtfully and pointed to Barry. "This fink's a Cubs fan." Chuckles and cheers met that beginning on both sides of the table. Steve, who wore a tattered St. Louis Cardinal sweatshirt, booed quietly. "He likes fudge ripple ice cream, and he's got two brothers—older, and three sisters—younger. Six kids, like in my dad's family. And the thing he has that's special is an old banjo his uncle had. He's never had a lesson 'cept what his uncle showed him one time, but he can pick out most any tune he knows."

"But once I figure it out in one key I can't do it any other way," Barry laughed.

"That's great. Both of you," said Mrs. Ramsey. The two boys smiled. "My guess is you found out you have some things in common—at least you think a little bit alike." They nodded. "Before we hear Barry talk about Terry, anybody from The Rods want to ask him anything?"

"Is Jared your brother?" Steve asked.

"Cousin. But anyway, he's like a brother. He lives at our house most of the time." Steve was clearly impressed. Jared, Mrs. Ramsey was told, was one of the best swimmers in the state.

The ice was broken. After Barry spoke about Terry, sharp shards of humor from Jack and Len punctuated the rest of the comments, but otherwise the brief discussions were well-received.

"Is anyone gutsy enough to say something about how you feel right now toward the person who introduced you?" Mrs. Ramsey waited through several seconds of dead quiet. Washington whispered something in Walter's ear.

Mrs. Ramsey looked toward the ceiling for an instant, turned to Washington, and asked, "Would what you whispered—uh—say something about how you feel toward Spike right now?"

Washington turned to Walter. Walter shrugged his shoulders and tossed his head slightly. "I told him, 'Too bad he's white.' I mean 'cause he be a good fighter," he added immediately.

"That's great," Mrs. Ramsey responded. "I really appreciate the fact that you *chose* to share that with us." Walter scowled. "OK, I asked you to share, but if it hadn't been all right with you, you wouldn't have." He nodded. Encouraged, Mrs. Ramsey pushed for a response from each of the boys. The responses indicated grudging, mostly positive feelings toward their counterpart across the table.

When that activity and the discussion that followed wound down, Mrs. Ramsey glanced at the card before her and began again. "Most of the time when we feel a lot of anger toward someone, we have some more positive feeling behind it. Like maybe with someone in your family—they couldn't make you so mad if you didn't care about their opinion."

"You lost me," said Steve.

Mrs. Ramsey fixed her eyes on him for a moment and rubbed her chin. "Well, stop me if you think I'm telling too much, Steve, but maybe this'll help. In the past you've talked with me and you said you get angry with your dad a lot, right?"

"No secret there," he said, sheepishly.

"When he makes excuses and doesn't take you to his new place, or bowling, or whatever he said he'd do with you on the weekend, you're annoyed." Steve nodded. "If you thought he was a nothing you wouldn't even want to go in the first place—you wouldn't care." He nodded again.

"What's that got to do with those guys?" Steve nodded toward The Cools.

"Maybe nothing. Maybe a lot." Mrs. Ramsey paused for several seconds, thinking of how to continue. She waved her hand toward The Cools and then The Rods. "If you guys really felt the others were 'nothings,' you wouldn't care what they did or what they thought. But you have some positive feeling behind that—at least you know they're strong and that they've got power."

"I don't see. . . ," Barry said.

"OK. Just try something with me, and we'll see if it makes sense afterwards." Shoulders shrugged. "One at a time I'd like to ask you to tell the person across from you something you admire, respect, or think is—maybe 'cool' about him."

After several chuckles and side comments of the you've-got-to-be-kidding variety, Mrs. Ramsey spoke again. "That's OK. I wasn't sure you'd be brave enough to do that anyway."

Barry had remained quiet through the brief melee. He nodded slightly. Mrs. Ramsey turned toward him and all eyes were drawn his way. "I have an idea," Barry said. "I get off on Terry's way of talking. He don't take any sh. . . , er, stuff from anybody—even teachers or the principal—but he does it just right—so nobody gets mad at him."

"Gr-ea-t," Mrs. Ramsey stretched out the word and patted Barry on the arm. "I'm tempted to go on, rather than mess with what you said, but I wonder if you'd be willing to turn to Terry, say his name, and tell him directly what you told us about him. It has more power if you say it to him."

In the middle of the first two tries Barry turned back to Mrs. Ramsey. Each time she thanked him heartily for his efforts and encouraged him to try again. Finally he kept his eyes on Terry, saying, "Terry, I think it's cool how you talk back to people, but kinda respectfully—so nobody puts anything over on you."

"Super. Just right." Mrs. Ramsey turned to Terry. "Before you say something to Barry that you admire, I'd like to invite you to tell him how that felt to you."

"It felt good."

"I'm sure it did. But tell that to Barry, not me—and maybe say his name, too."

"That felt good. . . Barry." Terry's eyes and Barry's met for a moment.

It took many minutes for each member of the group to say one positive thing directly to the person opposite. Mrs. Ramsey helped often with phrasing, and she gave frequent encouragement to the boys to make direct eye contact and to use names. Near the end of that discussion she returned to her original point. "Back several minutes ago when I started this, I was trying to say that there are some positive feelings under all the negative feelings you have for each other." Group members shrugged and were clearly not impressed, but no one took issue with the point.

Mrs. Ramsey looked at her watch and realized that well over half the fifty-minute period had ebbed away. She made a sweeping, admiring comment to all. "You're a gutsy bunch. Somehow I think we can lick this problem—because you're brave enough to do it."

"And you're some gutsy lady." Spike smiled broadly for the first time as he said that. It was clear that the group shared his opinion.

Along the way Mrs. Ramsey had added two notes to the worn-looking card she had touched and held and curled from time to time during the meeting. *Mess things up,* read one line; the other said *Do differently.* She looked down at those words.

"I'm not sure what I want to do next. There's not a lot of time left to get into the real issues between you. Besides I like the atmosphere in the room today, and I think it'd be just as well if we'd look at the nitty-gritty of the problems some other time." Heads nodded and smiles were exchanged within groups. "I tried something with some of the girls a few weeks ago. Maybe it'd work with you, too—though sometimes girls are a little freer to admit that what they do that causes problems." Quizzical looks met her eyes. "I wonder if you'd be willing to share what *you* do, *each* of you, that messes things up between the two groups—and if there's time, we can talk about what *you* could do differently, this week."

"Oh, man, my sister Jeanetta musta been there when you did that with those girls. I thought she'd never stop talking about it. She wouldn't tell me who, but she said a couple of the girls admitted they were too catty. Someone said she'd stop running to the teacher, and Jeanetta told me what she did—but maybe I'm not supposed to tell that in here." Len used the back of his hand to wipe a bead of sweat off his forehead, then rubbed his palms down the side of his sweatshirt and looked around.

Barry punched him lightly on the arm. "So, what do ya think? Should we try that?"

"I don't know. Don't see how it'd hurt," was Len's reply.

"It's cool with us," said Terry, again chuckling at his own use of the word cool.

"Who'll begin by saying what he does that messes things up."

For several seconds eyes looked in every direction but at Mrs. Ramsey, then Len looked at her and nodded, and all eyes fixed on him. "I been thinkin' about that, 'cause of Jeanetta. I like to tease the white kids. Mostly I tell 'em they ain't never gonna have a tan like mine. Stuff like that." He paused, but it was clear he intended to say more. The room remained quiet. "But sometimes I tell 'em I'll break their fingers if they don't gimme a buck." He looked at Mrs. Ramsey. "I'd never really do anything like that, ex-specially to the little kids, but . . . it sure is easy money with the ones that don't know that." He looked down at the table. "I guess I could cool it on that—this week."

"Yeah. He did that to my little brother. If he does it again. . . , " Spike began. Mrs. Ramsey held up her hand and interrupted.

"Excuse me, Spike." She waited for several seconds till Spike looked at her. "Leave off the threat and tell Len how you felt about that. Look at him. Say it to him. Use his name."

"That really made me mad—Len." The sound of Len's name was hissed. "I thought that was pretty chicken to pick on a little kid like him. That's one of the things that got *us* started." He waved his hands to The Rods. "We weren't going to have you guys picking on the little kids."

Len's jaw tightened and he clenched his fists. Before he could find words, Mrs. Ramsey cleared her throat; her voice was both kind and firm. "I'd like to thank both of you—Len for sharing what he did with us; seems like that took courage—and you, Spike; you let Len know really directly how you felt about that. Someday we'll talk about whether or not he can *make* you mad, but we won't worry about that today." She waved her hand toward Spike. "I want to be sure you heard Len say that he would hold back on that this week, Spike." Spike nodded.

Mrs. Ramsey invited other comments toward Len. Several were given. "Pretty gutsy," was Barry's offering.

Spike nodded as that discussion drew to a close. "Did you want to go next, Spike?" asked Mrs. Ramsey.

"No. Er. Uh. OK, sure," he said, and he drew a deep breath. "I guess I mess things up because, like my Mom says, I fight at the drop of a hat." He laughed. "Matter of fact, I don't need *that* much." Laughter and overlapping comments followed. Spike said he thought he could cut down the fighting, maybe even cut it out for a week. Subsequently each of the other boys shared something he did that caused problems and indicated what he would do that would be different over the next week.

As time wound down to the end of the period, Mrs. Ramsey scheduled the next meeting and complimented the group. "You've done a really good job today, and I'll let the teachers and the administration know that we've made a lot of progress. I know we've got a long ways to go, but we've started well, and I thank you for your help. You *are* gutsy kids." Several joking comments followed, but it was clear that the feeling in the group was positive.

"I might as well say it," she told herself after a brief pause. Aloud she said, "Some really terrible things have happened when gangs have gotten in wars with one another. I'm sure none of those gangs had any idea what might happen when they began, and I imagine some of them started with fellows about your age." Jack clutched at his throat, somebody chuckled, Terry raised a warning fist toward Jack, and the group was quiet. "If we can get together like we did today, I think we won't have to worry about those things happening here."

Mrs. Ramsey stood and so did the boys. She hesitated for a moment and conversations began on both sides of the table. She waved her hands for quiet. "I wonder if you'd be willing to end on handshakes today." She held up both hands, palms out. "But wait. This time don't do it because I'm asking you to. Only do it if it's an OK choice for you." Eyes were turned so that Terry and Barry were in the most direct line of vision after Mrs. Ramsey. Terry and Barry remained serious, but they thrust their hands forward at the same instant. Soon the two camps had exchanged handshakes all around.

The bell rang for the exchange of classes and Mrs. Ramsey said, "That's it. Thank you for your help today." She stood in the doorway and smiled as she watched the boys wending their way from her office. Words were being exchanged that she could not hear because of the noise of the throngs of students, but the movements she could observe appeared to be relaxed. She closed the door behind her, sat down, and sighed a long sigh of relief. She fingered her card and glanced again at the Choice Awareness poster. "I didn't identify them by name, but I got the boys to make a lot of enjoying choices, and sorrowing choices, too—when they shared what they did that messed things up."

Choice Awareness in the Group Counseling Process

Group counseling differs from individual counseling in one primary, significant way that has enormous impact on the process: there are many more variables to be taken into account by the counselor. At any given moment if eight clients are present there are eight peoples' needs to consider—nine when the counselor's needs are included; and the words, actions, thoughts, and the mixed feelings of any of those present are grist for the mill. In Choice Awareness theory the assumption is made that members of a group evolve a kind of society of their own. If the counselor does not take an active part from the beginning, that society will closely resemble the cliques and the "pecking order" that would have emerged if the counselor had not been present.

In individual counseling the counselor can function as a listener and a facilitator for many clients, moving gradually to more impact-oriented procedures only when and if they are needed. By contrast, if the counselor functions in the same way in group counseling, the evolution of the society, as opposed to the resolution of difficulties, is likely to become the focus of the group's attention. The counselor needs to act in ways that call the attention of the group members to the concerns that brought them together. To say it another way, if the *less is more principle* is to be applied effectively in group counseling, the counselor needs to be in control, to have impact, from the beginning of counseling. Direction is essential or much of the time of the counselor and the group members is wasted.

In the junior high school example cited here, Mrs. Ramsey took control immediately and continually. She was determined to discourage the fragmented society-building, rivalry, blaming, and arguing that she saw as inevitable if she did otherwise. (At an earlier time she had operated more non-directively until she realized that the "pecking order" that would have evolved had she not been present almost inevitably emerged; she intervened so that did not happen anymore.) She set up conditions in which she invited *initiation*, and then waited for the boys to shake hands, to talk with one another in pairs, and to state a strength of the person across the table. She also promoted the idea of initiation by encouraging the group members to speak directly and straightforwardly and use one another's names as they talked.

Mrs. Ramsey acted on *the principle of balance in self-interest and social-interest*. She used the challenge of courage, of guts, to encourage the boys to act in the social-interest, in the expectation that ultimately they would see such actions as in their self-interest as well. She responded selectively to the comments of the boys, focusing on the positive aspects of their communication, especially in the early stages of counseling. She saw that also as serving both the social-interest and the self-interest of the members of the group.

In the first meeting Mrs. Ramsey elected not to introduce *the five choice principle*. Except for her allusion at the end of the session to shaking hands if the boys saw it as an OK choice, she did not mention OK and OD choices or CREST choices. However, throughout the session, in her use of choice-focused language, she demonstrated *the choosing principle*, and she selected activities that were designed to encourage enjoying choices more often than sorrowing choices. The same activities took into account *the principle of three counseling levels: spa, learning, and relearning*. She placed the accent on achieving spa, assuming that a positive initial experience would best serve the needs of all concerned.

The cues on Mrs. Ramsey's hand-lettered poster (based on Nelson & Bloom, 1975, p. 44) were so integrated into her counseling style that she seldom glanced at them, though she could recall a time when she had depended on them greatly. She had not read the word *habit*—at least she had not been aware that she had—but she knew that word had guided much of her effort. She had vowed, if she could, that she would discourage the rerunning of old complaints and get the boys to communicate positively with one another—those were two things that lay well outside their usual habit patterns.

It had been Mrs. Ramsey's practice to begin every group session with her students with an activity that might relax the group members and provide a basis for communication in the present. She had not been certain whether or not to continue that tradition with the two emerging gangs, but the success of her first experiences led her to incorporate stimulus activities throughout the subsequent group counseling sessions. Some of the activities were informal and verbal like those she used in the first session, others were more structured and internally-focused. An example of the latter was animal identification: If you were an animal, what would you be, and why? She was uncertain that the boys would respond well to such an unsophisticated activity, but after a brief period of hesitation, they entered into it enthusiastically and said things about themselves that encouraged useful feedback from others. Using stimulus activities helped the group focus less on recounting history and past feelings and more on present-oriented, forward-looking communication. She came away from her experiences with the group confirmed in her judgment that stimulus activities move the process along in positive ways.

In subsequent sessions Mrs. Ramsey followed the model that characterized her first meeting with the group members. She remained in control. She encouraged the boys to speak straightforwardly to one another, and they did so—without anger for the most part. She used various stimulus activities to focus the attention of the group members and to create a genuine present-sense in the process of counseling. She helped the boys sort out their concerns—shifting from past history to present-communication whenever possible. She brainstormed with the group members possible ways of approaching their concerns; she worked with them as they chose the strategies they wanted to use, and she helped them evaluate their successes and failures. Her efforts to get the two groups to combine in some kind of positive effort, cleaning-up a vacant lot or volunteering in a nearby nursing home, fell on deaf ears, but the tensions between the two groups subsided. Ultimately it became evident that the needs that brought The Cools and The Rods into existence as gangs were being met in more positive ways; for a while the two groups took on the character of clubs more than gangs, then they faded away.

COUNSELING APPLICATION—JOURNAL ENTRY: Discuss the extent to which you believe it is important for counselors to use Choice Awareness theory in their work with groups of clients. Consider with at least one specific or hypothetical group how you might modify the counseling process to incorporate Choice Awareness. Head your entry CHOICE AWARENESS AND GROUPS.

Effective Choice Awareness group counseling requires the counselor to be a dynamic leader who implements the *less is more principle* through being in control of the process, and through seeking impact far more frequently than is seen here as being suitable in individual counseling. The Choice Awareness counselor understands that economical approaches that suit the early stages of individual counseling are likely to be counterproductive in group counseling. The counselor provides stimulus activities that focus the attention of the group, encourage clients to communicate directly and openly, and help them see that their behaviors in the group—and beyond—involve choices.

Afterword

Life is a continuous process of choosing. Although all of us choose our way through our lives, moment to moment, most of us have only a dim sense that we are doing so. Many of the clients who seek counseling have a cloudier vision than others of the opportunities they

---

have to choose. Lacking a clear vision that they *are* choosing, and that they *can* choose, they tend to build patterns of choices that block their full entry into their world. As a result they tend to feel bad about themselves and, in response to those negative feelings, they make even poorer choices both toward themselves and others.

Choice Awareness is a process that encourages people to see that in the small and the large matters of life they can make positive, effective, and responsible choices. Choice Awareness helps people shed the yoke of habit and free themselves to act in their own interests and in the interests of others. Choice Awareness helps people see themselves as choosers rather than as victims, as persons acting in their world rather than as persons acted on by others around them.

There is no human being on this earth who makes perfect choices all the time, nor is there likely to be. What *is* possible is for all of us to choose more effectively more of the time in our own world and in our interactions with those around us.

Most of us need to make changes in the ways in which we talk and act and think and feel about the people and situations we face, because whatever difficulties we have result at least in part from our choices. To say it another way, most of us need to make more effective choices in all three domains: the cognitive, the affective, and the behavioral. When we adopt more positive patterns of thinking, we are making more effective choices in the cognitive domain. When we tap the wellspring of positive feelings that often remains hidden inside us, we have the potential of making better choices in the affective domain. When we talk and act in ways that serve our positive, long-range goals, we are making better choices in the behavioral domain.

Life is a process of choosing. The world would be a better place if we lived our lives as if its quality depended upon our choices. It does.

The following motto is offered to you for yourself (Nelson, 1977).

.

And you may want to encourage your clients to take it as their own:

What I am is how I talk and act and think and feel
"unto others"—and myself.

What I do I choose to do.

What I say I choose to say.

How I feel I choose to feel.

What I think I choose to think.

What I am I choose to be.

Reference

Nelson, R. C. (1977). *Choosing a better way to live.* North Palm Beach FL: GuideLines Press.